Eden Seekers

Eden Seekers

THE SETTLEMENT OF OREGON, 1818-1862

Malcolm Clark, jr.

HOUGHTON MIFFLIN COMPANY • BOSTON
1981

Library of Congress Cataloging in Publication Data

Clark, Malcolm, jr., date
    The Eden seekers.

    Bibliography: p.
    Includes index.
    1. Oregon — History — To 1859. I. Title.
F880.C56   979.5'03   80-26236
ISBN 0-395-27622-5

Printed in the United States of America
    V   10   9   8   7   6   5   4   3   2   1

For
Shelley, Leigh and Tom

Acknowledgments

THE FOLLOWING organizations have kindly granted permission to quote from published texts and manuscript sources:

— The Lilly Library, Indiana University — four quotations from the J. Lane manuscripts.

— The Bush House, Salem, Oregon — four quotations from the Bush letters.

— The Hudson's Bay Record Society, Hudson's Bay House, Winnipeg, Manitoba, Canada — quotations from *Peter Skene Ogden's Snake Country Journals, 1824–25 and 1825–26* and *McLoughlin's Fort Vancouver Letters, 1844–46.*

— The Oregon Historical Society — twenty quotations from its manuscript collections; passages from *The Correspondence and Journals of Captain Nathaniel Jarvis Wyeth, 1831–36;* from *Oregon Argonauts* by the late Arthur Throckmorton; from "Diary of Jason Lee," *Oregon Historical Quarterly,* Vol. 17 (1916); from "Diary of the Rev. George H. Atkinson, D.D., 1847–1855," *Oregon Historical Quarterly,* Vol. 40 (1939); from "Diary of Samuel Royal Thurston," *Oregon Historical Quarterly,* Vol. 24 (1923); from "Diary of the Reverend George Gary," *Oregon Historical Quarterly,* Vol. 24 (1923); from "Correspondence of the Reverend Ezra Fisher," *Oregon Historical Quarterly,* Vol. 17 (1916); from "Archives of the American Board of Commissioners for Foreign Missions, Vol. 248 — Letter 28," *Oregon Historical Quarterly,* Vol. 22 (1921); from "22 Letters of David Logan," *Oregon Historical Quarterly,* Vol. 44 (1943); and an excerpt from H. H. Spalding's "Lectures: Early Oregon Missions, Their Importance in Securing the Country to America."

Quotations from *Robert Newell's Memoranda* are used with permission of Dr. Dorothy O. Johansen. All illustrations are from the magnificent

vii

photograph collections of the Oregon Historical Society and are used with the Society's permission.

A great many have helped in the making of this book. The author is deeply indebted to Thomas Vaughan, director of the Oregon Historical Society, for his initial aid, constant encouragement, and many kindnesses. Priscilla Knuth, executive editor of the *Oregon Historical Quarterly,* generously allowed the author to take up her time and borrow of her wisdom. Each is a valued friend.

It is not impossible that every member of the staff of the Society's Oregon Historical Center made some contribution. Those not named are here saluted. It is impossible, however, to pass over Susan Seyl, photo librarian, and Elizabeth Winroth, maps librarian. Paul Ewing, assistant photo librarian, spent a great deal of time helping to select pictures from the Society's voluminous archives. The entire library staff, counting down from Lou Flannery, chief librarian, rendered cheerful assistance. Special thanks must go to Arthur Spencer, who is not only catalog librarian but a walking compendium of Portland history.

The author is indebted to the staffs of the Literature and History Room, Multnomah County Library, Portland; the Lilly Library, Indiana University, Bloomington; the Illinois State Historical Library, Springfield; the California Room, California State Library, Sacramento; the Bancroft Library, University of California, Berkeley; the Henry E. Huntington Library, San Marino; the Nebraska Historical Society Library, Lincoln; and the Library of Congress. The late Martin Schmitt, formerly curator of special collections, University of Oregon Library, was unfailingly obliging.

Special people have made special contributions. Mabel Hoeye, sometimes of Des Moines, supplied an impressive file on Oregonians in Iowa. Edna Obinger typed a portion of the first draft of the manuscript.

The author has been fortunate in his editors. Anne Barrett, Jonathan Galassi, and John Russell each has the blessed quality of patience. Another Houghton Mifflin editor, the late Norman Berg, was generous with encouragement when the work was in its early stages. Janice K. Duncan shared her special knowledge of Margaret Jewett Bailey. Cathy de Lorge, lately the Oregon Historical Society's manuscript and rare books librarian, answered every query promptly and accurately.

Maxine Kirkland Clark typed this book — several times. The author's beloved companion, Barbara Serrell Friedman, advised some of the final revisions, wrote others, and shared the proofing.

Author's Note

There are, in this book, archaic modes, words and spellings deliberately used to help reproduce the flavor of nineteenth-century America.

Contents

Illustrations

following page 176

Eden Seekers

Introduction

WILLIAM FAUX was British by birth and by conviction, and by vocation a gentleman farmer. But he had a journalistic bent. Early in 1819 he crossed the Atlantic to look at the New World and to gather material for a book which would, he proclaimed modestly, "shew Men and Things as they are."[1]

He found both in bad order. Boston had achieved a certain culture and in Philadelphia the roast beef was excellent. For the rest the cities were garbage-littered and pig-infested, the roads disgraceful, the inns verminous, the land indecently fertile and the farms improvidently kept. Everything was new and crude and wore a look of impermanence. The Americans themselves were half-lettered nomads given to plunging off into the raw wilderness for any reason or for no reason at all. This universal restlessness troubled Faux's orderly insular mind, and the vast distances which allowed it overawed him. A three-thousand-mile journey, he remarked plaintively, was a matter of no moment.

In the fall he set off on an extended jaunt himself, traveling the Cumberland Road on his way to visit English settlements in Indiana and Illinois. It was the second week in October when he reached Wheeling. Despite the lateness of the season he discovered emigrant wagons still rolling in, gathering to await the flatboats and the autumn floods that would carry them down the Ohio. A little way on at Chillicothe, founded scarcely twenty years since, were decent homes abandoned and good town lots gone back to weed. By now Faux was convinced he was looking upon symptoms of epidemic mania and he set down for his readers a precise description of its nature. "The American," he wrote, "has always something better in his eye, further west . . ."[2]

In the year William Faux jolted along the Cumberland Road, taking his interminable notes and admiring the brooding grandeur of the scenery, more than two million Americans were settled in the Ohio and Mississippi valleys. One quarter of the nation lived beyond the Appalachians. In little more than two generations the West had become one of the hard, heavy facts of American life. The ever-increasing weight of it was dislocating existing economic and political combinations, sliding the pieces into new and unfamiliar patterns. That these changes were not the result of premeditated effort was little comfort to those who saw, or thought they saw, their interests threatened. The Louisiana Purchase persuaded a sizable number of Federalists that only by hacking New England free from the rest of the Union and reattaching her to the Mother Country could the purity of republican principles be protected from the contamination of frontier equalitarianism. It was a conviction which twice drew them to the edge of treason. In the end they contented themselves with joining their voices to those who cried out that expansion was error, even anathema; that the country would grow too big to be governed properly; that new lands opening meant the ruination of old. These arguments were repeated with vigor, and not infrequently with vehemence, for nearly half a century. To no avail. There was a current running from Atlantic to Pacific and the flow of emigration, though occasionally it thinned, never ceased.

The motivations which urged men west were very often personal and never after reduced to paper, or perhaps even to thought, and so are buried beyond discovery. But there was one which was held in common and so has come down to us. It was the vision of a fair land whose fat earth was fed by sweet waters and whose trees moved lazily to blessed breezes which blew warm from whatever quarter. Its name was Eden and it was the major apparition of the American Dream.

This it was which William Faux could not see but sensed that others saw. It was older than the nation. An act of communal conjuration raised it up while the first colonists were strung out along the Atlantic littoral. For two centuries it flickered above the upland ridges or blinked dimly from beyond the Appalachian gaps, damped by Indian raids and imperial policy. But after the Revolution it swelled prodigiously and any man might see it — any man whose eye was instructed by faith or impatience or necessity — simply by looking west wherever he happened to be standing. To the believer it was always visible but the vision was clearest in winter when storms howled along the ridgepole and wood was low. Or clearest when a child died, or a woman nagged, or a crop failed. Then the shining features became almost unbearably bright and the beck of them tugged with demanding fingers at the coat sleeves of the soul. And the believer, when he saw these things and felt these things, picked up and moved along, hurried by the knowledge that whatever the year or season a good part of the nation had picked up and was moving too.

The picture is not overdrawn but most of it must remain beyond the comprehension of twentieth-century minds. Our illusions are born of science, not of faith, and they are seldom comforting. Eden was aspiration. It has been replaced by concepts which may or may not be more valid but are unlikely to be more useful. The lure of those shimmering vistas peopled the wilderness, made necessary the building of towns and railroads, and held out a promise to five generations of have-nots. And the final fading, when it came, wrenched the national psyche with such violence the effects are still with us. The whole elaborate structure of the Welfare State has been erected to fill the void. It does not suffice. Security is a pale substitute for hope.

It is a pale substitute even when hope is illusory, or largely illusory, and floats mistily on the surface of a dream. The image of Eden was capable of endless variations, each nicely calculated to please the mind's eye of the beholder, but none approximated reality. The fat earth was never as fat as represented, and the fattest of it was too often swallowed up by land sharks who disgorged only for a profit. Nor was the frontier a safe haven from financial storms. Each new panic tumbled the rickety backwoods banks and tangled the lines of trade and credit. And finally, the living was never easy. It was not particularly easy anywhere in those times, save for the very rich, but the farther west you went, the fewer the available amenities, and at the verge there was little left but mules and muscle and woman power. Modern-minded literalists, adding up these facts, are inclined to discount the lure of Eden, and a few even deny its existence altogether. Their skepticism illuminates the intellectual and emotional abyss which separates the centuries. We are, today, preoccupied with reality. Our ancestors were dissatisfied with it and looked beyond it, projecting their ambitions. In the process they produced spread-eagle oratory; house-proud insularity; the vaporings of Mrs. Sigourney and Mrs. E.D.E.N. Southworth; antebellum cavaliers; some abiding variations on constitutional themes; a gaggle of sects; a respectable number of intellectuals and one honest-to-God philosopher; Stephen Foster and Edgar Allan Poe and the Christie Minstrels; stirpiculture; and a sizable body of first-rate literature that is now seldom read, except as literary exercise, because its writers speak to us from platforms so far removed that though we catch the words, we seldom grasp the meaning. Nineteenth-century Americans trailed after a dozen improbable prophets and embraced as many impossible doctrines. They found in themselves the stirrings of what has come to be called social conscience. They fought four major wars, one of them internecine, and half-a-hundred Indian campaigns and yet remained, by their own account, peace-loving. And in little more than a century they built a third-rate nation into a world power that stretched from ocean to ocean and reached on beyond.

This last was their major accomplishment. They achieved it because they were not drag-chained by reality. They were impelled, collectively, by the conviction that the present could always be improved upon. One way or another. They were unabashedly go-ahead and had not yet paused for self-analysis nor mixed together the compound of gloss and extenuation with which we less forthright moderns attempt to gild the flourishing but sometimes ill-favored lilies of materialism. Success was their central ethic. "What we should call cupidity," wrote Tocqueville in 1835, "the Americans frequently term a laudable industry; and they blame as faint-hearted what we consider to be the virtue of moderate desires."[3]

The redefinition sharpened at the lower reaches of the economic scale. Success was reduced to survival and the rule of life to an aphorism: Root, hog, or die. This was as true in the wilderness as it was in New York's Five Points but the implications differed. The slum-dweller seldom escaped the slum. A bare-knuckles society beat him back. On the frontier, however, there was nothing to prevent a man from walking away from failure, or from successive failures, drawn along by the conviction that something better would turn up farther on. In this way the westerners pushed back the West, going at it in stages, the whole process of a continental crossing taking years and even generations. Daniel Boone passed over the Yadkin Valley to Kentucky in 1767. Several of his children settled in Missouri. A grandson crossed the Rockies in 1846. A great-granddaughter married a territorial governor of Oregon. Morton Matthew McCarver, native of Kentucky, was a founder of Burlington in Iowa, Linnton in Oregon, and Tacoma in

Washington. For his excessive zeal may he be forgiven. The pattern had ten thousand variations but each was recognizable. Go a piece; bide a spell; hitch up and go again.

In their own time they were called not pioneers, but "movers." The term was derisory, poking at rootlessness. They were as indigenous to the frontier as the Indians they supplanted, and they were a special breed, though not in the romantic sense. Restlessness was their dominant trait. The gene of it was passed from father to son as a part of the act of procreation. The frontier was constantly reproducing itself.

At least until the discovery of gold in California it was a rare thing for an urban artisan or his rural counterpart to leave the Atlantic states and arrive at the verge of the wilderness in a single leap. More often he traveled only far enough to find and slip into a niche already prepared by someone who had impatiently hurried on. But go or stay, he could not avoid the effects of our westering on the shaping of the nation. The West was at once an expanding market and an overflowing reservoir of raw materials. More land meant more freedom of movement; it meant a counterweight, not always effective, against the power of property and special interest. A different soil needed different plows because the old plows could not break cleanly the tough sod of the prairies; and once the sod was broken the munificence it rendered up required new mowers and mechanical binders and an entire family of manufactured aids to agriculture. Even the distances were productive. A vast complex of transportation and communication must be erected; telegraph lines to wire the states to one another, railroads to connect producer to consumer. The progression was inexorable: more mines, more manufactories, more jobs, more opportunities — and more difficulties. The nation was growing too fast, growing beyond the imaginings of the most sanguine of the Founding Fathers. The simple administrative devices of Washington's day were already inadequate. Soon they would be anachronistic. Increasingly the federal government was called upon to cope with problems whose magnitude or complicated nature put them beyond the competency of the several states. Not infrequently it was necessary to stretch the Constitution thus, or twist it so, in order to tuck a practical solution neatly under. And each time the base of central authority was broadened.

The frontier was, then, an appetite, an opportunity, an anvil upon which the old forms were being hammered into new shapes. It was one thing more — a purge for discontent. Tocqueville recognized this and commented on it at length. And so, a decade before Tocqueville, did Theophilus Arminius.

His real name was Dr. John Floyd and we will meet him again in these pages. He was a pioneer, born the son of pioneers, and throughout his life the expansion of our boundaries was his principal preoccupation. In 1824 he wrote a letter urging the settlement of Oregon and the Methodizing of its Indians. His style was discursive (he was a politician as well as a physician) and at one point he departed from his text to fit the frontier into the pattern of American life:

> We must have a place to look to as the scene of new action. It is necessary to our free institutions, that, when effort fails in one part of the country, there will be another to resort to, which will carry away the irritation which proceeds from disappointment of any kind, and offer a place where new vigor and new enterprise may employ their ambition. If a man, for instance, in politics is disappointed, that sour and turbulent disposition which, if confined to the place where disappointed, would always be in a state of fermentation, if removed, is fully employed in virtuous pursuits, and stimulated by laudable ambition.[4]

Despite the complex sentences and uncertain syntax, the meaning is clear. The frontier was available to those whose characters or frustrations made them a danger to settled society, those whose failures burdened them, those who felt the need to start afresh where they would not rub shoulders with reminders of the past. It drew those who could not succeed or did not succeed in a society already organized and stratified and fenced about by conventions. This is not to argue that the frontiersmen were mental or physical incompetents. On the contrary, many of them were uncommonly active of mind, and those who survived the attendant hardships did so because the Lord provided them with reasonably sturdy constitutions. But a substantial number were social misfits — the rebels, the restless, the arm-swingers, the adventurous, the unruly — and more than one was a social outcast.

The reader of this book will do well to put from his or her mind the pioneer of legend. He is a virtuous afterthought, an idealization in spurious homespun, created by fabulists and romancers and set to music by the minions of Mr. Disney. Consider, instead, Ishmael Bush. Of all Cooper's characters he comes closest to the mark: crude, cross-grained, savage when it serves — and as remote from us as the dim brute that Millet painted in his *Man with the Hoe*. A reminder that each generation is raised up according to its own images; that we and our grandfathers and their fathers are connected by consanguinity, not convention; that every man must be judged within the frame of his time. The westering Americans were a bark-skinned lot — few saints if many martyrs — and all riveted fast to the main chance. No niceties impeded them. Where forks were luxuries, fingers would do. It was sweat, not perspiration, and soap did not place high on the list of necessaries. The whole of the corn ear had its uses: husk, kernel, silk and cob. Tongues ran to saw edges; vituperation was a fine art. The richest humor reeked of the hen run. None of this is derogatory nor even, to the judgment of history, important. It illuminates the pioneers' methods and their motivations but it does not touch upon their achievements. That they were crass and coarse-fibered does not mean they were ineffectual.

Nor were they simple. The frontier was never Arcadian. Not all who repaired to it sought pastoral paradise. Recall that Eden was variable — its promise adjusting to need. For those who were nearsighted the genius of the land speculator would produce whole towns on paper and impressive brochures urging the opportunity which awaited the mechanic or artisan or merchant or professional man who had sense enough to recognize a good thing and means enough to buy a town lot or two — on ridiculously easy terms — and settle down to grow with what would shortly be a flourishing metropolis.

And so they came: smiths and cabinetmakers, shingle weavers and leather workers, itinerant peddlers and small-town shopkeepers, book salesmen and dram sellers, doctors and teachers. Lawyers arrived in considerable numbers because when new country is opened title litigation is inevitable, and litigation is necessary to lawyers and they to it. After the lawyers came the preachers. This order was not everywhere observed but it was usual, perhaps because, as one wag suggested, sin must ever precede salvation. The lawyers and the preachers, antitheses buckled together by common interest, formed the most influential segment of every frontier community during the time it was struggling toward order and regularization. To a great extent they wrote the laws, edited the newspapers, were the arbiters of public conduct and the molders of public opinion. Both relied upon precedent, though they sought it in different books, and so operated to produce a political and legal continuum. The new states as they emerged were very nearly replicas of the old.

At the last came the accumulators. Capitalists in embryo — or some-times just out of embryo and fluffing their new financial feathers — looking for a comfortable nesting place and plenty of growing room. Their coming marked the end of one stage of frontier development and the beginning of another, which they would largely dominate. They were the wealth makers. With their passing the frontier would pass also. Even before their arrival the early comers were astir, prepar-ing to pull stakes and push ahead, either in person or by proxy in their children, to see what lay on the other side of tomorrow. Not all of them went, of course. Some remained because they had found success enough to satisfy them. And some because they were bone weary of searching.

The above reduces to simplest terms a process that was, in its opera-tion, neither simple nor always predictable. Any number of events affected western development and in some degree altered its course. And for the sake of clarity, the westering movement is here treated as a purely native one, which it was not. From the first days of the Repub-lic there had been European immigrants who debarked from the ves-sels which brought them and marched directly to the backcountry. After the Civil War their numbers increased wonderfully. These new arrivals carried from the Old World special modes and prejudices which tinctured the frontier culture. But the motivations which brought them made them immediately recognizable. Their compasses had a certain fix. They, too, were seekers after Eden.

One more point requires clarification. The Indians — the resident Americans — appear in these pages largely as they appeared to the whites who flocked to the frontier. This story is told from the viewpoint of the European American — not entirely from choice, though Eden was a European-American concept, but because history depends upon writ-ten records, and few American Indians north of the present Mexican border independently developed the arts of writing and record keep-ing. And so the attitudes expressed are — unless clearly editorial and so removed from context — contemporary white attitudes. Not all of them are unsympathetic. From the earliest days there were whites who recognized worthwhile values in Indian culture and realized with re-gret that the culture, like the Indians themselves, would be perma-nently battered by the brutal efficiency of Euro-American civilization.

One of the first adventurers to climb the Appalachians and look down upon the other side cried out in wonder that the land stretched on forever. And so it did — almost. As far as the Mississippi, and even beyond the Mississippi, it was fair and forested and beckoning enough to make the vision of Eden believable. But past Missouri the country changed. Past Missouri the plains began — vast, forbidding, overwhelmingly empty. Here were shallow, silt-stained streams and grass and buffalo and endless hypnotic vistas as characterless as sea waves. An icy hell in winter and a dusty desolation the remainder of the year, save when torrential rains beat the dust to mud. And treeless, which was important. The frontiersmen were conditioned to abundant wood. Wood was shelter and fuel and fences and furnishings. A savage could make do with a skin tent or an earthen hut. Civilization needed lumber.

Such was the popular conception and in 1819 Brevet Major Stephen H. Long, Corps of Engineers, was commissioned to confirm it officially. He was to lead a party of scientists and geographers up the Missouri to the mouth of the Yellowstone and on his return explore the valley of the Arkansas. The major and his entourage left St. Louis in June aboard the *Western Engineer,* a remarkable stern-wheeler especially designed to impress upon aboriginal minds the power of white sorcery. Its superstructure was decorated with flags and paintings and its bow was carved in the shape of a great serpent from whose gaping jaws smoke billowed. Three small brass cannon were added to convince any savage cynic inclined to scoff at machine magic.

The explorers moved at a leisurely pace, stopping at forts and villages to sample local hospitality. They did not reach the Platte until mid-September. A day or so further on, between Fort Lisa and Council Bluffs, Long decided he had had travel enough for one season and set up winter camp. He was not yet halfway to the Yellowstone and he would in fact never reach it. But already he was forming the conclusions which he eventually reported to his superiors and which would be published four years later. The whole of the western region, from the Sabine River to the 49th degree of north latitude and from Missouri to the mountains, was unsuitable for habitation by people depending upon agriculture and demanding such amenities as wood and water. It was nomad land, fit for buffalo, and wild goats, and Indians. Only the hunter could comfortably subsist there, and the hunted. The area's sole worth lay in the fact that its very desolation was an effective barrier against military invasion of the United States from the northwest quarter. There was no Eden.

But Thomas Hart Benton knew better. Benton was a young lawyer

— and, inevitably, a politician — who was just then embarking upon what would be a notable career as a Pointer-of-the-Way. In his political capacity he was a journalist as well, and back in St. Louis, during the very months Long was toiling sluggishly upstream, he was filling the columns of his paper, the *Enquirer,* with an interpretation of the faith according to his private reformation. Eden, he wrote, might not be found anywhere on the plains. But if a farsighted man looked West, shading his eyes against the setting sun, he could see an unmistakable glow rising from beyond the Rockies, out of the valley of the river geographers called the Columbia and William Cullen Bryant called the Oregon.

❧ 1 ❧

Across the Distant Mountains

1818-1824

THE READERS OF the *St. Louis Enquirer* admired a gaudy phrase, and in the winter of 1818–19 editor Thomas Hart Benton treated them to some of his choicest purple. "In a few years," he wrote, "the Rocky Mountains will be passed, and 'the Children of Adam' will have completed the circumambulation of the globe, by marching west until they arrive at the Pacific Ocean in sight of the eastern shore of that Asia in which their parents were originally planted."[1]

This was not prophecy. It was a statement of a truth as widely accepted in that time and at that place as the doctrine of original sin or Parson Weems's parable of young George and the cherry tree. It is improbable the circle of the *Enquirer*'s subscribers could have produced a single doubter. If there was one it is as well he did not stand forth and announce himself, for he would straightway have been damned as politically apostate. The territory of Missouri was Farthest West, and in the West the belief that the nation would one day stretch from ocean to ocean was only honored less than Holy Writ.

There was as yet no realization that the transcontinental passage would mean new departures in the frontier experience. Not because of ignorance but because beyond the Mississippi the accepted definitions lost meaning. There was general agreement that the plains were the Great American Desert and the Rockies the American Himalayas. So they had been described by Zebulon Pike and other, lesser, authorities, and so Stephen Long was finding them. The Biddle edition of Lewis and Clark's journals had been published in 1814 and contained precise descriptions of the country west of Council Bluffs, where Long said the desert began, and of the mountains into which the desert erupted. The journals were widely read and their contents were yeasting in the minds of movers and movers-to-be from Bangor to St. Louis, but something was lost in translation. "Mountains" became the Appalachians, and "Rocky Mountains" the Appalachians grown outsize, a thin line of peaks (on maps of the period, a string of unsightly blemishes running down the face of the continent) with convenient gaps provided. The desert was arid and barren, but it lacked the torment of wind-driven sand, the bits of alkali, the weight of space so heat-swollen it could smother you.

The Great Plains and the mountains beyond them were as far outside the imaginations of men who had neither seen nor felt them as were the landscapes of the moon. So were the distances which were, by past standards, astronomical. Daniel Boone had gone from the Yadkin Valley to Missouri, say seven hundred miles, and taken the best part of a long lifetime to do it. From St. Louis to the lower Columbia was three times as far and must be traveled between May and October. Here was an acknowledged fact. But it was a fact too heavy, too overwhelming in its implications, to be weighed without expert assistance. In 1819, and in the years which followed 1819, there were experts in numbers willing to apply themselves to the problem. Benton himself was one. John Floyd, sometimes Theophilus Arminius, was another. Floyd was a knowledgeable expansionist, a friend of William Clark (his cousin, Charles Floyd, had been the sole casualty of the great expedition) and a self-admitted authority on the trans-Mississippi West. Speaking on the floor of Congress, he was able to assure the nation that the way to the Pacific offered no special hardships or hazards, and could, indeed, be accomplished with ridiculous ease. Twenty-four days by steamboat would see you to the falls of the Missouri, and another fourteen in a wagon or coach would bring you to Clark's Fork of the Columbia River. You floated comfortably downstream for a week and you reached the ocean. Forty-four days in all, and the children of Adam need not raise a blister.

It wasn't a deliberate lie. It wasn't even, in the conventional sense, self-delusion. It was an attempt to reduce to comprehensible terms a reality too large in each of its four dimensions to be clearly comprehensible to any save the few who had wrestled bodily with it. There were men in St. Louis, and not only in St. Louis, who had been to the mountains and across them. They had seen the endless, empty, impersonal vistas of the plains and knew that they could not be crossed, nor the mountains either, by any large bodies of ordinary people, unless new techniques in travel were developed. They knew that some of these techniques were already being worked out along the upper Missouri by wandering traders and trappers, and if they could not know, they could guess with considerable assurance that before long the techniques of mountain travel would be worked out as well. They knew that even if these skills were of a high order, the whole of the backcountry could be inhospitable to the disciplined and deadly to the unwary. A few of them already knew that the short way west was along the Platte and not the Missouri, that the Platte was not navigable to steamboats or any craft which would not float on a few inches of thin mud, and that Benton's elaborate imagery was right. If the children of Adam were to reach the Pacific they must march there, and a good many of them were going to pull up lame or drop off along the way.

The men who knew these things could have corrected most of the errors which were being pumped into the collective mind. They did not because few of them were eloquent and none of them was literary. In the end it made little difference. Benton was wrong when he insisted, as he frequently did insist, that the plains were one great highway and that the tumbling torrents which are Rocky Mountain streams were in fact broad and navigable rivers. Floyd was wrong in believing there was a short cut to continental mastery. But both had grasped the central fact that the limits of expansion had not been reached, that the nation had only paused to catch its breath, and that one day it would pick up and go to the Pacific.

≈ II ≈

John Quincy Adams is not numbered among our national heroes. He was not a lovable man. But he was, after Jefferson, our greatest expansionist; he became persuaded of the manifestness of destiny while James K. Polk was still a schoolboy romping in the Tennessee hills, and it is impossible to write adequately or understandingly of the unfolding of the West without setting down some account of his services. He had no eye for Eden. But he was possessed of a vision of the nation's future which was broader, grander and of greater solidity. In the short span of a dozen years he formulated our national policy for the acquisition of the tramontane West and began its implementation.

President James Monroe brought him to Washington to be secretary of state in 1817. Adams was just turned fifty, a small man with all the asperities small men are apt to accumulate by their middle years: polished without being urbane, pathologically suspicious and overpoweringly able. Of himself he said that he was reserved, cold, austere and of forbidding manners. His enemies' judgments were harsher still. But few questioned his abilities and none his extraordinary qualifications. He had begun his foreign service career at fourteen, served as American minister to the Netherlands and to St. Petersburg and as one of the commissioners who hammered out the Treaty of Ghent, which brought an end to the War of 1812.

Adams was our minister to the Court of St. James's when word of his new appointment reached him. Not until late in the summer did he reach the national capital to take up his duties. Most of the problems awaiting his solution were territorial. Florida was Spanish and must not be. Whoever held Florida threatened New Orleans and had a hand at the throat of the vital Mississippi trade. And across the Mississippi, the West opened on air. Nowhere short of the Pacific was there a line traced to show where the sovereignty of the United States ended and that of Spain began. Fourteen years after the event, the southern and western limits of the Louisiana Purchase had not been delineated.

At the north the common boundary with the two Canadas was drawn uncertainly as far as Lake of the Woods, and past that not drawn at all. Parts of it had been subjects of controversy since Washington's day, parts would continue to be for decades to come, but the differences must be narrowed if possible on the near side of the Rockies. Beyond them the question was one not of boundary but of title. The Northwest Coast was the continent's dark corner, a brooding blank on contemporary maps, a repository of riches which could only be guessed at, a complex of rain forest and high desert thinly peopled by Indians of uncertain disposition. Spain claimed all of it, the United States and Great Britain most of it, and Russia part of it, though with small conviction. None could have defined the bounds precisely. It ran north — how far was uncertain — from California, whose northern limits had not yet been fixed. Its most celebrated physical feature was Robert

Gray's river, discovered by him in 1792 and named for his vessel, the *Columbia Redeviva*. One of Adams's first official acts was to draft instructions, to be sent on to a commissioner the President had already dispatched, to reaffirm the claim of the United States to the wilderness fortress which Mr. Astor's Pacific Fur Company had built at the river's mouth.

It was called, according to the loyalties of the speaker, Astoria or Fort George: no more than a log stockade surrounding a clutch of rude cabins. Even the Indians who traded there did not find it impressive. But the place was evidence of occupancy with a pretension to permanence and so a counter in the contest for control of the river and all the lands which lay within the river's drainage. During the War of 1812 it passed into British hands by forced sale, confirmed by the early appearance of a British gunboat. The Treaty of Ghent provided that places or possessions of either party taken by the other during the war were to be promptly restored. In the case of Astoria, restoration was to be an exercise in diplomatic symbolism. There was no intention to disturb or dispossess the current proprietor, the North West Company. But the flag which had come down must be raised again. After a necessary interval, it was. And when the American commissioner, who had arrived in a British sloop of war, departed as he had come, the Stars and Stripes were hauled down without ceremony and the Union Jack hurried up the staff. No matter. The world was put on notice that American claims to the Pacific Northwest were in no way diminished.

The accession of Florida was a more immediate concern. It might have been accomplished smoothly and even amicably but was not, because King Ferdinand VII of Spain was in equal parts stubborn and devious; because his advisers excelled in intrigue, not government; because Spanish pride took no account of the realities; and finally because Spanish sensibilities were rubbed raw by the congenital fire-eaters of the South and West who were endlessly announcing their intention to "liberate" some part of Spain's decomposing empire. These were the complications. None of them altered the central, unpalatable fact that Florida, in foreign hands, was a threat to national security. Americans were very nearly unanimous in insisting that its acquisition was both necessary and inevitable. But how to bring the inevitable to pass?

Down in Tennessee General Andrew Jackson, whose counsels were seldom watered by moderation, was prepared to bring it to pass directly with only the troops under his command. The administration filed that possibility where it could be found in case of need, and instructed the United States minister at Madrid to suggest that the matter of Florida and the adjustment of the western boundaries of the Louisiana Purchase were fit topics for diplomatic discussion.

Madrid was unenthusiastic, taking no pleasure in the prospect of negotiations which must inevitably cost her yet another part of her shrinking New World possessions. All through the fall — we are still in 1817 — she procrastinated, to no purpose. Nothing improved for her. The demands of the royal armies fighting desperately to put down half-a-dozen simultaneous rebellions in Central and South America reduced the tiny garrisons at St. Augustine and St. Marks below the point of impotence. In the arsenal at Pensacola there was not powder enough to fire a salute. Florida had already slipped beyond recall.

Winter brought the President an excellent opportunity to sharpen the point. A small nest of professional predators had located on Amelia Island, off the Florida coast just south of the Georgia line. They called themselves privateers, and some of them held letters of marque and reprisal issued by one or another of the rebel governments which were popping up like mushrooms all over Spanish America, but they preyed with a fine lack of discrimination upon ships of all registry, American included. In December Mr. Monroe let it be known that the United States government considered these freebooters to be a threat to this nation's peace, tranquillity and commerce. Since Spain, the President said, could not or would not eliminate this pest-hole, the United States Navy would.

The Navy would, and did, with dispatch. Amelia Island was occupied December 23. But Spain reacted even faster. The first Marine had not yet splashed ashore when the Spanish minister, Baron Luis de Onís, appeared at the State Department door. The territorial questions, he told Mr. Adams, which were troubling relations between their two countries might be fruitful subjects for official conversation. As it turned out, Onís meant less than he said. His employers were not accustomed to thinking clearly about colonial affairs, but at last they had come to an imperfect realization that Florida might be forfeit, and that if an accommodation was to be reached on the fixing of the trans-Mississippi boundary, some part of the king's lands along that border might have to be sacrificed. There was no disposition, however, to entrust matters which touched upon Spain's honor — and, parenthetically, upon Spain's weakness — to the uncertainties of head-to-head bargaining. Mediation, said Madrid, was far preferable, and Britain a suitable mediator. Washington might hurry matters along with an appropriate concession, a guarantee that the United States would withhold recognition from the revolutionary government busily engaged in dismantling His Majesty's empire.

Adams retorted coldly that a guarantee of nonrecognition was impossible and mediation was unthinkable; then he sat down to wait until Onís received fresh instructions. The delay irked the secretary of state but he made use of the time it afforded him to reorganize his thinking. He had begun by treating as distinct problems the issue with Great Britain over title to the Columbia and the Northwest Coast and the drawing of a western boundary. Now he saw they could be advantageously coupled, that one could be made to bear upon the other. He had arrived at a totally new concept. Not even that most sanguine of expansionists, Thomas Jefferson, had claimed the Louisiana Purchase pushed the limits of the United States farther than the summit of the Rockies, and there was a general assumption that any line drawn would follow the Continental Divide south from British North America, perhaps detouring to the east at the lower end to exclude Texas. What Adams suggested to the President, early in February of the new year, was that at some point above Texas the northern end of the line be bent due west, hitching the nation to the Pacific. Together Monroe and Adams laid out such a line on one of John Melish's maps, the best then available, and when they had done the President set down the boundaries they hoped for in a memorandum of instruction: north from Galveston Bay along the Trinity River to its source, thence to the Arkansas at its nearest point and up that stream to its headwaters, and thence west over the mountains to the ocean. They wouldn't get quite all of it. But they would get most of it and in doing so would set in train the events upon which James K. Polk would improve nearly thirty years after.

Seven hundred or so miles south of Washington, Andrew Jackson had made up his mind to set in motion his own train of events. For months he had argued that military considerations demanded the immediate seizure of Florida; nothing else would secure the southern border settlements against raids by the troublesome Seminole. At the end of 1817 he had sent off to the President a startling proposal. Occupation could be accomplished without the government's being in any way implicated. No official authorization was required. Mr. Monroe need only pass the word of approval to a mutual friend, say Congressman John Rhea of Tennessee, who would forward it privately, and the deed would be done.

This message was hardly on its way when the general received from the President a communication very nearly as remarkable. It ordered Jackson into Georgia to take command of the Seminole campaign, which was plain enough, but it contained also vague references to "great interests" and "other services" whose definition was left to Jackson's imagination. The general's imagination did not differ materially from his inclinations. He raised a brigade of riflemen to reinforce the troops already in the field, paying for some of their equipment out of his own pocket, and marched briskly off to the new assignment. He was bivouacked on Big Creek, forty-odd miles south of Macon, when a letter from Rhea caught up with him. It said, or Jackson construed it to say, that the President approved invasion.

Mr. Monroe afterward denied, and perhaps with truth, that he had read Jackson's letter — he was ill when it arrived — or that he had authorized Rhea to act. But he could not deny the shining phrases which had excited Jackson's expectations. And Jackson himself was undisturbed by doubts. By March 10 he and his army were descending on the Florida border. Except for the rivers, which were out of their banks, there was little to hinder them. The Seminole were pushed south of the Suwannee. Two British subjects suspected of giving aid and comfort to the enemy were captured, court-martialed, convicted and executed with soldierly dispatch. (Or indecent haste, depending upon the point of view.) St. Marks was occupied and at Pensacola the royal archives were seized and an American colonel installed as governor.

First news of these exploits began to descend on Washington at the beginning of May, report by report, like the early drops of an approaching storm. The storm itself arrived in mid-July. Onís set up a windy howling over the affront to Spanish sovereignty. The British minister rumbled his displeasure. As the clouds thickened, half Congress panicked, or pretended to. Jackson was a potential candidate for the presidency. There was the prospect the affair might be managed to his disadvantage. John C. Calhoun, secretary of war and also a candidate, persuaded most of the Cabinet, and very nearly persuaded

President Monroe, that the conquest must be disavowed, Florida returned, and the entire blame thrown upon the general.

Mr. Adams was for standing firm. He alone, of all the Cabinet, properly assessed the odds. Spain had neither strength nor stomach for war. Britain, bled white by the relentless cupping of the Napoleonic wars, needed peace and the comforts of commerce. Adams urged a vigorous approach. Jackson must be sustained. And as for Florida, it was no longer a piece on the board.

He carried the President with him, part way. Onís was told that General Jackson had exceeded his orders in taking St. Marks and Pensacola, but not further than necessity required. Both places would be returned, without apology, as soon as Spain could throw into them troops enough to protect them against Seminole attack. The message was more conciliatory than Adams had counseled, but not conciliatory enough to mend the damage to Spanish honor. Madrid continued to complain. Late in 1818 the secretary of state sat down to prepare a final reply. Spain, he wrote stiffly, was claiming the prerogatives of sovereignty without assuming the obligations. Florida was a derelict, Spanish in name only. It was the duty of the king's ministers either to maintain internal order in the colony and prevent the Indians from raiding north across the border, or to cede title to the United States. Until one or the other of these events came to pass, Washington would be governed, as Jackson had been governed, by the first law of nations and of nature — the right of self-defense.

It was a considerable performance, complete with documentary evidence that the executed Britishers and certain Spanish officers had intrigued with the Seminole. Sympathy for the Spanish position had been growing in Europe's chancelleries. Now it died for want of nourishment. The annexation of Florida was effectively accomplished, though the formalities remained. And if Spain was disposed to make difficulties over the fixing of the trans-Mississippi boundary, let her reflect that the right of self-defense could be exercised in any direction, west included.

The pieces were falling into place. Back in the middle of this strenuous year, the American minister to London, Richard Rush, had urged that proposed Anglo-American conversations include all matters at issue between the two nations. In expectation of this development Adams had in July drawn up a long memorandum of instruction for

Rush and Albert Gallatin, who had been ordered to England from his post at Paris to assist in the negotiations. The memorandum touched on a multiplicity of subjects — impressment, American fishing rights in certain waters off Newfoundland and the Labrador, indemnity for slaves carried off by British troops during the War of 1812, and the question of the northern boundary. The United States, Adams wrote, would accept the 49th Parallel west from Lake of the Woods to the summit of the Rockies, or even on to the Pacific. South of that line Britain could make no valid claim. And any disposition of the territory beyond the mountains could be binding only upon the contracting powers, leaving undisturbed the rival claims of Spain and Russia.

The resulting treaty was signed in October and reached Washington in December. It did not settle every difference between the parties, but it settled enough to be accounted a major accomplishment. American fishing rights were confirmed, machinery was set up to provide indemnity for the deported slaves, and the commercial convention agreed upon in 1816 was extended ten years more. The remaining provision was the most interesting. The line from Lake of the Woods west was drawn as the secretary had suggested in his memorandum as far as the Continental Divide. There it stopped. The land beyond — in the treaty it is referred to simply as the Northwest Coast — was to be open to settlement and trade by nationals of both countries for a period of ten years, without, however, prejudicing in any way the territorial claims of any other nation.

Unanimous Senate approval came in January (we are in 1819 now, the year in which Benton assumed his apostolic vestments), and Adams turned again with sour determination to his pursuit of Onís. Florida was in his pocket. Now he wanted to push the national borders to the Pacific. To achieve this, he and the President would, and did, give up on Texas. The line would go north along the Sabine, not the Trinity. When it reached the source of the Arkansas it would swing north or south (nobody was certain which) to the 42nd Parallel. To all lands above that line Spain conveyed to the United States such right, title and interest as she possessed.

Adams arranged the signing of the treaty for February 22, General Washington's birthday. When it was done he entered in his diary a short passage of self-congratulation. "The acknowledgement of a definite boundary to the South Sea," he wrote, "forms a great epoch in our history. The first proposal of it in this negotiation was my own, and I trust it is now secured beyond reach of revocations."[2]

⚜ III ⚜

Congressman John Floyd introduced his bill on January 25, 1821. It called upon the President to occupy that part of the territory of the United States lying along the waters of the Columbia River, to extinguish Indian title to an unstated portion thereof, to provide land for settlers, to open a port of entry and to make rather drastic changes in the management of Indian affairs and the regulation of the fur trade. The measure cost John Quincy Adams an unpleasant hour with the British minister and he regarded it as an iniquitous piece of political chicanery specially contrived for his embarrassment. Floyd's colleagues in Congress did not doubt the purity of the doctor's motives, but they thought the proposal was premature. It was in fact only just ahead of events.

The St. Louis fur trade had been crippled by the late war with England and by the long depression which succeeded that war, but now it was recovering strongly. In the fall of 1821 the Missouri Fur Company's Joshua Pilcher built a fort at the mouth of the Big Horn and called it for Tom Benton. Pilcher was a large man in the trade but the following year a larger emerged: William Henry Ashley, miner, militia officer, rural entrepreneur, presently brigadier general and lieutenant governor of the new state of Missouri. In the spring of 1822 Ashley outfitted 150 trappers, rivermen, clerks and hunters and sent them off to work the upper Missouri. Some of Ashley's people reached the Yellowstone and set up a post not far from Pilcher's establishment. Foothills country but in sight of the Big Horn range, which is a spur of the Rockies.

So we have arrived at the era of the mountain men, the greatest of American originals, textbook examples of environmental adaptation, more Indian than the Indians who, out of magnificent partiality, supplied them with allies, enemies and women. Jim Clyman, who was one of the best of the breed, said of his fellows that Falstaff's battalion was genteel by comparison. If it were so, their manners did not affect their usefulness. For a generation they would wander the mountains, trapping beaver along streams that ran cold enough to freeze a man's marrow even in summer heat; leaving their bones to whiten in lonely valleys when hostiles caught them unaware; discovering Great Salt Lake and the splendors of Jackson Hole and rediscovering Colter's Hell; making a thoroughfare of South Pass and pushing beyond it to Snake waters and the Columbia or to California by way of the Humboldt.

A party under Ashley's partner, Major Andrew Henry, might have reached the mountains in 1822, but it ran afoul of the Blackfeet — each one of whom was, by wilderness repute, as cruel and cunning as Ishmael, son of Nethaniah — and was racked repeatedly. Major Henry himself was experienced (he had trapped the Snake country as long ago as 1810) and competent, but he was luckless and the partnership did not prosper. One of the first two keelboats sent up the Missouri struck a snag near Fort Osage and promptly plunged to the bottom, carrying with her some $10,000 worth of supplies and trade goods and a sizable piece of the general's credit. The first year's hunt and trading did not bring in enough furs to meet expenses.

Eighteen twenty-three brought fresh and bloody troubles. The Arikaras, who controlled the middle river and were notable for their refractory natures, complicated matters by determining to halt all further traffic to the mountains. The result was a nasty little war which eventually involved most of the rival fur companies, a troop of Sioux and a detachment of regulars under Colonel Henry Leavenworth. The Arikaras were persuaded they had strayed into error, but the uprising convinced Ashley it would be safer to detour to the south of them in the future, following the course of the Platte and its north fork as far as the Rockies. At the time there was doubt the business had a future. Major Henry had resigned, weary of failure. Ashley was sole proprietor of a concern whose liabilities far exceeded its assets. The forbearance of his creditors saved him from bankruptcy and in September, 1824, at almost the last moment, his luck turned. Tom Fitzpatrick came out as far as Council Bluffs and sent word on to the general at St. Louis that early the previous spring he and Jedediah Smith had crossed the mountains and come down into a land abounding in beaver.

At twenty-five Tom Fitzpatrick was well on his way to becoming the grand master of all mountain men, but 'Diah Smith was the authentic giant of the breed. He was a New Yorker who had come west by way of Pennsylvania and Ohio. In the spring of 1822 he was in St. Louis, and hearing, as he later wrote, that General Ashley and Major Henry were outfitting an expedition to engage in the fur trade on the upper reaches of the Missouri, he hired out as a hunter. He quickly acquired a superb mastery of forest skills and in the Arikara war served with distinction, commanding a company of irregulars in the final battle. Thereafter he was Captain Smith to his subordinates, and the free trappers acknowledged him as one of their most distinguished leaders. It is strange that they did so for 'Diah was very much an outsider — a Bible reader among scoffers, pure-tongued among the profane, so-bersided among the harum-scarum. No Indian woman ever shared his lodge. For a time he carried about with him a young beaver tricked out in a scarlet collar, as both a pet and a symbol of the loneliness which surrounded him even in the midst of his company. But he was brave to rashness and had a genius for command, and these qualities allowed rougher men to overlook his inexplicable virtuousness. They even found a little satisfaction in his piety. In a country where death was never more than a step away it was comforting to know there was someone prepared to recite appropriate words should a man ever need burying.

In the summer of 1823, after the final defeat of the Arikaras, Smith and Tom Fitzpatrick led a detail of trappers west from Fort Kiowa. They would winter with the Crows, gleaning from them such information as they could about the country beyond, and when the weather lightened make a try at climbing the Rockies. They followed up White River to where it bends away to the southwest, cut across the south fork of the Cheyenne and a corner of the Black Hills and so into the grasslands beyond.

Somewhere short of Powder River a grizzly charged Smith from a thicket, peeling his scalp back to the skull and mangling one ear. Jim Clyman laid the insulted flesh back into place and sewed it down with a needle and common thread, but he balked at attempting to mend the shredded ear until ordered by his patient. When the operation was done the captain climbed aboard his horse and rode into camp. Ten days' convalescence and he was ready to travel. Jim's stitching was serviceable but it was not ornamental, and thereafter Jedediah wore his hair long, in deference to queasy sensibilities.

'Diah and his party found Crow lodges in the Wind River valley and wintered there. In February they attempted to cross the mountains through Union Pass but snow defeated them. They slipped off southwest to the Sweetwater and turned upstream, suffering terribly from cold and always on the near edge of starvation. Somewhere near the middle of March they found what they were looking for — what Benton and Floyd and other believers in the American Dream had long insisted the Lord must, in His infinite wisdom, have provided for the special benefit of His Chosen People — a broad, open way cut across the roof of the continent, with so little grade that loaded wagons could traverse it. South Pass. The Indians had known it for countless generations. Robert Stuart used it on his way home from Astoria in 1812. But Smith and Fitzpatrick were now connecting it permanently to the network of trails the fur trade was constructing to serve the mountain West, and so opening the path to Oregon. In time to come, the frontier would follow them.

❦ 2 ❧

His Majesty's Marches

1824-1831

I N 1821 the Hudson's Bay Company absorbed the North West Company, bringing an end to a competition which was also a war, the longest and most devastating of a series of such wars which bloodied the Canadian West for over half a century. A war fought at ruinous expense and with a demonic savagery which bemused the savages who were its spectators and, too frequently, its victims. The settlement gave His Britannic Majesty's government, which had urged it, a measure of ease. Those damned restless Americans were already at the eastern portals of the Rockies and must certainly soon appear on the western side. It would not do to have British North America divided by murderous contest when title to the Northwest Coast was in the balance.

Organization of the newly combined operation required adjustments, some of them delicate. Duplicate posts must be eliminated; the poor devils whom peace made redundant must be turned out to grass; endless sheets of accountings must be gotten through. Some of the Indians who had been clients of the late North West Company were mortally offended by the merger and it was necessary to repurchase their good will.

The whole process took three years and would have taken longer had not The Bay, as the company was called, found a wilderness administrator of rare genius. His name was George Simpson. He was squat, square, plump with self-esteem, still in his middle thirties and deficient in experience, for he had arrived in Canada as late as 1820. But he was a passionate authoritarian driven by ravening ambition, unimpeded by scruple, possessed of a sound instinct for corporate politics and a surface suavity fit to grease feelings wrenched by his

25

remorseless demands. By 1824 he had riveted his collar firmly on the collective neck of his immediate subordinates, the chief factors and chief traders whose responsibility was field command.

That same year he planned to visit England to seek a lady-wife to replace the half-Indian girl who presently warmed his bed and who would, before he had done with her, give him four children. He was unable to go because at London the executive committee of The Bay discovered a new and troublesome concern. The Columbia District, though it furnished one-fifth of all the furs the company collected, could show no profit. Simpson was ordered west on a tour of inspection and reorganization.

There was a geopolitical consideration as well. During the years immediately following the War of 1812 the conciliatory attitude of the British foreign secretary, Viscount Castlereagh, eased relations between the United States and the United Kingdom. But in 1822 threats of most odious blackmail overset Castlereagh's sanity and he cut his own throat to escape the dark terrors which pursued him. George Canning succeeded to the foreign office. Canning was, like John Quincy Adams, all imperial sensitivities. He was convinced Castlereagh's recognition of American title to Astoria was an egregious error and a needless sacrifice of imperial interests, and feared that it as good as perfected American claims to the Northwest Coast as far as the south bank of the Columbia. He was not disposed to retreat further, both because he regarded the river as an excellent natural boundary and because he thought the United States an upstart nation whose presumptuousness needed curbing.

In 1823 Canning advised the London committee of the Hudson's Bay Company that since occupation of the Astoria site depended upon Yankee sufferance, Fort George should be abandoned and a new post built at some suitable place on the north bank of the river where it would strengthen British claims. The suggestion was an acknowledgement of the partnership between Beaver House and Whitehall. Henceforth the company's rule of conduct in its relations with the Americans — and with the Russians in Alaska — was an expression of state policy. It was diplomacy on the cheap, defective because in the field, rules were not infrequently bent to accommodate the facts of commercial life, and because interminable miles and months separated London from Oregon. Close control was impossible. The system never worked well and could not have worked at all had not the Russians been irresolute and the United States government, after Adams and until Polk, been content to let the westering thrust of the frontier advance its interests.

Canning's proposal was forwarded to Simpson with appropriate instructions. The little governor was already at York Factory and on August 15 he set out west, traveling by the Nelson River to determine whether that way offered any advantages over the more usual route up the Hayes River to Norway House. Miserable weather and a lack of guides hampered him but he kept moving, as he always did, racing time. Beyond Lac la Biche and a little short of the Athabasca River he caught up with Dr. John McLoughlin, who was going to the Columbia District to be its chief factor and resident manager. They traveled the remainder of the way together, crossing the mountains in good season and reaching Spokane House toward the end of October.

Simpson's first impressions were unfavorable. From the earliest days of Astoria the Columbia traders had slipped willingly into habits of improvidence — the Nor'westers imported suits of mail and, for God knows what exotic reasons, laid in supplies of ostrich plumes — and despite the change in management the company's servants remained cheerfully unreconstructed, consuming quantities of European provisions brought in at enormous cost. They might as well, the governor remarked caustically, be eating gold.

His mood did not improve as the journey progressed. He wrote down Alexander Ross as empty-headed and bombastic and arranged that Peter Skene Ogden replace him as leader of the Snake River Expedition, the annual swing through the Snake country which produced some of the finest of the Columbia's furs. He mistrusted John Warren Dease because the man was "overly addicted" to tea, and when at last he reached Fort George he thought it altogether too grand in its fittings and appointments. By now he was convinced the district was overextended except for its trade and he was howling for economies. Farming would make the posts, or some of them, self-sustaining. Personnel must be cut drastically while at the same time a coasting trade must be pushed north at least as far as the mouth of Fraser's River, where he suggested a fort be erected, and overland brigades be regularly sent south to California.

It is difficult to avoid the suspicion that some of this was written for the benefit of the shareholders. Simpson knew when he set these suggestions down in his journal that there were Americans in the Snake country, but he did not mention them. They were the detachment of General Ashley's people led by 'Diah Smith. A group of Alexander Ross's free trappers, most of them Iroquois, had run afoul of a band of Snakes and come off second best. Smith happened on what was left of them, naked and plundered of their weapons, and offered to escort them back to Ross in exchange for the furs they had cached before the Snakes had jumped them.

So the story went. Nobody on the Hudson's Bay side was disposed to believe it. More important, Smith had talked his way to Flathead Post, where he proposed to winter, shown himself to the Indians there — some of the company's most valued customers — and, so suspicion went, spread subversion among the free trappers.

This was a major setback, though Simpson ignored it in his report. He had worked his way to the conclusion that the whole of the district's trouble was due to poor management and that now that he was running it, it would go. He spent a satisfying winter drawing up lists of instructions, investigating aboriginal lifestyles and otherwise acquainting himself with the area. Obedient to George Canning's directive, McLoughlin found a site on the north side of the Columbia, about eighty miles inland and almost opposite the mouth of the river called Multnomah or Willamette. Simpson thought the setting as magnificent as any gentleman's seat in England. On March 19, 1825, he broke a bottle of rum over the flagstaff, christening the place Fort Vancouver. He was on his way east and, after sharing a drink of celebration, departed, five months nearly to the day after crossing Athabasca Pass to the Pacific side of the Rockies.

It was a considerable visit. The governor had reason to be pleased with himself, and being Simpson, was. He had reinvigorated the district, laid out areas into which it could expand, and "prooned" with a vengeance. His appointments were excellent. Ogden was a vast improvement over Ross. McLoughlin was a great man, which handicapped him, and a good man, which handicapped him more, but he was a sound executive and a passable administrator. The presence of Americans west of the Rockies was regrettable, but stiff opposition would push them back. There remained the matter of firming relations with the mid-Columbia Indians, some of whom were fractious. At Simpson's direction Alexander Ross selected two boys, the sons of chiefs, one each from the Spokane and Kootenay tribes; the governor took them east with him to Red River Colony, where they could learn that salvation flowed from Jesus Christ and good works from the Honourable Company, The Kootenay died before long. The other lad, baptized Spokane Garry, lived and would return home one day, bringing trouble. But that was a worry locked in the future and as he climbed wearily over the mountains the governor could pause and look back with satisfaction. Britannia in the person of the Hudson's Bay Company was settled in on the north bank of the Columbia, and Dr. John McLoughlin had been duly installed as overseer of His Majesty's marches, Pacific Northwest division.

❧ II ❧

John McLoughlin is an important figure in this history and it is necessary to separate him from the legend he has become. He was a bear of a man, towering over most of his contemporaries, with a dramatic mop of white hair and imperious eyes. He was kindly, courteous and endlessly obliging but his nature was violent. He was not, as some latterday idolaters would make him, a saint. The fur trade produced no saints.

He was born at Rivière-du-Loup, Lower Canada, in 1784, the third child of John and Angelique McLoughlin, and christened Jean Baptiste, though he seems never to have been called by that name except, perhaps, during his short childhood. At fourteen he was apprenticed to a surgeon, and before he was twenty was licensed to practice medicine. That same year, 1803, he signed on with the North West Company.

He was engaged as a physician but in slack times turned his attention to trade, and found he had a talent for it. The Indians were awed by his size and impressed by his dignity, and treated him with a careful respect. He took a Chippewa woman. She gave him his first child, Joseph, her contribution to history. Very shortly the doctor put her aside in favor of Marguerite Wadin.

Marguerite was at least nine years McLoughlin's senior and had not the freshness of youth to recommend her, but she had other attributes. She occupied, by reason of her family and her connections, an advanced position in wilderness society. Her father, until he got himself murdered, was a Swiss and a trader of some importance. She herself had been consort to Alex McKay, who was the great Alexander Mackenzie's lieutenant in 1793 when Mackenzie led the first party overland to the Pacific. McKay had got a son upon her, Tom McKay, who would have a notable career in Oregon. In 1810 the elder McKay left Canada to join John Jacob Astor's Pacific Fur Company, taking his thirteen-year-old boy with him, and Marguerite found herself available. McLoughlin wasted little time in paying court. Terms were arranged and Marguerite moved in. In the summer of 1812 she gave birth to a boy, John McLoughlin, Jr. Two years later the doctor became a wintering partner in the North West Company.

McLoughlin was sufficiently active in the bitter contest with the Hudson's Bay Company to get himself arrested for alleged complicity in a senseless massacre at Red River. He was eventually found innocent but only after suffering near drowning while being carried to Quebec by his captors, and two years of legal harassment. Undoubtedly the incident tempered his thinking. The doctor became convinced that the war was a wasteful bit of business, interfering with trade and cutting back profits, and the incessant bloodletting did not pleasure him. He was not the only dissenter in the Nor'westers' ranks but he was the most important of them, for by 1820 he had become the acknowledged leader of the winterers. That year he fomented a rebellion against the company's Montreal managers. The rebellion failed but it was one of the pressures which hurried the merger of 1821.

McLoughlin had, then, a respectable career behind him when he reached Oregon, but his days of greatness were ahead. He had been honored with a command of inestimable importance and responsibility, but he entered upon it in a dour and skeptical mood. The trees of the coastal rain forest were enormous beyond belief and the undergrowth so rank as to be near impenetrable, but the doctor somehow persuaded himself the soil generally was thin, rocky and infertile. And if the winter weather was mild, it was so intolerably damp that in more than four months he did not look out on one clear, sunny day, nor see ten when it did not rain.

All these complaints he wrote to an uncle in March, 1825, and when he wrote he was already looking forward to going home on rotation three years hence. His reactions were partly predictable, for a winter's stay at the Columbia's mouth can be a depressing affair. But one also hears the echo of inner discontent. McLoughlin was not setting out on his new duties with notable enthusiasm. The reasons are not clear. It may be that the first weariness of middle age was on him, that time of life when men find the years running perceptibly faster. Or it may be that he was oppressed by a sense of isolation, the unhappy feeling that he was an exile in the land.

Whatever his personal dissatisfactions, he had little time to brood upon them. The *William and Ann,* which brought out the year's outfitting, brought also directives from the London committee: the ship was to be sent north to reconnoiter the coastal trade. She arrived in the river April 11, seasonably early, but what with repairs and refitting she did not get off again until early June. Near two months lost while McLoughlin reined in his impatience with difficulty. It was his first venture into maritime affairs and he prepared his instructions with special care. To small purpose. Captain Hanwell, who commanded, was no man of business, while the Indians he must deal with were already commercially minded when James Cook reached them, had now behind them fifty years' active experience in trade and figured their prices as closely as any Yankee shopkeeper. Hanwell tried unsuccessfully to soften their wits with rum and allowed himself to be patronized by an American coaster named Kelley who filled his ear with a select assortment of fleas. By September the Captain was back in the Columbia, bringing with him little but gloomy reports.

Hanwell had missed opportunities, underplayed his hand and been unduly impressed by Kelley's propaganda. The doctor saw this and saw too that the coastal trade, properly conducted, could drive a profit. But he had struggled through a summer of frustrations and the failure rankled. He might have enlarged on Hanwell's shortcomings more extensively had his attention not been suddenly distracted by news of an honest-to-God disaster: Peter Skene Ogden had lost nearly a thousand pelts and most of his free trappers to the Americans.

⚘ III ⚘

On the evening of October 25, 1810, Mr. Samuel Black and Mr. Peter Skene Ogden of the North West Company entered in at the east gate of the Hudson's Bay post at Île-à-la-Crosse. Mr. Black was carrying a

loaded gun and two pistols and Mr. Ogden had by him his dagger, and
both were conducting themselves in a rude and unseemly manner.
Peter Fidler of the Hudson's Bay Company intercepted them, ordering
them to go back, and when they did not, beat upon Mr. Black with a
stick. Whereupon Mr. Ogden cut two large holes in the back and side
of Fidler's coat, pricking his skin, and Mr. Black mashed his thumb
with a blow. The other Hudson's Bay Company servants did not interfere, being much afraid, and Black and Ogden continued to abuse Mr.
Fidler, even following him into his own room where he went to bind
up his wounds. When at last the two Nor'westers left, to Mr. Fidler's
considerable relief, they swore to see to it that the people at that place
spent a most miserable and unhappy winter. And they did.

Portrait of P. S. Ogden, aged sixteen.

His flavor improved with the passing of years. In 1818, because there
were warrants out charging him with sundry crimes, including murder,
he thought it discreet to cross over to the Columbia side of the mountains. He was still there, by now a wintering partner, when the merger
of the companies was arranged and he found himself jobless.

His old Nor'wester associates thought him a roaring good fellow, full
of pranks and eccentric humors, but the gentlemen of The Bay remembered him without favor. By the terms of the coalition agreement
both he and Samuel Black were excluded from employment. Simpson
wisely let them linger a year to humble their spirits, then personally
secured their reinstatement. He needed them in Oregon. Black was
detailed to Walla Walla, an anchor point, while Ogden's new assignment carried responsibilities of state as well as of trade.

London could not know, as Simpson knew, that 'Diah Smith had
reached Flathead Post, but London had its premonitions. Mountain
men were tramping the defiles of the Rockies, the frontiers were about
to overlap and the Convention of Equal and Open Occupancy had only
four years to run. London believed there was a possibility the line of
demarcation might be made to follow the Columbia east and north to
where it crossed the 49th Parallel. (No such possibility existed. After
1818 no American administration could safely have accepted less than
Polk accepted in 1846.) If London was right, the whole of the Snake
River drainage would pass to the United States, which made it pointless
for The Bay to conserve the area's abundant beaver. Simpson's instructions to Ogden were therefore conditioned both by the requirements
of trade and by the diplomatic imponderables. Henceforth the Snake

River hunt was to be a very nearly continuous affair, the brigades returning to fixed posts only when it became necessary to recruit, re-provision and deliver the catch, and the country between the Columbia and the Continental Divide was to be trapped bone clean. Not only would the company be assured a quick and certain profit but also, as Governor Simpson afterward explained to McLoughlin, the first step the United States government would take toward settling the Oregon territory would be through their Indian traders. If the Snake country, and the lands south of the Snake country, were exhausted of beaver, American trappers would have no incentive for crossing the Rockies. The Yankee thrust would be blunted.

Simpson was thus early slipping into misconceptions which would color his thinking in time to come. He failed to understand that the forces building along the American trans-Mississippi frontier were el-emental, not official, that Washington had no colonial policy (as distinct from a general policy of continental expansion) and that the mountain men were not settlers and would only become settlers under pressure of acute necessity and with reluctance. The colonists-to-be were still gathering stateside and when at last they set forth they would be lured along not by the prospects of beaver pelts but by a mighty vision. For the moment, however, none of these concerns was material, and the solution which the governor provided for the immediate problem con-fronting him was sound enough. The American fur trappers who were pressing through the Rockies must be contained in the high country and fenced off from the more valuable and vulnerable territories which lay west and north. To accomplish this goal he proposed to strengthen the Snake River Expedition by increasing the number of company servants to twenty-five. But in the end he provided only eleven. It was a profound blunder. It meant reliance must be placed on free trappers, who were unreliable by definition. Peter Skene Ogden's afflictions began when George Simpson came down with a fever of economies.

Flathead Post was on Clark's Fork of the Columbia near its conflu-ence with the Flathead in what is now Sanders County, Montana. Ogden rode out of it the afternoon of December 20, 1824, leading a decidedly mixed command. There were the eleven *engagés*. There was William Kittson for clerk; a plus, since he had served at Walla Walla and Spokane House, knew something of how the land lay and carried more than the ordinary complement of guts. There were forty-seven or forty-eight trappers and perhaps a half-dozen lads apprenticed to learn the trade. There were thirty squaws — tricked out in their finest beadwork to honor the occasion; next morning they would suit down to fatigues — and there were thirty-five children. In all, the party contained 125 souls and 268 horses. There would always be an Indian lodge in camp, sometimes two or more, and on the evening of December 29 the Ashley people led by Jedediah Smith joined up. Under the circumstances the Americans could hardly expect a rousing welcome (Kittson set it down that Smith was a "sly, cunning Yankey," a double redundancy in current British usage), but the caravan was about to enter Blackfoot country, which made for a community of interests. A country of war and murders, Ogden called it, where firepower was salvation.

His troubles with his free trappers had already begun. There were *métis* (half-Indian, half-French), and Iroquois, and one, astonishingly, was a Missourian left over from Astor's Pacific Fur Company — all of them feckless, undisciplined and almost beyond persuasion. They could not be taught to stake their horses properly. They refused to stand sentry duty or, what was worse, simply went off to bed in the middle of a watch. Ogden cursed them, cajoled them, issued orders they cheerfully ignored, stewed over their safety and damned their improvidence.

Somehow he shepherded them over Gibbon Pass into the Big Hole basin, where they wasted a joyous three weeks and much powder on a grand buffalo hunt. He brought them back west of the mountains by Lemhi Pass, the route Lewis and Clark had used when they were outward bound in 1805, and pushed off southwest. It was by now mid-February. Late storms, a poverty of grass and a slashed, bewildering terrain delayed him. The best of his horses were miserably poor. His returns were pitifully scant; most days he had to be content with a single pelt. Not until early April did he reach the Snake, not far from where the Blackfoot enters it.

For a little time it seemed his luck had changed. Somewhere near here, just where is uncertain, Smith and his party split off, though Ogden suspected them of lurking in the middle distance. But returns increased, the weather moderated and on April 19, just after crossing south from the Snake watershed, he reached Bear River just where it hooks around the northern tip of the Wasatch Range and starts southward toward Great Salt Lake. He was just counting his first thousand beaver, and three weeks later he had taken a thousand more. Not enough to make him sanguine, but his hopes were on the rise.

Despite his troubles, so far Ogden had experienced nothing insupportable, nothing outside the normal routine of a mountain hunt. Louis Kanatagan is shot dead by his wife. An accident, according to the only witness. So Louis is buried with solemn prayers and the witness moves in with the widow. Antoine Benoit is careless enough to lose his scalp and his life to the Blackfeet. Several children are born and perhaps one or two die, and a number of horses are run off because the free trappers will not guard them. Misfortunes, but none was beyond the commonplace and now things were looking up. By mid-May the brigade had reached what is since called Ogden's Hole and were trapping Ogden's River and the Weber which it joins. Here was rich beaver country, and Ogden was sufficiently encouraged to write, on the very eve of disaster, "I only wish we could find a dozen *Spots* equal to it." [1]

Next morning, May 22, there were visitors in camp: McLeod and Lazard, deserters from Flathead Post in 1822, bringing news that Taos was only fifteen marches off and the Spanish River (the Colorado) about three; that of the twelve others who had deserted with them three years earlier, only six survived; and that all of them were with a party no more than a day away. Ogden heard them without satisfaction. The country was getting overcrowded. A-crawl, he wrote sourly, with Americans and Canadians bent on the same object.

McLeod and Lazard reappeared the next day, bringing their companions, a party of about fifteen led by Etienne Provost, a French Canadian operating out of Taos. No formidable threat; but in the afternoon, in the middle of a territory to which neither of them had any valid claim, the empires collided. Twenty-five Americans marched in, parading the colors and accompanied, ominously, by fifteen of Ogden's free men who had been out with their traps.

The newcomers were more of the ubiquitous Ashley people and their leader was Johnson Gardner, nationalist in buckskin, spread-eagle patriot, and a man armored by his own virtues. He planted his flag a hundred yards from Ogden's camp and announced that all the country hereabouts was the property of the United States of America, and that any person indebted or under contract to a foreign corporation was cleansed and absolved from such obligation by having passed over into the Land of the Free, and that he was prepared to receive and protect any who might be fugitives from British despotism and would sell them what they needed at bargain rates and pay premium prices for their beaver. He must have extended these remarks with appropriate oratorical flourishes, for William Kittson commented dryly that when he was done night was coming on, and no more was said.

They were, all of them, in the valley of the Weber, a short march from Great Salt Lake and perhaps fifty miles south of the 42nd Parallel, former Spanish territory which was now Mexican. But the boundary question was academic. Gardner was preaching subversion, and he had the handle. Among Simpson's economies was a requirement that free trappers must pay Indian prices, which meant an outrageous markup on powder, lead, traps, tobacco and such other necessaries and comforts. It was impolitic gouging, one more grievance to unsettle minds already in a turmoil of discontent, and it added sweetness to Gardner's blandishments.

On May 23 fourteen of The Bay's free trappers resigned in a body — and not peaceably, for there were fierce little squabbles about horses and furs, and Gardner was energetic in promoting trouble. The Americans turned out to lend the deserters their support, both moral and profane and rather more of the latter. Nobody's hand got far from his gun but matters never quite came to a shoot-out despite Gardner's earnest endeavors. Ogden's account of the affair is abbreviated and rather confusing and in it he credits himself, and Kittson, too, with great firmness in the presence of the enemy. But it was firmness tempered with discretion, a little face-saving to relieve the sting of the whipping, and when the ordeal was over he laid plans to pull out first thing in the morning. There was nothing he wanted so much as he wanted to get away from that place.

He had lost perhaps a third of his furs, some horses and all the outfits unpaid for. He might have lost a great deal more had it not been for Alex Carson, the leftover Astorian. Carson was one of the few who had paid his debts before leaving and after dark he slipped over from the rebel side with a warning that the Iroquois and the Americans were planning to pillage Ogden's camp at daybreak. Ogden was ready when they arrived and what might have been big trouble degenerated into another round of name-calling. But before he broke camp five more of his free trappers deserted.

He was both humiliated and demoralized, his retreat north came near being a flight, and he was forced to submit to one more indignity. As he was prepared to cross the Bear three men left him, leaving behind their women, children, traps, furs and most of their horses, so possessed were they of the notion they must join the Americans. Ogden saluted their departure with appropriate expletives and pushed on north.

With him remained the *engagés,* twenty-three free trappers and six older boys, a total of forty-two counting Kittson and Ogden himself (to which add an equal number of camp followers of all ages who must be protected and provided for), and even the company servants had lost their enthusiasm. Too weak a party for adventuring, but somehow he managed it. Word came from the Flatheads, who were reliable allies, that many lodges were camped on the headwaters of the Snake, where there were many beaver. The news allowed Ogden to regain control of his people and he pushed them northeast, up Henry's Fork to the Snake. Blackfoot country again; but Blackfoot dispositions were unaccountably sunny early that summer. The beaver were fat and plentiful and the Flatheads were dependable. Kittson was dispatched in middle July to carry fur packs to Flathead Post. He left with sorrowful heart, distressed because he was leaving Ogden in dangerous country and with most of his men prepared to desert if opportunity offered. The assessment was painfully accurate. The unnatural good nature of the Blackfeet was wearing thin and the free trappers were increasingly frightened and increasingly rebellious.

Ogden himself was not indifferent to his trials. He raged that he was doomed to roam an unfortunate, cursed country and he wished all the villains who had crossed him were in Hell, if such a place there was. But he somehow beat his way to Fort Walla Walla, battling Indians and insurrection all the way, and reached that place about the end of October. A good many of the plews (beaver skins) he had with him were gathered on the east side of the mountains and in United States territory, which he must have thought sweet justice after his robbery by Americans, and shortly before he arrived he wrote in his journal that he was now hardened to reverses. He may have believed it, but it was not so.

John McLoughlin was awaiting him at Fort Walla Walla, full of bustle and decision and insistent that the party return to the field without delay. To strengthen it — of the original number there remained twenty men or fewer — he ordered that Ogden join Finian McDonald, out of Fort Vancouver since August with twenty-two company servants and four free trappers and at that moment trapping somewhere in the

Deschutes drainage — west more than one hundred miles and on the east slope of the Cascades. If the weary Ogden complained against these instructions there is no record of it, but surely his bones and his bowels protested. In a few days he was outfitted (inadequately, since Simpson's economies must still be observed) and on November 21 had set off again, downstream along the Columbia until he crossed the Deschutes, then swinging south, finding McDonald camped near the mouth of Warm Springs River.

The combined command was to work its way east and did so, across a beautiful, brutal land. High desert covered with sagebrush where the streams hid themselves in deep ravines. The men were still on the waters of Crooked River, a third of the way to the Snake, when winter hit them. What game there was, and there was never much, disappeared. McDonald had with him Tom McKay, McLoughlin's stepson, so accomplished an Indian killer that even the Blackfeet kept on his smiling side, and an indefatigable hunter. Without him the entire company would almost certainly have perished, and despite him very nearly did. Such deer as he flushed were pitifully thin. A week after Christmas there was not a pound of provisions in camp.

Without forage the horses became gaunt, and sharp ice and rimrock crippled their feet so badly that sometimes the hoof was worn away, leaving nothing but a sickening stump. The men were so reduced from want of food that often they were too weak to set out their traps. Even Ogden complained that all of them had been on short rations almost too long. The Snakes they met were faring no better, living on locust stored up from the previous summer, a few sparse roots and any ants they were able to discover.

Through January, and February, and half of March Ogden and his party crawled painfully eastward, winter attending them, constantly bone-chilled because they had no flesh left to warm, reaching the Snake and following it upstream while they doggedly trapped its icy waters. But on March 13, when they were close to Twin Falls and closer yet to the end of their endurance, word came from McKay's hunting party that thirteen elk had been killed, five of them by McKay himself. It was too late in the evening to haul the meat into camp and that night a violent storm brought rain which melted away most of the snow and two-thirds of the ice. Next day there was grass for the emaciated horses and a sufficiency of food in camp for the first time since the year began, and all settled in for a protracted feast. Never, Ogden said, had he seen men eat with better appetite.

A full belly and improving weather lightened his spirits but a week later he was all gloom again. Indians brought word of a party of Americans and Iroquois somewhere nearby. He concluded immediately that his hunt was damned, that he would lose what few furs he had and a good part of his free trappers and would be reduced to returning empty-handed. He need not have worried. The winter which had plagued him so sorely had dealt as violently with the opposition. When he came upon a company of Ashley's people some twenty days later he found they were as badly distressed as he was himself, and no better pleased to see him than he was them. A few of his deserters of the previous year visited his tent and he accepted eighty beaver to apply to their debts and traded from them the remainder of their furs at standard company tariffs. He thought correctly that they were already dissatisfied with their new arrangement and supposed it would not be long before they were back with the old concern.

His own people he kept in hand without difficulty, which convinced him he could deal sternly with any future rebelliousness. The opportunity came a few days later. Three of his free trappers proposed to take French leave. He promptly stripped them of their gear and horses and gave one a drubbing for what he termed impertinence but might more fairly be called poor judgment. From that time forward Ogden's command assumed a new character, a cohesiveness and esprit, and he took joy in it. He saw men working near-naked, in water that was barely above freezing, and making no complaint, and swore they were fit to be companions of John Franklin, the great Arctic explorer. When they sickened wholesale from eating beaver whose flesh was poisoned by a diet of wild hemlock, Ogden cured them, and himself, with heroic doses of gunpowder and pepper.

He pushed up the Snake as far as the Portneuf before turning back. Inward bound, he and his followers suffered a new season of starvation but did not falter, and in mid-July they reached Fort Vancouver — skeletal, weathered and in rags, but alive.

The Snake Country brigade had acquitted itself honorably. It had carried through a strenuous hunt without losing a man to Indians or accident, turned a handsome profit for the company and maintained its loyalties in the face of temptation. Ogden and McLoughlin could find satisfaction in all this, but no ease. In the mountains the Americans were asking two beaver for a three-point blanket. The Bay's price to Indians and free trappers was five beaver, with other prices in proportion, so high that some of Ogden's people had brought back as many as 150 plews without earning enough to pay their outfitting.

McLoughlin had no authority to cure these inequities. Price structures were fixed annually and were intended to be inflexible. But the doctor was not to be bound by regulations he believed unreasonable or which violated his sense of right. He arbitrarily increased the allowance per made beaver to free trappers who accompanied the Snake Country Expedition and he made some adjustment in the prices they must pay for their supplies. He did these things beyond undoing and afterward wrote his superiors what he had done. Results sustained his judgment and after some years, and much correspondence, both Simpson and the London committee gave their approval. But McLoughlin had shown an independence of spirit which George Simpson could not abide, for it challenged his own authority. The incident was prophetic of troubles to come.

Ogden allowed himself the luxury of two months' rest before setting out again. This time he turned south and east, visiting Harney and Malheur lakes and the Klamath basin before passing over the Siskiyou Mountains into the Shasta country, falling on the usual thin times. He saw no Americans that year, but the next he saw a number of them, near Great Salt Lake, and outmaneuvered them easily. Experience had given him a surer hand. But the relentless wear of privation had done nothing to make him philosophical. The Snakes crossed him too often. He came to hate them with a passion which can only be described as virulent and confided to his journal that he was prepared to sacrifice a year of his life, or even two, to exterminate the tribe, women and children excepted.

There were nights when he sat in his lodge nursing his discontent and wishing himself elsewhere. The success of Jedediah Smith, Bill Sublette and David Jackson, who had bought up General Ashley's business, filled him with dissatisfaction. They had been at the trade only six years and had cleared $20,000 in a single season. A common trapper in the American service could earn in a year what would take him ten years with The Bay, and then only if he practiced the strictest economies. He was thirty-four. Eighteen years of exposure to the hazards of the trade had eroded his spirit, and he had little to show for his pains.

Ogden set all this down in his journal, evidence that temptation touched him even as it touched his people. He thought the Americans careless and spendthrift and he believed, mistakenly, that they were not adequately trained in wilderness skills. But he envied them the money they were making, or the money he thought they were making. And more than that, a great deal more than that, he envied them their freedom.

⚘ IV ⚘

In 1825 representatives of the United States and Great Britain sat down in London to begin a profitless wrangling over title to the Northwest Coast which ended, two years later, in a solution which was in fact no solution. The Convention of Equal and Open Occupancy was extended indefinitely, or until either power gave twelve months' notice of its termination. It was also in 1825 that 'Diah Smith, returning from his visit to Flathead Post, found his way to the first of the annual rendezvous of the American fur brigades.

The rendezvous was the device General Ashley concocted to save him the expense of building and maintaining permanent posts. It was an open-air market where a man could be coaxed out of a year's hard labor in return for alcohol, supplies and baubles for his squaw, and it combined merchandising with the grosser features of the Donnybrook Fair. Both trappers and Indians attended and everyone looked forward to it with enthusiasm eventually accentuated by eleven months of enforced drought, and back upon it with fond recollections somewhat blurred at the edges. It was a time for monumental and murderous drunks, for acquiring a new wife or exchanging an old one, for counting coup sticks and trading boasts and remembering how the missing had walked unwarily when there were hostiles on the trail. This one was held on or near the Siskadee, which is now Green River, and from it Jedediah accompanied the general back to St. Louis. When

he returned, very late the same year, he was junior partner in the firm
of Ashley & Smith.

After a bad beginning the general had done very well. In 1826 he
did even better. At the rendezvous he picked up 125 packs of furs, 25
percent more than the previous year, and could count himself a man
of substance. He sold the mountain end of the business to Smith, David
Jackson and Bill Sublette, took up a contract as their supplier and went
home to pursue the political career which was his one enduring ambition. In time he became a three-term congressman, a Democrat with
Whig leanings and a bitter enemy of T. H. Benton.

Here begin the most remarkable of 'Diah Smith's journeyings. Once
the partnership was arranged, and the business with Ashley closed, he
led a party of eighteen south from the rendezvous (held that year on
Bear River), skirting Great Salt Lake and Utah Lake and trapping
upstream along Sevier River until he left it to cross the low divide
which separated him from the Colorado's drainage. Shortly he found
himself in a land of waste and desolation, almost waterless, and so
empty of game the party fed on horses whose debilitated and dehy-
drated flesh was tasteless as rope. Hardship, but nothing beyond the
normal requirements of western travel, and Jedediah drove his people
on, striking the Colorado where the Virgin empties into it and passing
down the east bank to arrive at the squat brushwood huts of a Mojave
village.

The Mojaves practiced a little at dry farming but they were soldiers
by trade. War was their profession, their entertainment and their consuming interest, and they rejoiced in violence. The savage disposition
could be, however, inconstant as the wind, and this summer they were
perversely peaceable. The Americans rested with them a little time,
gathering strength, and when they departed two native guides accompanied them to point the way.

They were traveling west now, following the principal trade road
between the Colorado and the Pacific, laid out by Indian engineers
long before Columbus sailed from Palos. It took them — by way of
Marl Spring and Soda Lake and the Mojave River — the width of the
Mojave Desert and over the San Bernardino Mountains to the valley
beyond, a place of agreeable fertility after three months of wandering
through unrelieved bleakness. On November 27, they came to the first
civilized community any of them had seen since leaving Missouri, the
Mission of San Gabriel the Archangel.

The Franciscan padres and their Indian charges were delighted to have visitors and received them warmly, but the Mexican authorities felt otherwise. They suspected the trappers of being spies, which they were not, and of being the advance guard of some future invasion, which they were, though not consciously. Smith was ordered to San Diego to explain himself. He managed to get a letter of good character from certain American hide and tallow dealers and he asked to be allowed to depart to the north, in order that he might visit the Columbia. This would give him a look at almost all of Alta California, and the governor, Don José María Echeandía, would not hear of it. The government he represented was new and frail, its hold on the province was feeble and the possibility of American infiltration held his eye like a persistent specter. He wanted Smith gone, by the way he had come, and quickly.

Jedediah agreed, but with silent reservations. Once in the interior he would be beyond the governor's knowledge or control. In due course he recrossed the San Bernardino Mountains. But on the far side he turned north to the Tehachapis, ascended them and dropped down into the lushness of the San Joaquin Valley. A hunter's paradise, with beaver aplenty and Indians so ignorant of the refinements of civilization they went without clothing and had never seen a gun.

Toward the end of spring he decided the time had come to return to Bear River to make the rendezvous of 1827, but the sheer spine of the Sierra Nevadas turned him back. After several attempts to find a suitable pass he put his party into camp, probably near Stanislaus River, and set off with two companions on what became one of the most harrowing trips in the history of western travel. Horses and mules gave out early and the three men were forced to walk a good part of the way and to make the first crossing of the Great Salt Lake Desert — seventy-five miles without a water hole and a shimmering hell in the summer heat. They were always hungry and near death from thirst, their sleep was tortured by dreams of magnificent meals and gushing mountain streams, but on July 3, exactly six weeks from California, they reached Bear Lake and the rendezvous.

Jedediah had brought with him no furs to contribute to the year's returns but he had left a great many in the San Joaquin Valley, together with the remainder of his party, and after ten days of transacting necessary business he set off to collect both. Leading eighteen men and a handful of the female camp followers who attached themselves to every fur brigade, he followed much the same route as he had the previous year, amending it only when a shorter or easier way presented itself, and paused again at the Mojave village for rest and refreshment. The villagers seemed as friendly and hospitable as before, but they were dissembling. For some obscure reason the tribespeople had become disenchanted with Americans, their hearts were black with malice and they were meditating wholesale murder.

They struck when Smith's people were crossing the Colorado, men and horses swimming and provisions on makeshift tule rafts. They killed ten men outright and badly injured another, and captured two of the women. Jedediah managed to beat off a second attack but his position was unenviable. He had five guns and little ammunition, fifteen pounds of food, a seriously wounded man to hamper his travel, no horses and 150 miles of Mojave Desert between him and the safety of the Spanish settlements.

He brought it off, aided by friendly Indians and more luck than is allotted most mortals in a lifetime. The latter nearly ran out when a Mexican officer arrested him at San José for illegal entry, and he was forced into a second round of negotiations with Echeandía. The governor did not greet him kindly. Smith represented a problem which could not conveniently be solved, ignored or passed on to higher authority. He also represented the very point of the American thrust toward the Pacific, and if he were shot or imprisoned that thrust might suddenly gather behind it official muscle. In the end Escheandía accepted a bond for Jedediah's good behavior, underwritten by four Yankee captains who traded at California ports, and hurried the mountain man off with admonitions.

A short march reunited 'Diah with his people on the San Joaquin and early in January, 1828, the combined parties passed over into the valley of the Sacramento, traveling north but looking east for a way across the mountains. A bear caught Harrison Rogers, Jedediah's clerk and lieutenant, and mauled him so badly that though he was treated with plasters of soap and sugar it was a week before he mended. The brigade continued north but the mountains offered no opening and somewhere above the present city of Red Bluff the captain gave up his plan of turning east and decided to strike toward the coast with the hope of following it to the Columbia.

The northwest corner of California is a tangled wilderness, choked with trees and undergrowth, cut by rocky ravines along which rivers run with mad abandon. Smith and his people got through, but only by brutal, bruising effort. It was the last week of June before they crossed the Windchuck, out of Alta California and into the Oregon country: nineteen men and an Indian boy for slave and interpreter, and a few horses and mules galled by hard usage and overburdened with fur packs. A good deal of trouble was behind them, and there was horror ahead.

All were, by that time, bone weary. The very country resisted them. They made no more than twelve miles on a good day, five on a poor one. Coos people, dissatisfied with prices offered, killed a horse and three mules and kept up a following action, requiring Smith to maintain a constant rear guard.

On July 11 the company reached the estuary of the Umpqua and the next morning passed over it — three hundred yards across deep water, the men and horses swimming, the furs and supplies piled in canoes or rafted — and pushed three miles upstream along the north bank. It was heavy going. Rain descends on this coast at whatever season and the ground was too boggy for comfortable marching. And in the afternoon a few Indians came into camp.

They were Kalawatsets, not a tribe but a congeries of tribal odds and ends — Coos, Kuitsh and Siuslaw — held together by the geography of the lower Umpqua valley. One of them, acting in accordance with the principle of community property to which all Indians subscribed, took an axe. Jedediah overreacted. He was tired, short-tempered and pushed by impatience past the point of sound judgment. He seized the offender, bound him and ordered him held until restitution was made. Standard fur trade practice but a grave misreading of the odds. The man was a chief and to lay violent hands upon his person was to offend savage dignity. The axe was returned and the hostage released. The Kalawatsets were polite and seemed forgiving. But thereafter the air was poisoned by ill will.

The next morning, July 13, it rained. The Americans drove their jaded, unwilling animals four miles through gelatinous mire and halted where Smith River, as it is now known, joins the Umpqua. The Kalawatsets visited them in numbers, fifty or more, to trade beaver and fresh berries and the information that fifteen or twenty miles further on there was good traveling across the coast range to the Willamette. They were cheerful and, on the surface, friendly. Jedediah rose early the following morning and set off with two of his men to find the trail of which the Kalawatsets had told him, leaving strict orders with Harrison Rogers that security measures required that no Indians be allowed in camp. Rogers was an experienced hand, but dusky smiles bemused him. The Kalawatsets crowded in, accompanied by women brought as a guarantee of peaceable intent. 'Diah and his two companions were just returning when the killing started.

𝇋 V 𝇋

The Fort Vancouver which John McLoughlin constructed in 1825 was a temporary installation. An unfavorable boundary settlement could make permanent construction wasted work, and with labor short other matters must be given priority. A rectangular palisade of logs, placed upright, strengthened by the usual blockhouse, it enclosed perhaps three-quarters of an acre. The hutments, workshops, storage lofts and apartments it sheltered were never quite completed. The fort was located on the south face of a wooded slope and the prospect from its front gate was magnificent, but it was an inconvenient mile and more to the river along a road which mired miserably once the rains set in.

It was an unimpressive capitol for so vast a territory but astonishingly cosmopolitan whenever the brigades were home. Delaware and Iroquois (undistinguished descendants of distinguished ancestors), Chinook slaves with normal heads, Chinook dignitaries whose deliberately misshaped skulls proclaimed their superior caste, sightseeing chieftains from the interior tribes, Kanakas from the Sandwich Islands whose soft smiles masked homesick hearts, métis from Assiniboine, Canadians bouncing with congenital garrulity and effervescence, artisans from Manchester or Aberdeen, seamen from Liverpool or London, all jostled one another in this courtyard. The men of business were, most of them, Scots by birth or extraction, and all of them gentlemen by company designation, though of the unpolished variety.

It was a mixed little society, rowdy, profane and turbulent. Lacking any natural cohesiveness it necessarily was held together by discipline. The doctor's rule was harsh (no one would reasonably expect it to be otherwise), but uneven and marred by temperamental outbursts. Ponderous Celtic dignity too easily dissolved into thunderous Celtic wrath.

He was not yet become the great McLoughlin of the literature, charming the lady missionaries, affable among their menfolk. Near associates quickly learned prudence was safer than dissent. Common servants were capable of more direct response. Two of them plotted assassination. The Indian lad hired to commit the deed took fright and confessed and the doctor escaped injury save to his self-esteem, but the incident was instructive. Not all his people loved him.

His early reports were recitations of complaints set down with a clucking concern. Supplies sent to him are too often faulty, inadequate or improperly packed against the misadventures of a long sea voyage. Seed corn is of poor quality, gunpowder too coarse. There is not salt or tobacco enough. Cattle do well, hogs poorly. The Indians in these parts are indifferent hunters, so there are not deerskins sufficient to cover the fur packs for shipping.

Clearly the doctor had not found himself. The country had taken no hold on him. He was uncertain, defensive and acutely aware that the American threat was not confined to invasion by land. Half-a-dozen Yankee traders were beating their way up and down the coast from California to Alaska, paying prices McLoughlin considered ruinous and still turning handsome profits. His relations with his own naval establishment, meantime, went badly. Naval persons were inclined to grog addiction and careless when they dealt with natives. Drunkenness disgusted the doctor and he recognized the dangers in what sometimes became a wholesale ship-to-shore trafficking in liquor and women. When whites mingled too closely with Indians the familiarity bred contempt — among the Indians.

Some of his cares were relieved in 1826 when Lieutenant Aemilius Simpson arrived to assume the superintendency of maritime affairs. The lieutenant was a shirttail cousin to George Simpson, a veteran of the Napoleonic wars, a competent commander and a decent if somewhat eccentric man. His flagship was the *Cadboro,* no longer than the great sea canoes of the north coast Indians and having less freeboard. In the summer of 1827 Simpson took her to the mouth of Fraser River to cover James McMillan while he constructed Fort Langley. The lieutenant remained until the walls were up, the bastions placed, and the gates hung and a storehouse built — by now it was mid-September — before he discharged his cargo and dropped down to the Strait of Georgia, turning north on a brief voyage of trade and exploration.

He was back at Fort Vancouver before November was out. Simpson had reached as high as Port Neville, two-thirds of the way to Queen Charlotte Sound, and on his return had coasted Vancouver's Island, finding prices high and furs scarce. But McLoughlin was not displeased. With a post on the Fraser and the *Cadboro* under capable command he was, for the first time, able to offer an effective opposition to the Americans who had until now monopolized the coastal trade. It could not have occurred to him that he had also arranged another, quite different confrontation. The seagoing Indians north of the Columbia's estuary were a warrior people, arrogant, avaricious and possessed of an acute sense of their territorial imperatives. That very winter a small tribe of them, the Klallam, committed an act of deliberate atrocity which could not be ignored.

They called themselves Nuxsklá-yem — Strong People. Little brothers of the wolf, having bad hearts and tricky humors, they lived on the south shore of the Strait of Juan de Fuca in great gabled houses constructed of vertical planks split from cedar logs. In January one of their great war canoes, on patrol north of Puget Sound, discovered the Hudson's Bay postal express from Fort Langley to Fort Vancouver camped on Lummi Island. The Klallam killed the five men in the party and perhaps ate parts of them in obedience to liturgical requirements, but reserved the heads, which they carried back to their village near New Dungeness. They took also an Indian woman, wife to one of the victims, as a slave and a hostage. The heads were driven down on the tops of tall, pointed poles already waiting to receive them, and turned so that the glazed eyes would look into the rising sun. Each morning for a week the warriors danced round them a solemn dance of victory while their women sang and beat time on the plank walls of the houses. When the celebration had ended the heads were thrown among the dogs and word was sent to the Columbia through the tribes that the Strong People were more powerful than The Bay.

McLoughlin was glooming over the failure of the mail party to return and a persistent rumor that Fort Langley had been sacked and its defenders put to the knife, when the challenge reached him — unaccountably delayed in transmission — sometime in May. He wrote afterward that only the emergent nature of the crisis prompted him to act without first asking instructions, but in fact only one course was open to him. To suffer passively under Indian insolence was to lose face, and face was essential to wilderness survival. Retribution must be visited upon the offenders. A few of them must be killed to make an example for the rest, the murders must be avenged and the woman retaken, alive, if possible. Otherwise the entire native population would look upon the company with contempt and its servants would be safe nowhere in the country. It was to be not a war (war could spread to other arenas, disrupting trade and pinching profits), but a police action with limited objectives. The doctor worked out an uncomplicated strategic plan and on June 12 Lieutenant Simpson in the *Cadboro* dropped down the river on the way to Fort Langley. On his return he was to make for Admiralty Inlet. The army, moving north by Cowlitz Portage and Puget Sound, would meet him there.

The army was mustered next morning, but necessary preparations took several days. The men were feasted to fatten their courage. Iroquois volunteers entertained with a war dance, muskets were polished and rations issued, and late in the afternoon of June 17 the force crowded into canoes and paddled downstream: fifty-nine privates and three lieutenants, all under command of Chief Trader Alex Roderick McLeod.

It was the kind of work for which Ogden was superbly fitted, but Ogden was not yet down from the Snake country. McLeod was a second choice, a poor one, and probably suspected it. He was secretive by nature, completely humorless, and he wearied himself struggling to impose discipline on troops as incapable of discipline as a flock of starlings. Their very gaiety jarred him. Target practice turned every campsite into a shooting gallery and a man who was called into the bush, for whatever reason, had an excellent chance of making the casualty list.

It was July 1 before McLeod reached Admiralty Inlet. In the afternoon the *Cadboro* found him and next day Simpson took a party of the expeditionary force aboard and towed the remainder behind in canoes until he anchored offshore from the murderers' village. At this point McLeod's hold on operations collapsed completely. His staff was for immediate attack, and Aemilius Simpson agreed. But McLeod procrastinated, unwisely allowing himself to be drawn into negotiations which dragged on for a week before his lieutenants persuaded him the enemy envoys were amusing themselves. He finally gave his consent for the strike. Simpson was allowed to bombard the village with the ship's six cannon; shocked Klallams streaked for the security of the forest; the army swept ashore, burned everything left standing and arranged the exchange of the kidnapped woman for a wounded chief captured in the assault.

In his report McLoughlin insisted the expedition had been judiciously conducted. In his heart he knew it was not so. McLeod had bumbled badly. But the matter was closed and it was pointless to brood over it. The doctor had fresh concerns to occupy him. Ogden had arrived with good news and bad: an excellent hunt but new losses to the Blackfeet. He was to be off again almost immediately and so was McLeod, who was to trap south into California. Fort Vancouver returned to peacetime footing and the doctor to the routines of business. But late in the evening of August 8 whatever complacency he had managed to gather was shattered. An American, come out of nowhere, had materialized at his very gates.

❧ VI ❧

The stranger's name was Arthur Black. He believed himself to be the only survivor of the Kalawatset attack on 'Diah Smith's company but a couple of days later Jedediah himself and two others walked out of the backcountry, having been passed along by the tribes. Smith blamed the massacre on the dispute over the axe and so did the Indians who brought him to Fort Vancouver, but they also said, or McLoughlin gathered from their manner, that the Kalawatsets reacted as they did because Smith's people were not servants of The Bay.

The central fact, of course, was that the murders could not be allowed to pass unnoticed. To do so, as the doctor put it, would lower Europeans in native estimation and diminish the general security. Americans were not exactly Europeans, but they were near enough. Once things were sorted out Tom McKay was sent up the Willamette to see what he could learn. Alex McLeod, bringing the remainder of the brigade which was to trap the upper Sacramento, followed on September 6. He was ordered to travel with dispatch, visit the Kalawatsets, recover such of the stolen property as he could find, punish the murderers if he thought it expedient and cross the mountains into California before bad weather set in. Jedediah went with him, holding a watching brief. They met McKay six days up the Willamette Valley and McLeod sent back word that the prospect of recovering any of Smith's goods or horses was dim. Thereafter the mists closed in.

On October 25 Governor George Simpson arrived on a tour of inspection.

He was Simpson improved. He had visited London in 1825 and if he had not yet found a new wife, he had taken some small part in preparations for diplomatic negotiations with the United States, and his counsel was sought by the government. He had acquired vice-regal tastes. He traveled as rapidly as ever — his *voyageurs* were the finest rivermen in the company's employ — but his accommodations were markedly improved. The servants continued to sup on pemmican but for the governor there were cold cuts and an occasional glass of wine which now and again some gentleman in the party was summoned to share with him. As each post was reached the entire company was formed into a procession. Simpson strutted in the van, done up in beaver plug and Micawber collar, and a piper led the way, a gigantic Scot whose kilts aroused among the Indian maidens an indecent curiosity. It was less wilderness tour than royal progress. The Little Emperor had come into his own.

When he arrived at Fort Vancouver the doctor could give him no recent news of McLeod's excursion or the problems raised by the presence in Oregon of Jedediah Smith, so the governor put these matters aside momentarily and applied himself to others. He wanted more posts built north along the coast and an expansion of the maritime effort. He even suggested that Cousin Aemilius consider hiring a few Americans who had seen service with Yankee coasters, both because they would have some knowledge of native dialects and because he believed Americans worked harder and demanded less in the way of shipboard amenities. He ordered the opening of trade in lumber and salt salmon with California and the Sandwich Islands. He had scarcely exhausted his list of instructions when, on December 14, Jedediah Smith returned. And McLeod returned with him.

McLoughlin had imagined the chief trader and his brigade safely across the Siskiyous and into California. He was intensely irritated by McLeod's sudden reappearance at Fort Vancouver, and the explanations he received did not soothe him. Instead of hurrying south McLeod had dawdled along the way, gathered a few beaver and a host of worrisome rumors that the whole of the Umpqua country was arming

against his coming. It took him six weeks to reach the fatal campsite
and very nearly six more to collect seven hundred of the stolen furs
— all of them in fearfully tatty condition — thirty-nine worn horses
and a ragbag of miscellaneous items. (Among the latter, to the advantage of history, were the journals of Harrison Rogers and of Jedediah
himself.) The Kalawatsets were respectful and insinuating. To their
recital of grievances they added the charge that the Americans had
told them that this land belonged to the United States and they presently would come in numbers and drive the British out of it. When
questioned, Jedediah replied that it could have been said but it was not
he who had said it, and he pointed out that only the boy slave spoke
the local tongue and was able to communicate other than by signs.

In the end the murders went unpunished. The Kalawatsets were a
tough outfit and it was clear that in a shoot-out they would be joined
by other tribes equally tough. McLeod was no coward but he was adequately supplied with discretion. He delivered himself of the warning,
little heeded, that any future transgressions would bring down a swift
judgment, and marched solemnly off, dragging a disgruntled Jedediah
behind him. By now it was nearly December, snow was heavy in the
Siskiyous and any passage over them must be delayed until spring
thaw, and so he put his people into winter camp and made the visit to
Fort Vancouver which so sorely nettled John McLoughlin.

Governor Simpson was not a man to approve dilatory conduct but
he did approve McLeod's forbearance in his dealings with the Kalawatsets, and he wrote London that any other course would have involved
the company in an interminable feud with the southern Oregon tribes.
He repeated a story, got from somewhere, that the massacre was
touched off when Harrison Rogers tried to force an Indian girl into his
tent. Highly improbable. Rogers's piety rivaled Jedediah's own. But the
story served to raise the murderers a few notches on the moral scale
and to make their crime seem less heinous.

With the dejected Jedediah Simpson dealt scrupulously and took
great satisfaction in doing so. He refused to make any charge for re-
deeming the stolen property, bought up the recovered furs and horses
at generous prices and persuaded Smith to give up a winter trip across
the Rockies and wait until spring when he could travel with Simpson's
party on its way east. It was a lesson in honorable dealing to a man
suspected of having encouraged Ogden's free trappers to defect in
1825.

A few weeks later the governor had the opportunity of delivering another lesson, this time on ethics and patriotism, to a countryman and sometime competitor of Jedediah's. Major Joshua Pilcher appeared at Flathead Post toward the year's end, leading a forlorn hope — the bankrupt remains of what had once been the Missouri Fur Company: total assets nine mountain men, a deal of mountain know-how and the makings of a proposition. The major wanted a grubstake. With it he would undertake to trap the beaver-rich tributaries of the Missouri — which as an American citizen with a valid license he could legally do — and to bring his fur packs back to Flathead Post or some other company establishment. Simpson cut the offer down with devastating precision. However rich the country in question, it was a part of the territory of the United States. It would not be reputable for the Honourable Company to acquire by subterfuge furs to which it had no legal right. Simpson's righteousness was alloyed with irony. Major Pilcher would have no tales of British sharp dealing to tell when he returned to St. Louis.

The governor was taking all the tricks that season. He took pleasure in his successes and saw in them confirmation that certain judgments at which he had arrived were sound, when in fact they were not. He was seeing his first Americans, looking down at them from his position as one whose word was sought by ministers of state, and from so great an eminence they appeared to him to be wholly insignificant. Jumped-up tradesmen he thought them, and common trappers, parading themselves in empty military titles; little men who formed thinly financed combines to conduct a marginal trade and be a nuisance to their betters.

He foresaw hardly more danger from the settlers. Smith told him there were men in Missouri who had heard wondrous tales of the fertility of the Willamette Valley and had a thought to go there, but Simpson assured his superiors there was little likelihood of their doing so. No settlers could come by way of Lewis Fork of the Columbia and the only other route open to them was from the big bend of the Snake to the Cascade Mountains, across the bitter land which so nearly defeated Ogden in the winter of 1824–25. Few would survive it and those few would arrive destitute.

These were grave misjudgments. George Simpson did not perceive that the mountain men were enormously expanding knowledge of the Pacific West and blazing the roads by which it might be reached. He

understood even less the character of the American frontiersman and
the strength and complexity of the visions which beckoned him onward. The Americans would come and Simpson would not understand
how it was they had come and would dimly suspect John McLoughlin
of being responsible for their coming. He would suspect McLoughlin
also, with rather more reason, for the fact that the overlanders did not
perish immediately they arrived in Oregon.

But for the moment the governor was all triumph and when he
started east, toward the end of March, 1829, his massive confidence
was only slightly clouded by late news from the mouth of the Columbia.
The *William and Ann,* arriving from London with the best part of a
year's outfitting, had gone aground after crossing the bar, with a total
loss of all hands and cargo. An ill-timed disaster. That very week a pair
of Boston merchantmen entered the river and were anchored off Fort
George, raising an opposition.

❧ VII ❧

The year 1829 was a hard year for John McLoughlin, a troublesome
year, the first of a set of such years that came to gall him. They would
not show him at his best. Before they were out he would complain
petulantly that he was persecuted and spied upon and that there was
none who appreciated the weight of his burdens.

The Bostons — as the Indians called all Americans — proved formidable opponents. They were the brigs *Owyhee* and *Convoy,* Captains
Dominis and Thompson commanding, owned by Marshall & Wilde, a
firm venerable in the North Pacific trade. John Dominis, the senior
officer, knew his trade and went about it briskly. Within days he had
driven the price of a musket from eighteen beaver to three, other
prices in proportion, and before summer was over raised a station at
The Dalles to contest the middle-river trade. McLoughlin had no
choice but to join in the price cutting though he struggled, without
total success, to maintain the old tariffs at his interior posts. Because of
the loss of the *William and Ann* he was badly hampered by shortages
just when he was confronted by an efficient and ably conducted opposition.

Eighteen thirty proved quite as vexing as 1829. The unfortunate McLeod returned with the appalling news that every last one of his horses had died or been run off during his return across the Siskiyous. The supply ship *Isabella* foundered on Sand Island at the mouth of the Columbia. Ogden lost five hundred furs and nine men in a boating accident; John Edward Harriot lost seven more in another. July struck a single bright note. Dominis sold off the remainder of his trade goods and sailed for Canton, bringing an end to his unsettling competition. But hardly had the Americans disappeared when a new and more enduring affliction descended, an epidemic of what came to be called, locally, cold sickness.

It was a malarial fever and it seems to have first broken out the preceding year among the Indians living near where the *Owyhee* was stationed, off Deer Island on the lower river. It reached Fort Vancouver in the summer of 1830, coming on with devastating force, prostrating even Ogden the iron-gutted, survivor of starvation, thirst, Blackfoot ambush and poisoned beaver flesh. At one time more than seventy persons were hospitalized — exclusive, as McLoughlin wrote, of women and children — and operations came almost to a standstill. When the resident surgeon made the sicklist, the doctor added medical duties to his other chores, dosing his patients with powdered dogwood bark when the cinchona ran out. A makeshift so successful that he reported only one man dead, and a few women, and two children.

But the Indians were nearly wiped away. They clustered in wretched, agued bands around the walls of the fort, pleading to be allowed to remain where there would be someone to bury them when death released them from their suffering. McLoughlin reluctantly ordered them driven off, believing them to be, as perhaps they were, an additional threat to the health of his own people. They went home to the bush to die wholesale. Entire villages were left devoid of life, save for the dogs who skulked and scavenged among the rotting corpses.

For John McLoughlin these were grim years. But they were years during which he found his place. The country took its grip upon him. Duncan Finlayson was sent out in 1831 to serve as understudy but by then McLoughlin had no thought of leaving. A new and more impressive Fort Vancouver was built in 1828–29, closer to the river and situated on a broad meadow. A sawmill was constructed upstream on the north bank of the Columbia to serve a projected traffic in boards to the Sandwich Islands. The Americans were being held back in the Snake country. Peter Skene Ogden — reduced from near three hundred pounds to a bony shadow — was succeeded by John Work, a highly competent journeyman. Aemilius Simpson died of one of the liver complaints which plagued nineteenth-century seamen, but there was no gap in command. The doctor thought a naval superintendent unnecessary. The malaria had become an annual affair, declining to no more than a seasonal nuisance among the servants of The Bay but eventually carrying off three-quarters of the natives on the lower Columbia and perhaps half those in the Willamette Valley.

So, by and large, things were going smoothly. And when he sat down, as perhaps he did during the winter of 1831–32, to consider causes for concern, McLoughlin could have given no thought to three which were unknown to him, but which posed the greatest threats to his security: the religious awakening which was stirring certain of his Indian clients; the plans one Benjamin E. L. Bonneville was whispering into certain ears in New York and Philadelphia, ears connected by the intricate pipelines of high finances to the ear of John Jacob Astor; and the visions marching in endless files through the muddled brain of one Hall Jackson Kelley.

❧ 3 ❧

Overlanders–
Pious and Impious

1831-1835

HALL JACKSON KELLEY was born in little Northwood, New Hampshire, educated at Middlebury College, and in 1817 was appointed by God to be special agent for Providence charged with carrying Christianity and civilization to the heathen of the Pacific Northwest.

The appointment seems not to have been arbitrary as to time. Kelley ignored it for nearly a decade while he busied himself with more mundane enterprises. He tried teaching and surveying and industry, and failed at each. An investment in a textile mill finally made off with what was left of his financial shirt, leaving him bitter, bankrupt and enmeshed in interminable litigation. He gave up business and became a weaver of dreams.

For that profession Kelley was admirably equipped. His imagination was unanchored. His mind never caught on the sharp edges of reality. His literary style had an apocalyptic eloquence. He set up a howl for the immediate colonization of Oregon, bombarding Congress with petitions and the press with letters and pamphlets, and careening from town to town like some vision-drunk evangelist, pressing the revealed truth on whoever would listen.

By 1829 he had collected about him a number of enthusiasts and organized them into an association which bore a resounding name: The American Society for Encouraging the Settlement of the Oregon Territory. Kelley was, as might be expected, the society's chief theoretician, its general agent and its publicist. The piety of the original

57

directive had, meantime, been diluted by a large measure of materialism. Kelley proposed to bring salvation to the savages, and at a profit.
There would be opportunities in the Promised Land for merchants as
well as missionaries. A settler might, as his option, work either the
Lord's vineyard or his own.

In 1831 Kelley produced a small pamphlet entitled (in part) *A General Circular to All Persons of Good Character Who Wish to Emigrate to the
Oregon Territory,* full of the sonorous nonsense beloved of real-estate
promoters; Oregon is the most healthful spot to be found on the face
of the globe and the noble savages inhabiting the lower Columbia are
always noble and never savage. In it he proposed that a large emigrant
party be formed, families and single men alike; be provided in advance
with laws and administrators; and march resolutely across the continent and settle on lands purchased from the Indians by a joint-stock
company formed for that purpose.

Given intelligent guidance and adequate financing the plan might
have worked. But financing and guidance were just what Kelley could
not provide. He procrastinated endlessly, fruitful of ideas but barren
of decision. Enthusiasm waned. Adherents drifted off. In the end
nothing was left but Kelley's unreasoning determination — and a virus.
Kelley had contracted history's first authenticated case of what would,
in another dozen years, come to be called Oregon Fever, and he was
incurably infected. In time he would find his way west only to discover
that for him the Land of Promise held no special blessings.

He did not go in 1832, the year appointed, but another sometime
member of the great colonization society did. His name was Nathaniel
Jarvis Wyeth, citizen of Cambridge, Massachusetts, and Yankee inge-
nuity personified. He was production manager for Frederick Tudor,
who pioneered the shipping of ice to the tropics, and while in Tudor's
employ invented contraptions so ingenious that they remained in use
so long as ice was harvested from lakes and ponds. At twenty-nine,
Wyeth had a certain future as Tudor's protégé, but he was impatient
in a business which cost him only six months' effort out of every year's
time. He was impatient also because, as he wrote, "I cannot divest
myself of the opinion that I shall compete better with my fellow men
in new untried paths than in those to pursue which requires only patience and attention."[1] The echo of Theophilus Arminius is strong:
the frontier was a magnet to draw the discontented.

Wyeth contracted the Oregon Fever from Kelley but he managed to avoid the delirium which was the most obvious of Kelley's symptoms. In Wyeth the virus had the effect of strongly agitating the ambition. What he proposed was to revive the plan evolved by John Jacob Astor some twenty-odd years earlier. He would establish a post on the Pacific Coast, supply it from ships sent out of Boston and send those same ships home with their holds stuffed with furs brought down from the Rockies and pickled salmon fished out of the Columbia. He worked out every detail carefully and in accordance with the information available to him, but he could not know that much of that information was pure error and most of the remainder was incomplete. He had no clear idea of the power and extent of The Bay's monopoly and so no way of knowing how long were the odds against success. Even if he had, it would probably have made no difference.

Wyeth's correspondence that fall and winter, the fall and winter of 1831–32, is varied, energetic and ceaselessly inquiring. He was intent upon cramming into his mind every fact which could in any imaginable way be useful to him, and both his mind and his imagination were capacious. He wrote Baltimore for information concerning the cultivation of tobacco. He needed to know the laws concerning commercial intercourse with Indians. He sought expert advice on the habits of salmon, asking at what seasons they entered the rivers and how they might best be caught and packed.

In a letter dated early in February of the new year and addressed to his uncle, Leonard Jarvis, Wyeth set down what is probably the clearest exposition of his scheme. He thought it improbable that the Convention of Equal and Open Occupancy would remain in force for any appreciable time because it operated almost exclusively to the advantage of the British. By being early in the field he hoped to establish himself so strongly that, once the convention was lapsed, he would enjoy a monopoly of American trade in the area, he and The Bay dividing the business between them after having eliminated all opposition by more economical methods. There is no mention anywhere of the moral or legal superiority of the American claim to the territory or the wisdom of supporting that claim by permanent settlement. He was thinking wholly in terms of self-interest.

The letter to Jarvis was long and carefully worded, for it was a request for financial assistance. There were a number of such requests. The breadth and complexity of Wyeth's plans hopelessly overburdened his slender resources and he was forced to levy on friends and even to mortgage his home. He had originally projected a joint-stock company with fifty partners working on shares, but recruiting went badly and he got no more than twenty, with himself as the twenty-first. Early in March he collected as many of them as lived in the immediate area, bivouacked them on Long Island in Boston Harbor for a short, intensive and inadequate course in forest craft, and hurried them off to Maryland where the National Road would lead them to St. Louis and the beginning of the great adventure.

They reached St. Louis in mid-April. That city, which had seen its share of remarkables, was treated to the sight of one of history's most colossal dude outfits: twenty-one green peas dressed alike in striped shirts, wool pants and rawhide boots, carrying bayoneted rifles and small bugles through which weary lungs were to blow courage into faint hearts. They had with them three boat-wagons — called amphibiums by the learned and Natwyethiums by the irreverent — cleverly contrived and beautifully constructed. But wise hands pointed out that the oven heat of the plains would bake open the seams. Wyeth got rid of the contraptions and wrote off the loss to experience, first entry in what would be a considerable account.

He chivvied his small band onward to Independence where Bill Sublette saw them, pitied them and took them in tow. There had been changes in the mountain trade. General Ashley was gone to Congress. Jedediah Smith was dead, caught by Comanche lances near the Cimarron. Bill himself was no longer an official mountain man. He had sold out to his brother Milton and others, doing business as the Rocky Mountain Fur Company, and he had joined with Robert Campbell in contracting supplies and bankrolling. Sublette's innate courtesy, which operated well enough when business interests did not inhibit it, led him into error. He saw Wyeth as an unimportant rival but not by the remotest stretch of the imagination a threat. The young iceman was unlearned but he had a retentive mind. Once taught he would be a dangerous man to cross. And it was fated that Bill Sublette would cross him.

But in the spring of 1832 there were no premonitions and no frictions. Wyeth was content that Bill led while he followed, eyes awake and ears open, missing little and forgetting nothing. The sun burned his hide to leather, the gnats ate him alive, he picked up the scalding phrases of the frontier, gorged on underdone meat broiled over buffalo chips — which imparted their own unique flavor — drank water thick enough to slice, suffered the inevitable flux and enjoyed himself hugely. But his company began to unravel almost within sight of the settlements. Two men deserted only twelve days out. A good part of the remainder were surly and mutinous and worked off their irritations by allowing the horses to wander off and by stuffing pots and pickets under the packsaddles so that the animals were rendered sore-backed and useless.

The rendezvous was held that year in Pierre's Hole, west of the Tetons, and they reached it July 8. Four days earlier Wyeth had crossed the Continental Divide, dipped his cup into a westward-flowing stream and toasted missing friends in the waters of the Columbia mixed with alcohol. He had reached the far side of the continent. But a week later nearly half his people voted to turn back, leaving him with just eleven men and his ambitions to sustain him. Wyeth presided over the meetings which split the party in a cold fury, for he regarded desertion as a deadly sin. What rankled most was that two of the defectors were members of his own family: his brother Jacob, who had come out as company surgeon, and a nephew, John, son of still another brother. For Nathaniel himself there could be no question of looking back. The only way he could outrun the disaster trodding at his boot heels was to reach the Pacific, pick up supplies from the ship he had sent to meet him and perhaps fill out his ranks with free trappers. He needed fresh horses and at the rendezvous collected eighteen of them (and a supply of jerked meat), in trade for beads, fishhooks, blankets and bells. Refitting improved his humor and on July 17 he set off once more, traveling for safety with Henry Fraeb and Milton Sublette, who were leading brigades of the Rocky Mountain Fur Company to the Humboldt. They moved no more than seven miles the first day and were still encamped next morning when the winds of violence struck them.

In the mountain wars the Blackfeet had no constant allies but the Atsinas, cousins of the Arapaho. A long time earlier the French out of Canada had given them the name Gros Ventres — Big Bellies — for their appetite for plunder was voracious. They were possessed of the same singular ferocity which possessed the Blackfeet, they had adopted the same tongue, and in fur trade annals they are identified as Blackfeet more often than not.

Two parties of them came out of the mountains to the south that morning and halted a mile from the trappers' camp to ponder the odds. They numbered, by Wyeth's estimate, two hundred braves. Fraeb, Milton Sublette and Nathaniel had between them only forty-two hands, including a small detachment of independent trappers, and a courier was hustled off to Pierre's Hole to call up reinforcements. Despite the advantage of numbers, the Gros Ventres were in no hurry to act. It was first necessary to practice the magic which would make victory a certainty, and to gain time for this a war chief was sent forward to arrange a temporary truce.

He was met on neutral ground by a métis whose father had been cut down two years since by Blackfeet, and by a young Flathead brave, born with hatred of the Blackfeet in his blood. They shot the chief in full view of the opposing armies, lifted his scalp, the tribal peace pipe he carried, and his handsome scarlet blanket and carried them back to the American camp in triumph. The peace pipe had magical properties; its loss was a tactical catastrophe, and the Gros Ventres needed time to make up a more potent medicine. They were still about it, whooping and hollering and hurling taunts and imprecations, when Bill Sublette came boiling up from the rendezvous bringing a mixed corps of Flatheads, Nez Percé and mountain men.

What followed was among the bloodiest, the most famous and the best reported of the battles the members of the Blackfoot confederation fought out during their long campaign against the rest of mankind. At least seven eyewitness accounts have come down to us and if they differ on detail, they agree on essentials. The Atsinas went to ground in a willow thicket, a boggy, almost impenetrable tangle grown up around an abandoned beaver dam. They forted up behind fallen timber, masked vulnerable points with blankets and buffalo robes, set their women to digging rifle pits and called loudly on their magic. Bill Sublette tried to root them out with a frontal assault, saw his volunteers shot up and was himself severely wounded and thereafter exercised command propped against a convenient tree. He had available to him a hundred or so Americans and twice as many Indians, but the initial repulse dampened military ardor and the engagement settled into a siege operation. A great deal of powder and shot was expended and a sizable number on both sides were struck off as casualties. Robert Campbell, Bill Sublette's partner, was wounded. James Sinclair, leader of the free trappers, caught a bullet and shortly expired. An unnamed mountain man was shot down close to the enemy position, dragged inside and turned over to the squaws for terminal surgery. As the day wore on the Atsinas ran short of ammunition and an attempt was made to burn them in their works, but it fizzled when rumor ran through the allied camp that other Blackfeet were raiding the rendezvous and half the investing army galloped back to Pierre's Hole, only to find all peaceful and unmolested.

Night came on before the detachment could return. The remaining besiegers sat down to await another day and inevitable victory but in the morning the Atsinas were gone. They left behind most of their belongings, a few dead and a woman with a shattered leg who pleaded insistently to be dispatched. The Americans would not touch her but a Flathead brave obliged by splitting her skull with his hatchet.

The allied dead were buried inside the fortified area where the bloody, trampled ground would discourage future seekers after a cheap scalp. The din of arms, Wyeth wrote, was then replaced by the yelping of masterless dogs and the sound of vultures come in search of carrion. The stench of rotten flesh oppressed him. Nevertheless the battle marked his acceptance into the elite of mountain society. He had been given a brevet commission and charge over Indian auxiliaries on the left flank, and he had led them with vigor. All respect to T. H. Benton and Missouri, it was a great day for Massachusetts.

Intelligence put more Blackfoot warriors somewhere out yonder and it was near a week before Fraeb and Milton Sublette moved, and Wyeth with them, across the passes and down into Snake drainage. They had not gone far when they stumbled on a late summer garden land, a hunter's paradise teeming with fat buffalo, duck, geese, trout that went a pound apiece and buckets of wild berries for dessert. The brigades stopped to dry meat and to enjoy God's marvelous bounty. The New Englanders had too few horses to use them up chasing buffalo and anyway Nathaniel thought meat-making a tedious business; but he joined with a will in the general banqueting until his belly, shrunken by deprivation, erupted in protest.

Whatever the momentary discomfort no one regretted the feasting, for lower down the country turned parsimonious. Chronic drought shriveled the vegetation and the air was so dry percussion caps exploded spontaneously. But there were crawfish in the creeks and the sage was thick with the enormous crickets favored by the Shoshone, so no one was in danger of starvation. Fraeb and Sublette were leading the way southwest, cutting across the southern tributaries of the Snake, and on August 28 they set Wyeth down on an upper branch of the

Owyhee along which he could find his way north again to the Snake, and bade him good-by. He was briefly saddened by the parting. His relations with Fraeb were cordial and he had become close to Milton Sublette. But dependency galled him and he resolutely assumed his own command.

The country in which Wyeth found himself was a chaos of cracks and chasms, and even with the river for a guide there were opportunities for going astray. But the natives adopted him (some even treating his possessions as communal property) and on the evening of October 14 he reached Fort Walla Walla. A post of no strength, he thought, fit only to frighten Indians; but it had a bull and a cow, a hen and cock, punkins, potatoes and corn in its garden — all of which was strange, and unnatural, and like a dream.

⚜ II ⚜

That winter the brig *Eagle* was to sail from Fort George, departing early November, carrying the year's returns to London. John McLoughlin had his accounts posted up against her leaving, and his report was signed and sealed October 28. But next day he reopened the mail pouch to add a brief, urgent message to his superiors. A Mr. Dwight (so he called him) had arrived that morning from Boston and St. Louis. He brought with him eleven followers and he talked variously of trying his hand at salmon packing, of bringing in furnishings to the American trappers by way of the Columbia and of returning home via San Francisco come spring. The doctor affected to accept these vague and conflicting explanations of just what motivated the expedition, but privately he reserved a suspicion. He believed it not impossible his new guests had some connection with plans for colonizing the Oregon country which had lately been much talked up in New England newspapers. Even at a remove of six months and three thousand miles, McLoughlin was informed of the gyrations of Hall Jackson Kelley.

Wyeth had come downriver in the H. B. express boat by favor of Pierre Pambrun, clerk in charge at Fort Walla Walla. He made the run in a holiday mood, gawping at marvels and thrilling to the exhilaration of the rapids, but at Fort Vancouver he found the worst of news awaiting him. The brig *Sultana,* outward bound from Boston with the supplies and trade goods he was depending upon to revive his fortunes, had grounded on a reef in the South Pacific. When she foundered his prospects foundered with her.

For whatever reason Wyeth makes no mention of this disaster in his journal. He says simply that the men who had remained faithful during the mutiny at Pierre's Hole now wanted their release. So he released them. He took the separation philosophically, writing that while he was alone and afloat on the sea of life without stay or support, he was yet in good hands. It is characteristic that he lists his own hands first, and after them, those of Providence and his hosts.

He did not waste the winter months. He would not have been Nat Wyeth had he done so. He earned the friendship and respect of John McLoughlin, asked endless polite but pertinent questions and paid house calls on the handful of retired *engagés* who had settled in the Willamette Valley. McLoughlin came to the conclusion that his guest was not colonial-minded, which was true enough, and that he would never be sufficiently well financed to mount a serious threat to the Honourable Company's hegemony. The doctor may be forgiven for having missed the point. Wyeth, wholly untrained in the techniques of overland travel and assisted only a part of the way by others who were masters of the craft, had successfully led men even less knowledgeable than himself from St. Louis to the Pacific. Thirty years after Lewis and Clark, the path across the continent was sufficiently marked and graded that even novices could follow it.

With the coming of February the weather in the lowlands moderated and Wyeth set off east at a trot, taking with him two of his former associates and traveling in company with The Bay's irrepressible Francis Ermatinger. They turned north from Fort Walla Walla since it would not do for so small a group to attempt the crossing of the Rockies so early in the season, and spent a month at Fort Colville, then commanded by Francis Heron. Both Heron and Ermatinger were notable convivialists and it may have been under the influence of a friendly bottle that Wyeth was persuaded to address a proposition to George Simpson, a proposition which did not differ materially from that put forward by Joshua Pilcher four years earlier, an offer to trade and trap on the American side of the Rockies and to market at Fort Vancouver all furs acquired. It was no more acceptable than Pilcher's and Simpson did not answer it directly, but after the usual delays a disapproving letter was got off to John McLoughlin, with instructions that should the iceman return he was to be met by a vigorous, well-regulated opposition and no accommodation of trade was to be entertained.

Nathaniel would have made no such an offer had he not been listening to the counsels of desperation. A year's effort had earned him nothing more than a liberal education. He was very nearly broke and had lost the funds entrusted to him by friends and relatives. He was not yet ready to admit defeat but plainly he must reverse his fortunes or be lost. In June he came up with a new combination. By then he was deep in the mountains and from somewhere northwest of the Tetons he got off a letter to Captain Bonneville, proposing a merger of interests and a joint hunt into California to be financed by Bonneville and led by Wyeth.

Captain Benjamin Eulalie Louis de Bonneville, U.S. Army, to give him full honors, was balding, humorless, efficient, assured. History had already brushed him. His father had been imprisoned by Robespierre and persecuted by Napoleon. He himself had been brought to America as protégé of those two gentle revolutionaries Lafayette and Tom Paine, and had been given an appointment to West Point. It was to be his destiny ever to rub shoulders with greatness, sometimes without realizing it. Years later he would achieve a left-handed distinction for his abusive treatment of a quartermaster captain named Ulysses Grant, whose comrades called him Sam.

Bonneville is one of the enduring mysteries of the mountain trade. Romantics would have him a government agent. Washington Irving wrote him up as a hero. He was, in fact, a young officer with excellent connections who managed to wring considerable financial backing out of Alfred Seton, a longtime associate of John Jacob Astor's, to float a mountain trading expedition. The venture was an impressive one. In the spring of 1832 Bonneville was well enough financed to sign on 110 hands and two first-class brigade chiefs, Manuel Cerré and Joseph Walker.

Bonneville himself was no novice. He had seen much service on the western plains, enough to come to the conclusion that pack trains were ruinously hard on animals and unnecessarily time-consuming. When he set out in 1832, a little in advance of Wyeth and Sublette, he had two years' provisions packed in twenty wagons that he managed to get across the Continental Divide and into the valley of the Green. It was his greatest contribution to the establishment of the overland trail, and his last triumph. Thereafter his luck soured. All his parties came to grief. He himself spent a wretched winter on the Salmon River. Everywhere he found Indians willing to love him for his virtues and suck up any amount of gifts and bribes, but he could not wean them from The Bay. Bonneville was still chewing bitterness when, at Three Buttes near the head of Godin's River, Wyeth caught up with him.

The captain took a single day to consider Wyeth's offer. That day happened to be the Fourth of July, 1833, and for the only time in the year's adventuring Nathaniel was afflicted by the blue devils of homesickness and doubt. He wrote to a brother that he was seated in an open prairie by a small brook, with no fire though the weather was freezing, and only dried buffalo for his supper. Wyeth wrote also, in this and other letters dated the same day, that he expected to be taking a party of trappers to California. Clearly he anticipated agreement with Bonneville. But none of these letters was ever sent and the day following he wrote briskly to McLoughlin that he was leaving immediately for the States.

He kept with Bonneville as far as Green River, where the year's rendezvous was held — four miles of brawling, racing, gambling, fornicating and socializing. Joe Meek, who had wide experience, remembered the occasion as an alcoholic's paradise, a fair gauge of its success. He had also a less agreeable memory of it. Rabid wolves attacked the camp. Twelve men were bitten and several died, but Joe gave out he was never much worried, he being so full of rotgut that any wolf which bit him would succumb to alcohol poisoning, or be cured on the spot.

Despite these diversions there was work to be done. A year's business must be got through in a week. Wyeth carved himself a small piece of it, a contract to deliver $3000 worth of goods to the Rocky Mountain Fur Company the year following. He accomplished this by persuading Milton Sublette, the RMF Co.'s most influential partner, that Sublette and Campbell's prices were exorbitant. It was only a modest triumph, but it brought Wyeth his second wind. He sold his horses, built boats of bullhide and floated down the Yellowstone and the Missouri to see what that part of the world was made of. And he did a larger thing, though unconsciously. He took with him to the States two Indian boys

to provide advertising copy for his revived enterprise. One was a mix
of French and Flathead. The other was a Nez Percé. The Nez Percé,
by singular fortune, was blessed with an oddly shaped head.

⚜ III ⚜

The Spokane Garry whom George Simpson carried east to Red River
in 1825 was taught to read and cipher, instructed in the catechism and
varnished thinly with civilized ways. In 1829 he was allowed a short
visit home, a walking example of the benefits The Bay could bestow on
the worthy.

He was only nineteen. But he had sojourned long in foreign parts
and even the elders listened when he spoke. He was, he said, a Christian, or shortly would be, and he had penetrated close to the mystery
which lay at the heart of the white man's religion.

Here was born a monumental misunderstanding. The Indian mind
was not equipped nor the Indian language structured to deal with
abstracts. Garry told his tribesmen that there was a Book, and the Book
was the key to a Better Life, and there were men who were adepts in
the use of the Book and eager to share their knowledge. His listeners
translated all this literally. A Better Life was exactly that — creature
comforts and material blessings. Religion, when it passed from French
or English to Salish or Sahaptin, became Medicine. Medicine was
theurgy, the art of controlling the powers of nature, seen and unseen,
in such a way as to squeeze benefits from them. Red Medicine was
dedicated to improving the lot of the tribe, with special emphasis on
matters economic and military: to securing plentiful game and good
fishing and fast horses and victory in battle and the making of rain or
fair weather according to need. White Medicine could only be the
same, though by overwhelming evidence it was immensely more powerful.

The roughest catalogue of the advantages the whites had gathered
to themselves was enough to convince the stoutest skeptic: inexhaust-
ible supplies of cloth, beads, ornamental glass, cosmetic vermilion and
rum; all manner of useful instruments fashioned from iron and steel;
watches in which was somehow encapsulated the essence of time; and,

most persuasive of all, firearms which they used to gain ascendancy over much land and many people. And yet they were mortal, just as Indians were mortal, born out of the same travail and dying when their moment was appointed. It could only follow that they had happened somehow upon the particular Medicine which was the key to wealth and power. And the source of that medicine was, on Garry's authority, the Bible.

This was an irony. The Spokanes were among the poorest of the people who lived along the banks of the middle Columbia, very nearly as impoverished as the Snakes whose eternal beggary and thieving so graveled Peter Ogden. The disinherited, and now with the treasures of the earth almost within grasp. It turned out to be much too big a secret to be kept. It was not long before word spread to the neighboring tribes, and the councils of the wise and dignified everywhere in the middle basin pondered the problem. Clearly the first need was to secure the services of a wizard of the Book, but there was none nearabouts and no man could say precisely where one might be located. Given time the tribes would certainly have applied to McLoughlin for assistance, and had they done so the course of history might have run a little· differently. They did not because the Nez Percé willed otherwise.

Of the chronicles of the native races few are sadder than is that of the Nez Percé. They were, and are, a handsome people, intelligent in the extreme and as close as any to the Noble Savage that Rousseau invented and James Fenimore Cooper copyrighted. They were the most enterprising of the horse Indians living west of the mountains — they seem to have been the only Indians, anywhere, to develop selective breeding — and they were prosperous according to the modest standards of the middle Columbia. But affluence had its disadvantages. The Blackfeet paid them unwelcome attention, ran off their livestock and their women, slaughtered their braves and in general made their lives a near approximation of hell. Nez Percé interest in getting to the bottom of Garry's mystery was particularly urgent. Magic which could produce weaponry to redress the military balance offered a way of salvation they could understand.

The Nez Percé were old and valued Bay clients but their diplomatic connections with the United States were older still. Numbers among their elders treasured the presidential medals Lewis and Clark had handed round a quarter-century before, and William Clark had come to be for them, as for so many western tribes, an elevated being — half oracle, half father figure. Nothing seemed more natural, in a matter of such fundamental importance, than that someone be sent to St. Louis to consult him.

Every year the Nez Percé crossed to the Missouri side of the mountains to hunt buffalo. They did so in 1831, traveling, as was their custom, with the Flatheads who were their neighbors and allies. Somewhere during the mountain passage the Flatheads learned of the decision to send a delegation east and suggested a joint venture. The suggestion was acceptable, and a commission of seven — four Flatheads, three Nez Percé — was selected, instructed in its duties and hurried on its way.

Standard procedure would have been to head for the rendezvous and connect up with one of the supply trains returning to Missouri, but that year, for reasons imperfectly understood, there was no rendezvous. The American Fur Company's Lucien Fontenelle said later that he fell in with the mission in what is now western Montana and took it in tow, and that at Council Bluffs three of its members, afflicted perhaps by homesickness or by bowels distressed by bad water, turned back. There are those who disbelieve Fontenelle, but his story may be true. The one indisputable fact is that sometime after the middle of 1831 four Indians from the Oregon country arrived in St. Louis. Three of them were Nez Percé, a senior chief called Black Eagle and two young braves, and the fourth was Man-of-the-Morning, a Flathead elder. It is probable, though not certain, they reached the city about the first of October, because shortly after that they met with William Clark, who received them in his dual capacity of superintendent of Indian affairs and honorary godfather of the western tribes.

Neither Clark nor his interpreter had Salish or Sahaptin, and everything must be reduced to signs. Despite this handicap the delegation managed to get across the essential points. The general understood that his guests were inquiring about the Bible, and about the efficacy of the Christian religion, and that they wanted a minister (later to be translated as priest or pastor according to the bias of the translator) to be sent among them. Clark answered them with the generalities of a practiced bureaucrat — there was such a book as they described, it did hold the key to a better life, and a teacher would come among them in due time — and after handing out the usual small gifts sent them on their way puzzled, dissatisfied and at least half-conscious of failure.

It was too late in the year to recross the mountains so they lingered on in St. Louis, moving with solemn purposelessness through the unceasing revelry of that rowdy little town. The two older men sickened with civilized diseases, were cared for by priests and shortly died. Both received Catholic rites and were buried in consecrated ground. The survivors, Rabbit-Skin-Leggings and No-Horns-on-His-Head, continued to wander the side streets of the town, living God knows how. No one took any notice of them.

Toward the end of the following March the American Fur Company's side-wheeler *Yellowstone* slipped her mooring lines and set off on a pioneering voyage: wedge of empire trailing a muddy wake. The year before she had gone as far as Council Bluffs and now she was determined to reach Fort Union, built just where the Yellowstone empties into the Missouri. George Catlin was on her, having come west to paint Indians because he found the faces of his New York subjects pale and uninspiring. Also on board were Rabbit-Skin-Leggings and No-Horns-on-His-Head, and at Fort Pierre Catlin learned they were personages of some importance. The plains grapevine had carried an account of their pilgrimage and the Sioux turned out to give the Nez Percé envoys full diplomatic treatment, fitting them with soft, beautifully made deerskin outfits, loading them down with amulets and giving them a ceremonial feast. Afterward Catlin painted them in their official finery and their faces have come down to us — handsome, proud and weary beyond description.

No-Horns-on-His-Head died a little further along, and at Fort Union Rabbit-Skin-Leggings left the river and cut off into the mountains alone, bringing back with him no wizard of the Book and no more than a vague promise that one would follow. His end is obscure. He passed out of sight and into legend. Fittingly. For within a year he and his three companions would be resurrected by the very magic they sought, rubbed against and could not understand.

❧ IV ❧

Gabriel Poillon Disoway was a wealthy New York merchant, an antiquarian of minor note, a prominent lay Methodist, a founder of the

Methodist Free Sunday School, the Methodist Missionary Society and Randolph-Macon College, an altogether mighty mover and doer. His friend William Walker was less notable but hardly less remarkable. He was part Indian, a member of the Wyandot nation, tolerably well educated, and Methodist agent to his tribe. In the winter of 1832–33 these two, operating at a remove of at least five hundred miles, collaborated in a piece of holy chicanery for the greater glory of God and the Methodist Episcopal Church.

The third party to this pious hoax was presumably innocent of guilty knowledge. The *Christian Advocate and Journal and Zion's Herald* was (and, under a mercifully abbreviated name, is) Methodist and enormously respectable, and during the second quarter of the last century its circulation among the godly and well-intentioned was formidable. The *Advocate* was not given to sensationalism — its usual contributors were elderly ministers shaving finer some fine doctrinal point or lamenting the penuriousness of congregations — but its issue of March 1, 1833, blew up a great wind of Christian zeal. For a good part of the front page for that date is given over to a long communication entitled "The Flat Head Indians," and signed "G. P. D."

The whole effort is in the form of two letters, the one introducing and then summing up the other. The first opens with a description of the Wyandot people and the government's efforts to move them from Ohio in accordance with established policy of resettling all of the tribes west of the Mississippi in an effort to simplify the management of Indian affairs — and the takeover of Indian lands. It tells of an inspection made by Walker and other Wyandot notables of a tract offered them on the eastern edge of what is now Kansas. It dates this inspection as having been made in the fall and early winter of 1832, rather than, as was the case, a year earlier. For the author this was a necessary falsehood. The sense of urgency must be maintained.

Inserted at this point is a "Dear Friend" letter from Walker himself, written with inspired artifice. After describing a scene of precious domesticity, his small daughter tugging at his handkerchief and his only son demanding help with his spelling book, he describes the background of the Kansas trip, misdating it as Disoway had done, and finally arrives at what he calls, with conscious restraint, an anecdote. Upon arriving at St. Louis, on his way west, he had waited upon General Clark to conduct necessary business and learned that three chiefs of the Flathead nation were in the general's house and were quite sick, and that one of them had recently died. Being driven by curiosity he stepped into the adjoining room and saw them and was struck by their appearance, which differed from that of any Indians he had ever seen. For they were "small in size, delicately formed, and [of] the most exact symmetry throughout, except the head."[2] The head, he explains, he had always thought would be flat on the top, but instead came to a point (a woodcut is provided to prove it, showing a forehead which sweeps directly from brow to crown). The Indians had come three thousand miles in search of religious instruction and missionary aid and had applied to the general for assistance. Though somewhat overset by the responsibility visited upon him, Clark had supplied his visitors with a complete history of man from Creation to Calvary, explained all the moral precepts in the Bible, expounded upon the Decalogue and instructed them in the role of Christ as Intercessor and the mercy of Divine Judgment. All in sign language, which must have been a challenge even to the practiced dexterity of William Clark.

This was too clumsy. Neither the Flatheads nor the Nez Percé are notably small, and neither made a practice of mashing the skulls of their offspring into unseemly shapes, that custom being almost exclusive to the lower Columbia region. (The heads which Catlin painted, and which have come down to us, are normal and even noble.) The long dissertation ascribed to William Clark is ponderous nonsense. Some of what Walker wrote surely came to him from Disoway and probably, by choice irony, from Catholic sources. Walker knew that a second Indian had died, and that the two survivors, though they were unwell, had set off to rejoin their people across the mountains. He knew this despite the fact he had left St. Louis months before Rabbit-Skin-Leggings and No-Horns-on-His-Head departed on the *Yellowstone*. Interestingly, the Most Reverend Joseph Rosati, bishop of St. Louis, wrote an account of the delegation at the beginning of 1832, an account published in France and probably elsewhere — and not impossibly in a periodical which reached the desk of Gabriel Poillon Disoway.

The Walker-Disoway correspondence was clumsily contrived. It could have been believed only by a generation which found Cooper believable — Cooper, whose Indians talked as impressively as Cato the Elder and died as stoically as Seneca — and anyway it wasn't long before someone turned up a biblical parallel: the Flatheads appearing at St. Louis was like unto the apparition appearing to Paul at Troas saying, "Come over into Macedonia and help us." The scriptural allusion was compelling. Multitudes were uplifted, not only among Methodists but among others as well. There was general agreement that the Word must be sent across the mountains. Wilbur Fisk had not waited on these events. Fisk was president of Wesleyan University, and a somewhat larger man in Methodist affairs than even G. P. Disoway, and on the very day the *Advocate* containing Disoway's unctuous humbuggery reached his desk he got off a letter to Stanstead, Lower Canada, offering leadership of the Oregon mission to Jason Lee.

❧ V ❧

Wilbur Fisk was born in downstate Vermont, graduated from Brown University and read law long enough to become convinced that the legal profession would be fatal to his religious character. He was tubercular, and had been warned that for his health's sake he must not overtax his throat, but he determined upon a career in the Methodist ministry. Early in 1818 he was licensed as a local preacher in his home village of Lyndon. Five years later he had become presiding elder of the Vermont district of the Methodist Episcopal New England Conference.

His rise was rapid both because he was exceptionally able and because he was university trained, a rarity among Methodist divines of that day. Methodists generally regarded higher education without enthusiasm and even with suspicion, believing that college life was surrounded by temptations contrived to deaden the piety of God-fearing youth. Fisk could only agree; he had attended the University of Vermont as well as Brown and found both rotten with secularism and conviviality, but he thought it need not be so. The student might be saved from debauchery and doubt, he said, if his instructors were unremittingly vigilant and kept always before him the immutable truths of Christianity and morality.

In 1826 Fisk succeeded to the presidency of Wesleyan Academy, a denominational secondary school recently removed to Wilbraham, Massachusetts, and promptly instituted measures to discourage recalcitrancy among his charges. The unruly were imprisoned, either in a room furnished only with a hard bed, single chair and naked table, or in a "dungeon" whose only amenities were the necessary pail and a sprinkling of clean straw upon the floor. Those who remained unreconstructed Fisk treated to a public caning. This was harsh treatment but Jason Lee, who was to become the academy's most notable alumnus, would recall its effectiveness when, years later and three thousand miles away, he would set up a school in the wilderness.

Lee was born in 1803 at Stanstead — then considered Vermont territory but a boundary correction threw it into Lower Canada — and grew up in mild adversity. At age thirteen he went to supporting himself, first as a common axman working the native hardwood forests, later as a gang boss. In 1826 he was "ushered into the liberty of the children of God,"[3] through the joint efforts of his nephew, Daniel, and an itinerant evangelist. Conversion stirred his ambition, but gently. It was three more years before he decided he must preach and enrolled at Wilbraham with the hope of filling some gaps in a necessarily patchy education.

Lee arrived for the summer term, 1829. Bits of the backcountry still clung to his clothes and his manners. But he was very tall, with an angular strength, and at twenty-six he was nearly a decade older than the other scholars. His coming caused a stir among the younger boys. With one of them, the seventeen-year-old who was to become Bishop Osmun Baker, he formed a lasting friendship. But it was poor, consumptive Wilbur Fisk who was most powerfully impressed. Fisk had a frail man's almost worshipful admiration for the sound-limbed and athletic. When he looked on his new pupil's great, gangling, sinewy frame he thought he saw not only the personification of muscular Christianity but the one man most superbly fitted to evangelize Indians. It was a sorry, though probably inevitable, misreading of character. Lee was deliberate, even-tempered, and his piety was genuine enough. But his nature was essentially chilly, and there was bred into his bones the flinty insensibility of his Yankee forebears.

Jason remained at Wilbraham only a year, afterward returning to Stanstead to teach briefly and do a little lay preaching. He corresponded regularly with Fisk, who had meantime moved on to Middletown, Connecticut, to become first president of Wesleyan University. Jason had already decided to enter the mission field and in 1832 applied to the London (Ontario) Missionary Society for a place in western Canada. He was still awaiting a reply when Fisk's letter reached him with its offer of the Flathead mission.

Fisk had laid down that Lee was the one qualified man and that settled it. No one else was seriously considered. On his part Jason very much wanted the post and thought himself equal to it. (He wrote Fisk that among the one thousand Methodist preachers in the States there must be one as well qualified; he did not suggest there was anyone better.) Late in May he forwarded formal acceptance. The task of finding a suitable associate turned out to be more complicated than anyone expected. Despite the drum beating of such as Fisk and Disoway, few clerical pulses were quickened. The prospect of a transcontinental tramp had its damping effect. So did the thought of spending season upon season surrounded by aborigines of mercurial disposition and insanitary habits.

Leaving the mission board to solve the problem, Lee visited south at the annual meeting of the New England Conference, was received into the Methodist Episcopal Church and was ordained a missionary. It was August before Daniel Lee's somewhat tardy application was accepted, and Jason had his companion. Though Daniel was Jason's nephew he was only three years younger and their relationship was nearer that of brothers. Daniel was tall and lanky, as Jason was, and he had some ministerial experience. But there the resemblance ended. Daniel was almost totally self-effacing. So much so that more than one of their contemporaries wrote him off as no more than his uncle's shadow. The judgment was unfair but hardly surprising. In an age which put a premium on drive, go-ahead and general aggressiveness, Daniel was wholly selfless. It was probably as well. Jason was stuffed with ambitions enough for both of them.

Back in April, replying to Fisk's original letter, Jason had written that he assumed any missionary selected would go to Oregon that very summer. That he would write this shows him to have been sadly ignorant of the planning and labor which must go into a journey across the continent. The mission board was no better instructed. The Lees arrived in New York in October to find that no real preparations had been made beyond the appropriation of $3000 for provisions. Things were hardly further advanced a month later when it was learned, quite by accident, that Nat Wyeth was at Boston, making plans for his second trip to the Columbia.

Jason hurried north to interview him. He was Captain Wyeth now, and the title was not simply an honorary one. Any man who had found his way over the mountains and back again had qualified for master's papers. He was still in hot pursuit of Fortune, and if the chase was wearying him he gave no sign. He had arranged new financing though to do so it had been necessary for him to mortgage all but his soul and be content with a minuscule portion of the new ownership, and the responsibilities of management. Not that his problems were solved. He had returned home to discover that the Platte River deserters were blackguarding him in print and that his nephew John, who turned back at Pierre's Hole, had authored a book in which Nathaniel appears as an energetic bumbler whose fur-trading scheme is a fool's venture. Despite the fact that he privately decried it as all "little lies told for gain,"[4] Wyeth knew perfectly well that his nephew was bent upon mischief and might very well make a good deal of it. He might even manage to sever the already tenuous line of credit upon which the captain depended. So sensitive was Wyeth to this danger that hardly had he arrived East when he began sending off letters defending himself. And now the chance appearance of Lee and Wilbur Fisk on his doorstep offered him an unexpected opportunity to improve his public image.

Wyeth put down none of this thinking. There is, indeed, no reference anywhere in his published correspondence to his conference with the two clergymen. The inference must be drawn from what followed, and from the way in which what followed was at odds with his private beliefs and the requirements of the business at hand. He was himself an agnostic, which set him outside the New England ethic. He had come to respect much of the Indian culture and he was too cynical to have faith that the application of a little Methodism would greatly improve Indian deportment. The most wearying of his experiences the preceding summer had been his endless efforts to hustle his amateurs along the trail, to impress upon them that safety depended upon discipline and success upon speed. For these reasons he had determined to hire only western men in the future, and his St. Louis agents were instructed to hire the best available. But his reputation had been rudely pricked and his ego wounded. Because he felt himself closed off from Yankee society and out of sympathy with its rigid morality, his vulnerability was even greater. There is no other acceptable reason that he would undertake to shepherd across the Rockies a pair of Sabbatarian parsons and their retinue — who at their best would be awkward guests among the company of resolute sinners, and at their worst might hinder his going — than that he hoped that by becoming a major benefactor of the mission, he could convince the respectables that he too was respectable.

Fisk and Lee could have suspected none of this. It was sufficient to them that the Lord had provided. On November 29 they gave thanks at a rousing meeting held in Boston's Bromfield Street Church. Wyeth's Indians were there on exhibit and Wyeth himself sat on the platform and even consented to speak briefly on the Oregon country and its inhabitants. Favorable notices of his remarks appeared in the Methodist press, and the captain himself was content with the effect of his performance, writing complacently to a brother that henceforth he would answer nothing to his detractors but let his character determine men's minds.

The Lees spent the winter on tour. After leaving Boston they set off in stately progression, pausing often to accept the hospitality of admirers and pleasure themselves in brotherly discourse, but moving always in the general direction of St. Louis. Daniel laid over at Alexandria long enough to be ordained an elder by the annual conference. Jason went on ahead, working the country, pontificating on the peaceable character of the Indian when in a state of nature (he had become translated, without appreciable effort, into an authority), never neglecting to pass the offertory plate, never omitting to note the take to the last copper.

At Cincinnati — it was now mid-March — he was joined by Cyrus Shepard. Of all the Oregon missionaries of whatever denomination poor Shepard was among the least offensive, and by long odds the most pitiable. He was that rarity, a cheerful fanatic. He had some education. He was four years older than Jason, which made him thirty-five in the year of their going, and he was an advanced consumptive. Jason found him teaching the village school at Weston, Massachusetts, spent a December afternoon lecturing him sternly on Christian sacrifice and by nightfall had won the Oregon mission's first convert. So Cyrus Shepard would submit his frail, unwholesome body to the rigors of overland journeying and the hardships of wilderness life.

Lee and Shepard traveled down the Ohio together, reaching St. Louis the last day of March. Shepard hustled ahead to Independence by boat to gather together an outfit, and Daniel caught up with his uncle soon afterward.

By this time the Lees were celebrities of some magnitude and the town turned out to give them a suitable welcome. Both paid courtesy calls on old General William Clark, and Daniel was curious enough to inquire about the Nez Percé delegation and the Macedonian call. From what he learned, he wrote later, William Walker's was a "high wrought account," and one containing many inaccurate statements, a judgment both shrewd and charitable. Daniel also attended meetings, and spoke when he was called upon, but it was Jason who was the principal attraction, the star turn, and for a solid week St. Louisans in large numbers turned out to catch his act, which closed with a spirited farewell service sponsored by the city's leading Protestant churches.

Two weeks later he and Daniel were at Liberty, coping with last-minute details. Jason rounded up horses, and cattle for beef and milk. Daniel rode to the nearby village of Richmond to hire a pair of additional hands, Philip Edwards and Courtney M. Walker. Edwards was an engaging and adventurous youth, just into his twenties and, like Shepard, a schoolteacher. Walker was thirty, unattached, a Pennsylvanian who had come as far west as the edge of Missouri and was willing to go the remainder of the way. Both, sad to relate, were doubters. But there was no helping it. If saints wouldn't enlist, sinners must serve.

❧ VI ❧

The winter and spring which saw the Lees parade across the land in pious triumph was for Nathaniel Jarvis Wyeth a time of vexation. He had chartered the *May Dacre* to carry goods and supplies, and some of the mission gear, but she did not leave Boston until January 7 of the new year, a month later than he had hoped and probably too late to reach the Columbia for the fall salmon run. Milton Sublette visited him that same month, having come in response to repeated invitations, but the welcoming celebration, if there was one, must certainly have been muted. For he was Milton sadly altered, distinctly unwell as the result of some obscure mountain accident which left him with a morbid excrescence attacking his left foot and beginning an inexorable crawl up the leg. A dismaying development. Milton was not only a friend, he was also guarantor of that all-important contract for the furnishing of supplies to the Rocky Mountain Fur Company, the contract which was the sheet anchor of Wyeth's new enterprise.

But no matter, Wyeth was not one to take counsel from his difficulties. While Milton spent a long month warming his aches before the hearth, and nursing an occasional glass of hospitality, the iceman hurried his plans ahead. Captain Joseph Thing, shipmaster on sabbatical, was signed on as second-in-command and hurried to Baltimore to expedite the flow of supplies from that port to Missouri. Two newcomers applied for passage to Oregon and were accepted; both were naturalists. Thomas Nuttall was forty-eight and the curator of the Harvard Botanical Gardens, but he was no ivory-tower sage. In 1811 he accompanied the Astor overland party as far as the Arikara villages, and in 1819 he joined the expedition of Lieutenant Stephen Long, the engineer officer who dismissed the Great Plains as a futureless wasteland. Nuttall was a respected authority on botany and ornithology and he had reached an age when he might comfortably have tended his exotic plants and delivered the occasional lectures required of him, but his youthful love for field work burned as brightly as ever.

John Kirk Townsend, Nuttall's associate, was exactly half his age, a Philadelphian, a practicing physician and a self-taught ornithologist. As an accomplished amateur, Townsend had contrived to secure sponsorship of the Academy of Natural Science and the American Philosophical Society, both of which were prestigious and each of which appointed him its representative. He was as ardent and judicious a collector as Nuttall (some hundred of his skins would allow John James Audubon to include far-western species in his monumental *Birds of America*), and he would write one of the most perceptive and entertaining accounts of the transcontinental crossing to come down to us.

Wyeth was without religion but he had a businessman's belief in the utility of science, and he was pleased with his new recruits, both because they brought distinction to his expedition and because one was an experienced plains traveler and the other a fine shot. He wrote as much to Nuttall from Boston, in a letter dated February 4. Six days later Nathaniel was at New York, where he paused briefly before continuing on to Philadelphia and then west, spinning off letters at every stop. Orders for rifles, spades, hunting knives. Instructions to Captain Thing to lay in a small, inexpensive supply of medicaments for clap and pox — palliatives, salves to reduce chancres, and perhaps laudanum to relieve the agony of stricture. He even managed a letter to his wife. It was short because, he wrote, "I . . . am unused to writing to ladys [sic] any way."[5]

This was the noontide of Nat Wyeth's expectations. From here, all the omens would be bad. At Louisville, or shortly beyond Louisville, Wyeth contracted cholera. He recovered quickly, but the disease left him wan and drained, and when he reached St. Louis he found himself awash in a spate of troubles.

He was already overextended. It had been necessary to double the capitalization of his new concern. Wyeth had somehow managed to delude himself that Bill Sublette was unaware that his brother Milton had passed a piece of the supply business of the Rocky Mountain Fur Company to his friend from Cambridge. But Bill had been tutored in chicanery by the Gros Ventres, the Arapahoes and the agents of Mr. Astor's American Fur Company. There were no better teachers. And he was aided by the minor knavery of Dr. Benjamin Harrison, son of one president-to-be and uncle and namesake of another, who learned that Wyeth and the Rocky Mountain Fur Company were planning a private rendezvous and leaked the information to Bill.

Which meant a race to the mountains. Which meant in turn Wyeth must have the best in horses and mules and must purchase them on a sellers' market. And Bill was showing his teeth. Sublette & Campbell refused to honor a draft upon which the Rocky Mountain Fur Company was depending, or would honor it only if Milton would undertake not to go to the mountains. It was unthinkable that Milton would not go and Wyeth was forced to purchase the draft out of his own pocket.

A rapidly emptying pocket. He managed to recruit thirty men but most of them were boozers who needed advance money to pay off their bar bills. His St. Louis agents proved less than thrifty. His ebullience was fading. At the end of March he wrote his wife a long letter of doubt and self-reproach, regretting he was denying her the pleasures of a marital relationship. But, Nathaniel said plaintively, "you know the success of what I have undertaken is life itself to me and if I fail in it they shall not say it was for want of perseverance."[6] So he described the succubus that would ride his shoulders to the bitter end.

He kicked his crew along to Liberty — his thirty and about twenty more going up as replacements for the Rocky Mountain Fur Company — cussed them into some kind of shape and on April 24, 1834, enjoyed his last triumph. Of all the brigades, Nathaniel Jarvis Wyeth's was first to set off for the mountains. He had read the weather right — the spring was soft and the grass early — and he was moving even before the energetic Bill Sublette was come to mark. But he was plagued by a dog's luck. Milton found sitting a horse excruciatingly painful and within ten days he was forced to turn back to the settlements. And three nights later Brother Bill, moving smooth as oil, slipped into the lead. Wyeth was dished.

But during the early weeks of that May, while Sublette and Wyeth raced west for a meeting with Tom Fitzpatrick, there occurred a truly momentous event. Jason Lee met his first "wild" Indians, and his psyche never recovered from the shock.

⚘ VII ⚘

They were Caws, cousins to the Osage, and they bore no resemblance beyond their color to Mr. Cooper's Uncas and Chingachgook. The adults among them were half-naked, the children entirely so; all of them were unwashed, and wherever they moved they were surrounded by a pack of mongrels as thick, noisome and pestiferous as a cloud of enormous flies.

A sizable troop of the tribe trailed in the wake of Wyeth's party for a week. They excited Cyrus Shepard's sympathy but Jason found for them nothing but revulsion and disgust. The very sight of them soured his charitable impulses. When they came begging he turned them away. He watched them closely lest they pilfer and blamed them for the loss of a wandering cow. They were, in fact, a poor people whose last corn crop had been lost to rot, who had been driven from their homes by cholera, who depended for sustenance upon Indian agents unremarkable for either honesty or efficiency. Their frugalities were the frugalities of perennial poor relations. They took what came to hand simply because they had no other way of getting what they needed.

Lee understood none of this, and could not have been expected to understand any of it. He was a copper-riveted product of the Protestant work ethic. The Caws toiled not; neither, so far as he observed, did they spin. They had not even the fragrance of the lilies of the field. Even after he discovered they were truly in a state of starvation he would not share an ounce of mission provender. "Lest," he wrote in his journal, "we should not have enough until we reach the buffalo."[7] First consideration must be given to the requirements of the master race.

Apologists will cry out that this comment is unjust, but it is no more than a recitation of the inevitable. Lee was not unduly fastidious. His tastes were not finicky. The sight of Townsend's gore-smeared face, when the young ornithologist drank buffalo heart-blood to relieve overpowering thirst, set him shouting with laughter. It offended him to travel on the Lord's Day, but he worked and traveled when that was required of him. He was sincere in his Christianity. In his journal he frequently and respectfully addresses the Lord God, and his sentiments are always impeccable. But, as his reaction to the Caws demonstrated, he lacked an evangelical essential. He was constitutionally unable to love the unlovable.

Jason was slow, but he was not stupid. A week in Indian company had destroyed his illusions. The reality which replaced them he found unappetizing and his mind worked, when opportunity offered, to find more agreeable accommodation. Opportunity seldom offered, because Wyeth was whipping the brigade along, making up to twenty-five miles in a day's journey so that four weeks out they reached the north fork of the Platte and exactly a week later, at the mouth of the Laramie River, came upon the founding of a post of major significance in the history of the Pacific West. Bill Sublette had detached thirteen men to raise a stockade and buildings on the level ground at the confluence of the two rivers. The place was christened Fort William but almost from the first it was called Fort Laramie. Sublette had placed it to attract the trade which moved through South Pass, as almost the whole of the transmontane trade did. When the time came the emigrants would pass that way also, and Fort Laramie would become the great way station of the Oregon Trail east of the mountains. Within a few months Wyeth himself would erect what would become the great way station on the western slope, and the whole process of overland emigration would be enormously simplified.

For Wyeth, however, the immediate consideration was that from this point Bill Sublette would be traveling light and could be overtaken only by prodigious effort. The captain demanded the utmost of animals and men alike. In the next two weeks he marched more than three hundred miles over harsh country. His horses foundered of fatigue and wasted on poor grass but on June 15 he reached Pacific drainage.

Four days later he caught up with Tom Fitzpatrick on the Green River. All effort wasted. Bill Sublette was already there and had exerted his leverage. Wyeth was told that because of Milton's absence the Rocky Mountain Fur Company would not honor the contract.

The rendezvous that year was on Ham's Fork, a dozen miles almost due west of where they were. Everyone paraded over and tented up. While his crew bivouacked Wyeth took Lee aside and told him that word was passing around the Rocky Mountain Fur Company camp that some of the boys were going to give the missionaries hell. He advised firmness and avoidance of offense. He also said the Lees and their lay assistants were under his, Wyeth's, protection. Jason replied that he feared no man, apprehended no danger from anyone sober and would stay clear of drunks. And he suggested they ride over to Sublette and Fitzpatrick's camp and clear the matter. Bill greeted them with his customary suavity, denied making any threats himself and introduced them around to some of those who had. And they all sat down for a nice talk about the problems of wilderness travel, polite enough to drink tea. Which was hardly surprising. Nat Wyeth was small but he was tough as bullhide, and the recent double-cross had curdled his disposition. And a missionary who stood six feet and weighed in at two hundred pounds was sizable even by mountain dimensions.

It was a small incident but Lee, by a little judicious twisting, shortly converted it into a useful one. He had never forgotten those Caw Indians, and the unsettling memory of them had driven him to the making of a remarkable decision which he now must justify. He did so in an adroitly worded letter to Wilbur Fisk. A long letter — Jason labored over it for two days — full of enthusiasm, self-congratulation and original spelling. And, carefully mixed in with the rest, this flat misrepresentation concerning his reception at the rendezvous:

> The Capt . . . came and informed me, that he had heard, that the *Indians* threatened to "give the Missionaries Hell," and that he had heard something of the kind himself, and advised us to say nothing to them on the subject of religion, for it was not possible to do them any good . . .[8]

The italics, as were the Indians, are supplied. Lee knew exactly who his proposed tormentors were. That is clear from his journal. But for his purposes it was necessary for them to be Indians, and so he transformed them. And he transformed them to bolster the opinion he now offered to Fisk: "It is rather my opinion that it is easier converting a tribe of Indians at a *Missionary Meeting,* than in the wilderness."[9] This time the italics are his own.

He has made his point. The wilderness is no place to convert Indians. The missionary to the Flatheads will not build his house among them.

During the whole of this period, almost from his arrival at the rendezvous, Lee was possessed by a strange lassitude of spirit. A delegation of Nez Percé and Flatheads wait upon him, dignified as so many bishops, to inquire as to his message and intentions. He is too busy to see them. They come a second time and he gives them perfunctory answers. He celebrates a birthday — his thirty-first — with a doleful summation of wasted life.

Whatever his burden he still carried it on July 2 when Wyeth saddled up and moved out on the trail, accompanied now by a distinguished guest — Captain William Drummond Stewart, veteran of Waterloo, more lately volunteer adjutant to Tom Fitzpatrick and baronet-to-be. The Nez Percé and Flatheads were also along, though for two days only, and once more they applied to Jason, asking whether he would stop among them and be their teacher. He was patently evasive but they were too polite to tax him with it and when it came time to part all crowded round to shake his hand. He said he was much affected.

Everyone, barring the religious, got drunk on Independence Day. Bonneville's people were in the area and Bonneville himself not far away, brooding on his defeats. On July 5 all of them set off north along the Bear, pausing when they reached it to pay the obligatory visit to Soda Springs. Jason roused himself from his torpor long enough to explore the phenomena and they inspired a long journal entry. He found the water acid, and impregnated with gas, and tasting not unlike the soda made with powders. Most astonishing was an aperture from which hot water spurted at intervals and with much force. His description is almost scientific, an indication of his mood. He is standing in the presence of a minor wonder and does not ascribe it to the glory of God.

This was on July 9 and later that same day Tom McKay rode into camp leading a small number of free trappers and a long string of pack animals, and John McLoughlin's Snake country strategy had taken a new turn. For nine years Ogden and John Work trapped the area as closely as Providence, weather and the Blackfeet allowed. But Work's last expedition, completed just two years earlier, was a near catastrophe. Eleven months of accidents and endless bloody skirmishes cost him a fifth of his effectives and a third of his animals, and brought in barely more than six hundred beaver. The Snake River hunt had become insupportably expensive.

There remained, however, the problem of containing the American threat. The doctor borrowed Wyeth's thinking; he would compete directly for the mountain trade. Early in 1834 McKay was commissioned an independent partisan (subterfuge to satisfy patriotic inhibitions mountain men might have about dealing with the British monopoly), equipped with an outfit and sent off to the rendezvous to run competition against the St. Louis suppliers. After that McKay was to find Bonneville, who was raising an ineffective but troublesome opposition in and around the Snake basin, and spoil his trade.

For reasons still obscure, McKay did not reach the rendezvous that year. But he found Bonneville. And he found Wyeth. Unexpectedly, because when McKay left Fort Vancouver McLoughlin had no intimation Wyeth was to return. McKay was faced with a command decision. He was too practiced a hand to bungle it. He visited Bonneville's camp, listened to Bonneville's people, and decided that the military gentleman's expectations were irreparably ruptured. Wyeth was another matter. He had a large store of goods, a respectable number of hands, intolerable energy and a plan for putting up a fort where it might well attract both Indians and free trappers unless it was actively opposed. When he broke camp and marched north, McKay marched with him.

Wyeth had chosen to build somewhere on the little plain which forms the south bank of the Snake between the mouths of the Portneuf and the Blackfoot. An easy five days' journeying. But Jason traveled it in dream state. Incidents flicker briefly in his journal. A grizzly charges crazily from cover and is met with yaps and hallooing and a hail of musket balls. Buffalo hurtle past the column. Jason gallops in pursuit but dust blinds him. He sets a few horseshoes but inadequate tools make the job laborious. Vagueness has invaded him.

Wyeth selected his site and on July 16 began construction. Shortly Jason's malaise took a more definite form. He got a wetting while hunting and came down with chills and high fever. For nearly two weeks he seldom left the comfort of his blankets. On one Sunday McKay asked him to preach. The audience was respectfully attentive but when it was over Jason could not remember whether he spoke well or ill.

At the end of July McKay set out, leaving Wyeth still working away at his fort and taking the mission party and Captain Stewart with him. Jason was still weak but his mood was improving and his journal is sprinkled with small pieties. That portion of the Snake Valley through which they were progressing was crowded with natural wonders — congregations of springs, sudden waterfalls and white-water cascades — and Lee saw the hand of God in the shaping of each one of them.

Travel became increasingly arduous as they toiled onward, and hunting was poor, but McKay saw to it that the mission camp was never without meat. And when he left them, a little past Shoshone Falls, he made the Lees a welcome present of flour and sugar, and set them all on the road to Fort Walla Walla. Then he went off to build a post where the Boise River joins the Snake, which he hoped would insulate the Nez Percé and the Flatheads from the attractions of Wyeth's new fort.

The second day after McKay's leaving there occurred an incident largely ignored in the literature. The caravan had found good pasture and halted early to allow the animals to graze. Jason was visiting Captain Stewart when word came that Cyrus Shepard was convulsing. Rushing to the mission tent Lee found the teacher cyanotic and unconscious, and beside him a pool of vomit in which were identifiable chunks of camphor and root of ipecacuanha — the first then a commonly used stimulant, the other a powerful emetic.

Cyrus was saved, though narrowly. In Lee's report to the *Christian Advocate* the affair is written off as an accident, which it could hardly have been. Camphor, in that day, was mixed with wax and shaped into small blocks from which pieces were pared as needed, the standard dosage being a paper-thin, inch-square wafer. It seems probable that the ailing Cyrus, his mind feverish and his body tormented both by hardship and by the tuberculosis which ravaged him, deliberately overdosed. Then, regretting his rashness, he choked down the ipecac in a successful effort to induce puking.

In a day or two, however, Cyrus had sufficiently recovered and they all went on, fighting their way up and down broken hills, driving cattle as footsore as themselves. The Indians were kind to them, however, which eased their way, and on September 1 they came to Fort Walla Walla. It was the oasis they had imagined. But the gentleman in charge, Pierre Chrysologue Pambrun, was hospitality itself. And a day later Wyeth caught up with them.

The captain was in a jovial mood. He had completed his fort and christened it, with the aid of a bucket of alcohol, Fort Hall, after one of his business associates. Thus had he evened matters with Bill Sublette and Tom Fitzpatrick. Fort Hall was admirably situated. It dominated the western approach to the Rockies quite as effectively as Fort Laramie dominated the eastern approach. So long as it was maintained the St. Louis traders could never gain a permanent foothold north of Bear River, and they would have difficulty hanging on even there. And if Nat Wyeth had not means to make his new post a going concern, he knew very well where he could find someone who did.

❧ VIII ❧

Wyeth, always moving at a gallop, reached Fort Vancouver on September 14. The others came in next day. McLoughlin sorted his visitors smoothly. Captain Stewart was an honored guest; he brought introductions from high places. Nuttall and Townsend were made comfortable and promised passage to the Sandwich Islands, where they proposed to winter. Jason Lee was told, with strict accuracy, that any mission established in the Nez Percé–Flathead country would be difficult to provision, costly to maintain and dangerously remote from such protection as The Bay could extend. It was advice received with gratitude and doubtless with relief. The Lees selected a site on the east bank of the Willamette, about sixty miles south from that river's mouth, and to it the Methodists adjourned to raise up a house which they would share with God.

There remained the matter of Wyeth.

Nothing was going to save Nat Wyeth from eventual bankruptcy but he was determined to run out his race. Within a week of his arrival he had erected a forge and charcoal house on Wapato (now Sauvie) Island, laid out a farm and given orders for the erection of a post to be called Fort William. For the first time since the departure of Captain Dominis some five years earlier there was an active opposition aimed directly at Fort Vancouver. It was on form an opposition with a certain leverage because Wyeth had stocks of raw alcohol and even the makings of a still, the latter presumably brought round the Horn on the *May Dacre*. He had only to broach a puncheon of booze and break open a bale of goods and McLoughlin would be forced to lay out outrageous sums in blankets, guns and gifts simply to maintain a grip on his home trade.

So the doctor wrote later in self-extenuation, and it was a fair appraisal. It was Wyeth himself who offered a short way out of a sticky situation, suggesting with some diffidence a division of the trade. What he got was a great deal less. McLoughlin would not increase the price paid at Fort Vancouver for salmon. In return, Wyeth would not trap west of the Cascades or north of the Columbia, nor trade for furs west of the Grande Ronde River, which divides the Wallowa Mountains from the Blues and flows into the Snake just north of the eastern end of the Oregon-Washington line. He was pushed irretrievably into a dangerous corner of the country and even here The Bay was free to oppose him. It was, as Wyeth wrote with sad precision, simply "an arrangement in regard to trade." [10]

Disarming Wyeth was a victory, but not one McLoughlin was disposed to celebrate, and the year's complications had not yet ended. A letter of state arrived from Don José Figueroa, governor of Alta California, announcing with displeasure that certain foreigners led by one Ewing Young had lately departed the California settlements for Oregon, driving off with them two hundred head of mules and horses which were the rightful property of Mexican citizens. These marauders, Don José suggested (using the standard epithet for wandering Americans), should be apprehended and given suitable punishment, or at the very least deprived of their booty.

Arrest, detention and dispossession were all beyond McLoughlin's authority. He had jurisdiction only over British nationals. But it would be diplomatically unwise to ignore an official complaint, and the doctor was not prepared to accept meekly the invasion of his precincts by men charged with outlawry. He publicly posted Young and his associates as horse thieves and he forbade the company retirees settled in the Willamette Valley to have business dealings with any of them. He was busy arranging this interdiction when he learned that Young had passed over the Calapooya Mountains to the headwaters of the Willamette, and that among his companions was Hall Jackson Kelley.

It had taken Kelley nearly two years to go from Boston to Oregon. His accounts of his travels (he wrote several) are vague, contradictory and crowded with the chimeras which took residence in his disordered

brain. Frauds bilked him. Assassins stalked him. All, he insisted, hire-
lings of The Bay. The bulk of Kelley's valuables disappeared down the
Mexican customs service's labyrinthine ways. Despite monumental difficulties, real and imagined, he eventually came to La Paz, near the tip
of Baja California, and worked his way north the length of that bleak,
arid and inhospitable peninsula. From San Diego he made it by ship to
Monterey and there he would have stuck had he not been taken up by
Ewing Young.

Young was a Tennessean who had once been prominent enough in
the Taos trade to joint-venture with the Sublettes and David Jackson,
but for several years past he had led a small company up and down
Alta California, trapping beaver and doing a desultory trade in mules
and horses. He was not thriving. Kelley, still full of pretensions as agent
of a long-defunct Oregon colonization society, full of promises that
Young and his people could become rightful inheritors of a waiting
empire, appealed strongly to his ambitions.

So in August, 1834, a little column filed out of San José, driving
animals to which Young claimed indisputable title. Kelley, Young and
the five men of Young's command were joined a short way along by
nine hard cases who volunteered themselves and the horses with them,
and were accepted because there was no safe way they could be refused.

So far everything is put together from Young's version, and Kelley's
versions, but from this point there is little dispute. The late joiners
were vicious as wild dogs. They murdered, raped and plundered with
chilling jocularity the Indians they came upon. In the Sacramento Valley everyone was stricken by malaria, and the horrors Kelley witnessed
were magnified by fever. Being Kelley, he came down the sickest of all,
and his associates were debating the wisdom of abandoning him when
the party collided with the returning Bay California brigade commanded by Michel LaFramboise. LaFramboise took the schoolmaster
in charge, dosed him with Peruvian bark and venison broth and on
October 27 helped him through the gates of Fort Vancouver.

Where he proved an awkward nuisance. Hall Kelley arrived in Eden
to find himself unacceptable as errant Adam. His libels against the
Honourable Company preceded him. He had been in company with
men denounced by properly constituted authority. None of this altered
his expectations, which were to dine at high table and be put to bed in
fresh linen, though he had none of his own. Instead there was an

abrupt, unsatisfactory interview with Dr. McLoughlin, who assigned him to a hut outside the fort's palisade with food and medical care laid on. He was not to be received in the bachelors' hall where visiting dignitaries were customarily housed.

To McLoughlin this seemed a sensible arrangement. It would be inhumane to turn a sick man away. And because this sick man was an announced enemy, it would be absurd to magnify his importance with comfortable quarters and fat living. But Kelley convinced himself he was the victim of corporate persecution and his agitation increased when even the Americans avoided him. Only Cyrus Shepard came. Only Cyrus had the patience to listen again and again to the long litany of Hall Jackson Kelley's woes.

Ewing Young, meantime, stomped into Fort Vancouver in November, full of denials of thievery or other wrongdoing. A profitless interview. McLoughlin would not accept simple disclaimers. Young and friends would continue to be banned from dealings with all Bay employees, current or retired. No doubt the doctor hoped that Young would depart discouraged, taking his aggravation with him, but the American had his own mulishness. He laid out an enormous claim on the west side of the Willamette, built a neat cabin, put out his animals to graze, gave employment to his companions (always excepting Kelley, whom he blamed as author of his difficulties) and sat down to sulk.

This was the end of Kelley's enterprise, though over the forty years which remained to him he would never admit it. In March 1835, he sailed for the Sandwich Islands on a Bay vessel, with a purse of walking-around money which was a gift from John McLoughlin. He had picked up a bit of scabrous gossip and would retail it, to McLoughlin's disadvantage, in Honolulu. Somehow he would find his way back to New England, taking eighteen months to do so, and he would never return to Oregon. But he would be fixed in his conviction that he was the sole architect of Oregon's colonization, would write pamphlets defaming the Lees, Wyeth and McLoughlin, and would levy unsuccessfully on an ungrateful Congress for a suitable reward. And in his eighties, having long since slipped into the abyss of madness, he would believe that even the urchins who jeered him along the streets of Three Rivers were agents of The Bay.

❧ 4 ❧

Oregon as Eden

1835-1838

THE SITE which the Lees selected is still known as Mission Bottom. Then it was level grassland, impossibly lush and broken by groves of oak, ash, fir and western maple. They laid out a claim (two miles from north to south, paralleling the shining waters of the Willamette, and half a mile in breadth), and near the northern edge, a few rods from the riverbank, set about establishing their station.

The first Mission House was thirty-two feet long and eighteen wide, with two rooms below for living and a half-story attic for storage. It was built of oak logs hewn smooth on the inner side, with a split-log floor and shake roofing. Subsequently a wing nearly as large as the original structure was added. John McLoughlin loaned the missionaries oxen for clearing and plowing, and a few cows and calves to replace those left behind at Fort Walla Walla, and a bull to service the heifers. At planting time he supplied them with seeds of all kinds. When the Lees needed extra hands the doctor hired them company Kanakas — Hawaiians — at company scale, and the settlers on French Prairie were infinitely obliging. By late spring — it is now 1835 — the mission had thirty acres fenced and under cultivation, a decent barn up, and neat pens for the livestock.

Cyrus Shepard spent the first winter at Fort Vancouver, too ill to risk exposure at Mission Bottom and too frail to be of help. He was still seriously ill when Jason fetched him upstream in March, but strong enough to cook and clean. Three months later Courtney Walker, his contract expired, went off to join Wyeth, who was somehow still afloat. It was a disquieting thinning of the ranks, and not long after the Lees found themselves entertaining the debris of disaster.

In the spring eight men and the trail wife of one of them left San Francisco to ride overland to Oregon. They did well enough until they reached the south bank of the Rogue where they were attacked by the tribal cousins of two young warriors wantonly murdered a year earlier by the Young-Kelley party. Two of the whites were killed outright and two more so badly damaged they could not travel and were abandoned. The remainder escaped, though one was hideously wounded. His name was William J. Bailey. He was a young Britisher, trained for medicine but driven to vagabonding by an importunate thirst. His entire body was battered and slashed and an ax blow had sliced through his lips just below the nose, split both jaws and driven deep into his neck, narrowly missing the carotid artery. He somehow managed to stumble three hundred miles in this condition, holding his shattered face together as best he could, bound up in a filthy handkerchief, and arriving at Mission House with his bone and flesh half-healed into lumpy distortion beyond the power of surgery to repair.

Bailey and his companions had hardly passed on to Fort Vancouver when the entire mission family came down with malaria. All of them were miserably ill, but Daniel developed an infection of the lungs with symptoms so alarming that Dr. McLoughlin hurried him off to the Sandwich Islands to recuperate. This was in October. That same month Philip Edwards took a school on French Prairie at Capement du Sable, a dozen miles from Mission House, and Jason and Cyrus were left to cope. They struggled manfully to survive and managed because their neighbors were helpful. And so, occasionally, was Providence. The dog chased a deer among the cattle and the cows hooked it to death. Its flesh was tender and excellent, and furnished a seasonable supply of meat, which was a rare commodity.

Despite his constant preoccupation with the business of hacking out a living, Jason kept the Sabbath. Every Sunday he was able he walked two miles through thickets to the home of Joseph Gervais to hold prayer meeting. Gervais was a man of influence, and the most considerable of the retirees settled at the south end of French Prairie. The little congregation which gathered weekly was made up of French Canadians and the families of French Canadians. Those who had religion were Catholic. But they were a friendly, cheerful lot with an ingrained respect for reverend gentlemen, and in the absence of priests allowed the Methodists to marry the willing, baptize the infants and dying — too often one and the same — and bury the dead. When Jason organized the Oregon Temperance Society a number of the men took the pledge, though it went against their natures.

These were proper, even laudable endeavors. But Jason had been sent out to preach the Word Made Flesh to savages, not the semicivilized. He had not done so. He had carried the Gospel to no Indian village, and converted not a single heathen to belief in Jesus Christ. He had garnered no sheaves.

There were of course the children, who were Indian, or largely so. The first of them arrived in November, 1834, and thereafter there would always be children at Willamette Mission. The missionaries cleansed them — all were filthy and most were verminous — and fed them, prayed over them, exhorted them, worked them remorselessly — for work is central to the Protestant ethic — and taught them when time allowed. But gave them no love. Daniel might have supplied the deficiency, but he had little opportunity. Jason had no love to supply. Cyrus Shepard was kindly but scrofulous; tuberculosis was devouring him and his mental state was often unsettled. So the mission children lived in a stern and joyless world, wan and dismal-eyed, the blameless victims of the well-intentioned. Caught in a prison from which there was no escape save by "absconding" (the term is borrowed from a mission journal) or dying. Seventeen youngsters were taken in before the end of November, 1835. Before that year was out one had run away, one was removed by anxious relatives and four were dead. God's Providences, says the mission journal, are sometimes dark and mysterious.

In March, 1836, word came from Daniel that he was mending but would stay in the sun a little longer, and the gentlemen at Fort Vancouver contributed to the mission a total of £26 (above $100 at the local rate of exchange), which was a handsome and unexpected boon. Despite these encouragements Jason's mood was troubled. That same month he sent a letter to his old friend and mentor, Wilbur Fisk, in which he laid bare his concerns. He was writing, he said, unwillingly, and only out of a sense of obligation, for he had no triumphs to report. He could not claim that hundreds of Indians had been brought to a belief in God or even that he and his associates had been instrumental in the saving of a single soul since crossing the mountains. There were times when his courage was diminished and his faith weakened, though neither had yet failed entirely.

The admission agonized him and he hurried on to self-justification.

He had become satisfied, he wrote, that expectations for the success of his mission were unduly elevated even before he left the States (more accurately, when he met the Caws near Kansas Crossing), and that many must suffer great disappointment. Now he was convinced the disappointment would be even greater than he had anticipated. For himself, he was content that he had acted conscientiously under the burden of heavy handicaps. Since expediency required him to spend almost every day either farming or building, he had not the time to visit even the nearest Indian villages. In addition there was much sickness at the mission station, and the nearest physician was sixty miles away.

Jason had previously written both Fisk and the mission board that he needed a farmer, and that Daniel's intended should be forwarded without delay, and that an unspecified number of families should be sent out as reinforcements. He wanted no single men but men with wives because the example of good women could best bring the benighted to accept the advantages of civilization and Christianity. He needed help so that he could be released from temporal cares to devote his full energies to evangelizing natives, and so that he could establish a large school for the benefit of generations yet unborn. For, Jason insisted, there was no place on earth where missionaries were more needed than in Oregon. But then he added a somber and contradictory appraisal:

> That the Indians are a scattered, periled, and deserted race, I am more and more convinced; for it does seem, that unless the God of heaven undertake their cause, they must perish from off the face of the Earth, and their name be blotted out from under Heaven . . .[1]

❧ II ❧

For John McLoughlin, the same years which tested Jason's faith were marred by minor aggravations. Maritime matters took up an unconscionable amount of his time. Frank Ermatinger arrived at the 1835 rendezvous in advance of the St. Louis caravans but on his return lost three men to hostiles and came perilously close to losing his whole command. Letters from Canada brought the disturbing word that John

McLoughlin, Jr., the doctor's eldest child by Marguerite, had turned spendthrift and ne'er-do-well. And on March 19, 1836, the *Beaver* stood in over the bar of the Columbia. Three weeks later she had worked her way upriver to Fort Vancouver.

Though she would be the first steamboat to operate in Pacific waters, the *Beaver* impressed the doctor not a whit. He had protested fiercely against her being sent to his district, arguing that she would be outrageously expensive to operate and maintain, and that fixed posts supplied and supplemented by sailing vessels could most economically control the northern coastal trade. When she arrived he inspected her with sour disapproval. She was a side-wheeler, just over one hundred feet in length and mounting five small cannon. She was brought out under sail carrying her paddle wheels in her hold for installation at Vancouver. She carried also an admonitory letter from London. While a matter was under discussion McLoughlin was free to advance his opinions, but once a decision was made he was expected to accept and implement it. This injunction came with special reference to naval affairs. McLoughlin's reaction was waspish and his reply lacked grace.

Wyeth dropped by in May, bringing a fresh proposal. His last, and one which was the measure of his extremity. He was prepared to surrender Fort Hall in exchange for a contract to trade and trap south and east of that place, on both sides of the Continental Divide, buying his goods at Fort Vancouver and delivering his furs there. McLoughlin thought the proposal had merit — he was particularly anxious to acquire Fort Hall — so he tightened its terms and sent it off for approval by higher authority. He was not empowered to do more, and for Wyeth it was not enough. His time had run out. He broke up his establishment at Fort William, auctioning off the furnishings (selling, among other things, a huge iron cauldron to Ewing Young), and ordered Captain Thing at Fort Hall to liquidate business there if contrary instructions were not received within a year. Having made these arrangements the unhappy captain started home to Cambridge, via Taos, carrying little in his saddlebags but reminders of indebtedness.

The *Neriede* dropped anchor off Fort Vancouver in September, outward bound from London via the Sandwich Islands. Daniel Lee was aboard her, as was the Reverend Herbert Beaver, Church of England, and his wife, Jane. Mr. Beaver was London's chaplain-designate to Fort Vancouver. He would shortly become John McLoughlin's personal cross. It was to be a month for visitors. Jason appeared to collect Daniel.

And on the twelfth a freight canoe manned by company Indians slipped smoothly up to the fort's landing and five white strangers clambered stiffly out: Dr. Marcus Whitman and his wife, Narcissa; the Reverend Henry Harmon Spalding and wife Eliza; and young William Henry Gray. It is a moment in which the future is reflected as in a crystal. The Americans are not only crossing the mountains. They are bringing their women with them.

All the newcomers were Presbyterians sent out by the American Board of Commissioners for Foreign Missions, a cooperative enterprise jointly supported by Congregationalists, Presbyterians and the Dutch Reformed Church. They had come to evangelize the horse Indians of the Great Basin, the same whom Jason Lee had found utterly unacceptable as prospects for conversion. The men stayed at Fort Vancouver only briefly before hurrying back through the Cascades to build their stations — Whitman at Waiilatpu, about twenty-five miles east of the confluence of the Columbia and the Walla Walla, and Spalding at Lapwai, where the Clearwater joins the Snake. (Gray, as carpenter-mechanic, was to have no station of his own, a fact which caused him continuing anguish.) The ladies stayed on as McLoughlin's guests for hardly more than a month before moving to Fort Walla Walla, despite the doctor's urgent pleas that they winter with him, for Narcissa Whitman was markedly pregnant.

McLoughlin was urging them to stay on just when London was criticizing him for his helpfulness to the Methodists and his hospitality to Americans generally, and most particularly for the agreement he had struck with Wyeth in 1834. His reply was hotly indignant and stiffly self-righteous. He had done nothing for missionaries or others not required by common decency. As for Wyeth, the man was defeated and departed. Nothing remained of his enterprise but Fort Hall, which could not support itself. And this had been accomplished without costing The Bay a farthing.

The doctor solicited supporting documents from his subordinates (Chief Trader Robert Cowrie, who expressed mild misgivings, was summarily dragooned into line), and enclosed them with his letters of justification, which are dated November 16 and 18, 1836. He might reasonably have expected to be finished with Americans, at least for the remainder of the year. But on December 22, the Yankee brig *Loriot*, just out from Honolulu, entered the Columbia, carrying no freight and only the passenger who had chartered her. He introduced himself as

William Slacum, tourist. McLoughlin correctly suspected him of being a spy.

Slacum managed to help shape history without ever completely emerging from the mists of anonymity. He was a Virginian, a Mexican businessman, and a purser in the U.S. Navy with some service in the Pacific. He was at Washington in the summer of 1835 when he recommended himself to President Andrew Jackson as a suitable confidential agent to survey conditions on the Columbia, and after some delay the President commissioned him to do so.

John Quincy Adams, who seldom approved one of Jackson's appointments, thought Slacum to be a very observing man. He was a plausible one as well, and could blend truth, half-truth and self-serving fiction with a judiciousness which marked him an expert in the field of intelligence. McLoughlin, who saw no need for secrecy, answered questions, overlooking the occasional impertinence, and put guides at this visitor's disposal. He even found a way of using the Virginian to solve a problem just then agitating the Willamette settlement.

Ewing Young had used the great iron pot he bought from Wyeth to construct a still. Early in January, 1837, he and Lawrence Carmichael, a member of the Young-Kelley party, announced their intention of distilling and purveying booze, operating under the name and style of Young & Carmichael. The missionaries were horrified. Jason hastily convened an emergency meeting of the Oregon Temperance Society which voted an offer to reimburse the partners for all expenses to date if only they would abandon their plans. A total of $51 and twelve bushels of wheat was pledged, and the mission guaranteed to make up any deficiency.

John McLoughlin was quite as opposed to traffic in liquor as were the Lees. Slacum, who was planning a trip up the Willamette, was authorized to assure Young that if the distillery project was given up, the interdict McLoughlin had pronounced against Young two years earlier would be lifted, and Young would be allowed to trade at Fort Vancouver on the same terms as any other settler. Slacum not only passed along this word, he offered Young $150 toward the purchase of a decent outfit. And so he got himself involved in a transaction of much larger significance.

That winter the missionaries and other members of the Willamette community had frequently discussed among themselves the sending of a company to California to purchase cattle and drive them north to

Oregon. Nothing definite had been decided, nor could be until spring thaws cleared the mountain passes, but now Slacum offered prospective cattle buyers free passage aboard the *Loriot* as far as the Russian post at Bodega Bay. Acceptance was immediate. A mass meeting was held at Mission House in mid-January and the Willamette Cattle Company was organized. Young was elected captain — both an act of appeasement and a piece of good judgment — and Philip Edwards was chosen secretary. Shares were sold. McLoughlin subscribed $500 and James Douglas and Chief Factor Duncan Finlayson pledged $300 between them. Jason Lee put up slightly more than $600 in mission funds. Ewing announced the dissolution of Young & Carmichael in a letter in which he both refused to accept the reimbursement tendered by the temperance society and roundly damned John McLoughlin as a tyrant.

Despite Young's ill-natured blast, the doctor must have been relieved that a potentially nasty situation was so tidily arranged. The drovers were hurried aboard the *Loriot.* Most of them disembarked at Bodega Bay, where they had little trouble finding a winter's employment. Slacum left Young at Monterey, struggling to persuade the Mexican authorities to grant him a license for the purchase and export of cattle, and sailed south to San Blas, writing the account of his adventures and observations along the way. His memoir pokes sharply, and legitimately, at the Indians' practice of slavery, but it also accuses The Bay of inciting Indians to attack American trappers, though Slacum himself was certainly aware the charge was a flat lie. On the whole, the account is long, shrewd, sometimes accurate and highly quotable. For nearly a decade western congressmen would rise in their places to denounce the Hudson's Bay Company as the great murderer of American mountain men, and they would cite William A. Slacum as their authority.

⚘ III ⚘

The *Loriot* had hardly crossed the bar of the Columbia when epidemic struck Mission House. Daniel Lee thought it might be influenza but it was probably septic sore throat, for it attacked only the children. All of them sickened of it, four of them died, and the survivors frequently

1837

relapsed. Seven of the patients were still ailing, curled wanly on damp straw pallets spread on the draughty floor, when an express brought word that the bark *Diana* was in the Columbia and nearing Fort Vancouver, bringing a Methodist reinforcement to Oregon. Daniel was anxiously expecting his hometown sweetheart, Elvira Rogers, but it was Jason who hurried to the fort to learn what God and the Methodist Board of Foreign Missions had provided.

Even on brief acquaintance the newcomers were an ill-assorted lot. Dr. Elijah White, who led them, was sleek, of dubious sincerity and busily officious; he came accompanied by an adoring and exceedingly pregnant wife, their small son and a teen-aged stepson, George Stoutenburg. Carpenter William H. Willson was single, entertaining, ingratiating and very nearly irresistible to females of whatever age. Blacksmith Alanson Beers was stiff-necked, puritanical and an inveterate psalm-sayer. His wife was placidly obedient, as was required of her, though his three youngsters were not. Daniel's Elvira was not in the party. She had decided that her dedication was not strong enough, nor her soul sufficiently resolute, and so had declined the honor. But there were three other maiden ladies: Elvira Johnson, who had come to teach; Susan Downing, who had come to teach and to marry Cyrus Shepard, to whom she had long been promised; and Anna Maria Pittman, who had come to marry Jason Lee, though no one troubled to inform him of the fact in advance of her arrival.

The brothers told him now, privately, and by his own account he was not pleased. He had met the woman once, briefly, at New York in the winter of 1833–34, and had not found her prepossessing. He found her no more so now. She was very near as gangling as he was, and long in the jaw. And, at nearly thirty-four, getting long in the tooth as well. His new associates urged upon him that she had traveled a monstrous great way in the expectation of becoming his wife. He replied loftily that though a lady might travel the world over with that end in view he would not have her unless convinced the marriage would result in mutual happiness and the greater glory of God.

There was, meantime, work to be done. The *Diana* was burdened with supplies and the clothing and furniture of the new missionaries. The vessel's second mate, Josiah Whitcomb, expressed a desire to stay in Oregon. Jason hired him, put him in charge of organizing transportation and gave him Beers and Willson for assistants. Everyone else, including Captain and Mrs. Hinckley of the *Diana*, made the trek to

Mission House, where they found Cyrus doing housework in a smock and Daniel exhausted from tending the sick.

A concerted effort brought some kind of order out of chaos. Dr. White purged the sick. Susan Downing nursed poor Cyrus, who had come down with an inflammatory fever. Miss Johnson took over the teaching. Mrs. White and Anna Maria managed the household, providing pies and gingerbread and even a cloth for the one table, the same table on which Dr. White performed his surgery. The cargo of the *Diana*, when it arrived, provided a few small luxuries. The crowding, of course, was intolerable. More than twenty Indian children, seventeen missionaries and missionary offspring (Mrs. White gave birth to a son in June) and perhaps a hired Kanaka or two were jammed into a space which could not comfortably have held half so many. But everyone turned to with a will and for a short interval Mission House seemed the realization of Jason's dream of a Christian colony: kindred souls blessed by the tie that binds.

But it was a brief illusion. Immediately he arrived from Fort Vancouver, Brother Beers brought charges of unchristian language against Dr. White.

It was Jason's first real crisis and he did not handle it well. Beers was a rigid Sabbatarian; White was inclined to be worldly. Eleven months in one another's company during the long sea journey had exacerbated the differences between them and words passed. It was the kind of petty disagreement which should have been forgotten once the reinforcement reached Oregon but Beers was both vindictive and tenacious. Jason was forced to hold three hearings of interminable length before rendering a decision which satisfied no one.

There could be no privacy at Mission House, and the place was always filled with a confusion of noises: the crying of little Jason White, the drone of scholars at recitation, whines of the sick and a constant clatter from the kitchen area. Despite the handicaps which surrounded her, Anna Maria conducted her courtship of Jason Lee with a calm efficiency. She was born again, but she was no prude. She was even willing to take a little wine for her stomach's sake. Her one failing was an urge to produce poesy. She had not been put off by Jason's initial refusal to acknowledge her as his intended. She was content to rely, just as the mission board relied, on the power of propinquity. She was pathetically in love with a man capable of no more than a little chilly passion, and who was attracted to her only because she was available.

When he proposed, as he very shortly did, she asked for time to pray
and counsel with the Lord. She had come nearly twenty thousand miles
in the hope of marrying Jason, but she would not be denied one last
coquetry.   *1837*

Her acceptance, when she granted it, was in verse with a footnote
from the Book of Ruth. Daniel married them on July 16, with a grove
of trees for a chapel; then Jason joined Susan and Cyrus and one
Charles Roe to Miss Nancy, native American. A camp meeting followed. Almost the whole of the Willamette settlement attended, for
this was its first social occasion of magnitude. It marked the beginning
of a new order. The community of saints which Jason had envisioned
just three years earlier at the rendezvous had come into being.

There was, however, no evangelical surge. After a difficult crossing
of the Coast range, the newly wed Lees and Shepards honeymooned at
the seashore, in the hope that Jason and Cyrus, who were much fa-
tigued by their labors, might recruit their strength. At Mission House
the new arrivals contracted malaria and disillusion almost simultaneously. They had submitted to a dangerous and uncomfortable voyage for no other reward than the bringing of heathen souls to Christ,
only to discover that their prospective proselytes clung stubbornly to
their cultural prejudices and the gods of their ancestors.

Frustration eroded the missionaries' sense of high purpose. Hardship made them inharmonious. It should be emphasized that conditions in Oregon, the extreme isolation aside, did not differ greatly
from those elsewhere along the American frontier. But these were not
frontier people. Most had been gently bred and had acquired a taste
for social niceties. Antebellum America was by no means a sanitary age,
but it had certain standards of neatness and polish. The natives regarded dirt as an element of nature; they took baths — steambaths —
only for therapeutic reasons and saw no disgrace in being hosts to
smaller forms of life. But to the mission ladies filth was evidence of sin
and contrary to John Wesley's dictum that cleanliness is next to godli-
ness. Perhaps the more vigorous among them discharged their spiritual torment by currying down the hapless, helpless inmates of the
Indian school, who were, if not sanctified, painfully purified in the
process.

Living conditions were materially worsened in September by the
arrival of a second reinforcement, as ill-assorted a mixture as the first.
From New Hampshire came the Reverend David Leslie, with his

chronically ill wife and three young daughters; from Maine the Reverend Henry K. W. Perkins; and from Massachusetts yet another maiden lady, Miss Margaret Jewett Smith. Leslie, at forty, was senior in age and ministerial experience to every other member of the mission. And an enigma. Publicly he was prayerful hands, pious intonation, and rectitude perfumed by cloying sanctity. Privately he was a self-indulgent scold whose ambition was strangled by indolence. Twenty-three-year-old Henry Perkins was an innocent idealist of volatile temperament who had already written, or would shortly write, letters which caused his home conference to suspend him as being unsound of faith.

Margaret Smith was the most interesting of all. In a day when young ladies were expected to be silent and submissive, Margaret was neither. She had attended Wilbraham Academy against the wishes of her father (who believed that advanced education for women was heresy, if not abomination), and had prevailed upon reluctant members of the Methodist mission board to appoint her a teacher for the Oregon mission. Under some private arrangement she nursed Mrs. Mary Leslie and looked after the Leslie children on the voyage out. Things did not go well between her and the good reverend, who treated her as a social inferior and visited upon her a variety of petty harassments, and long before the party reached Oregon the two were no longer on speaking terms. Hardly had she been welcomed at Mission House when Margaret filed allegations that Leslie had subjected her to oppressions unworthy of a minister of Jesus, and at the same time demanded that her tenure as teacher be recognized.

Jason's reaction was uncharacteristically harsh. The memory of the White-Beers altercation was still fresh in his mind. He flatly refused to entertain charges against David Leslie. And he told Margaret in blunt terms that his mission staff was overrun with female schoolteachers and he didn't intend to have another on his payroll.

This disposed of the matter temporarily and allowed Jason to attend to the provision of additional housing, now desperately needed. Cabins were built and the Leslies, Whites and Beers moved into them, and Margaret Smith went to washing for Mrs. White. In October the cattle company returned from California, bringing 630 head out of the 800 originally collected and a variety of tales, not all of which made pleasant hearing.

It was also in October that Anna Maria wrote a chatty letter to her brother George, describing something of life at Willamette Mission. There were pumpkins — she was just then baking pies — and a vegetable garden which had produced a beet weighing eleven pounds, and the beginning of an orchard, though such few apples as were available came from Fort Vancouver. Although there was no fat for making soap, by being industrious the mission people might eat the good of the land. Most significant of all was Mr. Lee's acumen in investing substantially in the cattle company so that now the mission would have more than eighty cows and plenty of milk and butter. Mr. Lee, she wrote importantly, was a man of business, and pressed down with care. This letter reads like a proud wife's distillation of her husband's confidences: Jason congratulating himself on the abundant fruits of his investment; Jason straining his unsupple mind to deal with the unfamiliar intricacies of simple accounting; and Jason oblivious of the fact that there was much carping among his associates.

His marriage took up a good deal of his time — Anna Maria was already pregnant — and that may have dulled perceptions never particularly acute, but it seems extraordinary that Jason recognized no signs of a rising storm. Dr. White, his energetic mind double-charged by contempt for Lee and his own imperative ambitions, was busily plotting a coup d'état. Brother Leslie thought Jason parsimonious, penurious and without a drop of human kindness in his blood. Brother Beers continued to brood upon his private discontents. When Henry Perkins married Elvira Johnson in November, the wedding took place at Mr. Leslie's, rather than at the mission station, and Leslie officiated, not Jason Lee.   '37

The blow fell in December, the month when much church business was customarily transacted. The Missionary Society of the Willamette Settlement was duly organized. A sum of money was subscribed for the benefit of the Calapooyas, who were in need. David Leslie was given a certificate of good character signed by both Lees, Perkins, Beers and Whitcomb, specifically repudiating Miss Smith's earlier charges against him. And then the mission conference was handed a petition, doubtless prepared and circulated by Dr. White, urging that Superintendent Lee journey to the States on sabbatical in the hope that mingling in polite society might improve his manners.

It was an unthinkable affront. Jason reacted with such a crying out and a wringing of hands that the embarrassed petitioners voted to withdraw their own petition. What they did not withdraw was their very nearly unanimous disapproval of his management of the mission. Apart from his disposition to curtness, the principal complaint seemed to be that he was uncommonly tightfisted. That he was imposing too much austerity. His associates yearned for more civilized comforts and contrivances.

They were, most of them, homesick and unhappy, and they blamed Jason as the author of their unhappiness. He had lured them to the ends of the earth to Christianize Indians and they found no Indians willing to be Christianized. They were, in fact, no worse off than tens of thousands of other settlers in a thousand tiny villages on the Mississippi side of the mountains, but their capacity for self-pity was infinitely greater, perhaps because they realized they were rapidly losing the evangelical purpose which might otherwise have sustained them. This much Lee should have understood. He had been oppressed by the same doubts and suffered through the same weakness of commitment. But the sheer rancor of the opposition to his governance dismayed him. He had established this mission, built a good part of it with his own hands, ploughed its fields and harvested its crops and provided it with numerous cattle. And barely six months after the arrival of the first reinforcement his own people had repudiated him.

The impact of that repudiation was traumatic. He was possessed by confusion and vacillation. He felt urged to visit the States in the hope of recovering his self-confidence but he was unwilling to go under pressure of that infernal petition. For nearly three months he labored to invent a suitable excuse. He would go in the hope of improving his health; repeated attacks of malaria had weakened him and he was probably already tubercular. But this, of itself, was not sufficient to justify his abandoning the woman who was carrying his child. For his excuse he needed an overriding cause of unquestionable importance to the missionary effort, and in seeking it he succumbed to the imperial impulse.

What Jason proposed was a massive expansion of the mission's field. New stations were to be established near Astoria, at the lower end of Puget Sound, and the falls of the Willamette and The Dalles of the Columbia and elsewhere. Their stated purpose was to serve the needs and save the souls of the heathen inhabitants of these areas. But Jason was also thinking colonially. Most of the sites considered, and every one at which a mission station was eventually erected, was a place of great commercial potential.

Quite obviously none of this could be accomplished without the recruitment of a sizable force and the expenditure of large sums of money. It seemed unlikely the mission board would be willing to undertake either unless Jason was on hand to stress imperative need. In his diary he says the question of his going was much argued among the mission family that winter. White and Leslie undoubtedly urged him to be gone. Their sole concern was to rid themselves of his presence. Anna Maria refused to advise him, saying the decision was his and she would accept it without complaint, for she had not married him to hamper him. But he must have sensed the anguish in her heart. Jason's own mood was one of tormented ambiguity. He dawdled and temporized, watched with growing apprehension the child swelling in his wife's belly, and made an unproductive twenty-three-day trip south to the Umpqua River valley. By his return he had come to a conclusion. On March 14, 1838, Daniel and Henry Perkins set out for The Dalles to establish Wascopum Station, first step in the projected program of expansion. Twelve days later Jason was on his way to Fort Vancouver and the States.   3 - 26 - 38

He took with him, for purely promotional reasons, two boys from the mission school: Thomas Adams, who was probably a Calapooyan; and William Brooks, a Chinook of good family who boasted the high forehead and pointy skull of the well-born. Philip Edwards also went along, going home at last, and at Vancouver the party was joined by a certain F. Y. Ewing who the previous season had crossed the mountains for the benefit of his health and knowledge, and now proposed to cross them back again.

Though he makes no mention of it in his diary, Jason carried in his luggage a document of some historical importance, the first of a long series of petitions Oregonians would rain upon the Congress of the United States during the next dozen years. Philip Edwards wrote it down, though he was certainly not its sole author, and its tone is uncommonly mild. It speaks well of the moral influence so far exercised by the Hudson's Bay Company, enthusiastically about the Oregon country's climate and resources, and weightily of the area's importance to future American trade in the Pacific. Toward the middle of the text there appears a brief but revealing passage: "Our interests are identified with those of the country of our adoption. We flatter ourselves we are the germe [sic] of a great State . . ."[2] Here is the meat of the matter. Oregon's natural advantages would bring the inevitable wave of immigrants. The United States should therefore take possession of the country, extend over it the protection of federal courts and statutes, regulate Indian affairs and create a climate favorable for American business, so that only the industrious and law-abiding would be attracted to the infant community.

The statement was innocuous enough. Nine French Canadian retirees subscribed to the petition without receiving any reprimand. But James Douglas was skeptical. Here was Jason Lee departing for the States with the announced intention of bringing out a vessel freighted with merchandise and carrying a large complement of passengers composed of mission workers and perhaps other adventurers (Douglas correctly made no distinction between the brethren and ordinary fortune hunters) drawn by the hope of gain. It seemed to Douglas's critical eye that the Methodist mission in Oregon was being rapidly transformed into a commercial concern, and that the Methodists nourished secret plans which were at variance with the best interests of The Bay. In all of which he was correct. When the small company reached The Dalles Jason conferred so convincingly with his nephew that Daniel was moved to write a long, involved letter to the mission board, complete with cost estimates and profit potential, urging the Oregon mission to form a combine with maritime and mercantile interests and engage actively in trade. Daniel's letter is an astonishing document, both because it gives evidence of considerable talent for business, and because Daniel Lee was a totally selfless man who never, apart from this occasion, demonstrated the slightest interest in financial affairs.

From Wascopum the travelers journeyed to Fort Walla Walla, where Jason left his people while he visited Dr. Whitman at Waiilatpu and Henry Spalding at Lapwai. On April 25, back once more at Walla Walla, he wrote Daniel a crisp assessment of the A. B. C. effort. He was impressed by the number of natives who had been converted, if not to the Gospel of Jesus Christ, at least to rudimentary farming. Their industry astonished him. He reported that both Whitman and Spalding whipped their Indians, which he approved, and he urged his nephew to be as firm in enforcing discipline. He acknowledged that some of the Nez Percé and Cayuse had acquired some knowledge of the Scriptures and seemed anxious to be taught. But, he wrote, "the truth is they are Indians."[3] It is the clearest statement to come down to us of the unalterable prejudice which possessed him.

Jason was too full of his colonial vision not to share it with his Pres-

byterian friends and he described it in terms so glittering they were
hypnotized into committing an act of egregious fatuity. Spalding wrote,
and Whitman approved, a letter to the American Board proposing the
establishment of a string of mission stations from Puget Sound to the
Snake River country. To accomplish this Spalding asked for the immediate dispatch, preferably by ship, of 110 farmers, mechanics,
schoolteachers, physicians and ministers, all accompanied by their
wives and children. These new recruits should bring with them machinery for a forge and gristmill, several tons of iron and steel to be
worked into implements, three hundred hoes and fifty ploughs, and a
supply of trade goods to include, incredibly enough, two thousand gun
flints, large quantities of powder and musket balls and one hundred
scalping knives.

This absurdity (at the time of its writing the American Board was
supporting a total of only 360 missionaries at stations scattered all over
the globe) was entrusted to Lee, who would see to its delivery and who
would, should he visit Boston, be prepared to describe — so the letter
puts it delicately — the peculiar state of affairs in Oregon. It was an
odd performance, a tribute to Jason's inspired persuasiveness. Henry
Spalding was a man of eccentric passions and capricious enthusiasms.
But Whitman was more than ordinarily hardheaded and a long way
from being a romantic.

Early in May, when thaws were melting the snow pack in the mountain passes, Jason and party left Fort Walla Walla for Fort Hall, now
property of The Bay, and went on from there to the rendezvous,
traveling with the Snake country brigade. Frank Ermatinger was leading it but Tom McKay went along part of the way, escorting his three
oldest sons, who were going east to get a New England education.

The rendezvous that year was on the Popo Agie near where it joins
Wind River to become the Big Horn. East of the Continental Divide
and indisputably American territory. Nonetheless Ermatinger was
made welcome and did a tolerable business with free trappers galled
by the monopolistic yoke of the American Fur Company, which had
outlasted all competition. And there was a meeting of saints. W. H.
Gray and his new bride were on hand, leading west the only official
reinforcement Marcus Whitman would ever receive — three Congregationalist ministers and their wives and a lank young New York lay
assistant named Cornelius Roger. Lee showed the Spalding-Whitman
letter to Gray, which was a mistake. Gray was contrary by nature and

acerbic by disposition. He was also aware, having recently come from the States, that a major business depression had severely reduced the American Board's resources. Instead of approving the grand design, as Lee obviously expected, he got off a vigorous critique of his own opposing it as impractical.

William Gray's disapproval was a setback, but not a fatal one. Within a few days Gray and the Congregationalists were on their way west with the returning Ermatinger, and Lee and company had joined the caravan packing furs to Missouri. At the settlements Edwards and Ewing said their farewells, while Jason and the five boys put up at the Shawnee mission near Westport for a few days of rest before continuing on. They were still there when, very early on the morning of September 8, special messengers from Oregon brought word that Anna Maria and her little son were more than two months dead.

Jason wrote out an incomplete journal of his trip across the mountains in 1838, and it is appended to his earlier diary. It opens, without any assigned explanation, with an extended description of Anna Maria's arrival in Oregon, his first impressions of her, their courtship, their wedding and their married life together. In the whole of that eight months, he writes, their affections for one another steadily increased; their souls beat in unison; they had no difference of opinion, however slight; never did they exchange a cross look or an unkind word; always they were happy in one another's company. Only the demands of duty could have persuaded him to leave so loving a companion, especially since she was six months gone in pregnancy. And she, firm in her trust of the promises of God, resigned herself to separation with Christian submissiveness, for "it becometh the Christian, *ever* to say, not *my* will, but thine O god be done." [4]

All this is dated as of July 28, at the north fork of the Platte, weeks before word reached him that Anna Maria was dead. But it reads strangely like an apologia, and throughout it Jason speaks of his late wife in the past tense.

❦ IV ❧

John McLoughlin also went east in March of 1838. It was his first vacation in fourteen years and he must have embarked upon it with weary relief, for he had lately been much vexed.

He not only had defeated Wyeth, but had bought up all the furs Captain Thing had collected at standard prices and acquired Fort Hall for a pittance. Until the arrival of the U.S. Army, the western portal of the Rockies would be a possession of the Honourable Company. He thought, reasonably enough, that these were achievements of some worth. But his superiors accused him of erring on the side of moderation. Any future American competition was to be eliminated at whatever cost.

As it happened, the question was academic. European artisans had developed a process for felting silk. The stovepipe hat was replacing the beaver and declining demand was depressing the price of peltries. There would be no more organized efforts to contest the Snake country trade, though bands of mountain men would continue to trap that torn and tangled land for years to come.

Charges that he had mismanaged affairs with Wyeth put the doctor in a passion but there was another matter which greatly embarrassed him. Back in 1835 Hall J. Kelley arrived at Honolulu as a guest of The Bay and immediately repaid kindness with defamation, swearing to an affidavit which charged that McLoughlin had ordered the emasculation of an Indian. It was an accusation based upon an actual incident, and for that reason difficult to deny effectively. There was an Indian. It was his habit to dress himself in woman's clothing, go aboard the ships tied up at Fort Vancouver and offer his body for the delectation of the seamen. Beatings and floggings did not discourage him. The sailors, weary of the fellow's importunings, applied to the post physician, Meredith Gairdner, and a number of them held the poor devil down while Gairdner performed castration.

Dr. Gairdner was a Scottish Calvinist whose horror of sin was sharpened by terminal illness and he was not, therefore, altogether accountable. John McLoughlin, when he heard the details a short time after, reproved the surgeon sharply. But he did nothing more because he could think of nothing to do which might serve any useful purpose. The operation was irrevocable. There was no way of making restitution. He resolutely put the matter out of his mind and made no reference to it in his next dispatch. But word of Kelley's affidavit reached London and McLoughlin was called upon to defend himself. He did so, but rather clumsily, and the episode confirmed his conviction that Hall Kelley was no gentleman.

But of all John McLoughlin's trials during these years, none tested his patience so severely as did the antics of the post chaplain, the Reverend Herbert Beaver. They first broke openly over control of the Fort Vancouver school. It was McLoughlin's position that the whole of the district, and all those employed within it, were under his general authority. Beaver, on his side, accounted himself answerable only to God and the established church, and if it pleased him, to the governor and committee of The Bay. The doctor was not listed in this chain of command. Beaver would therefore take no part in the teaching of the scholars save on his own terms, which included instruction in the Anglican faith as a part of the curriculum. When he was not allowed to do this, McLoughlin sensibly pointing out that the parents of a high percentage of the scholars were Roman Catholics, the little parson withdrew from the classroom in a huff.

In the ranks of the church militant, Herbert Beaver could have qualified as a particularly stiff-necked sergeant major. He was strictly obedient to clerical forms. His Christianity was all rubric. He refused to conduct the burial of a dead child because she had never been baptized. He refused to baptize another because she was not, in his sight, properly catechized. He denounced trade or common-law marriages as concubinage and civil marriages as unlawful and iniquitous. He damned his erstwhile parishioners as villains and John McLoughlin as the chiefest villain of them all.

He enlarged on these matters in his official reports and in a letter to Benjamin Harrison, who was deputy governor of the London committee and a personal friend. But he was happiest when discoursing on his favorite subject; the personal tribulations of Herbert Beaver. He complained of the food. He found his apartment at the fort inadequate in size and incompletely furnished. He wanted competent servants to look after his needs and those of his wife, who seems to have been quite as difficult as he was himself. And he protested, bitterly and repeatedly, that his liquor allowance was inadequate for his needs.

As his hatred of McLoughlin intensified, Beaver broadened his criticism into matters which were not his concern, and of which he had imperfect knowledge. Punishment of the insubordinate was harsh. (So it was, of necessity, and by no means as harsh as that practiced routinely in the navies of that day.) Business affairs were sloppily managed. The agricultural establishment was inefficient. John McLoughlin was not a fit man to administer the Columbia District.

Matters between McLoughlin and his chaplain had very early reached so prickly a point that for months they communicated only in writing. But a physical confrontation might still have been avoided had Beaver shown an ounce of judgment. Instead, immediately prior to the doctor's departure on leave, the little pastor handed in a report in which he made an invidious attack on the character of Marguerite Wadin McLoughlin, who had lately entered into a civil marriage, performed by James Douglas as justice of the peace, with her husband of more than twenty-five years. As a matter of routine this document crossed the doctor's desk. He read it and sent for Beaver, who ignored the summons. The doctor sought him out and when Beaver turned away, refusing conversation, kicked the pastor's backside; and when Beaver raised a heavy cane to defend himself the outraged McLoughlin wrenched it away and used it to hammer its owner's shoulders.

The day following McLoughlin publicly offered his apologies. The Reverend Beaver curtly refused to accept them and was thereupon relieved of his duties.

Once McLoughlin was started for Canada, James Douglas, who succeeded to command, ordered the chaplain's reinstatement. Douglas was smooth and reasonably flexible, and for a time there was peace. But by now Beaver was intent upon returning to London to bring formal charges against the doctor, and in November he sailed for home.

By this time there were few at Fort Vancouver who bore him any love, or he them, and his parting report is an extended and immoderately phrased diatribe in which he inveighs against irregular marriage, company officials consorting with fallen women (their trade wives), uncivilized living conditions, rampant immorality and, one last time, the insufficiency of his liquor supply. Even the diplomatic Douglas found his patience at an end, and in a covering report he completely demolished Beaver's catalogue of complaints. Taking up the matter of potables, he gave a final accounting which, it may be, explains why the chaplain seemed to see things more than slightly out of focus. In the approximately eight hundred days of his stay at Fort Vancouver Herbert Beaver was issued 14.25 imperial gallons of brandy, 65 imperial gallons of high-proof wine, and 146 imperial gallons of porter, not a drop of which mellowed his disposition. To his last day, he wanted more.

※ 5 ※

Germ of a
Great State

1838-1840

IN 1834 AND AGAIN in 1835, the Canadians of French Prairie peti-
tioned the bishop of Juniopolis at Red River Colony, asking that a
priest be sent to minister to their religious needs. John McLoughlin
concurred, the bishop was willing, but company management was
unenthusiastic. Thinking there were already missionaries enough in
Oregon, it feared the Indians would be stirred up by sectarian rivalry
in a day when the confrontations between Catholics and Protestants in
both Great Britain and the United States were too often marked by
unchristian violence. Several years passed before London accepted the
doctor's argument that Catholics had a right to the benefits of their
own clergy. Not until late November, 1838, did Father Francis Norbert
Blanchet, vicar general to Oregon, and his single associate, Abbé Modeste Demers, come down the Columbia River to Fort Vancouver.

They were a formidable team. Demers, still in his twenties, was practical, equable and capable of endless itinerating from station to station
and tribe to tribe. Blanchet, at forty-three, had labored for fifteen years
among the Indians and Acadians thinly scattered through New Bruns-
wick's forests. He was a man of superior intellect, mercurial disposition,
a modesty which did not interfere with his ambitions and religious
inflexibility. He could pity the heathen. For the heretic he had only
contempt.

As a condition of furnishing transport for Blanchet and Demers,
The Bay stipulated that the two must establish their mission station on
the Cowlitz. The motives for this provision were mixed. There was a

genuine desire to avoid a collision of creeds. And there was the hope that Bay retirees living in the Willamette Valley would be attracted to the Cowlitz by the presence of priests and would settle there, strengthening British claims to the land north of the Columbia. So Blanchet and Demers went to the Cowlitz. But settlers from the Willamette did not follow them. It was not a matter of faith, but of common sense. The valley of the Cowlitz is narrow and its soil is thin. The Willamette cuts through one of the world's richest alluvial basins. As Dr. McLoughlin later warned Governor Simpson, no sensible person would be content to farm on the Cowlitz when he could have a claim on the Willamette.

James Douglas, meantime, was keeping an anxious eye on the Willamette settlement, which was growing in size and importance at such a rate he feared it must soon exercise a greater influence than was desirable over the conduct of company affairs. By the end of 1838 the settlement possessed an abundance of domestic animals and was producing a substantial surplus of grain. A gristmill and a sawmill were already in operation and a second gristmill was nearing completion. Most of the independent American settlers, those not a part of the Methodist mission, were doing passably well and Ewing Young seemed on his way to becoming a wilderness entrepreneur, dealing in cattle, hogs, peltries, lumber and grain. And while no sort of manufacture was yet introduced, the restless Americans were talking expansively of improvements to navigation, the building of steamboats, the erecting of machinery and a multitude of other schemes which would seem laughable if put forward by a less venturesome people.

So Douglas saw things, and so he described them to London. It was the Methodists who were providing the financial impetus behind all this unfortunate enterprise. Their mission had expended, in less than twelve months, over £500 on land, structures and livestock, so inflating prices that the cost of a horse had almost doubled and during harvest season men were demanding ten shillings for a day's wages. The missionaries themselves were busy as ants, though few of their activities seemed related to religion. From Wascopum Station Daniel Lee and Henry Perkins itinerated doggedly among the middle-river tribes, and Perkins, at least, was making a strenuous effort to learn trade Chinook and the Walla Walla version of Sahaptin. But at Willamette Mission no one troubled to study native languages or evangelize Indians. The missionaries kept up the school. They nursed the sick, who were always numerous, and patched the occasional victims of savage feuds. They preached to one another, and to the residents of French Prairie and to those few American settlers who were spiritually inclined. But mostly they accumulated comforts.

Dr. White, in particular, accumulated. The doctor managed to gain an unhealthy influence over the lethargic Reverend Leslie, who was acting superintendent in Jason's absence, and used it to advantage. He added little conveniences to his house, at mission expense. He traded cattle on his own account. He began construction of a hospital of his own design. (It was needlessly large, impossibly expensive, delayed in completion and never used as a hospital.) And he projected with Leslie plans for a "literary institution" — a school at which missionary children and those of immigrant families could be educated, safely segregated from the earthy morality and social gracelessness of their red-skinned contemporaries.

There were also the incidents and accidents of frontier life. Daniel Lee came down in September to drive a herd of cattle back across the Cascades to Wascopum. Marcus Whitman stopped by, and so did some ladies and gentlemen from Fort Vancouver. And throughout most of October, 1838, the Methodists were privileged to entertain an authentic, self-advertised notable: Captain John A. Sutter, or so he inaccurately introduced himself, half rogue, half genius.

Sutter was no Napoleonic veteran, as he sometimes professed to be. He was a failed Swiss tradesman pursuing his own special vision of Eden. He told the missionaries he would import cattle from California and families from his native Switzerland and found a Swiss colony in Oregon. He was to find his place in the Sacramento Valley and keep none of these promises, but at the time his listeners found them inspiriting.

Still, the habitués of Willamette Station had little to cheer them at year's end. Anna Maria Pittman Lee and her little son were long in their common grave. Mrs. White lost her newest child to the rapids of the Columbia while returning from an unnecessary excursion to Wascopum. And on December 19, 1838, the Reverend David Leslie's house caught fire and burned to the ground, the flames consuming the better part of its contents. A sorry record for a sorry year. Surely the hand of the Lord lay heavily upon the heads of His servants. And there was worse to come. That same winter would produce a scandal among the saints.

❧ II ❧

Margaret Jewett Smith, the same who brought accusations against Leslie and to whom Jason Lee refused teacher status, voluntarily withdrew from formal mission activity about the time Jason departed for the States and was given a position as teacher at Fort Vancouver. After roughly a month Leslie appeared to beg that she give up her self-imposed exile and return to the bosom of the Methodist family. She agreed, but only upon condition she be allowed to teach in the mission school. A tremulous harmony was achieved, though Margaret's awesome lack of inhibition and lively zeal constantly threatened to transpose it into discord. One Sunday she invited some Indians to church services. When they marched in, their presence preceding them, the Reverend Leslie asked them to sit outside on the front steps where they would be ventilated by the breezes. They went away, knowing that they were not welcome at that place, and Margaret thought it unlikely they would ever return. There is no record they ever did.

She was hell on pretense. She became a principal organizer of the Oregon Female Benevolent Society, formed to teach the Indian women to sew and, by charitable example, improve their general lot. When Leslie and White refused to allocate to the society bits of cloth and other necessities, Margaret wrote to friends in the East asking for special contributions. In doing so she explained that apart from castoffs doled out to the children of the mission school, the mission customarily *sold* clothing and other goods donated by the faithful in the States. Janice K. Duncan, who has written knowledgeably and entertainingly of Margaret, describes her as a totally liberated woman misplaced in time. Liberated she certainly was, and had she not been a woman she would not have fallen victim to the artifices of William Holden Willson.

Willson's background was strange for a missionary. He had served as cooper on a whaler, knocking together the barrels in which oil was stored. He had seen a great deal of the world and experienced adventures. He was cheery; he was helpful; he was ingratiating. And very shortly after she arrived, he set off in pursuit of Margaret Smith. When she felt herself cut off, as she generally did, from the remainder of the mission community, it was Willson who comforted her. He was kind when others were irritated. He sympathized with her in her dispute with Leslie, though so discreetly only she was aware of it. He won her trust and her confidence. He omitted to tell her, however, that he was already promised to a young lady in Connecticut named Chloe Clark.

Margaret's withdrawal to Fort Vancouver temporarily blighted the budding relationship. Willson, who seems to have been moved by an overpowering need to marry, wrote his Connecticut fiancée care of Jason Lee, urging her to come to Oregon with the next reinforcement. Yet when Margaret returned to the mission he was as attentive as before. Not with immediate success. Margaret had learned of Chloe's existence and the fact that Willson had dispatched a letter of proposal, and she was not amused. Willson found himself in the classic dilemma of the inconstant lover: instead of having two hearts on his string, he could very well end up with none.

The untimely death of Anna Maria Lee gave him an opportunity to wriggle free. At the mission's request James Douglas was sending special couriers to notify Lee of his wife's passing. Willson offered to send by them (though he apparently never did) a request that Jason not deliver that letter of proposal to Chloe Clark. Margaret was sufficiently infatuated to accept the carpenter's assurances of honorable intent and from thenceforth — we are now near the end of June, 1838 — she considered herself betrothed. But she stubbornly refused to agree to marriage until she had proof in hand that the invitation to her rival in the States had been truly withdrawn. None arrived by the onset of winter when it was decided that the two, Margaret and William, should share a single cabin.

The Reverend David Leslie, who was responsible for the moral and spiritual purity of the mission family, must have approved this arrangement. No one else raised a question or an eyebrow. Margaret herself made no serious objection. Her confidence in God's amazing grace sustained her. Brother Willson was more than willing.

At the outset they got on well enough, better than might have been expected of an engaged but pious couple crowded together in a tiny log cabin whose principal inner partitions were, in all probability, muslin or Osnaburg cloth. But as the nights lengthened and the weather turned chilly, Willson's urges rose like tidal forces. He became increasingly importunate, insisting Margaret marry him without further delay, arguing that they were already living together as husband and wife except that they were denying themselves an important and blessed benefit of holy wedlock. Margaret replied firmly that there could be no question of matrimony so long as doubts remained over

Willson's Connecticut commitments. To which Willson retorted that immediate marriage would be excused, even should the young lady from the East subsequently appear, *if certain circumstances could be admitted.*

So Margaret described his proposition later. He may have been more explicit but even if he were not, there was no mistaking his meaning. She told him hotly that no "certain circumstances" existed, that none would ever exist, and that their engagement was at an end. Her outburst so maddened Willson that he ran from their house shrieking that he would revenge himself upon her reputation, and sought out Brother Beers, the sternest of the saints, to announce himself in sad trouble. He had sent for Miss Chloe Clark to be his bride, but he had since sinned grievously with Sister Smith.

The missionary hive boiled up in joyous indignation; nothing stirs the enthusiasm of the godly like the downfall of the uncompromisingly righteous. Willson was urged to repeat his confession and did so on divers occasions, loud in his lamentations, tearful in his repentence. But Margaret proved recalcitrant, protesting innocence. Brother Leslie, at once sad and stern, waited upon her to demand she admit to carnal sin. She refused. He tried sly reassurance: two Methodist preachers of his acquaintance were guilty of the same error before marriage, but they confessed and it was passed over. This example of ministerial permissiveness did nothing to persuade Margaret, and Leslie was forced to issue an ultimatum: she must acknowledge her transgression, *for the brethren would accept no less.*

The implication was clear. She was trapped in the outback, twice betrayed and without prospects, and dependent upon the mission for shelter and sustenance. Having no recourse, she signed the confession prepared for her.

For Leslie it was a sweet triumph. His long struggle with Margaret Smith's independence was at an end. She had been forced to admit to wantonness which, in a woman, was beyond forgiveness of the mission family. Not long after, she married Dr. William J. Bailey, he of the scarred and misshapen face. As for Brother Willson, he was welcomed back into the mission fold with that fervor reserved for the returned prodigal. Shortly thereafter he was licensed to preach.

⚵ III ⚵

Eighteen thirty-eight became 1839 and Brother Leslie roused himself to conduct a full-scale camp meeting. A few of the students of the Indian school became so emotionally distraught by hell-fire exhortation and hallelujah shouts they rushed among the worshipers crying out for forgiveness, and for a time there was rejoicing that they had been brought to Jesus and were born again. But it proved a transitory aberration.

Spring came and crops were planted and the new hospital grew larger but no nearer completion. Indians everywhere in the valley died in depressing numbers, carried off by malaria or by the consumption which had become endemic to them. Native boys kept absconding from the school. In August George Stoutenberg drowned while trying to swim a horse across the Willamette and his body was not found for twenty days. In September Susan Shepard wrote that the French Canadians seldom came to prayer meeting now that there were priests in the country.

But at Wascopum it seemed that the persistent ardor of Daniel Lee and Henry Perkins had worked a wondrous miracle. The spirit of revival ran like a bright flame through the mid-Columbia tribes. The people collected in multitudes to listen to the Word and wonder at its power, to proclaim their sinfulness, to engage in the ritual washing of feet (and, equally remarkable, the daily washing of their hands and faces), to retire to their lodges to pray for further illumination. And the Lord sent precious aid in the shape of an unlikely instrument. The Reverend Ben Wright turned up, a Methodist lay preacher who had lately departed Texas just ahead of an indictment for selling liquor to Indians, and who stayed on to help with the exhorting. This was God's work, and it was good, and there was great rejoicing. Word was sent east to the faithful that the idols were tumbling, superstition was routed and the day of salvation of the heathen was near at hand.

The country was filling up. Fifteen mountain men drifted into the Willamette Valley that summer, some of them with families, Indian wives and Yankee prejudices. Messrs. Geiger and Johnson appeared, just out from Illinois, and unaccountably introduced themselves as advance agents for a colonization society, which they were not. Two more missionaries, advertised as "self-supporting," managed to get over the mountains, but by the time they reached Fort Walla Walla they discovered they could neither support themselves nor abide one another. Whitman and Spalding gave them employment to save them from starvation.

Douglas was too acute to miss the significance of these constant arrivals from the States. The Americans, particularly those settled along the Willamette, were rapidly building a community. And the nucleus of that community was the Methodist mission. For some years both the London committee and Her Majesty's government had tacitly agreed that any boundary settlement would give the south bank of the Columbia to the United States. Douglas presumably thought likewise, though it certainly went against his grain to let the Willamette go by default, and it must have given him satisfaction to inform Father Blanchet in October that the original restrictions were lifted, and a second permanent station could now be established on French Prairie.

Blanchet was shrewd enough to wonder whether he was being used as a geopolitical pawn, and cautious enough to ask that the authorization be put in writing. Douglas willingly did so, for he was acting on orders, McLoughlin having persuaded the governing committee that the presence of a priest among the retirees might be advantageous to the company. Having cleared his ecclesiastical skirts, Blanchet hurried to his new assignment to comfort his people and strengthen them against the perils of Protestantism.

Blanchet had been on the Willamette before, of course. And he had carefully remarried those whom the Lees had married, and rebaptized those whom the Lees had baptized, rousing rancor in Methodist breasts. The Methodist missionaries (presumably White and Leslie) received him with professions of Christian fraternity which he immediately found to be duplicitous. For he learned that the Protestants were circulating abroad that abomination of abominations, *The Awful Disclosures of Maria Monk*.

It is, mercifully, an almost forgotten book. The invention of an indefatigable wanton who claimed to be a nun escaped from the Hotel Dieu convent in Montreal, *Maria Monk* is a pornographic account of supposed orgies indulged in by priests and nuns with the inevitable byproducts of this wholesale dalliance buried in a hole in the cellar — though only after being duly baptized. The book became a best seller solely because it was endorsed by a committee of Protestant clergy and laity of great prominence and small conscience who thoughtfully arranged for its publication.

Blanchet not unnaturally considered *Maria Monk* a libel on his faith and a reflection upon his own devotion to priestly vows. He considered the Methodists guilty of monstrous indecency in giving it circulation, and his bitterness overran his cup. But there was worse to come. He might combat effectively outrageous slander, but how could he save himself from the inventions of Thomas Jefferson Farnham and the slippery tongue of Elijah White?

Farnham was a late arrival. He was the principal instigator and deposed leader of what has been designated the Peoria Party, a collection of sixteen tin-pot adventurers, largely from that Illinois community, who had heard Jason Lee lecture on his way east in 1838 and set out the following year to drive the Hudson's Bay Company from the Columbia and rescue the Oregon country for the United States. The group fragmented even before it reached the mountains, Farnham was relieved of his command, and some of the faint-hearted returned to the safety of the States while most of the remainder wintered in the mountains and drifted into Oregon or California the year following. Only Farnham and Sydney Smith (whose contemporaries called him Blubbermouth) reached the Willamette Valley in 1839 — but not together, for they found one another impossible and parted company at Fort Walla Walla.

Farnham was a lawyer by training and glib by nature. At Wascopum Station he joined Daniel Lee, who was on his way to visit the Willamette, and a little further along they fell in with John McLoughlin, just then returning from his sojourn in Canada, Great Britain and France. The doctor was in an expansive mood. He had visited with his younger brother, Dr. David McLoughlin, court physician to Louis Philippe. He had been entertained by members of the London committee. A project of his proposing, a semiautonomous cattle-raising subsidiary of The Bay, the Puget Sound Agricultural Company, was organized and he given the management of it, with an annual gratuity of £500. The title of superintendent was created for him, to acknowledge his lordship over all that area in which The Bay operated, as far north as Russian America, south to Alta California, and west to the Sandwich Islands.

It was, after fifteen years of devoted effort, a proper triumph, and the doctor would not let the moment pass. He invited both Daniel and

Farnham to be his guests at Fort Vancouver. Because Farnham had been forced to trade off his clothing for decent horses, McLoughlin gave him an outfitting and even furnished him with a formal suit so that his guest would not be out of place at dinner. And he agreed that the young lawyer could have passage on the company ship *Nereide,* shortly to leave for Honolulu. These arrangements took less than a week and Farnham hurried off for the Willamette settlement, where the missionaries greeted him effusively. They were pondering another petition to Congress, one quite different from that sent east with Jason Lee, and they needed a practiced hand to give it a legal style and persuasiveness.

The Farnham petition (so called, though Farnham was doubtless responsible for little more than its form, language and a certain law-yerly disregard for the inconvenient fact) is an exercise in cooperative mendacity. The petitioners describe themselves as being citizens of the United States or persons desirous of becoming citizens. They represent that each of them settled in the Willamette Valley believing it to be a part of the public domain of the United States, but find themselves denied the protection of the United States government. As a consequence they and their families are exposed to be destroyed by the savages around them, and by "others that would do them harm."[1] (These last being, as even the uninstructed understood, the lawless legions of the Hudson's Bay Company.) That they have no protection other than self-constituted tribunals or force of arms, and neither of these is a sufficient safeguard against a current wave of thefts, murder, infanticide and certain undefined et ceteras. Nor have the settlers means to protect themselves from a foreign monopoly which is cutting down American trees, ploughing up American soil and trading in American furs, all to the disadvantage of the United States government and the present memorialists.

The entire production was unadulterated humbuggery. But it spoke in support of "higher purpose," and Americans to the present day have had a weakness for those higher purposes by which the means can be made to justify the end. Farnham wrote later, in an effort to absolve his clients, that none who approached him was connected with the Willamette Station. But Dr. Bailey (who married Margaret Smith and who was by now, because of a temporary religious spasm, a mission attaché) later claimed a hand in the Farnham petition's preparation. The Reverend Leslie certainly contributed more than his signature.

Elijah White actively solicited subscribers. And when the numbers gathered from the mission brethren and the American settlers did not seem impressive enough he personally took the petition to French Prairie, where he maintained a wide medical practice; by insisting, in flat contravention of the truth, that it differed in no major particular from the petition sent by Lee, to which neither Douglas nor Mc-Loughlin had raised any objection, White persuaded a very considerable number of Bay retirees to append their signatures or marks.

Farnham sailed on the *Nereide* in December, his passage courtesy of The Bay. From Oahu he sent the petition ahead to Washington, with a cover letter composed of incendiary poppycock. He returned to the States by way of California, where he managed to get himself involved in a revolutionary plot, and for the price of his adventures published several books. He was no Oregon boomer. He thought the area east of the Cascades too dry, that west of them too wet. The mammoth trees of the coastal rain forests struck him as indecently large. He thought no better of California but half a dozen years later he returned there — just in time to die.

⚜ IV ⚜

On the last day of 1839 Cyrus Shepard died. He had lingered overlong. When he took to his bed in November it was plain he was ready for release, but the doctors insisted he submit to one last, unnecessary agony. White and Bailey, assisted by the ubiquitous Brother Willson as surgeon's apprentice, sawed away one leg above the knee. But Shepard's great, attenuated frame was rotted from within. After the amputation he roused himself sufficiently to write a postscript to one of Susan's letters, signing himself "part of Cyrus," a sad bit of gallows humor.

They buried him January 2 in the mission burial ground to which had already been committed so many of the children given into his charge. The mission family, including Susan and the two tiny daughters Cyrus had fathered upon her despite the increasing gravity of his condition, attended him to the grave. So did most of the Americans residing in Willamette Settlement. But the *Canadiens* of French Prairie, though they had been invited and though the gentle Cyrus was widely admired among them, did not come. They had consulted Blanchet and he was set against their going.

The priest's position was understandable, but highly impolitic. It marked the first real crack in a community which could pull itself apart only at great cost to its disparate elements. Leslie and his associates predictably issued indignant outcries, charging bigotry. Blanchet was self-insulated by the knowledge that his erring brothers had offended both men and God by promoting *Maria Monk*. He wrote airily to Demers that his decision to cut all religious communications between his charges and that pernicious set at Mission House had been inspired by heaven. But shortly came a disturbing letter from Fort Vancouver. James Douglas wrote that much bad feeling had been excited among the Americans and that the French Canadians, Blanchet's own parishioners, were so stung by reproaches they laid the whole blame upon their priest. Blanchet's reply was long, defensive and not always dignified. At the end of it he offered Douglas the assurance that this time of troubles would pass; that the Americans would come to realize they must allow others the same liberty of conscience in spiritual affairs that each had the right to enjoy in temporal matters. Whatever his other virtues, the good father lacked the gift of prophecy.

A greater storm blew up almost immediately. John McLoughlin somehow learned the nature of the Farnham petition, and his wrath reached operatic ranges. He refused, or affected to refuse, to believe that the signers had been bamboozled by Dr. White's perfidy. An infuriated McLoughlin was awesome enough to make even a vicar-general quail. Blanchet, though the necessity for doing so must have purged his ecclesiastical bowels, applied directly to White for an admission of the truth in the matter. He was turned away with a shrug, a smirk, and the assurance that the entire business was of no moment. The priest was still choking down this effrontery when he received a breezy note from Elijah asking Blanchet to attend the upcoming meeting of the Oregon Temperance Society, and expressing the hope that all small differences between them could now be forgotten.

To the tormented Blanchet it must have seemed that the enemy was delivered into his hands. His reply was a model of polite invective. Temperance, he wrote, was a virtue and a general obligation, and not subject to the rules of some self-constituted organization. As for the "small differences," he took them up *seriatim*. There was the circulation of *Maria Monk*. There was the fraud and misrepresentation involved in tricking the French Canadians into supporting the Farnham petition. And finally, there was the matter of a certain Methodist physician (White) who had visited a Catholic woman without any great necessity or the permission of her husband, under circumstances which might wound her modesty, expose herself and said physician to temptation and cause her husband sorrow.

He was so proud of this production he sent copies to Fort Vancouver. John McLoughlin thought it severe. James Douglas raised a more worrisome point. The letter accused immoral conduct and might be construed as libel. If Blanchet's offended parishioners were unwilling to testify in some future civil suit, the priest was in trouble. Blanchet was badly frightened by the threat of litigation, but his concern was needless. No one at Mission House had sufficient French to make an adequate translation of his diatribe, and Elijah wrote happily to The Bay's Dr. Tolmie that while the priest did not attend the meeting of the Oregon society, he sent in a splendid letter on the subject of temperance.

There was little else in the early months of 1840 to give the Methodists real satisfaction. By May the great revival conducted by Daniel Lee and Henry Perkins had come to an inglorious end. A chief was murdered. Tribal code required bloody reprisal but Christian morality forbade it. The conflict between old laws and new preachments proved irreconcilable. Converts slipped away, and the brief brotherhood of spirit was replaced by sullen mistrust. Henry Perkins stayed on to serve a diminishing number of prospects; Daniel canoed down to the mouth of the Columbia to carry the gospel to the Chinooks. He had scarcely arrived among them when the ship *Lausanne* scudded in over the bar, bringing the Great Reinforcement, the New Departure, the Society of Saints whose example would soothe the savage breast and tame the savage heart, bring the heathen to the Communion table and the benighted to the judgment seat, after first firmly establishing the rule of civilization in the wilderness. All under command of Superintendent Jason Lee who had, besides himself, fifty-one recruits of all ages, machinery for the construction of a gristmill and a sawmill, and $5000 worth of trade merchandise. The Great Reinforcement had arrived.

❧ V ❧

When, nearly two years earlier, word reached Jason at Shawnee Mission that Anna Maria was dead, he allowed himself no time for official mourning, but almost immediately rounded up a canoe and paddled down the Missouri. At Alton he marched unannounced into a meeting of the Illinois Methodist Conference, his Indians and the McKay brothers in a file behind him, delivered an impromptu address on Oregon and his mission and passed the hat. He was learning the uses of theater.

It was the first stop of a barnstorming tour. He was selling God, Methodism, Indians and the Oregon country, but the mix had changed since 1834. Oregon may not have moved up in the billing, but it was given a larger part of the act. Whatever his conscious intentions (there are reputable historians who argue that Jason's first priority always remained the salvation of heathen souls, and that his involvement in empire building was an accidental by-product of his missionary endeavors), Lee was pitching for emigration. Text from Joshua 23:4: "Behold, I have divided unto you by lot these nations that remain, to be an inheritance . . . even unto the great sea westward."

They called in at St. Louis, then marched northward the length of Illinois. Thomas Adams sickened at Peoria and was left behind. Jason and the remaining youngsters persevered, pausing wherever an audience could be gathered to preach the crusade and take up a collection, and at Chicago boarded a lake steamer for New York State. William McKay was dropped off at Fairfield Medical School, near Utica, where he was to pursue his studies. The rest arrived in New York City on October 31, 1838, and were given a handsome welcome, complete with an official reception by Mayor Aaron Clark.

That affair was the first of a series of exhilarating triumphs. The mission board listened respectfully, if a trifle anxiously, while Lee outlined his plans for expansion. When he visited Washington, statesmen gravely consulted him. At Wilbraham, where he deposited the two remaining McKay boys, he was greeted as a distinguished alumnus. Everywhere he lectured, admirers thronged to hear him. The religious press gave him rave reviews. At Middleton poor Wilbur Fisk literally climbed from his deathbed to share the platform with his former pupil.

Jason had left the Willamette shaken by confusion and inner doubt and this celebrity was balm to his being. His confidence was restored. He found Miss Marie T. Ware at Lowell, judged her suitable to marry Daniel and persuaded her to accept engagement by proxy. Since he had himself inconveniently lost the wife the mission board selected for him, he looked about for another of his own choosing. At Montpelier, Vermont, where he preached on Oregon and Indians, he was introduced to Miss Lucy Thompson. She came highly recommended by Jason's old Wilbraham classmate, Osmun Baker, and a single meeting was sufficient. Miss Thompson withdrew to her home at Lower Barre to prepare her trousseau and wait out long months for her husband-to-be, the Reverend Mr. Lee, whom she would not see again until he returned to Vermont for the wedding.

In Massachusetts, meanwhile, Jason had been taken up by the wealthy Cushings of Newburyport. They were a shipping family who traded largely into the Pacific, especially to the Sandwich Islands, and for some years old John Cushing, company president and patriarch of the clan, had looked upon Oregon as a potential market. Jason and the Cushings found areas of mutual accommodation and sometime that summer entered into an arrangement. Its precise terms have never been revealed but plainly it was based upon a quid pro quo, Lee undertaking to advance Cushing mercantile interests in the Pacific Northwest in return for any influence the family could exert at Washington in support of the Methodist mission's secular aspirations. It was Congressman Caleb, the political Cushing, who sponsored the Oregon petition in the House of Representatives. And it was to Caleb that Lee wrote a letter intended to be used as a document in support of that petition, a letter in which Jason incautiously revealed the direction of his thinking. A large majority of the members of the Methodist mission were, he wrote, and after the new reinforcement would be, of the laity: farmers, mechanics, teachers and physicians. And while the exclusive object of the mission was to Christianize the Indians, to accomplish this end it would be necessary "to cultivate the soil, erect dwelling houses and school-houses, build mills, and, in fact, introduce all the necessaries and helps of a civilized colony."[2]

Here we are at the tipping point. Had Jason gone no further his apologists, past and present, could be content. But two paragraphs later he spoils his purity of purpose:

> We need a guarantee from the Government that the possession of the land we take up, and the improvements we make upon it, will be secured

to us. These settlements will greatly increase the value of the Government domain in that country, should Indian title ever be extinguished. And we cannot but expect, therefore, that those who have been pioneers in the arduous work will be *liberally* dealt with in this matter.[3]

The Methodist Board of Foreign Missions had meantime approved the dispatch of seventeen additional missionaries, with families, and appropriated $30,000 for their travel and support. It was eventually necessary to appropriate $10,000 more. The size of the contingent created considerable newspaper comment and its cost caused unhappy muttering even among Methodists, who were being asked to contribute heavily at a time when jobs were scarce and business poor. The mission board, when it issued a call for volunteers in April, 1839, thought it judicious to include a disclaimer that it was planting a colony in Oregon, or acting in concert with any colonization society. Out in St. Louis the Missouri *Republican* put the matter in proper perspective. The sending of so large an expedition would expedite the settlement of Oregon, and sustain the hope that a moral and religious character would be given to the people of that territory.

In July, 1839, Jason hurried north to Barre to marry Lucy Thompson on what was, so far as the record shows, only their second meeting. The *Lausanne* sailed from New York in October: the usual interminable voyage; the usual green and sweaty faces lining the ship's rail; the usual squabbles born of boredom. But at Honolulu Jason turned a bit of business. He was granted an audience with King Kamehameha III, with whom he discussed the opening of regular trade between the Sandwich Islands and the American settlements in Oregon, to be carried, of course, in ships provided by the Cushings. When the interview was over the king remarked that Jason was a very persevering man.

He was also a man altered by circumstance. The Jason Lee who sailed into the Columbia in May, 1840, was not the Jason Lee who had fled east some two years earlier. Recognition in high places had worked changes in his personality which were fatal to his expectations. He had lost a good part of his humility and with it any real understanding of his own inadequacies. He had exchanged what little empathy he had for an aloofness which would cut him off from his own kind as surely as he had already cut himself off from the Indians. Daniel, one of the first aboard the *Lausanne* when she anchored near Fort George, found his uncle in a great pother and so full of importance that he would not remain aboard while the vessel beat her way to Fort Vancouver, but the next day was off in a canoe, traveling to Mission House as rapidly as possible. There he was promptly guilty of unpardonable and unnecessary affront. His flock was expecting a disconsolate widower, still mourning the lost Anna Maria. Instead, when they gathered together to welcome him, he produced a copy of the ship's passenger list to be handed about. At the top was entered "The Reverend Jason Lee, and wife, *New England Conference.*" He offered no explanation. They asked none. But he had contrived, by the brusqueness of his announcement, to make his new wife's position painfully difficult. There is no reason to believe that Lucy Thompson Lee was other than a most estimable young woman. Yet Anna Maria became, and has remained, the admired martyr of Oregon Methodism. Lucy, though she served Jason three times as long and bore his only surviving child, is scarcely mentioned in the missionary correspondence, even her death receiving only passing notice. She is now largely forgotten.

It was a bad start. There was worse to follow. The reinforcement had reached Fort Vancouver and been taken in by the hospitable McLoughlin. Weary, peckish, drained of strength, the new arrivals confidently expected to be invited to Willamette Station for a season of prayer, recuperation and renewed fellowship. But Jason intended no delays in the implementation of his plans. He returned to the fort, officiated over the wedding of Daniel and Marie Ware and issued marching orders.

He was treating his people as soldiers of the Lord when they were in fact a mixed crew of touchy individualists bitterly resistant to imposed discipline. But Lee was mindful only of his own priorities. He was particularly anxious to establish a station at Nisqually Plains, just below the southernmost reach of Puget Sound. It offered little as a field for religious endeavor. Most of the Indians who formerly lived there had moved elsewhere. The local Hudson's Bay post, Fort Nisqually, served principally as headquarters for the Puget Sound Agricultural Company, and its employees were Catholics who received instruction from Father Demers. But there was no American settlement anywhere north of the Columbia. A station must be raised at Nisqually, not to serve an evangelical need, but to answer a geopolitical imperative.

The Reverend Dr. John P. Richmond was dispatched to Puget Sound and went unwillingly. With him went an ailing wife and four small children, and Miss Chloe Clark who had, after all, received from Jason's hand William H. Willson's letter of proposal, and come out in response to it. (Brother Willson shortly went north to marry her and to help Richmond complete a dwelling.) Farmer Henry Brewer and his young wife and Dr. Ira Babcock and family were sent to raise muster strength at Wascopum, where the Indians were increasingly obstreperous now that they had lost their brief enthusiasm for Christianity and returned to the naturals of their ancestors. The Reverend J. H. Frost was assigned to Clatsop Plains, to proselytize Chinooks. The remainder of the new recruits were taken up the Willamette and housed in Dr. White's still unfinished hospital. Most of them promptly contracted the prevailing fever, but sickness excused no one from necessary labor unless his case was terminal, or very nearly so. And there was much to be done. Jason had determined to move the principal facilities of Willamette Mission about ten miles upstream to a broad plain which the Indians called Chemeketa, and the missionaries named Mission Mills (and which is now situated within the city limits of Salem). The sawmills and gristmills were to be set up there, on a stream called Mill Creek, and Oregon's most imposing edifice raised to house an Indian manual-labor school.

All this would have been a tremendous undertaking for a well-ordered community. The Methodists were not well ordered. Partly because they lacked any real cohesiveness. Partly because Jason's capacities for organization and management were sadly overtaxed. The logistical problems alone were nearly insuperable. The entire cargo of the *Lausanne* — machinery, equipment, tools, goods and furnishings — must be packed into canoes, paddled upstream to the falls of the Willamette and then unpacked, portaged, repacked, wearily pushed another fifty miles against the current. At Mission Mills came the seemingly endless chore of uncrating, sorting, storing or assembling. None of the women and not above half the men were up to it. The old-timers, after three years in a malarial country, were woefully debilitated. The newly arrived, almost without exception, were dispirited. And in July open warfare broke out between Superintendent Lee and the effervescent Dr. White.

Back in 1836, when word reached Elijah's home in Havana that he had been selected for the Oregon mission, the pious ladies of that community protested against his going, for they feared their infant church would collapse without his sturdy support. The doctor's creditors also raised objections, though for quite different reasons. This is not to say that White was dishonest. He was simply careless with money, whether his own or another's, a fact which bothered him not a whit. His belief in his own financial acumen was unblemished by the slightest doubt, and his powers of self-justification were superb.

White's arrogance helped make his resounding clash with Jason as inevitable as it was unseemly. So did the fact that for two years the doctor had been acting as managing director of the mission, operating under color of Leslie's authority but overlooking no opportunity to enlarge his own field of operations. When William Geiger, hired to replace the departed Cyrus Shepard, resigned to attempt a crossing into California, Elijah became master of the Indian school. And when Jason asked to see the business records covering the period of his absence in the East, it was White who produced them, confidently expecting *pro forma* inspection and routine approval. But Jason laid the books aside, remarking that he would require time to complete a thorough audit. Elijah immediately took loud umbrage, crying out that the very suggestion of an audit was a slur upon his character and an imputation against his integrity. He harangued the imperturbable Lee for the rest of the day and through most of the night before stomping home to write a letter announcing his intention of visiting the States as soon as opportunity offered, promising that an explanation would shortly follow.

It was almost a week in arriving. The early paragraphs are marked by a restraint which must have cost the doctor great effort. He even manages to include a blatantly insincere expression of sympathy for the cares which burden Jason. But very soon his own grievances intrude. The press of duties domestic and secular laid upon him during Lee's absence have caused him to neglect theoretical advances in his profession, and he feels the need to return to the States to refresh his knowledge and at the same time raise men and means for the establishment of a literary institute in Oregon (the segregated school he and Leslie so long projected). Even so, the fact that Lee's Great Reinforcement had included so few professional men would have persuaded him to stay on did he not consider himself virtually dismissed.

From this point Elijah is in full cry. Lee, because he is woefully inadequate as superintendent, is ordered to resign at once and help in the search for a suitable replacement. If he does as he is bid, the doctor will give him a character reference. If he does not, White will act accordingly.

Jason's reply is mild, which must have cost him some effort also, and to the point. He is unaware of having dismissed the doctor, either virtually or otherwise. He asks an explanation. What he got instead was a letter which he characterized as abusive, and another which he characterized as threatening. He answered neither, and received yet a third demanding an immediate reply under promise that if one was not forthcoming, the doctor's next would unfavorably compare Lee's deficiencies with White's virtues.

Jason sensed that his adversary had reached a manic phase. He waited three days before penning a long, gently ironic letter, with a sting in its tail. White would either report himself for duty within two days or be considered as having deserted his post, and the mission board would be so advised. This was on August 3. Elijah's replies — two, because one did not suffice to release his outrage — end with the threat that if Jason does not resign within two days, the doctor will punish him most severely.

There the matter rested for a little time. In mid-August Lee and the Reverend Gustavus Hines, who had come out on the *Lausanne,* left on a tour of the Umpqua Valley to determine where a mission might best be established on that stream. White went along. Uninvited, but to the doctor's second application the long-suffering superintendent replied that it was usual for free men to travel where they would in the Oregon country. Elijah was with them only six days, turning back at the middle courses of the river. Lee and Hines continued downstream but did not find the people friendly (they had not been since settling accounts with 'Diah Smith's party), and decided an unprotected station could not be safely maintained. Jason and Hines themselves had a narrow escape from permanent indignity at the hands of ill-disposed natives and were saved only by the intervention of Madame Gangier, wife of the clerk of a small Bay post in the area, who was acting as their interpreter.

Dr. White, meantime, had returned to the Willamette Valley and was improving upon opportunity. During Jason's sojourn in the States the doctor had built up a considerable practice among the settlers on French Prairie by waiving his fee. Jason, when he discovered this, was much displeased. White was a salaried employee and any sums due him for outside practice were payable to the mission. He ordered White to collect. Elijah was unwilling, and hit upon an artful dodge. He passed among his patients offering full forgiveness of the fees in return for pledges to support of his "literary institute." And he drew from the grateful *Canadiens,* all of whom preferred a future promise to immediate and disaccommodating settlement, a testimonial to the excellence of their beloved physician, with the request that, once he had visited the States, he be promptly returned to them.

White had finally overreached himself. At the beginning of his troubles with Lee he had a considerable support among the missionaries. But he took to reading aloud choice excerpts from his letters that his followers might share his joy in Lee's discomfiture. As his conduct became more disordered, and his language more intemperate, his supporters crept away. Isolation made him irritable and erratic. When Lee and Hines returned from the Umpqua Elijah offered a nervous compromise. Let the correspondence between himself and the superintendent be burned, and he undertook never again to derogate any member of the Willamette Station, seven of whom he named specifically. But it was too late. The Reverend Alvan Waller, who would prove himself the most determinedly litigious of the Great Reinforcement, was appointed to draw up a bill of indictment against Elijah White.

Trial was held September 12. Jason Lee, chief complainant, presided. The Reverend W. W. Kone, outraged party, served as recording secretary. Waller prosecuted and a committee of six was impaneled as jury.

By this time White had lost his contrition. He interrupted Waller's opening statement with a growl that it was best to get on with the proceedings, which proved an error in tactics. He was found guilty of improper conduct and disobedience to church order, technical peculation, abandonment of his duties and libeling the person and character of Jason Lee. He was found innocent of an attack upon the virtue of Mrs. W. W. Kone, three other ladies testifying that he had treated them for medical problems without ever offering insult or impropriety. Despite this hollow victory, White was voted expelled.

He was already committed to depart. But he was not disposed to do so in repentent silence. And he had his own constituency. He arranged with Father Blanchet that on the day following his trial, a Sunday, he could call a meeting at French Prairie's Catholic church to say farewell to his longtime patients. Though Blanchet afterward wrote placidly to Demers that he had no understanding of White's true intentions, the priest could hardly have been unaware of the upheavals wracking the Methodists. White invited Lee to be present at this meeting, but warned him to come alone. Jason, who read Elijah's mental state accurately, took along a few mission friends. It was the first public tribunal summoned in Oregon and the doctor intended to dominate it. Encouraged by his wife he fired off volleys of abuse against Jason and the brethren. But his mania betrayed him. He urged that Lee be ridden upon a rail (to which Jason replied with mild humor), and finally thundered that Lee was not fit to live. It was an open appeal to lynch law. Even Mrs. White protested and Blanchet, after a quiet consultation with Lee, calmed the restless. In the end, after demanding not only violence but monetary damages, Elijah was forced to accept a vote of good character.

This should have been, but was not, the end of it. Elijah and his family boarded the *Lausanne,* now ready to return to New York. But before he left the doctor sent a final word to his late associates. As soon as he reached the States he intended to bring as much trouble down upon their heads as he conveniently could. There was not the least reason to doubt his sincerity.

🌿 6 🌿

The Children
of Adam

1840-1845

IN MID-JUNE, 1840, just a month after the arrival of the Great
Reinforcement, Captain John Couch, outward bound from Boston
in the brig *Maryland* and representing Cushing & Company, entered
the Columbia and proceeded directly to the falls of the Willamette,
where he spent three unsatisfactory months seining for salmon. He
took away with him no more than one hundred barrels of salt fish but
he left behind young George LeBreton, who had campaigned for Congressman Caleb Cushing and was a Cushing protégé. Oregon had acquired its first political wire-worker.

It was also in 1840 the last rendezvous was held, somewhere on the
Green. A meager affair by ancient standards because there were few
beaver and fur prices were so badly depressed no one could raise the
cost of a decent spree. But three more self-supporting missionaries
showed up, complete with wives, as well as eight emigrants from Missouri, Joel Walker and a family which included five children. Moses
("Black") Harris, a mountain man of considerable experience, arranged to pilot this combined party as far as Fort Hall, though for an
exorbitant fee. Robert Newell was just then preparing to lead a small
brigade of independent trappers along the same trail. Newell, univer-
sally known as Doc Newell because of his skill in herbal cures and
minor surgery, offered his services as guide at a substantially lower
figure and was given the contract. Which so irritated Black that he took
a pot shot at his old friend, but being either bemused or liquored,
unaccountably missed.

Doc led his people as far as Fort Hall, where he purchased two of Marcus Whitman's abandoned wagons and drove them through to Fort Walla Walla. Here the missionaries found themselves no more capable of self-support than had their "self-supporting" predecessors, and were parceled out among the American Board stations. The Walkers went on to the Willamette. So did Newell and a handful of trappers determined to exchange their old trade for another which offered greater security and less peril. Among them was Joe Meek, Doc's brother-in-law (they were married to Nez Percé sisters); at thirty he was twelve years a mountain man and now on his way to becoming legend.

The Methodists did not receive their new neighbors with particular enthusiasm or charity and Newell, Meek and some of their more impoverished companions were forced to swallow their American prejudices and apply to Fort Vancouver, where McLoughlin loaned them supplies enough to see them through the winter. The experience soured Meek somewhat but as it happened the Methodists were not, just then, looking upon one another with notable enthusiasm or charity. Matters were not going well. Brother Waller had been appointed to supervise construction of the mills at the Chemeketa site. The sawmill worked well enough when it worked, but was frequently down for repairs. The gristmill was useless without major modification. The holy mechanics had set the burrs improperly. The missionaries were forced either to send their grain elsewhere for milling or reduce small quantities to flour in coffee grinders, a time-consuming process.

Members of the Great Reinforcement had come expecting a measure of hardship and inconvenience, and might have coped with these, but none of them was prepared for wholesale disillusion. They had been told they were being sent to rescue thousands and even tens of thousands of souls from the abysmal darkness of paganism. Now they learned it could never be. And for the most elemental of reasons. There were not Indians enough. The field white for the sickle had been gathered by a grimmer reaping. During the years of Jason's absence, malaria, consumption and venereal disease had brutally savaged the tribes. Lodges were emptied. Whole villages were depopulated, the inhabitants dead or dispersed. The survivors had little fear of hell — they were experiencing it. They had even less interest in a salvation they must die to enjoy. They wanted no part of Christianity. The old ways were best. Gambling, which was their consuming passion, was a better anodyne than prayer. White Medicine worked no better cures than Red. The Great Reinforcement was redundant before it arrived.

The realization that this was so caused profound and widespread shock among the new recruits. They were, almost all of them, ordinary people who had allowed themselves to get steamed up with a religiosity which kept its heat well enough in civilized surroundings but cooled quickly when exposed to a savage counterculture. They had given up homes and friends and creature comforts, and each had engaged to spend ten years in mission service, and all had exposed themselves to a dangerous sea voyage. They had done those things that they might raise the banner of the Lord in the wilderness and convert the heathen for the greater glory of Jesus Christ and Him Crucified. Now they discovered there were no candidates for conversion.

In any consideration of the future development of the mission, this disillusionment is a central fact. The missionaries were much criticized in their own time, and have been much criticized since, for abandoning the evangelical cause and turning instead to secular activities. But at its beginning this shift of emphasis was simply an exchanging of the impossible for a viable alternative. Some of them eventually went a good deal further, straying into commercialism and even into chicanery, and that is to be regretted. But the remainder were merely struggling to salvage a decent existence out of the ruins of their exalted expectations.

There were those who refused to make this compromise. The Reverend W. W. Kone and wife were sent to Clatsop to aid the Reverend Mr. Frost. He found Frost and his family sharing an unroofed cabin with James Birnie — The Bay's clerk at Fort George — Mrs. Birnie, and an astonishing number of little Birnies. With the help of a pair of old Wyeth hands who were homesteading in the area a black seaman named Wallace who had deserted Couch's ship to adventure in a new land, and the inevitable helpful Indians, Frost and Kone managed to put together a station of sorts and begin preaching. But before the winter was out the Reverend Kone, discouraged by the thinness of religious prospects and dismayed by his wife's declining health, announced his intention of resigning as soon as he could book passage to the States.

At Nisqually, the Reverend Doctor John Richmond was also loud in his complaints. Richmond was an Illinois physician and minister who had heard Jason preach during Lee's tour across that state in 1838 and had come down with the notion that he, Richmond, was of the stuff missionaries are made. Now he blamed Jason for having led him into error. There were even those who could see no good in the land itself. Hamilton Campbell, another Illinoisan, wrote home shortly after his arrival that the Willamette Valley (a place of incalculable fertility) was poor farm country. But Ham was a man of suspect judgment.

Despite undercurrents of dissension the business of the mission proceeded, though George Abernethy — steward, accountant and storekeeper — was frequently confounded by Jason's unbusinesslike behavior. In the fall of the year Alvan Waller was sent to Willamette Falls to set up what would, as it shortly turned out, be more mercantile establishment than mission station. In one respect, however, the Reverend Waller was more persevering than his ministerial brethren. The site of his station was just east of the falls, where the river is dominated by stony heights below which the soil is not overly fruitful. A mile or two to the north, at the junction of the Clackamas and the Willamette, is a small section of bottom land of marvelous richness. It was then the domain of the Clackamas, a minor tribe much reduced by the epidemics which were sweeping the Indians from the country. Before long Waller adopted the Clackamas as his Indians. He visited them on the occasional Sunday and preached to them through an interpreter who understood Brother Alvan's English somewhat better than he understood Wesleyan theology. Waller also introduced his new charges to the beginnings of agriculture. He selected a choice plot, had it fenced and announced that he would plant it come spring and share the harvest with the Clackamas.

Elsewhere, however, it was for the Methodists a winter of minor discontents. The incessant rains depressed them. The damp invaded their bones. They quibbled peevishly among themselves. Certain lay brothers were increasingly restive because they were allowed no voice in mission management. And finally there was general dissatisfaction that despite three petitions to Congress the federal government had taken no steps to annex the Oregon country or to extend to it the protection of American laws.

This last issue was particularly irksome because there was a confusion of legal and quasi-legal authorities. In a technical sense, Oregon was outside the law. But the Hudson's Bay Company was empowered to act as an extension of the British North American judicial system and certain chief factors were granted magisterial powers. James Douglas was justice of the peace at Fort Vancouver, though his author-

ity extended only over British subjects. Father Blanchet, whose judgments were touched by benignity, exercised moral and apostolic
jurisdiction over his French Prairie parishioners. And as early as 1838,
for no assignable reason, the members of the mission and certain
American settlers had elected David Leslie justice of the peace.

The missionaries had no particular quarrel with Douglas, nor with
Blanchet so long as he confined himself to adjudicating differences
arising between members of his flock. But when a French Canadian
was found in possession of property belonging to an American, Lee
demanded the man be tried by the civil authorities (that is, Leslie),
though Blanchet had already arranged return of the goods and sen-
tenced the poor culprit (whose Indian wife had found the stuff floating
in the Willamette and claimed it by right of salvage) to a stiff penance.
The result was an acrimonious exchange between priest and pastor
and a firming of Methodist resolve that a code of laws must be adopted
and a government established to enforce it. All that they waited upon
was an urgent excuse for acting.

Conveniently, early in February, 1841, Ewing Young died.

He was not a believer, though in his last days he was quite mad, and
there were those who took this to be a sign of awakening faith. In all
events he was by far the wealthiest independent settler in the country,
and the Methodists buried him with due care and reverence — sometime prior to February 12, because on that date the official appraisers
were already at work on the estate — and after he was safely planted
they retired to Mission House to confer among themselves as to what
must be done. There were no heirs apparent, or none whom they were
prepared to recognize. (Young had lived with a woman, but she was
probably Indian. And there was a mysterious José Rownaldo Young
who brought suit against the estate, and afterward disappeared
abruptly from history.) Clearly some kind of apparatus must be erected
if the late lamented was not to be deprived of his right, bestowed by
God and confirmed by the laws of the United States, to have his worldly
goods divided and distributed in accordance with the dictates of law
and equity.

No minutes of that first meeting survive, but that it was a purely
Methodist affair is confirmed by a note in the Oregon Archives. David
Leslie was apparently at this time selected administrator of Young's
estate, and a committee of arrangements was appointed to draw up
plans for a public meeting to be held on February 18.

On February 17 a second planning session was held at Mission House. Like the first, it was a semiprivate affair. Lee was chairman, standing in for David Leslie, whose wife had died just two days earlier. Gustavus Hines was secretary. The first order of business was the election of George LeBreton as an additional member of the committee of arrangements.

He was, of course, the same LeBreton who had come to Oregon with Couch. He does not figure largely in histories of early Oregon because until the moment of his unfortunate death he had the useful quality of unobtrusiveness. From this point we may regard him as resident manipulator. The evidence that he exerted powerful backstage influence during the two years of maneuvering which preceded organization of a provisional government is largely circumstantial but wholly persuasive. The orchestration of events is marked by a professionalism certainly not possessed by Lee or any other member of the American community.

Once George had been suitably elevated the meeting moved rapidly along. It was resolved that a committee be selected at the public meeting next day to draft a constitution and code of laws, and that the protection of those laws be extended, upon application, to those settlers north of the Columbia who were not connected with The Bay. The committee of arrangements was instructed to propose the making of certain offices and nominate a slate of suitable candidates. Nothing was left to chance. When, the day following, very nearly all of the male residents of the valley met at Mission House, the Methodist machine was oiled, organized and instructed.

Things did not go, however, precisely as planned. Father Blanchet showed up to look after the interests of his constituency, and he proved a tenacious and resourceful adversary. David Leslie, his three days' private mourning for his late wife apparently at an end, was elected chairman. Hines and Blubbermouth Smith were made secretaries. But when the Methodists' carefully prepared package was presented, Blanchet was dumfounded to learn it proposed the election of no fewer than seventeen officials, from governor right down to two overseers of the poor, and that he himself was nominated chairman of the committee to write a constitution. He immediately rose to protest the proceedings as illegal on the ground that the committee of arrangements represented only a minority of the valley residents, which was certainly the case.

The Methodists had the organization, but Blanchet had the votes, and a compromise was arranged. Dr. Ira Babcock, who had moved down from Wascopum after White's precipitous departure, was elected supreme judge with probate powers, and LeBreton became clerk and recorder. A Bay retiree, Englishman William Johnson, was made high sheriff and given three constables to assist him in keeping the peace, two of them French Canadians. Blanchet, though he did nothing to conceal his lack of enthusiasm, accepted chairmanship of the constitutional committee, whose report he managed to put forward until the following June.

The priest was plainly shaken by these developments (a letter he wrote Demers is almost panicky), but he managed to keep his peace which must have been difficult. A developing squabble with the Reverend Alvan Waller did nothing to improve his opinion of Americans generally or Methodists in particular. Like Waller, Blanchet carried his mission to the Clackamas. When Waller objected that these were his Indians, Blanchet retorted that it was both his right and duty to carry the True Faith to every heathen he could reach, not excluding those Brother Alvan regarded as his special charges.

The contest began in February and continued for some months. On neither side was it conducted with dignity or Christian charity. Father Blanchet was disagreeably supercilious. Waller was insufferably self-righteous. Both resorted to threats, blandishments and bribes. But Waller was at a disadvantage, as were all Protestant missionaries confronted by Catholic opposition in Indian country. His sermons, uninspiring in the original and interminably dull in translation, were far less appealing to the Indian mind than the drama of Catholic liturgy. And Waller himself was guilty of two serious tactical blunders. In April Blanchet gave one of his adherents a flag, bearing a white cross on one side and on the other the letters *M. C.* (for Mission Catholique), with instructions it be raised in the village each Sunday. Waller, on his next pastoral visit, ordered it cast down, an act resented by the Clackamas and disapproved even by some of Brother Alvan's Methodist associates. And when he came to harvest his garden plot, Waller refused to share the proceeds, keeping everything for himself.

All of this acted to confirm Blanchet's conviction that Protestants were beyond trust. When June arrived he reported to the adjourned meeting at Mission House that his constitutional committee had never once been called into session, and tendered his resignation as its chair-

man. Dr. Bailey was elected to replace him, with instructions to call a
meeting no later than the first Monday in August. He was also instructed to consult with Dr. McLoughlin and the commander of the
United States Exploring Expedition, Lieutenant Charles Wilkes, as to
the propriety of forming a government to regulate the affairs of the
community.

❦ II ❧

The United States Exploring Expedition was the most ambitious scientific venture the federal government had to that time undertaken. It
was equipped with every manner of modern gadgetry and accompanied by artists, surveyors and scientists of every discipline and at
least one of several: Titian Peal, the most versatile of a family of ge-
niuses, who was painter, naturalist and paleontologist, and had gone
with Stephen Long up the Missouri a generation earlier.

The expedition sailed in August, 1838, and before reaching the
Northwest Coast had surveyed both coasts of South America, explored
a part of Antarctica and visited the Sandwich Islands. In May, 1841,
the explorers reached Puget Sound, at which point Wilkes added espionage to his other duties.

Slacum's report, and the increasingly intemperate petitions sent to
Congress urging a government presence in Oregon, had generated
indignation among expansionists and caused President Van Buren to
forward instructions that the lieutenant determine the precise state of
affairs in the Oregon country. From the purely political standpoint,
Charles Wilkes was not an ideal choice. He was an officer and a gentleman. He was a scientist in his own right, having studied oceanography
under the great Ferdinand Hassler, and as a child he had enjoyed the
advantages of moderate wealth. His intentions were correct but his
prejudices patrician, and his judgments, from the Methodist view, were
too evenly balanced.

Wilkes sent a party overland from Puget Sound to the A. B. C.
missions, whose members entered no complaints against Hudson's Bay
Company treatment. A supply ship, the *Peacock,* dispatched to the Columbia, foundered entering the river. No lives were lost but her sinking

was an embarrassment. The lieutenant came down in his flagship, the
Vincennes, to sort things out, and his mood could not have been at its
best when he met his first missionaries, the Reverend and Mrs. J. H.
Frost of Clatsop Plains. Frost he put down as a shoemaker gone to
preaching, with a reputation for being idle and tightfisted, and though
Mrs. Frost was an active, smart little body neither of them had, in
Wilkes's opinion, much desire to convert Indians. Snobbery, but not
inaccurate. At Fort Vancouver Wilkes found the hospitality baronial.
Dr. McLoughlin was at his patriarchal best. James Douglas was full of
suavities. Even Sir George Simpson turned up, being then on the first
leg of a journey around the world. They entertained him handsomely,
were solicitous of the comfort of his men and sold him supplies at 80
percent above London cost, which is to say, at wholesale. His one complaint about management at the fort was that wives were not allowed
to eat with their husbands, though he thought them entirely worthy to
do so.

The lieutenant found a number of missionaries lounging about the
place. Asa B. Smith and wife were departing the A. B. C. mission at
Kamiah after less than three years of service. The Reverend Harvey
Clark and the Reverend John Smith Griffin, also with their wives, had
come out as self-supporting Congregationalists but found the effort
onerous and were now nonpaying guests of The Bay. (Wilkes thought
Griffin a stupid man and a bad preacher, which was a charitable assessment.) Both were discouraged, considered returning to the States and
asked the lieutenant's advice. He suggested that they homestead on the
Twality Plains, and eventually they did.

But the Methodist operation disappointed him. He thought Jason
Lee an ordinary-looking man and one unfit for his situation. At Mission House he was shocked to see expensive farm machinery left out to
rust and acres of unharvested fat wheat rotting in the fields. At the
Indian manual-training school at Mission Mills he was shown no more
than a handful of half-naked louts lounging in convenient shade.

The constitutional committee waited on him and he recognized them
immediately for what they were: governors, legislators, judges and
placemen in embryo. Wilkes advised against the setting up of a provisional government — 116 Canadian settlers had only just arrived from
Red River and were to be given farms on the Cowlitz or herds on the
Nisqually Plains — and pointed out that with Ewing Young's estate well
in hand, there was no real need for organization.

It was not the answer the missionaries expected and they went away disappointed and resentful, but he was invited to dine, as he said, *à la* Methodist. They fed him well — salmon, pork, potted cheese, hot cakes and tea — but they smelled. And they charged for everything, while John Turner, who had escaped two massacres, made a gift of a slaughtered beef.

On his way back to Fort Vancouver Wilkes heard Alvan Waller's complaints that The Bay's monopoly was ruining his trade. He listened without sympathy because he thought that business was no part of the mission's proper endeavor and that Waller was the dirtiest man he had ever seen, dirtier than any Indian. The observation summed up his opinion of the Methodists. They were low, vulgar and unclean. He excepted their women from this general condemnation, but he could not understand why even they could put up with their husbands.

When the lieutenant returned to Fort Vancouver he discovered he was indebted to John McLoughlin for a great service. The loss of the supply ship was a serious matter, for after picking up an overland exploring party at San Francisco, the squadron was to sail for the South Pacific. But in May the American coaster *Thomas Perkins* — Varney commanding — entered the Columbia to raise an opposition. McLoughlin immediately arranged to exchange Varney's goods for salt salmon already in stock, then helped transact sale of the *Perkins* to Wilkes, who renamed her the *Oregon*. When Charles Wilkes sailed south in September he had reached the conclusion that the Honourable Company was conducted as benevolently as good business practice would allow, and that the Methodist mission was a sadly overdone and undermanaged concern.

In this last judgment he was not alone. The Reverend Joseph Williams was no silver-spooned New Yorker. He was born in Pennsylvania in 1788, converted to Methodism in 1801, and admitted as a circuit teacher in 1803. Williams was strong on Biblical injunction. On two wives he begat sixteen children. But he had energies still untapped. At sixty-three, though he suffered painfully from the rheumatics, he set off from Indiana for Oregon. At St. Louis he learned that the party he had intended to join had broken up but that there was another forming at Independence, clean the other side of Missouri. Williams determined to catch up with it and did, in Pawnee country, having traveled on some days forty miles by his own reckoning and with no other protection but a little powder and ball, and a gun which proved worthless. Father Pierre de Smet, who was a member of the company, invited him to dinner, and the next day sent venison to his tent. A woman urged the old man to sing and pray, which he did.

The emigration of 1841 has been largely ignored. It was a scrambled affair. At one time during the previous winter some five hundred citizens had formed the Western Emigration Society, each of them pledging to meet on the Kansas River the following May. But wide publication of Tom Farnham's discouraging letters about Oregon and California caused most of the faithful to fall away. There was no mass rendezvous in May, only a thin gathering of hard-core enthusiasts, some of them for California and some for Oregon, held together by the energy of John Bidwell, one of the emigration society's principal organizers.

None of them knew what to do. They had come to the end of civilization but there was nobody among them who could tell them how to step off into mystery. They might have broken up and gone home had not Father de Smet come along at precisely the proper moment. The father had spent the previous season among the Flatheads, paid a quick visit to St. Louis to collect help and was now returning to form permanent missions. And he had taken the wise precaution of hiring Tom Fitzpatrick to pilot him.

It was a routine passage. Marked by the usual Indian alarums and the standard violent weather, with a small twister thrown in. There were two marriages — Reverend Williams and Father de Smet split the honors between them — and there was the shock of sudden death: a young man accidentally shot himself and died, after two hours of agony, calling out for his mother and his old Kentucky home.

Along the way Williams and de Smet engaged in a continuing dialogue, conducted on Williams's part with imperturbable good humor, and on de Smet's with alternating amusement and irritation. Williams was the ultimate ecumenist, more than a century before ecumenism would become fashionable. His favorite text was Ephesians 4:5, "One Lord, one faith, one baptism." At a time when bigotry was an accepted tenet of every Christian persuasion, he was almost completely devoid of it. It was his fundamental belief that the love of God could only be achieved through understanding and universal brotherhood. De Smet, though he was admirably tolerant himself, thought Williams carried toleration past absurdity. It was a curious and revealing encounter, which could come to nothing. Both were remarkable men, and they were traveling along converging lines of our cultural heritage, but those lines would be a long time intersecting.

A few miles above Soda Springs the party split. Those going to California (thirty-two men, one woman and a child) followed south along Bear River. The emigrants for Oregon pressed on to Fort Hall. And the priests marched north to do battle with the Devil, the Congregationalists and the Presbyterians, in approximately that order.

By now it was mid-August. Frank Ermatinger guided Williams and the new Oregon settlers as far as Waiilatpu. There were Indians everywhere, for the salmon were running in the Snake, and at the mission Brother Williams admired Whitman's well-behaved congregation. Further along, at Wascopum, he was kindly received and concluded that Daniel Lee and Henry Perkins were decent men who were making some progress. They were almost the last Methodist missionaries he would approve. Those he found in the Willamette Valley he wrote down as cold, starchy and overly influenced by the world and speculation. At Chemeketa the Indian school was barely operating. When he openly disapproved, his credentials were declared unsatisfactory and he was denied the right to preach. Jason visited the old gentleman one evening with the warning that Williams was a stranger in those parts and had best restrict his remarks to subjects of which he had certain knowledge. Williams felt he had certain knowledge that these people were imperfect Christians.

He was witness, or near witness, to a curious tragedy. Asahel Munger and his wife had come west in 1839 as lay assistants to the "self-supporting" Reverend John Smith Griffin. Griffin treated the Mungers shamefully and even tried to abandon them at Fort Hall. Finding Munger stranded at Fort Walla Walla, Marcus Whitman engaged him as carpenter and cabinetmaker at Waiilatpu. The man was an excellent worker but by spring, 1841, it became obvious he was suffering from religious mania. Whitman tried to send him, with his wife and infant child, to the rendezvous, in the hope he could be taken to the States for treatment. But there was no rendezvous and the Mungers went instead to the Willamette, where the Methodists hired Asahel to be smithy. By December he was persuaded that should he die the Lord would raise him to life in three days, and to convince skeptics he determined to nail himself over his own hearth. He managed to pin one hand to the wall before pain and heat so overcame him he fell in among the coals, which cured him rapidly of his error but burned him so agonizingly he died shortly after. How careful, wrote Brother Williams, one must be to escape the delusions of Satan.

That winter the Devil tested Williams's own steadfastness. He tried to build a small house on the Twality Plains, but found it would not do. Thereafter he was forced to live around in the mission settlement. There were hard and dry times, but despite the chill of his reception he was shocked by the infinitely more pitiful condition of the Indians. He saw a band of them come upon a dead horse and cut it up with joyful looks and glad hearts though it was so stinking a white man could not stand downwind of it and the pigs and dogs had given off worrying the putrid flesh.

Williams set out for home in March, 1842, forced to go by way of Taos so that he did not reach Indiana until the following winter. The next year he published a little book of his travels. He thought himself then to be very near death and transfiguration but he lived on for almost two decades — a tough, vigorous, honest old man simple enough to believe that every man is every other man's brother.

❧ III ❧

Governor George Simpson became Sir George Simpson in 1841, courtesy of his gracious Queen and a little lobbying by the Honourable Company. That same year he embarked on an overland journey around the world which would see him cross both the North American continent and the Eurasian land mass from east to west. But he had business to conduct along the way, most particularly in the Columbia District, which he had not seen since 1829 and where he felt things were going unsatisfactorily.

He arrived at Fort Vancouver in late August and shortly after set out on an inspection of the company's North Pacific posts and a courtesy visit to the Russians at Sitka. He spent only a few hours at Fort Stikine, but he made one fateful decision. The fort's chief officer was John McLoughlin, Jr., and in this brief, initial inspection Simpson found affairs in such good order he dispatched Roderick Finlayson, young

McLoughlin's second-in-command, to Fort Simpson to stand in for an ailing clerk, promising to send a replacement from Fort Vancouver. Dr. McLoughlin was much upset when he heard of these arrangements, arguing that the company servants at Stikine were a gallows crew in a trade and country which attracted the violent and unprincipled. Simpson waved off these fatherly concerns. The governor had complaints of his own to pursue.

Complaints especially about the Americans, and most particularly the Methodists. He had visited Willamette Settlement and found it prosperous and promising and the missionaries busily engaged in almost every enterprise but that of proselytizing Indians. He blamed McLoughlin. If the first missionaries had been allowed to starve, as they assuredly would without the help they received from Fort Vancouver, they would not have multiplied like so many cursed rabbits. Now they had become a competition.

For more than a decade McLoughlin and Simpson had dealt at arm's length, depending upon correspondence that kept them months apart. Under these circumstances they had been able to maintain the amenities. But since 1829 the doctor had grown more independent, and the governor more imperious. A collision was unavoidable, but there is considerable evidence that Simpson, whose character did not measure up to his capacity for business, set out to bait McLoughlin by way of bringing the doctor to curb. And to do so he was prepared to dismantle the commercial fief McLoughlin had so painstakingly assembled.

In November, when Simpson sailed to inspect the company holdings in California and the Sandwich Islands, the doctor accompanied him. A year earlier, in obedience to instructions sent him, McLoughlin had opened a hide and tallow business at San Francisco and sent his own son-in-law, William Glen Rae, to manage the establishment. Rae had been promised regular transport to and communication with Fort Vancouver. Neither was ever given him, and he seems to have been a dependent personality. Simpson found little in the San Francisco operation to please him and by the time he and McLoughlin reached Honolulu he was stuffed with new directives. Rae's venture was a failure. It must be liquidated immediately, at fifty cents on the dollar if need be. Nor was this all. Sir George ordered the programmed closing out of most of the North Pacific posts, the reduction of Fort Vancouver to a secondary base, the establishment of the district's central supply

district at the southern end of Vancouver Island and future depen-
dence upon the marine arm, in particular the *Beaver,* to command
coastal trade. The doctor was stunned. Everything he had worked so
hard to achieve was to be swept away.

When they parted company their relationship had reached a precarious point. McLoughlin, very near rebellion, returned to Fort Vancouver. Simpson sailed directly from Honolulu to Sitka with a bill of goods
he had sold the Russians, then went on to supply the company forts
south of Alaska. At Fort Stikine he found that, four days before his
arrival, John McLoughlin, Jr., had been murdered by his own servants.

Beyond doubt, Sir George panicked. He had lived too long believing
in his own infallibility. His one way to justify his poor judgment in
removing Finlayson and leaving young McLoughlin to deal unaided
with a band of cutthroats was to justify the murder, and the murderers
were eager to assist him. He believed them, or affected to believe them,
when they swore the young man had been drunk for months, mouthed
threats, careened about the fort waving pistols. He did not forget that
the doctor's son had raised problems earlier, before he was an employee of The Bay, spending money unwisely and getting himself involved with a crackpot adventurer named James Dickson, who had
styled himself Montezuma II and proposed to raise an Indian empire
in northern Mexico and Alta California with the aid of métis recruited
at Red River. So the governor wrote McLoughlin announcing John
Jr.'s death in a drunken fracas, accusing the deceased of brutality,
disorderly conduct and bad business practices, and giving it as his
judgment that the murder was justified.

It was an odious performance, even for a man so small-souled as
George Simpson. McLoughlin was beside himself with grief and outrage. He conducted his own investigation and was able to show conclu-
sively that the charges against his son were false, and that the killing
was a wanton act by men properly denied access to the women of the
Indian villages near the fort. The matter became an obsession with
him, and he pursued it interminably, though without result. Simpson
was wrong — his superiors admitted it privately — but he must be sustained. Yet his inflexibility was a gross blunder. The great American
migration, so long expected, had seen its last rehearsal. Just when John
McLoughlin's loyalty to the Honourable Company was compromised
by deep and unforgiving resentment.

❧ IV ❧

Jason Lee once told John McLoughlin that before he brought out the Great Reinforcement, all the missionaries worked; and that after the Reinforcement, none of them worked. It was a complaint, but it was also an admission of personal failure. Beginning in 1841 Jason struggled manfully to prevent the collapse of his enterprise, but time and circumstance opposed him and his own inadequacies betrayed him. His people were slipped from his control. He could neither lead nor command them.

By fall, 1841, Alvan Waller had given up on his Clackamas Indians and resigned them to Father Blanchet. (To whom they gave more trouble than satisfaction; for they preferred gambling to instruction and had a disconcerting habit of dying before completing their catechumenate.) Thereafter Waller spent his time making improvements to the mission holdings at Willamette Falls, causing John McLoughlin, who claimed the east bank of the river at and below the falls for himself and the Hudson's Bay Company, to make inquiries of Lee as to Brother Waller's intentions. Lee replied with assurances that neither the mission nor Alvan Waller had any intention of jumping McLoughlin's claim.

It was the first exchange in a controversy whose merits have been argued by historians for well over a century, and which will be considered later in these pages. But McLoughlin's concerns were hardly quieted by subsequent events. George Abernethy, the accountant who came out on the *Lausanne* as mission steward, persuaded Jason that the various mission stations could not be adequately supplied from the middle Willamette, arguing that the falls of the Willamette were more centrally located — which they undoubtedly were — and before the year was out the mission goods were moved into a warehouse there. Abernethy immediately set up a store in connection, dealing, though circumspectly at first, with the American settlers and in competition with Fort Vancouver. And not long after, the Island Milling Company was formed, heavily dominated by Methodist missionaries though some shares were offered to mission-connected settlers, to build mills on what was to be known as Abernethy's Island. This was near the eastern shore of the falls, where McLoughlin had some years since

blasted out a millrace to perfect his claim. Alvan Waller's station had
ceased to be a missionary establishment and become the nucleus of a
business center.

Certainly this development did not disturb Jason overmuch. But
deaths and disaffections did. The Kones departed in late November of
this same year. The Reverend Dr. Richmond was promising to do the
same at any early date. Munger immolated himself. And in March,
1842, three weeks after giving birth to a girl child, Lucy Thompson
Lee died — "fallen victim," in the late Arthur Throckmorton's imper-
ishable phrase, "to the ardors of frontier life."[1]

Jason had little time to grieve, for shortly he found himself presiding
over shrill disorder. The mission's financial affairs were in a hopeless
muddle despite the canny Abernethy's best efforts. The children of the
Indian manual-labor school were rebellious and riddled by civilized
diseases. (It must have been about this time that Jason harkened back
to Wilbur Fisk's Spartan discipline. The dying were allowed to die. The
dissenters were dealt with abruptly.) The Reverend Dr. Richmond,
after a stormy exchange in which he announced himself Jason's sworn
enemy, took passage for the States. W. H. Willson moved to Willamette
Falls, and shortly resigned from the mission. Susan Downing Shepard
had sometime since married Josiah Whitcomb, the seaman turned
farm supervisor. But like the lamented Cyrus, Whitcomb was tubercular, and now Susan was carrying him home to die. Dr. Bailey and his
Margaret went off to visit in the East. David Leslie was given leave to
take his two middle daughters to the Sandwich Islands to arrange for
their schooling, leaving the two youngest behind with their married
sister, fifteen-year-old Satira, lately wed to Cornelius Rogers. And at
the end of September the ubiquitous Elijah White returned, somewhat
ahead of an immigrant party of more than one hundred and boasting
the title of Indian subagent to all lands west of the Rockies and north
of California.

White had done his best to keep his promise to make trouble for his
late associates. He had half-convinced the mission board that Lee was
incompetent, and he had managed to persuade the New England Conference, Jason's own, to pass a resolution condemning White's expulsion as illegal. But he was forced to admit to the board that he had
abandoned his post. He was censured for desertion, and certain expenses of transporting his family from Oregon were disallowed. Elijah's mania for outrage overtook him. He demanded exoneration,

remuneration and even reimbursement for his wife's recent miscarriage, under threat of exposing alleged sharp fund-raising practices of the church. Being denied his demands, he went about representing himself as a certified money-raiser for the Oregon mission, and pocketed the proceeds.

White was, in fact, poor to the point of bankruptcy. But Fortune opportunely elevated him. In January, 1842, he was picked, as Jason had been picked by the Cushings, as a useful man to represent certain commercial interests in Oregon. In this case his sponsors were Alfred Benson & Bro., of New York. Elijah was ushered to Washington and interviewed by John C. Spencer, secretary of war, who appointed him Indian subagent at a salary of $750 per annum. When White thought this amount insufficient to maintain his dignity (or pay off his creditors), Spencer promised that a bill increasing the salary would be put through Congress. No such bill was ever introduced.

Elijah later claimed credit for the emigration of 1842 but it gathered in advance of him. It gathered because all the variables had slipped into conjunction, because the American people, or that segment of the American people which exercised its energies in pushing the line of the frontier west across the continent, had decided the time had come to push that line over the mountains to the Pacific. The senators from Missouri were acutely aware of the gathering momentum. Lewis Linn already had a bill pending before the Senate providing for the raising of a regiment to guard the emigrant trail, the extension of federal laws to afford protection to all Americans residing beyond the mountains from 54°40' north down to the Mexican border, and the allotment of 640 acres to every male white inhabitant over the age of eighteen who would undertake to cultivate his grant for a term of five years. And Lieutenant John C. Fremont, who was Tom Benton's son-in-law, was preparing to have his first look at the new Eden. (Kit Carson was his guide, but that year Fremont would march behind the movers.)

For Jason, White's triumphant return brought nightmare specters of renewed harassment, and indeed Elijah could not wait to spread the word that the New England Conference had voted a charge of irregular proceedings against Lee. Despite this provocation, Jason handled his adversary gently. A meeting was called, White was politely requested to display his credentials and a resolution was passed thanking the United States for the favor of his appointment. Noncommittal, and intended to be. But Elijah characteristically overplayed his hand. Hearing talk of new plans for the formation of a provisional government, he first opposed them implacably, insisting that by the terms of his commission all governing power was vested in himself. This was patent nonsense and he shortly shifted his position. The settlers might have their government — so long as he was governor.

In his dealings with the colonists White's everlasting officiousness was merely irksome, but when he acted in his official capacity the effects were pernicious. He visited the Nez Percé, the Walla Wallas and the Cayuse during the fall of his arrival, rumors having come down from the American Board stations that these tribes were meditating mischief. He took Tom McKay along, knowing McKay's presence would give pause to the most troublesome. But he did not consult with McKay, and his failure to do so led him into dangerous error. He persuaded the Nez Percé to accept a criminal code of his own devising, complete with a schedule of fines. whippings and hangings to punish various breaches of the peace. And he replaced the existing tribal council with a head chief and twelve subchiefs. For head chief he chose one Ellis, who was too young to have the full respect of the tribal elders and was mistrusted by the American Board missionaries, but who had attended school at Red River Colony and could speak some English.

White was immensely proud of his accomplishments but he had, in fact, sowed the seeds of calamity. His penal code was in violent contravention of Indian custom. He had unwisely injected himself into Indian politics and tried to restructure Indian society. And he had written into the Nez Percé code that should a white man be guilty of breaking its statutes, he was to be reported to the subagent, who would himself arrange condign punishment.

He met also with the Cayuse and the Walla Wallas but their mood was surly. They lived along what by now had become the Oregon Trail and they had watched increasing numbers of Americans crossing into the country. They had been told it was American practice to drive out the resident Indians and appropriate their lands, and the younger and more excitable were spoiling for a fight. A deputation of them asked McKay privately what The Bay would do should they make war on the settlements and McKay told them The Bay would stand with the colonists. It was an answer which did not improve their dispositions, though it temporarily cooled their enthusiasm for a violent solution. But they did not believe White's assurances that the immigrants were no threat to their lands or their security, and they refused to accept the laws he pressed upon them.

In the end Elijah had done little that was good and a great deal that was iniquitous. His promise to secure the punishment of whites who violated Indian rights or persons was injudicious in the extreme, since it was a promise beyond his keeping. It would shortly lay him open to the imputation of bad faith, and that imputation would eventually be extended to the entire American community of Oregon.

V

When Dr. White returned from his peace mission he settled at the falls of the Willamette and entered practice in partnership with W. H. Willson, whom Elijah had given a quick course in the healing arts during his earlier sojourn in Oregon, and who henceforth styled himself, with seasoned impudence, Dr. Willson.

Most of the immigrants who came that year had set forth poor, and arrived impoverished. McLoughlin kept them alive with generous extensions of credit, selling them provisions, tools and seed for the next spring's planting and taking back unsecured notes. He employed one of them, J. M. Hudspeth, to survey his Willamette Falls claim, which he christened Oregon City, and he authorized a transplanted Ohio attorney and professional promoter, Lansford W. Hastings, to deed a town lot to every responsible person who applied for one. (The lots were given free, but Hastings charged each applicant a $5 legal fee.) The place grew rapidly. Where there had been three buildings, there were now thirty. John Couch returned to manage Cushing's store. Very shortly Francis Pettygrove set up shop for the Bensons. And the Methodists, operating as the Island Milling Company, had jumped McLoughlin's claim to Abernethy Island and were busily erecting sawmills and gristmills. The doctor made no attempt to dislodge the interlopers. But he commenced construction of a sawmill on the river bank, and let it be known he would build a gristmill as well.

In the spring word came from east of the Cascades that the middle and upper tribes were contemplating attack on the immigrant trains expected the following fall. White hurried off to convene a new council to sort things out. Everywhere he found the Indians much exercised, and at Waiilatpu the younger Cayuse chiefs were calling for immediate assault on the Willamette settlements, though the old men counseled caution. But a sizable number of Nez Percé arrived at the council and their mood was peaceful. They wanted no part of an adventure which might bring them into collision with The Bay. Ellis promised to persuade the Cayuse and Walla Wallas to accept Elijah's Indian code, and did so. (He also announced he expected a salary as head chief, and by his own reckoning had already earned enough to make him well-to-do.) All understandings were ratified by a grand feast and the doctor took his leave, convinced he had averted war. The danger was probably never as great as he imagined. But the trouble blew up at a time when the shifty machinations of the Reverend Alvan Waller threatened to divide the whites in the country against themselves.

The controversy had its own history. During the winter of 1828–29, years before Waller assumed ministerial vestments, McLoughlin and Governor Simpson visited the falls of the Willamette and agreed that it was an important industrial site — Simpson reported to London that enough saws could be installed there to load the British Navy — and the doctor was ordered to secure title for the Honourable Company. Seeing no urgency, he went about doing so in a desultory way. He put up small buildings (the Indians burned them), he blasted his millrace on Abernethy Island, and he cultivated part of the land lying along the east bank, planting it with potatoes. But in 1838 the increasing restlessness and enterprise of his American neighbors, and particularly Jason Lee's departure to secure a large Methodist reinforcement, roused the doctor's apprehensions. He ordered a warehouse erected at the falls to serve as a subsidiary summer post, trading largely for Indian salmon, and had timbers hauled to the island for the publicly stated purpose of building a sawmill.

That same spring McLoughlin left on his sabbatical and the venture was not pressed. In 1840 Jason Lee applied at Fort Vancouver for the loan of some of those timbers that the Reverend Waller might build a house against advancing winter. McLoughlin agreed, but in his letter of consent he informed Lee of his own prior claim, and he sent Dr. Tolmie, who was down from Nisqually, to point out the metes and bounds.

McLoughlin was being uncharacteristically devious. He was acting as trustee for The Bay. But throughout the extended broil which followed he maintained steadfastly that he was himself the true claimant. He did this because, as he later explained to his employers, the Americans were so ill-disposed against the company they would refuse to honor any claim it made to land south of the Columbia. It was wasted deceit. Waller saw no distinction between a hated British monopoly and a hireling of that monopoly who was not only a British subject but a Papist to boot. Neither, in the pastor's view, had any rights which a Protestant American need recognize.

It is probable Brother Alvan had designs on the falls site almost from the moment he settled there, but he made no overt move until October of 1842. Rumors reached Fort Vancouver that he was proclaiming himself sole proprietor of Oregon City. Jason Lee, when queried, denied it. So did Waller, though there was hard evidence to the contrary, insisting that he intended no contest but meant only to make clear his intent to file should McLoughlin's claim be withdrawn. But he wanted a deed to the lots he was occupying, and wanted the doctor to confirm the transfer of other lots Waller had already conveyed to third parties, and there was his labor and expense in clearing, on his own motion, a part of the town site. With some help from Lawyer Hastings, a settlement was worked out. Waller and those to whom he had conveyed lots were granted deeds. Waller himself received $25 for clearing the land; by the acceptance of which sum he tacitly acknowledged McLoughlin's ownership, a legal quiddity which meant nothing to Alvan, even if it was explained to him, which it probably was not. He had no intention of honoring the agreement or giving up his pretensions. He simply shifted the direction of his attack.

Robert Shortess was a Missourian, a member of the Peoria Party, and leader of the mutineers who deposed Tom Farnham. He was a man of some education, his humor was vinegary — he would one day lapse into misanthropy — and his principles rabidly nationalistic; but he did not write the petition to Congress which he circulated, and which bears his name. (Much later Shortess tried to father it on George Abernethy, but the copy in the Oregon Archives is in Alvan Waller's hand; David Duniway, former state archivist, believes Waller to be the author; and certainly it was a contrivance got up for Waller's benefit.) After a long introduction which repeats, at wearisome length, the alleged outrages visited upon innocent Americans by John McLoughlin and the infamous company he represents, the petition boils down to two major charges: that the doctor, by building mills in opposition to the Island Milling Company, is guilty of unfair competition, and that he has unlawfully usurped a land claim which is the Reverend Alvan Waller's by right of preemption.

Sixty-five persons, indulging their prejudices, lent their names to this egregious humbuggery. Daniel did not sign. Nor did Jason. Neither did either of them raise a word of protest. The only Methodist clergyman who expressed outrage was Henry Perkins, who threatened to resign from the mission if the petition was forwarded to Washington. It was forwarded and he did not resign, so it may be he was merely clutching at pretext. For he had grown mightily bored with Indians.

The petition is dated March 25, 1843. McLoughlin learned of it two weeks later, when Hastings alerted him. The doctor twice applied to Shortess for a copy but one was refused him, though he had learned enough from his attorney to have a fair idea of the contents and was both hurt and indignant. But when Hastings, already planning to remove to California (three years later he would achieve unenviable fame by persuading the Donner party to follow the trail which led it to macabre disaster), suggested the getting-up of a counterpetition, McLoughlin was uncertain. Grief for his murdered son and the running dispute with Sir George Simpson had thinned his spirit. He was still trying to decide when history caught up with him.

On May 2 a mass meeting was held at Champoeg — formerly Capement du Sable. The settlers voted to organize a government; and we have reached a moment gilded by pioneer legendry. Joe Meek, his rags and moccasins made dingier by a resplendent vest, hollering, "Who's for a divide?" and the issue settled by two apostate French Canadians who voted for organization while the remainder of The Bay retirees lined up solidly in opposition.[2] The truth, taken from the official minutes, is more prosaic. It was the resourceful LeBreton, stage manager of the affair, who moved a division. At least seven *Canadiens* voted for organization. The minutes say the motion was carried by a large majority. Doc Newell, who was present and truthful, put the count at fifty-five to fifty. There is general agreement that once the issue was decided most of the dissenters withdrew.

The late Bernard De Voto, describing the founding of the Bear Flag Republic just three years after events at Champoeg, says that it was conceived by a combination of legitimate immigrants and common adventurers, and its birth was by proclamation. And that there were those present between conception and proclamation who thought the process looked very much like a general drunk. The Oregonians, by contrast, were sober as beadles and efficient as ants. A. E. Wilson, Cushing employee, was elected judge, LeBreton became clerk and recorder, Joe Meek was chosen sheriff and Dr. Willson treasurer. Three magistrates were elected, and three constables, and a clutch of militia officers given rank though there were no troops to command. Most important, a committee of nine was delegated to write the new government's organic laws, and to deliver its recommendations on July 5, to which date the meeting was adjourned.

The legislative committee had been carefully selected to insure it acted with the necessary bias. Five of its members had signed the Shortess petition (Shortess himself was a committeeman), as had LeBreton, who became committee secretary. They met in two sessions between May 16 and June 28, and the document they produced was, in the main, respectable enough. It provided for a three-man executive committee in addition to the nine-man legislative committee. The franchise was extended to every white man and every free male descendent of a white man above age twenty-one. Expenses of the government were to be met by voluntary contribution, no provision being made for taxes. The rights of Indians were to be respected, their property not taken from them without their consent nor their lands invaded "except in just and lawful wars."[3] Euphemism stretched to the ultimate. The section on land claims came toward the end. No individual was allowed to claim more than 640 acres, exclusive of town lots. But,

> No person shall be entitled to hold such a claim upon City or Town lots, extensive water privileges, or other situations necessary for the transaction of Mercantile or Manufacturing operations and to the detriment of the community.[4]

And the provisional government is exposed as one more device to lever McLoughlin out of his Oregon City claim.

Jason Lee had taken no very active part in the move to organize. He even argued, though temperately, against it. The reasons for his lack of enthusiasm are obscure. He may have felt a minority government could become an inconvenient luxury should its control fall into other, and unsympathetic, hands. Or that the very existence of a governing body, however ineffective, might reduce pressures in Congress for the annexation of Oregon. But he was present at the July 5 meeting, and after listening to the reading of the land laws he spoke emphatically to

LeBreton and LeBreton dutifully moved an amendment to be tacked onto the paragraph aimed at McLoughlin:

> — provided that nothing in these laws shall be so construed, as to affect any claim of any Mission of a Religious character made previous to this time of an extent not more than six miles square.[5]

There was no one present who was not aware that this was a Methodist swindle of noble proportions — Blanchet and Demers had founded only two permanent stations, each upon a tract of modest size — but it was whooped through anyway. The Americans had their government — but it wasn't operable. Having no power to tax, it had no certain supply of funds to meet the expenses of running it. It was supported by less than half of the community over which it claimed jurisdiction. McLoughlin, for any number of obvious reasons, refused to recognize its authority. Most of the French Canadians stood apart from it. Tinkering would eventually put the new institution into working order, but for the moment it was just what its critics decried it as being: a purely Methodist concern.

❧ VI ❧

By the summer of 1843 it was plain even to Jason that his mission was collapsing of its own weight. Desertions were routine. The Frosts were preparing to depart. So was Daniel, a greater shock and an infinitely greater loss. Jason pleaded, but his nephew was unmoved. He had served out his term and his wife's health was precarious. David Leslie had returned from the Sandwich Islands in April — to discover that his married daughter, her husband and one younger sister had been swept over the falls in a runaway canoe. But Brother Leslie, even after he had given over his mourning, was not of much use around the mission. His attentions were elsewhere, for he was in panting pursuit of the fascinating Adelia Judson Turkington Olley, whose husband had drowned at the end of the preceding year.

Jason's own position was increasingly difficult. He could be sure that Brother Kone and Dr. Richmond, once in New York, would lay charges before the mission board just as Elijah had done. And he knew that there was much dissatisfaction within the mission family and that he was thought not only inept, but guilty of speculation and a preoccupation with worldly affairs.

Daniel and Frost and their families sailed from the Columbia in August. (They shortly coauthored a book remarkable in Oregon missionary literature for its moderation, good sense and lack of scurrility, chiefly because Daniel wrote two-thirds of it.) The month following Jason learned from letters received that the board disapproved of his governance. He must have expected something of the sort, but one item of complaint stunned him. He was accused of being delinquent in his accounts of disbursements to the amount of $100,000.

During October he composed a long letter of defense. He denied his mission had become secularized, though honesty forced him to add a qualification or two. He denied the accountings were irregular, and insisted that any delay in forwarding them was chargeable to George Abernathy, as mission steward. He regretted that he had already much exceeded the appropriations made for that year, but prophesied that the Methodist Church, as the fruit of missionary effort, would receive out of Oregon more than all that had been expended in the years of his management.

Jason began the letter at Wascopum, where he went on tour of inspection. Before he had completed it he was visited by Dr. Whitman, lately returned from the East. Whitman told him of hearing, while in the States, that Jason was to be removed. The news, and more particularly the manner of its transmission, put a considerable strain on the bonds of brotherly love, and the tone of the remainder of the letter is occasionally harsh. Jason complained, with justice, that instead of writing him directly of his imminent dismissal, the board had chosen to publish it in the ears of missionaries of other societies.

He was discouraged and disgruntled and now there were whispers that Gustavus Hines, who was his good right hand and loudest upholder, had written a letter to the board in which he deplored the shortcomings of Jason Lee. And what was worse, had read this letter to others of the disaffected. Treachery was getting close to the throne. Jason, who saw the dagger at his back, decided to sail for the States, and to take his little daughter and the Reverend and Mrs. Hines with him. And had he not permitted himself to become the servant of Alvan Waller's unhallowed schemes, he might have left the Oregon country with most of his honor intact.

About 850 persons crossed the mountains into Oregon that year. Most of them were Eden seekers, or the wives, children or numbed survivors of Eden seekers. One was a bird of passage. He styled himself John Ricord, attorney-at-law and councillor to the Supreme Court of the United States. Though he was only thirty-one he was already halfway through a picaresque career. The son of a prominent New Jersey family, he was admitted to practice in New York State, but it was his nature to wander. Before arriving in Oregon he had been confidential secretary to two presidents of Texas, and a refugee from the laws of that republic. He was on his way to becoming attorney general of the Kingdom of Hawaii, where he would distinguish himself by petty tyrannies and eccentric conduct.

To a conniver of Ricord's genius the McLoughlin-Waller controversy offered obvious opportunities. He had not been long in the Willamette Valley before he delivered himself, assumedly on his own motion, of a legal opinion: John McLoughlin, being a British subject, could not hold claim to any part of the Willamette Valley, since that was territory of the United States. Which was patently absurd. What was or was not territory of the United States was yet to be determined. But poor, harassed McLoughlin was enormously impressed, and tried to retain Ricord to get around Alvan Waller.

Ricord was willing to try, for a fee of £300. McLoughlin need only cede the Reverend Mr. Waller five more acres of Waller's selection, give up all claim to Abernethy Island and cede to Jason Lee, as agent for the Methodist mission, certain lots, the number and location of which were not specified.

The doctor observed dryly that this seemed an expensive way of business, but asked time to consider. In November he rejected the terms and asked whether Ricord continued to represent him. This, it turned out, Ricord could no longer do. He was about to leave for Oahu and asked passage on the next company vessel to that place.

Very shortly the lawyer turned up at Fort Vancouver in company with Gustavus and Mrs. Hines and Jason and his tiny daughter, Lucy Anna Maria, all of them en route to the Sandwich Islands. Dr. McLoughlin, still anxious to compromise, offered additional concessions and suggested that contested issues be submitted to arbitration, but both Lee and Ricord denied they were empowered to act for Waller. This was on December 11 and that same day the lawyer and the mission party took canoes downriver to board the Hudson's Bay vessel *Colum-*

bia. Contrary winds detained her and not until February 3, 1844, was she able to put out across the bar. Three weeks later a letter to McLoughlin was handed in at Fort Vancouver. It was dated December 8 and it was signed by Ricord, as attorney for A. F. Waller. It respectfully informed the doctor that his nationality and his position as an officer of the Hudson's Bay Company disqualified him as a claimant, that Waller was filing on the Oregon City claim with the United States Land Office, and that any conveyance of any part of that property by McLoughlin would be unlawful. At the same time Ricord's *Address to the Citizens of Oregon* was circulated throughout the Willamette Valley. In it McLoughlin is described as a representative of tyrannous wealth from whose rapacity no honest American's land is safe. All of which caused the doctor to grumble that the Methodists had come to Oregon to preach that thou shalt not covet thy neighbor's house, nor his ox, nor his ass, but they neglected to put their preaching into practice.

Ricord acted throughout in accordance with his principles, he being a professional scoundrel. No such excuse is available to Jason, who actively abetted this unwholesome chicanery. He had known since the previous April that Waller did not intend to honor his first agreement with McLoughlin and still was bent on securing the entire Oregon City claim, and he wrote Waller that he found this decision "satisfactory."[6] It was he who would file Waller's claim with the land office and at Oahu he paid Ricord $250 on Waller's behalf.

It was Lee's last ingratitude. Not long after, he heard that his superintendency was terminated and his replacement on the way. Now he was in a fever to confront the mission board and determined to go by way of Mexico. The Hines and little Lucy Anna Maria were sent back to Oregon, for Jason could take no excess baggage, whether ambulatory or otherwise. He shipped on a small schooner bound for San Blas. It was near the end of May, 1844, when he reached New York. The general conference was much agitated by the slavery question and had no time for him, so he went to Washington to file Waller's claim and lobby a bit with such as Tom Benton. In July he appeared for three days before the mission board, struggling to vindicate himself, and after strenuous argument was acquitted of speculation or other wrongdoing. But he was offered no position, only confirmed in his title of missionary to Oregon and told that any future employment was up to the episcopacy.

It made little difference. Jason was already gravely ill and by the time he reached home in Stanstead he wanted only rest. In November he roused himself to deliver a sermon in the local chapel — his last. Daniel visited him and found him wan, emaciated, coughing heavily and in constant pain. He was suffering both pulmonary and intestinal tuberculosis, his lungs badly ulcerated and his bowel constricted at two places. He died on March 12, 1845, being then in his forty-second year. According to his gravestone he died in peace. The term is relative.

❧ VII ❧

The Reverend George Gary was born in Middlefield, New York, a place not otherwise celebrated. He was licensed to preach before he was fifteen, and reached Oregon halfway through his fifty-first year. He was a bookish man with a wry wit and Yankee ethics.

Gary arrived at Oregon City on July 1, 1844, in time for the annual meeting of the Oregon mission. On the third of the month he sat in council with the seven members, lay and clerical, who were present, and told them the feelings of the mission board: that the prospects for benefiting large numbers of Indians had been overstated; that this had misled the board into making too heavy appropriations for the mission; that too little information concerning the mission's fiscal and spiritual condition had reached New York; that he, Gary, had been sent to learn the true state of affairs and, because the board found itself financially embarrassed, to institute a policy of retrenchment.

He then invited comments and the missionaries present complained that the immigrants of 1843 had brought with them a strong prejudice against the mission because of the number and location of its land claims, and this prejudice was heightened by the officers of the Hudson's Bay Company, who met the immigrants cordially, cooperated with them and treated them well. And second, that the Waller-McLoughlin dispute had divided the Oregon community, and that as a result of it some of the mission's own claims had been jumped and the political climate was such that it would be unwise to protest the jumpings. This was a sound conclusion though the opening premise was deliberate falsehood. The immigrants brought with them no bias against the mission. They acquired it after arriving.

Three days later Gary inspected the Chemeketa site, where he saw impressive holdings; a sawmill and a gristmill, a parsonage, a claim filed on sixteen sections — 10,240 acres — of land, and the Indian manual-labor school. The school was an ambitious three-story structure, seventy-one feet long and twenty-four wide, with two wings twenty-four feet square; but the weatherboards were not on and the cornices not placed. Gary estimated that it already represented an investment of $8000 to $10,000, and would cost $2000 or more to complete.

He thought these immoderately large outlays for the housing of an institution which had graduated only four pupils in nearly a decade since its founding. Even among his brother missionaries it was agreed that the chief good accomplished was that those who died had been exposed to religion, and might possibly go to heaven. He was appalled to learn that the children who ran away, if they were brought back, were severely whipped, put in chains and guarded and imprisoned behind a high enclosure. Wilbur Fisk's disciplinary methods adjusted to meet missionary requirements. And there was medical evidence that the boys and girls sometimes indulged in criminal intercourse with one another, passing among them an offensive disease.

In order to cut the overhead, which was impossibly high, there was discussion of letting out the school to its superintendent, Ham Campbell, to run on a contractual basis. But now Gary was told privately that Campbell had been found in a compromising position (caught, quite literally, with his pants down) with one of his Indian girl students. Since the mission would be held responsible for the moral character of the school it would not do to trust its management to Brother Campbell.

For nearly three weeks the Reverend Gary wrestled with the problem. There were then just twenty-three pupils in the school. Seven others had died in the past seven months. Almost all the survivors were tubercular, their necks disfigured by scrofular abscesses, and several were failing so rapidly they could be expected to live only a little longer. At the end he decided the only sensible solution was to abandon the enterprise and sell off the unfinished building. His luck was in. In 1842 a group of Methodists had joined to organize the Oregon Institute, whose stated purpose was to provide education for the children of white men. W. H. Gray, who had quitted the A. B. C. missions to the undisguised relief of his former associates, and moved to the Willamette Valley, was engaged to superintend construction of a school-house on Wallace Prairie, about three miles north of Mission Mills. He had been at it for more than a year, but the project languished. And when Gary offered to sell the institute the manual-labor school and the claim upon which it stood — reserving only that part occupied by the parsonage and the mills — the directors were delighted to accept.

Gary had now made up his mind to dismantle the secular arm of the mission as rapidly as possible. He had already sold Clatsop Station to the Reverend Josiah L. Parrish, a member of the Great Reinforcement, in exchange for six months' preaching and quittance of Parrish's right to return passage to the States. He now sold the mills to John Force, acting as agent for Brother Lewis Judson and Dr. Willson, for $6000, and was satisfied, for he thought the milling operations not thrifty. He sold all the cattle and horses at Mission Mills to Ham Campbell, hence-forth to be known as Cow Campbell, for about $4250, secured by a mortgage, but did so with reservations. He thought Brother Campbell a man who would bear much watching. And in mid-July he sold the Mission House farm, with stock, tools and smithy, to Alanson Beers.

By now Gary had come to two conclusions: first, that the sending out of the Great Reinforcement had been a sad and costly error; and sec-ond, that in Oregon the Methodist mission was considered more a secular than a religious concern. This second point was shortly borne in upon him, for he found himself entangled in the Waller-Mc-Loughlin controversy.

The entanglement was deliberate. He thrust in his fingers after the matter was presumably closed. In April, 1844, the dispute had been submitted to arbitration. In order to quiet title the doctor, largely influ-enced by James Douglas, was prevailed upon to grant $500 and five acres to Waller, and fourteen city lots to the Methodist mission. Three months later George Gary, intent upon liquidating the mission's earthly holdings, took up the matter of the Oregon City lots. The Methodist church occupied two of them, but the remaining twelve Gary considered dispensable — and valuable, for they were centrally located. On one of them stood the house Waller built in 1840 with lumber borrowed from McLoughlin and never paid for. Gary priced the house at $100, other improvements and the land at $5900, and offered the package to the old doctor, warning that delay in acceptance would result in sale to the highest bidder.

McLoughlin complained that he was being put upon. The grant to the Methodist church had not been a matter of business, but an act of charity. Lee had frequently denied that the mission intended to contest for the Oregon City claim. Gary's answer was sharp and uncompromising. The mission had as good title as was available without a boundary settlement, and that title was traceable to McLoughlin. The doctor could either meet the terms or bid for the lots on the open market.

The doctor met the terms and the good reverend congratulated himself, for it was understood that McLoughlin would assume mission indebtedness to The Bay equal to the amount of the purchase price. It was an instructive performance and settles the question of whether the close and sometimes slippery bargaining of Waller, J. Lee and other early Methodists was peculiar to them. It was not. George Gary took a healthy pleasure in this transaction, which was quite as insupportable as any which had passed before it.

It was too insupportable to be borne silently by Dr. White, or by Asa Lawrence Lovejoy who, with Frank Pettygrove, was proprietor of an embryonic community they called Portland. Or by the Reverend Henry Perkins. Curiously, most of the outrage was aimed at Alvan Waller. White formally charged Waller with treating John McLoughlin in an unchristian manner, forcing Gary to hold hearings and take evidence. Lovejoy chaired a meeting at Oregon City which openly questioned the validity of Waller's submitted evidence and demanded that every deposition entered be read publicly and the deponent allowed to affirm it by his signature. Henry Perkins announced he would resign.

Gary did not greatly admire Waller, but he strongly disliked White, and he had no intention of involving himself in an unseemly squabble. He decreed that there were not enough traveling ministers in Oregon to conduct a trial and posted Alvan to the Genesee (N.Y.) Conference, to which place the evidence and depositions would be sent. Lovejoy's protesters were politely told they might apply either to the Devil or to the Genesee Conference if they wished to mix into purely internal church matters. As for Perkins's threat, the unimpressed superintendent said it might make so tremendous an explosion it would blow him, George Gary, higher than a cat's back.

But when Perkins persevered in his intention, Gary was momentarily dismayed. His solution was to call back Waller, who had hurried with his family to Fort George in the hope of catching a vessel but had missed his sailing, and assign him to Wascopum. Waller would remain there until 1847 when he abandoned the station and Gary sold it to Marcus Whitman.

There remained the disposition of the mission store at Oregon City. Gary offered its accounts receivable, discounted to a mere $27,000, to Dr. McLoughlin, but McLoughlin would have none of it. Early in 1845 George Abernethy bought out the entire business, both stock and accounts, and the great liquidation was completed.

The Reverend Gary remained on in Oregon until 1847, plagued by old unpaid bills which continued to float in, grumbling that the mission was a "leaky concern" and had been shamefully managed. His sympathy for the departed Jason grew with time, for he decided that Jason's former associates were a difficult set of men. He boarded with David Leslie and found him elbowish and rough-tongued to his family, and not kindly to his young wife, the former Widow Olley. He tangled with Alanson Beers over ownership of scrap metal lying about the smithy and Beers threatened to take him to law. He discovered that Brother Abernethy considered himself above opening the church door or making a fire in the church stove before divine services. And he reached the conclusion that the local ministry used too little care in issuing licenses to preach, after listening to a sermon by an unnamed brother. "It was," he wrote, "an excellent cathartic for me." [7]

❧ VIII ❧

The while the Reverend Mr. Gary amused himself with secret drolleries, John McLoughlin's world was turning upside-down. The desire to avenge his murdered son embraced his soul like some personal demon. He arrested the murderers and sent them to Quebec, only to be told he must personally bear the costs of any prosecution and that Canadian jurisdiction was doubtful, Fort Stikine having been erected on Russian territory. He posted letter after letter, supported by reams of evidentiary documents, accusing Sir George Simpson of having made an inadequate investigation and having passed a shameful judgment. He continued to do this even after he was told he must desist; the matter was closed. His shrill insistence both displeased and embarrassed his

London superiors. They had privately concluded the doctor was right, and the governor wrong. But Simpson was indispensable, McLoughlin was not. Early in 1844 it was decreed he must go, and Sir George was so instructed.

It was not simply that the doctor refused to give up his feud. His habit of independence had betrayed him into insubordination. He stubbornly refused to close down Rae's hide and tallow operation in San Fransciso, despite peremptory orders to do so. And because a large part of the country had been deliberately overtrapped, Columbia District returns declined after 1840. They did not decline precipitously but they did so at a time when the European market was soft and prices sliding; Simpson, sharpening his pencil to an almost impossibly fine point, refigured the district's accounts for Outfits 1841 through 1843 and slashed a reported profit of £61,682 to an estimated loss of £5685. The London committee, having no one else to blame, blamed McLoughlin, though it was Sir George who had ordered the streams west of the Rockies and south of the 49th Parallel closely trapped until they were bare of beaver.

And there was the matter of Americans. In Simpson's view, McLoughlin treated them with damned, unbusinesslike benevolence. Sir George was all for letting them starve. London was less bloody-minded but even London was not overjoyed to hear that in 1842, and again in 1843, when numbers of immigrants had congregated at The Dalles, unable to find transport to take them downstream, the doctor had sent canoes to ferry them as far as Fort Vancouver. And London experienced acute corporate shock when it learned that by spring of 1844 McLoughlin had advanced to settlers more than £6600 in credit.

His reasoning (set forth in a letter written late in 1845) was sound enough. If he left the settlers to winter in a part of the country where Indian anxieties were already raw and Indian dispositions uncertain, there was bound to be conflict. Americans would be killed and in the States it would be charged that The Bay had put up the Indians to killing them. And once the immigrants arrived it would have been inhumane to refuse them the assistance without which most of them would have perished, and London would have been the first to censure him.

He might have said, though he did not, that there was also danger to be averted. He was dealing with true Eden seekers. Frontiersmen whose patina of gentility was thin as tissue and as readily torn. Men who accepted the sick fantasies of Hall Kelley and the lies of Slacum and Waller as being sober truth. They reached Fort Vancouver, their tempers beaten sore by loss and hardship, expecting to find that place an outpost of His Satanic Majesty and British tyranny, which were one and the same. They were prepared to forcibly expropriate what they needed for survival if it could not be acquired by legitimate means. McLoughlin recognized this. He recognized, too, that the credit he extended and the gracious treatment he gave them did little to soften those whose prejudices were deepest rooted. In the fall of 1843 he requested that a gunboat be sent to the Columbia to protect company property.

Perhaps because it was hoped that the doctor would recognize the impossible situation he had created and would voluntarily resign, the Northern Council of Chief Factors and Chief Traders over which Simpson presided in 1844 did no more than remove the Sandwich Islands from the jurisdiction of the Columbia District. McLoughlin was well enough pleased. Efficiently managing an unfamiliar business at so great a remove required more time and attention than he could profitably spare. Oregon was opening up at an astonishing rate. Fourteen hundred Americans poured over the Rockies in 1844, and a few more came by sea. The fat, deep bottom land of the Willamette Valley attracted them as would a magnet. (The colonists from Red River — those Britishers who had come out in 1841 — drifted south of the Columbia after an unproductive year on the Cowlitz or at Nisqually Plains. Already their interests were merged with those of the Americans.) Oregon City had become a market town, with shops and mills and even a hotel. Two ferries crossed to Linn City, on the west bank of the river, beginning point of a rough road blazed as far as the Twality Plains.

McLoughlin opened a company store at Oregon City in 1844, with the irrepressible Frank Ermatinger in charge, to compete with Couch (who had returned to represent the Bensons), and Frank Pettygrove, and George Abernethy once Abernethy bought out the mission store. And the doctor continued to deal in town lots, despite Waller's pretensions and Ricord's threat, but he was increasingly troubled by the irregularity of his claim. He had recorded it under the laws of the provisional government, taking title in his own name, but he had built improvements with company funds and he had done so in contravention of company policy announced in 1842, when London accepted that there was no possibility of a settlement fixing the boundary south of the Columbia and ordered major investment in the Willamette Valley discontinued. And in a letter dated June, 1844, Sir George Simpson wrote the doctor stiffly that while the Honourable Company would endeavor to maintain its rights, it was not in the business of buying off pretended claims (Waller's), or feeing individuals who professed to be lawyers (Hastings, to whom McLoughlin had paid £150 for legal advice).

This letter reached Fort Vancouver after McLoughlin closed with Gary, and the doctor was caught in an uncomfortably tight place. Early in 1845 he tried to extricate himself, offering to buy the Oregon City claim — less the company store and its stock in trade — for the cost of the improvements. It was an offer hedged by an ambiguous qualification; he wrote that at his time of life he was not desirous of beginning a new business, and he hoped he would not be made to suffer for acting to further company interests and extend British influence. If by this he meant his tender as a sham, or made in the expectation it would be refused, he would have been wiser to speak frankly. And certainly he was incautious to send with the letter two drafts, totaling nearly £4200, representing payment in full.

It was a shaky beginning to what would be, for John McLoughlin, a dark year. In February an obstreperous American named Williamson occupied part of Fort Vancouver's grazing land, posted a claim and put up a log hut. McLoughlin tore down the sign and ordered the hut dismantled and when Williamson returned the following month, bringing a surveyor, the doctor delivered himself of a stern lecture on property rights. Williamson listened defiantly and replied disrespectfully, but when other Americans then visiting the fort — Dr. White, Frank Pettygrove and Gustavus Hines among them — refused to support him in his trespass, he decided to withdraw. Pettygrove advised McLoughlin to report the incident to the executive committee of the provisional government. The doctor did so, and received back a reassuring letter including even an acknowledgement of Oregonians' obligations to him for his furtherance of their peace and prosperity. But he continued anxious and wrote to the British consul general at Oahu asking again that a gunboat be sent to the Columbia.

After long months of resistance, the doctor was at last ready to close down the hide and tallow business at San Francisco, and when the *Cowlitz* sailed there in March she carried instructions to Rae to liquidate. But that year nothing would fall right. The ship returned in June with the sad news that McLoughlin's son-in-law, addled by drink and hopelessly entangled in the Byzantine intricacies of California politics, had committed suicide the previous January, leaving company affairs in a disorderly state. In his report the doctor put the best face he could upon the matter, but it was a blow to his self-esteem. And it came just when he was informed by London that his reign as superintendent was ended, that new arrangements were being made for command of the district and that the additional £500 in salary allotted him annually was discontinued effective May 31, 1845.

The doctor did not immediately comment on his demotion though he knew it meant an end to his service with the company, and the thought was bitter as bile. He was convinced that London, misled by distance, time lapse and Simpson's insinuations, did not understand the complexity of the problems with which he was wrestling. Most particularly he believed that London did not understand the relentless nature of the forces which drove the movers westward; the irresistible allure of a vision which could compel a man to risk the whole of his fortune, whether great or small, and the lives of his wife and children, to the perils of a two-thousand-mile journey across the Great Plains and over the roof of the continent. Once he himself had been skeptical. Now he was half-convinced he would one day see prairie wagons disappear into the waters of the Pacific and later hear they had surfaced along the coasts of the Orient.

He was embittered by what he felt was undeserved injustice but bitterness did not yet affect his loyalties, and he continued to watch vigilantly over the company's interest. There was much to occupy his eye. The American community bubbled with fresh political ferment. George LeBreton had been killed in the spring of 1844 while foolishly trying to arrest a drunken and bellicose Indian whom a pair of settlers had cheated out of a horse. The Methodist party lost its only capable organizer and in the elections held the following June lost control of the provisional government as well. Lost it to a loose coalition of mountain men and immigrants of 1843 whose most effective leader was Peter Hardeman Burnett, destined to become first governor of the State of California.

Burnett was thirty-seven, tall and spare, with ropy muscles and a grave wit. Born in Tennessee and brought up along the frontier, he settled in Liberty, Missouri, in 1832. He did not thrive among the

Pukes. His business ventures failed and his wife sickened. He read law and built up a modest practice, but his income was not enough to support his debts. In 1843 he set off for Oregon, having first obtained the consent of his creditors, who prayed hopefully that he would find improving fortunes.

He did, though not immediately. Jointly with that compulsive town founder Morton Matthew McCarver, he became proprietor of Linnton and laid out a claim on the left bank of the Willamette, about five miles south of the Columbia, at a point that he and McCarver mistakenly believed was the head of navigation. By May of the next year Burnett had decided the place would thrive. He bought a farm on what was now called the Tualatin Plains — the Indian names were being rapidly Anglicized — and settled down to work it. He was there when he was elected a member of the new legislative committee.

Not until he arrived at Oregon City to take up his official duties did Burnett first read the original organic laws. He saw immediately that they were an inadequate base upon which to build a sound government, but the question immediately arose as to whether the committee had the power to amend them. Burnett argued that it did, of necessity. The new members of the executive committee agreed with him, and on June 18 they addressed a long memorandum to their legislative counterparts suggesting appropriate changes. There seems no direct evidence that Burnett had a hand in preparing these recommendations, but they closely follow his reasoning and the language in which they are framed has a legal taint. None of the executive committeemen was trained for the law. Dr. Bailey had considerable schooling, but largely in medicine. Peter G. Stewart, immigrant of 1843, was a studious watchmaker. Ex-Wyeth hand Osborne Russell, like so many others, like even the Falstaffian Joe Meek, had attended what Os himself named the Rocky Mountain College — long sessions of reading and debate to fill the empty hours when winter snows besieged the lodges and only a good book, a roaring fire, a rousing discussion or an eager woman was proof against chill and ennui.

Whether or not Peter Burnett aided Bailey, Stewart and Russell in the preparation of the recommendations, it was he who pushed through their adoption, though not without some difficulty. Not all members of the legislative committee were certain that amendment of the original organic laws was a proper exercise of their powers, and even the committee chairman, Burnett's old partner, McCarver, had reservations. But Doc Newell was stoutly supportive and so was the committee's only other lawyer, young Asa L. Lovejoy, and by December, after two working sessions, a substantial reorganization had been accomplished. The section on land laws was tightened; the Methodist land grab and the interdiction against private ownership of town and manufacturing sites were eliminated. Importation, manufacture and sale of liquor was prohibited. The marriageable age for girls was lowered from fourteen years to twelve to increase the pool of eligible maidens in a society which numbered three males for every two females. The courts were restructured. Five counties were organized, all of them south of the Columbia. The executive committee was to be replaced by a governor, who would also be commander-in-chief of the armed forces, and would be elected for a two-year term. The legislative committee was to give way to a somewhat larger legislature, its members to be elected annually. Provision was made for appraisal and assessment, and a tax of one-eighth of one percent was levied on mills, town site improvements, domestic animals, clocks, watches, pleasure carriages and goods imported for use in trade.

These changes were so extensive that it was thought discreet to tack a call for a constitutional convention onto the June, 1845, ballot. At that election George Abernethy was elected governor, over a badly divided opposition and to the satisfaction of the Reverend Gary, who hailed it as a victory for the Methodist Party. But The Bay's Frank Ermatinger was elected treasurer; Dr. John E. Long, both British-born and Catholic, was returned as secretary and recorder; Joe Meek, never numbered among the saints, was reelected sheriff; and Burnett, just become a Catholic after a two-year process of self-conversion, was elevated to the supreme bench. The call for a constitutional convention was defeated. In July, however, a popular assembly overwhelmingly approved adoption of the new organic laws. The provisional government had at last evolved into the Provisional Government.

From north of the Columbia John McLoughlin was closely following the progress of events. In 1843 he had opposed organization of a government as being unnecessary to the maintenance of order in so small a community. The pressure of public opinion was enough. But Waller and Lee had taught him to doubt the effectiveness of public opinion and meantime the country had grown uncomfortably populous. Most of those who came overland McLoughlin thought responsible and respectable. And the majority of these abandoned their prejudices against Britishers and The Bay once the calumnies which had excited them were exposed. But there was a minority whose super-nationalistic principles locked them into permanent antipathy.

He was being pushed, unwillingly, toward approval of organization. The conviction grew in him that Americans would abide by laws of their own making, and were prepared to have these laws evenly administered. Late in 1844 he withdrew his objections to French Canadian participation in the government. The following March he and Douglas heard that certain of the immigrants of 1844 were proposing that every man with an Indian wife be driven from the country and that no child of mixed white-Indian parentage be allowed to hold real property. Nothing came of this unappetizing scheme but its very suggestion convinced Douglas that no people could be more prejudiced and nationalistic than the Americans in Oregon and he wrote Simpson that he was more suspicious of their designs than of the wild natives of the forest.

Despite Douglas's misgivings it was becoming increasingly obvious to both him and the doctor that The Bay would be safer as part of the Provisional Government than outside it, if suitable terms could be arranged. This once McLoughlin set out to justify himself in advance of taking action. In July he wrote London that he had the previous spring sent furs stored at Fort Vancouver to Fort Victoria, on the southern tip of Vancouver Island, for safekeeping. He complained, not for the first time, of the systematic slanders which poisoned the minds of the immigrants against him. He reported that a man who had left the country said that his one regret was that he had not burned down Vancouver before leaving, for he had come west with that intention. Many of the immigrants were worthy, upright men, but many were of a quite different character. The Provisional Legislature, however, had recently addressed a new petition to Congress (Dr. White carried it to the States, departing, as usual, in a cloud of controversy), in which it was admitted that the British had an equal right to settle in Oregon. It was the one bright spot in an otherwise gloomy recital, but less than six weeks later he wrote again to acquaint his superiors of the general state of tranquillity which reigned in the country, and inform them that The Bay's servants had yielded to the wishes of the most respectable colonists, British and American, and joined the Provisional Government.

The Provisional Legislature had met in July, passed its petition and adjourned to await the outcome of negotiations which they hoped would bring the Hudson's Bay Company under the government and sorely needed additional revenues into the Provisional Treasury. McLoughlin demanded two concessions — that only Bay goods sold to colonists should be subject to taxation and that a new county to be organized north of the Columbia be named for George Vancouver — and these were promised him. But there remained the thorny issue of national fealty; some acceptable formula must be devised which would allow both British subject and American citizen to support a shared government.

Jesse Applegate came up with the solution. He was a member of the new legislature, a quirky man who too often confused capricious dissent with independence of spirit, but an innovative thinker. He had come west with the announced intent of driving the Hudson's Bay Company out of Oregon, but his friend Burnett introduced him around at Fort Vancouver where McLoughlin and Douglas charmed him. On August 14 he handed McLoughlin a letter in which he inquired whether the gentlemen of The Bay were willing to become parties of "articles of compact" by the payment of taxes and in other ways complying with the laws of the Provisional Government.[8] When the doctor discussed the matter with Douglas, neither of them could see anything in the proposal which violated their duties as British subjects or the honor or interests of the Honourable Company, and they decided to accept. Peter Skene Ogden, who was in the field, could not be reached for his opinion. When he returned he expressed disapproval, but the thing was done.

These maneuvers McLoughlin described at great length in a letter to London dated November 20, 1845, the last he would write in his official capacity as chief factor. By now he learned that he had been replaced by a board of management, to consist of Douglas, Ogden and himself until the end of 1845, when he was granted a year's furlough (during which time John Work would replace him), and that after two additional years' leave he was to be reassigned east of the mountains. He also learned that Simpson had accepted his offer to buy the improvements at Oregon City and kept the drafts, which caused him anguish, for he complained that his true intentions were misunderstood and that his capital was to be seriously depleted at a time when his income was sharply curtailed.

McLoughlin moved to Oregon City permanently at the beginning of 1846. Shortly after, he wrote Simpson that he intended to retire

Dr. John McLoughlin (1784–1857),
an honorable victim.
Daguerreotype, *Oregon
Historical Society Collections*

Fort Vancouver, 1845. From a watercolor by J. M. Warre.
Oregon Historical Society Collections

Anna Maria Pittman Lee (1803–1838).
Marriage martyred her.
Oregon Historical Society Collections

Jason Lee (1803–1845).
The apostle of muscular Christianity
had a chilly nature.
Oregon Historical Society Collections

The *Lausanne.*
Ham Campbell's sketch of the vessel which brought out the Great Reinforcement.
Oregon Historical Society Collections

The *Lot Whitcomb*, Milwaukie's pride.
Oregon Historical Society Collections

Peter Skene Ogden (1794–1854).
Brass knuckles and an iron gut
in the service of The Bay.
Daguerreotype, *Oregon Historical
Society Collections*

William Henry Gray (1810–1889).
He did not overvalue truth.
Oregon Historical Society Collections

James Willis Nesmith (1820–1885),
the pioneer personified: rowdy,
robust, ribald, and irrepressible.
Oregon Historical Society Collections

General Joseph Lane (1801–1881),
the Francis Marion
of the Mexican War.
Oregon Historical Society Collections

Thomas Jefferson Dryer (1803–1879),
"the Sewer Man" of the *Oregonian*.
Oregon Historical Society Collections

Asahel Bush (1824–1913),
a power-broker more feared than loved.
Oregon Historical Society Collections

Oregon City, 1857. Falls, upper left; Linn City, upper center; river, center right.
L. Lorain photograph, *Oregon Historical Society Collections*

Oregon City, 1857. Linn City is to right of falls; Abernathy Island,
to left. Millstream passed just beyond house in left foreground.
L. Lorain photograph, *Oregon Historical Society Collections*

Judge Orville C. Pratt (1831–1902),
an equal blend of egotism and deceit.
Oregon Historical Society Collections

Governor John P. Gaines (1795–1857), a
Whig among Democrats.
Oregon Historical Society Collections

Portland, Front and Stark streets, 1852. The main street ran from forest to forest.
Oregon Historical Society Collections

Abernathy's store, Oregon City.
The former governor is standing in the doorway at left. The building,
built around 1850, was destroyed during the great flood of December 1861.
Daguerreotype, *Oregon Historical Society Collections*

Delazon Smith (1816–1860).
They called him "Delusion."
Oregon Historical Society Collections

David Logan (1824–1879),
advocate and alcoholic.
Oregon Historical Society Collections

Oregon's Justinian, Judge Matthew P. Deady (1824–1893), with sons Edward Nesmith and Paul Robert and wife Lucy Henderson Deady.
Oregon Historical Society Collections

Portland, Independence Day Celebration, July 5, 1858.
Volunteer fire companies and general citizenry at rear; local brass band
at center left; Mayor A. M. Starr and Chief Engineer Charles Hutchins
at right. One of the volunteer artillerymen at lower left was
seriously injured while firing a salute.
Oregon Historical Society Collections

from the service. Oregon had captured him. He would not go east in any event. Marguerite would be unhappy there and he could not leave her. She was an old woman and they fitted comfortably together. The Bay treated him generously. His £500 salary was continued until June, 1846, and he continued to draw a full chief factor's share of the company profits through 1851, and one-half share for five years after that. None of this softened the doctor's resentment. He spoke with open contempt of his longtime employers, though he continued on proper terms with Douglas, Ogden and Work. And from the day he moved to Oregon City, McLoughlin labored to identify himself with the American community. But he labored unavailingly, for he remained unacceptable to the Protestants, who mistrusted him for his Catholicism; the nationalists, who could not forgive him his place of birth; and the manipulators — political, commercial and ecclesiastical — who were determined to steal him blind. Toward the end of his life he would lament that he had given his best years to the development of Oregon, and for thanks was treated worse than any dog.

❦ 7 ❧

Oregon, California, Texas and Polk

1845-1847

EARLY IN THE summer of 1845 Colonel Stephen Watts Kearny took elements of the crack First Dragoons from Fort Leavenworth to South Pass, and back by way of the Santa Fe Trail, in a sweep intended to impress upon the tribes east of the mountains the wisdom of peaceable behavior. That same year some three thousand emigrants departed Independence and St. Joe for Kansas Crossing and the Oregon Trail. Most of them hailed from the border states and the old Northwest. But an entire company (fifty-two wagons) of New Englanders serenely refused to travel on the Sabbath. Thirteen years after Nat Wyeth's first expedition the transcontinental passage had become a commonplace.

Credit the remarkable adaptability of nineteenth-century Americans. Joel Palmer, who went to Oregon that year, left a description of his countrymen's capacity to adjust to the unfamiliar. The division he was leading followed the south fork of the Platte and on June 14 halted early to rest its teams. Hunters raised a buffalo herd and the next day was spent jerking meat. Women took advantage of the layover to wash, iron and bake. A couple of fiddlers scratched out tunes. The literarily inclined read novels. The pious pored over their Bibles. An impromptu chorus sang the old sweet songs, the doleful harmonies Stephen Foster's genius would shortly transform into the unmistakable and unforgettable music of the antebellum generation. A Campbellite preacher recited a hymn preparatory to holding holy service and the fiddlers put aside their instruments in deference and organized a game of cards. It was, Palmer said, a miniature of the great world they had all left behind them when they crossed the line separating civilization from the wilderness. The movers, like the Romans, carried with them their lares and penates, their peculiarities and their prejudices, their customs and their political institutions. This intellectual baggage, however, did not always arrive intact. Some of it, impractical and therefore expendable, would be discarded along the way. Some would be altered, roughened by coarse circumstances. Palmer's miniature of the great world was also a subtly changing one.

At Fort Laramie they met Indians. They had met Indians before but these were Sioux, people of account. Several of the trains — Palmer's was one — entertained them at a formal banquet. The calumet was passed; there was an address by the principal chief and a reply by Palmer (the usual diplomatic language — protestations of eternal friendship balanced by judiciously muted bluster); and bread, meat and coffee served on spread buffalo robes. The descendents of Bradford and Brewster sitting down with the inheritors of Massasoit and Squanto.

But beyond South Pass the natives were less respectful and occasionally murderous, the plodding column dangerously attenuated, stretching out over more than a hundred miles of trail, and a discomforting rumor circulated that the mid-Columbia tribes, made angry and apprehensive by the numbers of Americans crowding into the country, were discussing infamous designs. At Fort Hall a California land agent was waiting. Caleb Greenwood, doyen among mountain men, past eighty but still rugged as the Rockies; sent by John Sutter to guide those parties already decided for California and to lure as many more as he could by chanting the praises of Sutter's New Helvetia. Caleb was no hand at selling real estate but he had spent a long lifetime in the wilderness and his pronouncements had a patriarchal weight. He told the families he would take them to Sutter's Fort in perfect safety but that the trail to Fort Vancouver was perilous and brutally rough. The worst of it, he said, was the nearly impossible traverse of the Blue Mountains, and beyond the Blues there was danger of Indian attack. It was enough to convince frailer spirits. Thirty-five wagons turned off to follow the old man southwest to the Humboldt and across the Sierras, in addition to the fifteen originally outfitted for California. Most of the defectors would beat their way north to the Willamette the next spring, to the open satisfaction of Joel Palmer, who all along insisted that old Greenwood was well stuffed with humbug. But Stephen H. L. Meek, who had several times made the transcontinental passage, knew otherwise; he knew that the final leg — Fort Hall to Fort Vancouver — was demanding far beyond anything so far encountered by the trains. And the knowledge made him thoughtful, for he saw in it an opportunity to improve his personal circumstance, which had become necessitous.

Stephen Meek was Joe Meek's older brother. Like Joe he had entered the mountain trade. He had never distinguished himself, but he had learned the basic wilderness skills and become a competent journeyman. At forty he could boast of an impressive variety of adventures, firsthand knowledge of the trail from Missouri to the Willamette and even proprietorship of lots in Oregon City. When, the previous May, emigrants congregated near Kansas Crossing to organize into companies and elect officers, only Meek could say that he was on his way home.

He was hired to pilot one of the larger companies for $30 in hand and $220 to be paid upon arrival at Fort Vancouver, and on the strength of this contract married seventeen-year-old Elizabeth Schoonover just two days later. But by the time Meek reached Fort Hall the company which employed him was shattered, as almost every overland company shattered, torn apart by impatience, inexperience, resistance to discipline and general cussedness. It was no longer a cohesive, nor even an identifiable, unit. Meek was a middle-aged man newly burdened by the responsibilities of marriage, and his prospect of collecting the balance due him was rapidly diminishing.

He resigned his commission and hurried west from Fort Hall, taking Elizabeth with him, to catch the families already toiling down the Snake toward Fort Boise, 280 miles away. Riding with trail captains by day, hunkered down with the menfolk around campfires by night, he explained that a part of what Greenwood said was true. The Blues were fearsome; crossing them would put intolerable strain on nerves and sinews and exhausted teams already lean and sore-footed. And there was always the danger you would be jumped by hostiles — Cayuse or Walla Wallas.

The men gathered around those campfires were road-worn and fearful and when Meek told them that there was a better way, a way which avoided both mountains and Indians, they listened. And some of them believed. He offered for $5 a wagon to lead them up the

Malheur, cross-lots to Crooked River and from there to the Deschutes and Wascopum Mission. One hundred fifty miles saved, and no mountains.

He signed on two hundred wagons — upwards of one thousand souls of all ages, encumbered by more than two thousand domestic cattle, eight hundred oxen and one thousand goats; and got the first of them started northwest from the Snake on August 25. But Meek had claimed familiarity with country with which he had only slight acquaintance. The forks of the Malheur confused him. His internal compass went awry. He thought himself farther north and west than he was and turned south into high desert parched by six successive years of drought. Even the goats had trouble finding forage. The availability of water dictated direction, drawing the trains still farther south. Provisions ran low. Those who had cattle killed them for food. The destitute were reduced to eating grass, thinly salted.

Members of the company muttered against Meek and made threats on his life, but he somehow managed to get them to Crooked River and the Deschutes. The van of the column was only a day's march from Wascopum when he took Elizabeth and hurried on ahead. A rescue party organized by Black Harris gathered in the stragglers. Since leaving the Snake, twenty-four had succumbed to starvation or to a fever which was probably tick-borne; as many more lingered only briefly before passing. One poor devil overloaded his belly and died of glut. And the survivors had not done with ordeal. At The Dalles, the south bank of the Columbia was jammed with jostling immigrants waiting for passage to Fort Vancouver, their numbers having hopelessly overtaxed the available transport.

A little band of adventurous men, Palmer among them, beat a rough trail through a pass high on the south shoulder of Mt. Hood, down the awesome declivity known as Laurel Hill and into tangled thickets of huckleberries, rhododendron, vine maple and scrub fir and so on to the Clackamas and Oregon City. Drovers took cattle by roughly the same route, and a few enterprising families followed. It took Palmer almost a month of walking and riding to travel the approximately 130 miles. But next year that trace would be the Barlow Road (after Sam Barlow, who helped survey and improve it and was one of its first proprietors), and most future trains coming by the northern route into Oregon would use it rather than risk the run down the Columbia.

The immigration of 1845 doubled the number of Americans in Oregon, and Reuben Gold Thwaites, writing sixty years ago, said its arrival guaranteed that the Oregon country, north to the 49th Parallel, would become territory of the United States. Thwaites was an accomplished scholar and his contribution to western history is vast, but on this occasion patriotic fervor seduced him into accepting pioneer myth. The American colony was certainly a counter on the diplomatic scales, but not one weighty enough to tip the balance. And just as the immigrants of 1845 reached the Willamette there was grave danger the boundary question would be put to the test of war. It was not, because fortuitous circumstance damped British resolution and because James Knox Polk, though somewhat belatedly, recognized the limits of brinksmanship.

⚜ II ⚜

Back in 1811 John Quincy Adams wrote that it was this nation's rightful expectation to become "coextensive with the North American continent, destined by God and nature to be the most populous and most powerful people ever combined under one social compact."[1] He was thus early expressing a conviction which would, in little more than thirty years, become a tenet of our national policy. It is called Manifest Destiny. James Polk was its most effective instrument.

Polk was not a great man. His mental perspectives were narrow. He was irrationally partisan, sour of disposition and devious beyond need. But he was almightily purposeful. He had set four great goals for his administration (he would achieve them all) and in March of 1845, the month of his inauguration, confided them to his secretary of the navy, historian George Bancroft. Two were domestic: reduction of the tariff and establishment of an independent national bank. The other two touched on foreign policy and are important to this history. The President wanted settlement of the Oregon boundary question. And he wanted California, by which he meant everything south of Oregon and west of Texas: all of what is now Arizona, New Mexico, California, Utah and Nevada, and as much of Wyoming and Colorado as lies west of the Continental Divide. An area comprising close to half of all the territory over which Mexico claimed sovereignty, though throughout most of it that sovereignty was thinly spread.

Bancroft said later that the President should have added Texas to his list. The omission was almost certainly deliberate. Annexation had been a key plank in the Democratic platform and Polk certainly wanted it, wanted it enough to endorse the Texans' wholly spurious claim to the land between the Neuces River and the Rio Grande. But by the time he was explaining his program to Bancroft the President considered annexation already an accomplished fact and Texas, to the line of the Rio Grande, territory of the United States.

A year earlier, then secretary of state John C. Calhoun had negotiated a treaty providing for annexation and the admission of Texas to statehood with emissaries sent to Washington by President Sam Houston. It failed of ratification in the Senate. But in the dying days of his presidency John Tyler managed to push a resolution of approval through both houses of Congress. An irregular procedure — Tom Benton thought it unconstitutional — but it was enough to satisfy Polk. There would be no negotiations with Mexico over Texas.

There would, in fact, be no meaningful negotiations with Mexico on any subject. The President was possessed of the notion that he could buy what he called California, and enough Mexican politicians to confirm the purchase. It was a delusion born equally of cynicism and ignorant contempt. He misunderstood the fierce quality of Mexican national pride. He knew only that that country was being governed by a succession of military gangs whose members were so openly venal as to seem artless. They were quite as venal as Polk imagined them to be but by no means artless, and each had a strong sense of survival. A politician caught conniving at the sale of Mexican territory risked prompt and permanent termination of his career.

So what Polk expected to acquire for a few tens of millions judiciously distributed was to cost the United States a nasty and not wholly honorable war and a century of hemispheric ill will. But war could not come at once because Mexico's treasury was empty, Mexico's army unpaid, ill-trained and lacking in military hardware; and because Mexico's diplomats hoped to persuade France and Great Britain, both of whom had substantial commercial interests in Texas, to intervene against annexation. More than a year was spent in dodgy maneuvering and shabby intrigue, none of which is germane to this history save as it exerted leverage on relations between Britain and the United States.

The Democratic platform of 1844, upon which Polk had been elected, called for the "reoccupation" of the whole of the Oregon country to latitude 54°40' north. This was pure cheek — no more than a scattering of Americans had yet settled north of the Columbia, none north of the 49th Parallel — and could be discounted as domestic political demagoguery until Polk defeated the heavily favored Henry Clay.

It was a victory, rumbled the London *Times,* of all that was evil in the United States over all that was good. Even the British foreign secretary, Lord Aberdeen, suffered a certain bilious distress. He was an amiable man (the most "ladylike," detractors said, in Sir Robert Peel's Conservative cabinet), and for months he had treated quietly with Edward Everett, American minister to London, to settle upon extension of the existing boundary of latitude 49° north from the Continental Divide to the Pacific, but with a bend at the western end to exclude the southern tip of Vancouver Island. Not until shortly before the American elections did Aberdeen learn that Peel would accept no such compromise. The prime minister was much influenced by his eminent minister-without-portfolio, the Duke of Wellington, whose militancy was undimmed by age, and by the officers of the Hudson's Bay Company. Sir Robert wanted the north bank of the Columbia, and he deprecated Aberdeen's fears. Let the Americans vent themselves of intemperate threats; a gunboat at the Columbia's mouth would be sufficient answer. And if negotiations failed, let the issue be submitted to impartial arbitration.

But the outgoing Tyler flatly rejected arbitration and Polk, in his inaugural address, took a seemingly uncompromising stand: title of the United States to Oregon was clear and unquestionable. He was careful not to claim title to the *whole* of the Oregon country, a point so fine it was missed on both sides of the Atlantic, as the President patently intended. He was rewarded by a gratifying uproar. The British press went into editorial convulsion. In Parliament Her Majesty's loyal opposition (notably the ever-belligerent Palmerston, who would replace Aberdeen if Lord John Russell's Liberals overturned the Peel ministry) bellowed outrage. The unhappy Aberdeen thought a peaceful solution improbable, if not impossible, and Peel reluctantly agreed. The prime minister did not yearn for war, as did Palmerston, but he knew his duty. The admiralty was given necessary instructions. And a pair of military officers, Lieutenants Henry Warre and Mervin Vavasour, were outfitted in mufti and sent overland from Canada to conduct a quiet reconnaissance.

In the States the tides of excitement ran nearly as high. When Ohio's Congressman William Allen rose in his place to holler, "Fifty-four forty or fight," he was echoed by a grand diapason from every corner of the frontier West. The dying Jackson wrote urging Polk to stand firm against British hectoring. The President's answer was reassuring, but he already had a tight grip on reality. He could not reasonably ask, nor expect to get, more than Monroe had been willing to accept in 1818 or J. Q. Adams in 1826. It was less that he was bound by the concessions of his predecessors than that he was embarrassed by them. Or so he rationalized. Secretary of State James Buchanan was ordered to tender to the British minister to Washington, Richard Pakenham, a formal offer to fix the Oregon boundary along the 49th Parallel. It was anticipated that Pakenham would refer the matter to his superiors for instructions, where Lewis McLane, who had replaced Everett in London, could privately explain to Aberdeen that the proposal was flexible and that the President was prepared to entertain any reasonable counteroffer. A carefully orchestrated plan, but it failed to take into account Pakenham's impatience with official protocol.

The British minister was an old diplomatic hand. But he had the arrogance of one whose family connections were impeccable, and the reputation of being excessively clever, and these were factors enough to lead him into error. He had the well-born Englishman's automatic contempt for Americans generally, and American politicians in particular. He had served in Mexico before being posted to the United States and he knew to a certainty that the Mexicans would not accede to the annexation of Texas without a fight. He had no way of knowing the breadth of James Polk's territorial ambitions but he was canny enough to recognize an imperial design. By now — we have reached the end of July, 1845 — the Texas senate had ratified the annexation treaty; the Mexican congress was debating war; and General Zachary Taylor, commanding a small army stationed at Corpus Christi near the mouth of the Neuces River, was informed that the Rio Grande had become the southern border of the United States. A storm was blowing up and Pakenham thought to take advantage of it. Instead of forwarding Buchanan's proposal to London he rejected it on his own authority, in a less than respectful letter. Polk promptly decreed the conversations at an end. Henceforth he would settle for nothing less than the whole of Oregon.

Pakenham was shaken, and diplomatic rockets from London did nothing to comfort him. His ineptness had given the initiative to the Americans. He was ordered to reopen discussions, using Buchanan's tender as a point of departure. The President would not hear of it. When the frantic secretary of state, whose congenital suppleness of spine was intensified by his desire to succeed to the presidency, argued that simultaneous wars with Britain and Mexico would carry incalculable risks, Polk blandly replied he expected the government to do its part and would leave the rest to God and the country. And on December 2 he asked Congress for a resolution authorizing him to give notice of intent to terminate the treaty of joint occupancy.

Her Majesty's sloop of war *Modeste* was anchored in the Columbia, covering Fort Vancouver. H.M.S. *America,* mounting fifty guns, was patrolling the head of Puget Sound. It was reported out of Liverpool that military and naval preparations were the greatest since Waterloo. War seemed only a spark away. But the potato crop had failed in Ireland, opening the years of devastating famine still remembered as the Great Hunger. Peel was so anguished by reports of wholesale starvation that Wellington wrote he had never seen a man suffering greater agony. To alleviate the distress, the prime minister proposed repeal of the Corn Laws, protective tariffs which had effectively blocked the importation of grain for fully thirty years. When his cabinet refused him its unanimous support, Sir Robert handed his resignation to the queen.

Throughout most of December Britain's will was paralyzed by cabinet crisis. For two weeks Lord John Russell labored to form a government, but could not. On the twentieth the queen sent for Peel, and he returned to office, with his options sharply limited. War with the United States was become unthinkable. Repeal of the Corn Laws would be a hollow gesture unless American grain was available for import. Aberdeen must settle the Oregon question on the best available terms.

Now it was Polk who raised difficulties. By using Pakenham's blunder to lay claim to the whole of the Oregon country he had made himself a popular hero throughout the Mississippi West and excited the expectations of western congressmen whose support he would need in the event (now made almost certain by the ordering of Taylor's army to the Rio Grande) of war with Mexico. The President found himself awkwardly boxed. He was prepared to compromise on the Oregon boundary, but it was politically impossible for him to give the appearance of doing so.

For five months the diplomats in both London and Washington struggled to rescue Peel and Polk from their respective dilemmas. In the course of this sometimes frantic exchange of arguments and advices occurred one of those apparently inconsequential events whose future significance history is prone to overlook. In mid-February Pakenham received a visitor from Oregon. His name was John M. Shively. He was a Kentuckian and had gone overland in 1843 to Oregon, where he had staked out a claim at what was once Astoria — and would be again — and was presently called Fort George. Now he was returned to the States to arrange the publication of an emigrant guide, which he hoped would encourage other Americans to settle in his newly platted community.

Shively urged that both the United States and Great Britain withdraw all claims of title, allowing Oregonians to govern themselves for a period of five years, at the end of which time a plebescite would determine whether the country would be British, American or independent. He argued that the distances involved made it unlikely that Oregon could, whether divided or not, be effectively governed by London or Washington. There is small evidence that Shively was speaking for any organized party. But he was expressing a separatist point of view which would remain strong until the Civil War attached the Pacific Northwest firmly to the Union.

The bemused Pakenham, whose instructions were to exercise the caution which had earlier deserted him, could not seriously treat with Shively as the representative of an independent power, and in any case the major issues were already being pushed to settlement. McLane, as impatient as Aberdeen for a peaceful solution, magnified British naval preparations. Polk let it be known that any reasonable compromise based upon the 49th Parallel would be referred to the Senate for ratification. The final offer excluded the southern tip of Vancouver Island and granted the Hudson's Bay Company free navigation of the Columbia through the term of its charter, on the same basis as American vessels. Polk, avoiding responsibility, passed the proposed treaty to the Senate. Tom Benton supported it with one of his most effective and tedious speeches (it took him three days), by explaining that Oregon did not include New Caledonia. On June 15 the boundary settlement

was signed at Washington. Zachary Taylor's troops were already south
of the Rio Grande, Americans had raised the Bear Flag in California
and a month had passed since Congress declared that a state of war
existed between the United States and Mexico.

⚜ III ⚜

With the ratification of the treaty the boundary ceased to be an issue
except in Oregon, where word of the settlement would not arrive for
months. Americans and British watched one another with wary mistrust. The military spies, Lieutenants Warre and Vavasour, were too
obviously inept and antic to be suspected of conducting espionage.
They roamed the countryside, splendiferous in beaver hats, frock coats
with figured vests and beautifully tailored buckskin pantaloons, all gen-
teelly scented by rich tobacco and rosewater, bringing comic relief to
the humdrum lives of resident Oregonians. Warre painted acceptable
water colors and Vavasour reduced miles of magnificent scenery to
scarps, counterscarps, ridges, spurs and headlands, and positioned
endless gun emplacements never to be built. A fondness for brandy
made them indolent. Their report did not reach London until after
the treaty was signed.

The presence of the *Modeste* at Fort Vancouver was a more serious
matter.

The sloop first visited the Columbia in July, 1844. Late in October of
the following year she returned to the river to remain for the duration
of the crisis. She would remain on after, departing in May, 1847. James
Douglas was not impressed by her officers. They were courteous and
agreeable young men but inattentive when he lectured them on the
grave national interests involved in the Oregon boundary question.
Captain Thomas Baillie, commanding, was less outspoken than Captain John Gordon of H.M.S. *America,* who damned the entire country
as not worth five straws. But Gordon could allow himself license; he
was Lord Aberdeen's brother. Baillie was discreet, but he did not think
Oregon worth a war and he exerted himself to avoid any inflammatory
incident. His crew was kept strictly in hand. He produced theatricals
and sponsored balls and picnics and otherwise entertained the local

ton. On Washington's Birthday three of his young officers visited Oregon City to take a respectful part in the observances.

There could never, wrote one observer, be any real congeniality between an American frontiersman and a British naval officer, but Baillie's efforts helped reduce friction and his social events were reported in the columns of the *Oregon Spectator,* whose first issue was published February 5, 1846. It was printed on a press ordered from New York and owned by the Oregon Printing Association, but got up to further the interests of Governor Abernethy who, with like-minded friends, held a controlling interest in the association's stock. Its editor, for the moment, was William G. T'Vault.

T'Vault was a lawyer, a former Indiana sheriff, a great sinner (as he once confessed to the Reverend Mr. Gary, who commented in his diary, "public opinion will sustain him in this position"), and a Jeffersonian Democrat.[2] His tenure was brief. On March 19 he printed an editorial supporting Asa Lovejoy as a suitable candidate for member of the Provisional Government's house of representatives. Lovejoy was an officer of the Oregon Printing Association but he was also George Abernethy's most resolute political rival. In the issue of April 2 — the *Spectator* came out every second Tuesday — T'Vault announced his involuntary retirement in an angry valedictory in which he blamed his dismissal not on his inability to follow standard rules of syntax and orthography, but upon his failure to bend to the wishes of the local aristocracy whom he described as a "class of mungralls [*sic*], neither American nor anti-American — a kind of foreign hypocritical go-betweens."[3] The application to Abernethy is biting. The governor carefully ingratiated himself with the gentlemen of The Bay, while privately excoriating all things British.

T'Vault was succeeded by H. A. G. Lee, of the Virginia Lees, a man of superior attainments and a modesty which approached diffidence. But he quit the editorial chair in August with obvious relief and the prediction that while the paper would one day give satisfaction to the majority of its subscribers, it would never please all of them.

George Law Curry was twenty-six, a jeweler by trade but widely read, and in St. Louis he had acquired some experience as a journalist. He would shortly marry one of Dan'l Boone's great-granddaughters and for his eagerness and impetuosity would be known as Young Curry to the end of his days.

Curry arrived in Oregon in the fall of 1846 and almost immediately was given charge of the *Spectator,* announcing in his salutatory that he would take a firm and consistent American tone, but open his columns to all. Under his direction the sheet flourished, though there was so little real money in the country that a law had been enacted making wheat, bills drawn on solvent merchants and scrip issued by the Provisional Government legal tender. The scrip was valueless, and while bills drawn on The Bay were accepted at face, those drawn on other houses were considerably discounted and not infrequently refused, particularly by rival establishments. Joel Palmer said of the American merchants that their mode of dealing was to ask whatever their avarice demanded and the necessity of the purchaser would bear, and that were it not for competition from The Bay, prices would double. Doubtless he was right. Since pickling was the only way of preserving meat and fish, salt was an important commodity. During the summer of 1846 the supply at Fort Vancouver ran short, forcing up the cost per bushel from 62¼ cents to $2. Frank Pettygrove and his new associate, Benjamin Stark — as indefatigable a pursuer of the dollar as might then be found west of the Mississippi — refused to sell any of their abundant stock in the hope of cornering the market and gaining control of the salmon-packing industry. M. M. McCarver accused the two of monopolistic practices. Most Americans, following their patriotic prejudices, blamed the Honourable Company. But the high price of salt was a temporary vexation, and during much of 1846 the colonists were occupied with a matter of graver concern.

Oregon was Eden; it was an outpost of empire; it was, as Theophilus Arminius had it, a place to which the failed might go to purge their discontent. It was also an immense real-estate speculation the success of which depended upon a constant flow of immigrants hungering for land. Most Americans in Oregon had come there by wagon train, traveling the usual route. They knew that in describing the trail west of Fort Hall, Caleb Greenwood had been guilty of nothing worse than mild hyperbole, and that a safer and less toilsome route must be discovered. By any measure the road to Oregon was daunting, and with the increasing possibility of a Mexican war, California was becoming a competitive lure.

We have met Jesse Applegate. He was the youngest of four brothers, three of whom reached Oregon in 1843, but he was imperious. His siblings deferred to him. He was possessed of original, if increasingly perverse, genius, but his physical appearance so displeased him he would never sit for painter or daguerrotypist. The only portrait which survives was done by a relative from memory. The face is homely, the ears jug handles and, as Jesse's most enduring enemy once wrote, "he had not head enough."[4] But Jesse knew — with a special poignancy, for both he and his brother Lindsay had lost sons when a boat overturned in swift water below The Dalles — that a less hazardous road to Oregon must be found. During the spring he consulted with his neighbor, Levi Scott. And on June 22 these two, with the infinitely accommodating Black Harris for guide and interpreter and twelve of Polk County's landed gentry, left La Creole (now Rickreall) and turned upstream along the Willamette.

They followed the regular Fort Vancouver–Sacramento Valley trail as far as the Rogue, turning up that river's south fork till they reached, and crossed, the height of land north of the division the Klamath cuts between the Cascades and the Siskiyous. From there they wound through the lakes strung out along the Oregon-California line, finding no serious difficulties. But beyond Mud Lakes, in the extreme northwest corner of what is presently Nevada, they came upon a somber and uninviting land. Desert, and they explored it twice, finding a few springs which could be enlarged to make water holes. They pushed ahead to the Humboldt and an intersection with the California Trail, from which a detachment hurried north to the Snake. On August 8, Black Harris, David Goff and Jesse himself rode into a large camp of movers just past Fort Hall to announce that a new, shorter and safer route had been discovered from that place to the Willamette.

The line surveyed by the Scott-Applegate party, somewhat modified, would shortly become the standard route to Oregon. But for the roughly one hundred wagons which took it in 1846 it was the road to near calamity. Jesse had underestimated the distances involved. The settlers' oxen were worn lean before they left the Snake and some were badly handled by unskilled drivers. Most important, the immigrants were deadly tired by the time they reached Fort Hall, and some were sick, and almost all were so demoralized they had lost discipline and become lethargic. Urging could not hurry them. They persisted in traveling in small groups, which made them prey to the Diggers, who were thievish, and the Modocs, who were bloody-minded. It was the second week in October before the greater part of them reached the middle Rogue and turned north. Rain caught them as they were toiling over the Umpquas. They suffered less than Steve Meek's people, but they were sorely tried. Not until January did the last of them reach the settlements.

The world had meantime changed. The previous July the U.S.S. *Shark,* Lieutenant Neil Howison commanding, scudded across the bar of the Columbia and worked her way upstream to Fort Vancouver, showing the flag and greatly delighting those patriots who were piqued by the continued presence of the *Modeste.* Howison exchanged compliments with Baillie, was romantically impressed by the beauty and accomplishments of James Douglas's fifteen-year-old daughter and at Oregon City was greeted by a salute fired from a hole drilled in the village blacksmith's anvil. With Governor Abernathy he toured the Willamette Valley, finding it as lovely country as nature ever provided for the virtuous.

The *Shark*'s visit cheered the Americans as a token Washington had not forgotten them, but the circumstances of her leaving caused chagrin. Howison's orders required that he put out from the Columbia on September 1. He was late arriving at the river's mouth. No pilot was immediately available, so he decided to chance the passage of the bar using the maps Charles Wilkes had prepared six years before. The wash of tide and current had shifted the channel, however, and the schooner ran on Clatsop Spit and shortly broke to bits, though no lives were lost. Captain Baillie and James Douglas sent aid immediately, not waiting on requisition, and the unhappy Howison was reduced to chartering The Bay's *Cadboro* to carry his crew to San Francisco. He was still awaiting transport when the *Toulon* arrived from Honolulu, carrying word of the boundary treaty.

IV

Eighteen forty-seven blew in on a storm, bringing much snow. Wolves and panthers came down from the hills to ravage the flocks. The Reverend Mr. Gary sat in his house at Oregon City mourning absent friends and the lack of innocent gaieties, and wished himself home in New York State. But in January he was pleased to make the acquaintance of the J. Quinn Thorntons, who were refined above the average. Mr. Thornton was Virginia born and London educated, and had practiced law in Missouri and Illinois, though with imperfect success. Nancy Thornton was genteel. Both were delicate. He was asthmatic; she suffered from "female complaints." They had come to Oregon in 1846 seeking improved health. Beyond Fort Hall they had taken the Scott-Applegate road.

J. Quinn spent most of a day describing the travail of that journey, causing Gary to write that it was "truly suffering and perilous."[5] The Thorntons' sufferings were real enough. They had lost almost everything but their lives and their greyhound, Prince Darco; jettisoned a fine library, furnishings, personal effects and the wagon which brought them, for their team broke down between Klamath Lakes and the Rogue. Thereafter they walked, beating their way over tilted, twisted country, stumbling down icy, rushing mountain streams, falling so deep into despair Nancy was stricken briefly with hysterical blindness. The immigrants who hurried ahead reached the Willamette without undue hardship but the Thorntons and those behind them would have perished had not Black Harris and others dispatched by the road company brought south cattle and provisions, which were parceled out at Oregon prices. Thornton was given the loan of a horse and acquired a second, though at the cost of a fine suit of broadcloth, which maddened him. He became and ever after remained convinced that the road hunters were a piratical crew who had deliberately deluded the immigrants to reduce them to want, so as to squeeze a profit from their necessity. And of this company of villains he settled upon Jesse Applegate as the most heinous.

George Gary rather liked Thornton and was pleased when the lawyer joined Gary's congregation. He must have been equally pleased when Brother Abernethy appointed Brother Thornton to the supreme court. This was done in February, and the next month Gary learned that Indians around Wascopum had become increasingly threatening. In April he wrote Alvan Waller and Henry Brewer to sell the station to Whitman, if Whitman would have it, and bring their families to the safety of the settlements. Waller protested, but the superintendent was adamant. It was useless for the Methodists to remain longer at The Dalles.

Gary was nearing the end of his term, though he could not be certain of it, and his last days were enlivened by a brief anxiety and a brush with adventure. In May forest fires threatened Oregon City. The season was unnaturally dry; only favorable winds saved the village. And early in June the old gentleman found himself on the uncomfortable edge of an affair of honor.

The Thorntons had come down from their middle Willamette claim so that the judge could hold court, and were staying with the Garys. Thornton had, since his first visit, aired his charges against Applegate and associates in the *Spectator,* in language most intemperate. A reply, appearing over David Goff's name, robustly defended the road finders and in passing remarked that Thornton was a man so odious that of those with whom he traveled, scarcely one would have raised a hand to defend his life or dig a hole to hide him were he dead. The irate Thornton scolded Curry (in another letter) for opening his columns to filth and scurrility and declared that Goff, whom he characterized as an absolute illiterate, could not have written what was attributed to him. This charge brought the judge into collision with James W. Nesmith, recently married to Goff's fifteen-year-old daughter, Pauline.

Nesmith was probably the real author of the offending letter. The language is Nesmithian. He practiced at law, and like Thornton was in Oregon City for the sessions. There resemblance ended. Nes was self-taught, his legal training was imperfect, but he was a prodigious pleader. He once convinced a jury that a man who, while crossing the plains, exhumed the body of a dead Indian to steal the blanket which served as winding sheet had no right to title in Oregon land. He was ten years Thornton's junior and the quintessential pioneer — rowdy, ribald, rough-hewn and a palpable menace. The judge took to carrying a bowie knife and a six-shooter. To the admiring Gary he was a model of Southern courage who would rather die than retract. But when Nesmith proposed a duel, Thornton prudently refused. Whereupon Nes published the judge an arrant coward in a pungent broadside tacked up all over Oregon City and its environs.

The Reverend William Roberts arrived shortly after to take over superintendency of the Methodists, and the Garys departed with grateful relief, leaving only a single piece of business to be concluded. Waller and Brewer were arranging the sale of their station to Marcus Whitman for $600, but they and their families were still at Wascopum in August when a sharp skirmish broke out between Indians and immigrants, causing casualties on both sides. Governor Abernethy hurried up to arrange a peace. The outbreak was significant because natives around The Dalles were seldom violent against whites — Dr. Whitman trusted them enough to make his eighteen-year-old nephew, Perrin

Whitman, sole custodian of the station less than a month after this incident — but Oregonians generally were more excited about the security of their land claims. Most were displeased with a clause in the Oregon treaty which guaranteed The Bay title to property it occupied below the boundary line, and quietly countenanced the jumping of company claims and those of McLoughlin and the French Canadians settled at French Prairie. But earlier immigrants were dismayed when later arrivals began to invade even American claims registered with the Provisional Government, either upon the ground that the treaty invalidated all titles, or by force. Anti-claim-jumping meetings were called in every county and there was a general move to deny the vote to any candidate who supported claim-jumping (causing the newly elected auditor to object against vigilante law), and more petitions were got off to Washington, praying for the extension of the laws of the United States to cover Oregon.

The *Spectator* divided its attention between these efforts and the late news of the Mexican War, which was, except in the case of happenings in California, very late. It missed the quiet departure of Judge Thornton, who embarked for the national capital in October, by way of San Francisco, bearing a petition which the governor approved. The general public did not hear of the judge's leave-taking until December, when the legislature met, and by that time word had come down the Columbia of the murder of the Whitmans and many others by the Cayuse. The Oregon colony, like the United States, had a war on its hands.

⚜ 8 ⚜

Most Horrid Butchery

1847-1849

THE REVEREND HENRY PERKINS, who knew them both, wrote of Marcus and Narcissa Whitman that they were ill adapted to missionary work. He thought Narcissa had been haughty and discontented away from the refinements of polite society, and Marcus so independent, mannerless, incapable of compromise and overbearing that his Indians feared but did not love him. All true. Narcissa might, with perfect sincerity, name herself an unworthy sister in the Lord; but she could not sustain the role. The doctor was arrogant and arbitrary. Yet near the end, the imperiousness which so long supported Whitman deserted him. He remarked morosely that it was probable his death would do as much good for Oregon as his life could. He was forty-five when he said this, and had two days to live.

We know a great deal about what Marcus Whitman did during the hours which remained to him. We can only conjecture as to how his thoughts ran. Clearly he recognized his peril. There is no evidence he feared to die. But the imminence of death is awesome enough to turn the bravest man contemplative, to set his mind to a casting up of life's accounts. Not all Whitman's memories could have been comfortable ones. Just eleven years before, he built at Waiilatpu the first Oregon station for the American Board of Commissioners for Foreign Missions. During the first six of those years the mission family had been divided by bitter acrimony. Certain of the brethren were difficult. William Henry Gray, who was the least of them, had no demonstrable interest in evangelizing Indians, no ambition save his own advancement, no close acquaintance with truth. His major talent was for troublemaking. Of the three Congregational ministers who came out with their brides in 1838, two — the Reverends Elkanah Walker and Cushing Eells — were decent men of limited ability. The third, the Reverend Asa Bowen Smith, was a doctrinaire Calvinist who could not imagine an Indian qualifying for Election to Grace. At Kamiah on the upper Clearwater he dourly told his Nez Percé parishioners, when they proclaimed themselves Christians, that they were the victims of a dangerous delusion.

The Reverend Henry Harmon Spalding was both the most effective of the American Board missionaries and the most deeply flawed. He was illegitimate and the shame was a stain upon his spirit. Brought up by unfeeling strangers, he could barely read or write when he reached his majority. Yet he managed to graduate from Western Reserve College and spend two years at Cincinnati's Lane Theological Seminary. He was a failed suitor for the hand of the uncommonly beautiful Narcissa Prentiss — who became Narcissa Whitman — and instead married lean, sallow, saintly Eliza Hart. He was capable of acts of humanity which Asa Smith found intolerable, such as baptizing dying children that they might pass on with some hope of salvation. But when a Nez Percé girl he had married to a mountain man ran off to escape her husband's brutal treatment, Spalding ordered her given seventy lashes. So mercurial were his moods that certain of his associates thought him unbalanced.

But during the early years of Henry Spalding's ministry he was a magnet to the Indians. So many attended a camp meeting he conducted at Lapwai in February, 1839, he was forced to call in Smith and Walker for assistance in preaching and crowd control. His approach to missionary teaching was pragmatic. It was Nez Percé practice to trek yearly to the buffalo grounds for an annual hunt. Spalding sought to settle the Indians permanently near his station, persuading them to clear small tracts which he taught them to cultivate, and giving them peas, seed potatoes, hoes and even cattle in the hope of converting them into farmers. Much of what he did was in contradiction of mission policy, but had he been more personable and less intolerant of criticism, he might have worked at least a minor miracle. Instead his obdurance and abrasiveness so alienated his colleagues that most of them wrote letters to the American Board complaining that Henry Harmon Spalding was unfit.

Marcus Whitman was one who wrote, though his true differences with Spalding were personal. But when, in 1842, the A. B. C. ordered abandonment of Waiilatpu and Lapwai and called Henry Spalding home, it was Whitman who undertook a dangerous winter passage overland to Boston to seek recision of the closure orders and save Spalding from dismissal. The mission, Whitman was able to tell the board in April, 1843, had become harmonious. Asa Smith was gone to the Sandwich Islands, taking his ailing, unhappy wife; forty years later the Nez Percé would still remember her as "the weeping one." Mr. Gray had retired to the Willamette to take employment with the Methodists, Mr. Spalding had composed his difficulties with the brethren (chiefly Whitman, though the doctor did not say so), and undertaken to correct his ways. As for the Indians, Whitman was careful to avoid exaggeration. The prospects for instructing them were good. When the season was right a hundred might attend worship. And he raised a specter; there were priests in the country whose pernicious influences must be opposed. On one point he was positive: "Many emigrants from the U.S. are expected."[1] He had passed through Missouri as recently as February and knew the whole frontier was burning with Oregon Fever.

Dr. Marcus Whitman in a righteous humor could be formidable. The board withdrew the offending orders. The doctor hurried to Rushville, New York, to visit his mother and persuade a fourteen-year-old nephew, Perrin Whitman, to accompany him back to Oregon, promising the boy a gun, saddle and mule. Toward the end of May the two caught up with the emigrants, some thousand of them, a few days' ride beyond Independence.

Memory is adaptive. In remarkably few years Marcus Whitman held himself forth as the guide and inspiration of the emigration of 1843, when he was neither. James W. Nesmith, himself orderly sergeant of the emigrant train, said a generation later that Whitman joined up with only a ham for subsistence, and when that was consumed survived by inviting himself to other people's dinners. Nes was a professional iconoclast but the yarn will do for a corrective, both for Whitman's anxious pretensions and for the romantic fictions religious writers later constructed upon them. Peter H. Burnett was duly elected commander of the company and Captain John Gantt, sometime army officer and long-time mountain man, was hired as guide. Whitman was no more than a knowledgeable and hard-working member of the caravan.

Yet the doctor did make one essential contribution to western travel. On May 28, not far from the Shawnee mission, he wrote brother-in-law Galusha Prentiss that this year the wagons would go all the way to the Columbia; and along the way he did his best to convince leaders of the overlanders, men like Burnett and Jesse Applegate, that it was possible to take covered wagons over the Blues. He himself had managed to wrestle a light wagon, cut down to a cart, only as far as Fort Boise in 1836. But four years later Doc Newell dragged two rigs from Fort Hall to Fort Boise, and even shipped one by boat to Fort Vancouver. What mountain men could do, Marcus Whitman reasoned, movers could do.

He carried his point. He did not lead the way, appointing a reliable Cayuse, Chief Sticcus, to serve as guide before himself hurrying ahead to Lapwai, where Eliza Hart was ailing, and to Waiilatpu. The experiment was a qualified success. The effort involved in pioneering a road across the jumbled cliffs and canyons of the Blues debilitated both men and animals so terribly that half the immigrants might have perished at The Dalles had not John McLoughlin acted promptly to rescue them. But the way to the Willamette was opened.

In May of the following year Whitman wrote triumphantly to Asa Smith at Honolulu that the Oregon country was not surpassed by any in the world and the work of the American Board missions was become more interesting and important. For whether or not the Indians survived (he thought probably they would not), the missionaries would be needed to aid the new settlers, as indeed they were already doing, and to found and sustain institutions of religion and learning. Circumstances had converted the doctor to colonialism. His letters east were crowded with new urgencies. American settlement of the country was inevitable; arrangements must be made for the missionaries to perfect title to mission lands; a threshing mill was needed at Waiilatpu, and more plows, a wool carding machine, a qualified mechanic. Alanson Hinman, immigrant of 1844, had been hired to take over the mission school — whose pupils were not Indians, but members of the mission family. Attempts to teach English to the natives had failed. The Papists were becoming immoderately active.

East of the Cascades relations between Protestant and Catholic missionaries were, if never warm, generally correct. At Tshimakain, among the Spokane people, priests took tea with the Walkers and dined with the Eells, though not frequently. Priests and parsons sat at table together at Fort Walla Walla. Father de Smet gave Marcus Whitman a Douay Bible, no doubt with a hope of curing the doctor of his heresies. But at Lapwai there was no fraternizing. Henry Spalding studied under that notable anti-Papist Lyman Beecher at Lane Theological Seminary, and Beecher implanted in Henry an abomination of Catholicism which would eventually grow to inexorable passion.

Because the original Jesuit mission was opened among the Flatheads, Spalding felt acutely threatened. The Flatheads and his own Nez Percé were close and ancient allies, and they mingled freely. It was unavoidable that the Nez Percé be exposed to Romish errors. When, after 1843, religious attendance at Lapwai slackened and the young braves became increasingly hostile, Spalding blamed his troubles on Papist subversion. Certainly the sectarian contests were not always conducted with dignity or Christian forebearance. But there were graver causes for Indian disillusionment. Elijah White's penal code and his appointment of Ellis as head chief seriously undermined the powers of the subchiefs who had historically maintained routine discipline. The equality of justice under White's imposed laws was brought into question early in 1845 when Elijah Hedding, son of the Walla Wallas' Chief Peu-peu-mox-mox and a former student at Jason Lee's Methodist Indian school, was most deliberately murdered by Americans at Sutter's Fort. Ellis hurried to the Willamette to remind the Indian subagent that penalties of the code were to be invoked against all wrongdoers, whether native or white, and a much-concerned Whitman wrote that he feared for the safety of his mission station, so great was the anger of the tribes. Dr. White smoothed Ellis with fair words and duplicitous promises, including an offer to give the aggrieved chiefs $500 from his own pocket the following fall so that they could buy cattle. But when fall came White was safely on his way to the States and the pledge unkept.

If the Indians were losing interest in the American Board missionaries, the missionaries, Spalding apart, were losing interest in the Indians. At Tshimakain Walker and Eells busied themselves raising crops and families. Three times a day Narcissa set places for twenty, most of them youngsters. The Whitmans' only child, little Alice Narcissa, had died at two, drowned in the Walla Walla River in 1839, only yards from her parents' door. Thereafter Narcissa accumulated waifs — a bush baby she named David Malin; Mary Ann Bridger and Helen Mar Meek, daughters of distinguished mountain men; and the seven Sagers, orphaned when both father and mother died coming out with the immigration of 1844. Managing so large a family took up the whole of Narcissa's time. Her sewing and knitting classes for the Cayuse and Walla Walla wives were discontinued.

Marcus, apart from his medical practice, busied himself with commercial and agricultural affairs. Waiilatpu ceased to be a mission station and became a frontier town, complete with mills, houses, sheds and artisans' shops, and surrounded by pastures and cultivated lands. Spreading out across country to which the Cayuse laid claim by right of prior occupancy and through which annually trooped increasingly long armies of Americans. Narcissa wrote with amusement that the natives were awed by the sheer numbers of the immigrants. A dangerous misconception. The tribes felt not awed, but threatened.

Marcus Whitman knew he was critically circumstanced. As early as 1844 John McLoughlin had warned that the Cayuse were ill disposed, and other Indians also, because Whitman identified himself openly with the settlers' interests. Certain chiefs had approached McLoughlin for approval of a plot to wipe out the American settlements on both sides of the Cascades. McLoughlin issued a stern warning against any such undertaking but succeeding immigrations, after having passed through the Sioux and Blackfeet without incident, found themselves harassed and abused by the supposedly peaceable and Christianized Cayuse and Walla Wallas.

Whitman's motives for buying Wascopum from the Methodists are uncertain. He first offered the station to Elkanah Walker but Walker, cozily dug in at Tshimakain, refused to move. In the summer of 1847 the doctor hired Alanson Hinman, then teaching at the Methodists' Oregon Institute, to be secular agent at The Dalles and reinforce nephew Perrin. This was clearly a temporary measure and it is not improbable that Whitman intended eventually to retreat to Wascopum himself.

The Catholics, meantime, were pushing south from the Kootenay-Flathead country. Walla Walla had a bishop, the Most Reverend Augustine M. A. Blanchet, brother of Alvan Waller's Francis Norbert Blanchet, now archbishop of Oregon City. Apart from normal religious rivalries, the conduct of Bishop Blanchet and his missionaries was carefully correct. They entered the Cayuse country by invitation. When Indians offered them Waiilatpu for a station they refused to displace the Presbyterians, and established themselves by the Umatilla on a tract granted by a local chief. Whitman was not pleased to have an opposition encroaching on his precincts but the bishop treated him with disarming courtesy. Presently the doctor was confronted by graver concerns. The immigrants of 1847 brought with them a virulent form of measles and a highly infectious flux which may have been typhoid-related. Though the whites, having developed natural immunities through generations of exposure, usually recovered, the diseases ran among the tribes as far north as Fort Colvile. But it was around Waiilatpu the epidemics took their most terrible toll. Half the Cayuse people were cut down. The mortality among the children was appalling.

The native mind is direct. Both whites and Indians sickened of measles and dysentery and were doctored by Whitman. Most of the Indians died. Almost all the whites recovered. The odds were against coincidence. According to one account three braves, two sick and the third feigning illness, were sent to the doctor for treatment. He gave them medication and next morning all three were dead. Rumors were spread that Whitman carried two kinds of pills in his bag; white for Americans, black for Indians. And the black pills were fatal.

Those who survived the last months at Waiilatpu said that Narcissa did much crying and the doctor's mood was somber. His situation was daily more precarious yet he unaccountably urged late arrivals from the States to winter at Waiilatpu. Eight families obliged him and were put up in outbuildings or apartmented in one of the several residences. By the last week of November there were sixty-nine whites living at the station, too many to move quickly should some emergency arrive and too many to house at The Dalles, where no accommodations were available. But, sadly, too few to defend against an attack. Four-fifths of them were women and children.

On November 27 the doctor rode to Umatilla to attend some sick natives. Henry Spalding, who had just brought his ten-year-old daughter from Lapwai to attend the school at Waiilatpu, rode with him. The following morning Whitman's old friend, Chief Sticcus, warned the doctor to leave the country immediately, for the young men of the tribe had bad hearts and could not be controlled. Though it was a Sunday, Marcus Whitman traveled back to his station, leaving Spalding at Umatilla. The next morning the doctor officiated at the burial of three children of Chief Tiloukaikt. That same afternoon an Indian, with Tiloukaikt's assistance, drove a tomahawk into Marcus Whitman's skull, a signal for the massacre to begin. Narcissa was also killed, the only woman who was. Shot repeatedly, and a brave whipped her face and flanks with a braided quirt and she was rolled in the mire of an irrigation ditch where, after long hours, she was released by death.

In eleven years of effort, turmoil, prayer and sacrifice, twenty-two natives had been accepted into the First Presbyterian Church of Oregon — twenty-one Nez Percé, and one Cayuse. So great a price.

≪ II ≫

On November 30 William McBean, commanding at Fort Walla Walla, sent a momentous letter to James Douglas and Peter Skene Ogden at Fort Vancouver. Early that morning, McBean wrote, an American had appeared at the gates of the post. He was half-naked, much bloodied, carried a gun and said his name was Hall, and that the day previous a most horrid butchery had taken place at Waiilatpu. Dr. Whitman was dead and others, though it was uncertain who or how many. That he, Hall, had escaped by snatching the gun from one of the attackers and diving into the bush.

Though he left a wife and children at the mission station, Hall's great objective was to reach the safety of the Willamette settlements. McBean furnished him with food and other necessaries, and a Hudson's Bay cap and coat, and the man set off down the north bank of the Columbia. He was not seen again.

Because Hall's account was incoherent and incomplete, William McBean immediately sent his post interpreter for additional details, and these he included in his letter. Eleven were dead and three, counting Hall, were wounded. Apart from Narcissa, all the dead and injured were men and older boys. McBean blamed the outrage on the devastating effects of measles and dysentery. His interpreter was told by the murderers that Andrew Rodgers, schoolteacher and ministerial candidate, confessed to overhearing Spalding and Whitman plotting the poisoning of the entire tribe in order to take over the Cayuse lands, horses and cattle. Poor, terrified Rodgers was shot anyway and McBean — himself half-Indian — wrote bluntly that "no person can believe the doctor capable of such an action without being as ignorant and brutal as the Indians themselves."[2]

He continued that only Cayuse were involved in the killings: Tiloukaikt, Tamsucky and certain young chiefs. The Walla Wallas were calm
and Chief Peu-peu-mox-mox was counseling peace, for which offense
the Cayuse, it was said, intended to kill him on the morrow. There
were also rumors of a strike at Fort Walla Walla, where McBean had
only five men but promised a stout defense. The gates were closed
night and day and the bastions in readiness. He signed as "most obedient humble servant" and sent the letter by special express, warning
his messenger to say nothing of the massacre until he was well below
The Dalles lest the Wasco and Deschutes people, who had been restive
of late, be excited to uprising.

The story of the Whitman massacre has been told often enough. As
massacres go, it was not a large affair. Fourteen Americans, counting
the unfortunate Hall, lost their lives. Louise Sager and Helen Mar
Meek, who were ill, died of inattention. Numbers of women and some
children were ravished. It was a grievous event, but an event less important to this history than the use to which it subsequently was put.
There are incidents, however, which cannot be ignored. One immigrant was spared because he was needed to work the sawmill; de-
mented by terror, he not only urged his fifteen-year-old daughter into
the tent of a Cayuse brave, but also countenanced the abuse of girls
who were, in Henry Spalding's infelicitous phrase, "so young the knife
had to be used."[3] Joseph Stanfield, a Whitman employee, was passed
over because he was part Indian. Stanfield twice prevented mass
slaughter of the remaining women and children — once by diversion,
once by defiance. He saved a young woman from rape by pretending
to be her husband, and helped a wounded man escape to Lapwai. But
Stanfield was Canadian and Catholic. After he reached the Willamette
with the other survivors he was charged with complicity in the massacre. And there was a final irony. Henry Harmon Spalding avoided the
martyrdom Marcus Whitman achieved through the intervention of a
courageous priest.

Apart from McBean's interpreter, the first outsider to reach the
Whitman station after the massacre was the Reverend Father John
Baptist Abraham Brouillet. On November 30 Brouillet departed the
Catholic mission on a pastoral visit to the Cayuse and perhaps to explore further the possible purchase of Waiilatpu, a subject he, Whitman and Spalding had discussed during the recent visit of the latter
two to Umatilla. It was evening when he reached the camp of Tilou-

kaikt's band and learned of the murders. That night he spent in fear and trembling. But early next morning, supported only by his interpreter, he rode resolutely to the scene of carnage, offered such cautious comfort as he could to the frozen-faced survivors and buried the slain with the help of Joe Stanfield, whom he found washing the mangled and mutilated bodies. Then, knowing Henry Spalding was expected, Brouillet set off to intercept him, accompanied by Edward, a son of Tiloukaikt, who rode along as uninvited guest.

They met Spalding just three miles from the Whitman station. Brouillet, putting his own safety at risk, persuaded Edward not to kill the Presbyterian without prior approval of the chiefs. When the brave galloped off to consult with his superiors, the priest, after rapidly describing the horror which had taken place at Waiilatpu, gave Spalding his own tiny supply of bread and meat, and with difficulty, for Spalding was panicky almost to paralysis, persuaded the minister to flee. Minutes later an execution party thundered up, furious to find its victim escaped and dangerously displeased with Father Brouillet for interfering.

Henry Spalding was six days reaching his station, six days crowded with hardship and terror. He traveled under cover of darkness, sometimes wandering in confused irresolution. He managed to lose his horse and was forced to walk the last ninety miles, his feet wrapped in rags for protection against the frozen land because he had discarded his boots. Lapwai, when he arrived there, was abandoned. William Canfield, the wounded man given aid and direction by Stanfield, had already brought word of the massacre. And Cayuse emissaries had come to demand that the Spaldings be surrendered for disposal. The Nez Percé refused but it was thought safer to move the mission family to William Craig's place, about eight miles distant. Bill Craig was a mountain man with a Nez Percé wife, Indian sympathies and an open distrust of evangelicals. Henry Harmon Spalding, in his ministerial capacity, had frequently damned the man for an infidel and scoundrel, but just now he was happy enough to accept Craig's protection.

On December 10 Spalding got off a long letter to Bishop Blanchet of Walla Walla, whom he addressed as "reverend and dear friend." The Nez Percé, he said, were prepared to protect their missionaries from harm so long as the Americans in the Willamette Valley kept the peace. He therefore pleaded that no reprisals be taken against the Cayuse and begged the bishop to forward this recommendation to

Governor Abernethy. From Canfield the Spaldings had learned that the charge Whitman was poisoning the Cayuse people was first circulated by a half-breed vagabond from the States (Joe Lewis, described as part Penobscot), who had some grudge against the doctor. "We think," Spalding wrote, "that the Cayuse have been urged into this dreadful deed. God in mercy forgive them, for they know not what they do."[4] The tone is taut as a controlled scream but at one point the anguish bursts forth: "Our help, under God, is in your hands, and the hands of the Hudson's Bay Company. Can help come from that source?"[5]

The couriers who brought this told the Cayuse that the Nez Percé had no heart for war, which was unsettling. Peu-peu-mox-mox and his Walla Wallas not only would not fight, it was even reported they had hanged a Cayuse who boasted of taking part in the killings. At Tshimakain, the Spokanes promised to protect the Walkers and the Eells. The Cayuse themselves were of divided mind; two of their senior chiefs, Camaspelo and Sticcus, disavowed responsibility for the murders, and Sticcus had warned Whitman of the danger. Bishop Blanchet, taking advantage of the growing indecision, suggested a tribal council to discuss possible peace terms.

The council was held December 20 at Umatilla, the bishop and Father Brouillet being present in consultative capacities and to reduce results of the deliberations to writing. After the obligatory speechifying, the chiefs voted for peace, abjuring the Americans to forget the late murders even as they themselves had forgotten the murder of Elijah Hedding at Sutter's Fort, and promising that no more harm would come to the prisoners, all of whom would be released immediately a formal treaty was arranged, with commissioners to be sent by the colonists. Scarcely had the tribes adjourned when word was brought that Ogden was at Fort Walla Walla and had called a general meeting of the Nez Percé, Walla Wallas and Cayuse. A separate message requested the presence of Bishop Blanchet and his priests. It was politely phrased, but was command rather than invitation. Under such circumstances, Peter Skene Ogden was not one to issue invitations.

McBean's messenger reached Fort Vancouver the evening of December 6. Next day James Douglas sent notice of the tragedy at Waiilatpu, enclosing a copy of McBean's communication and remarking that Mr. Ogden, with a strong party, would shortly leave for Walla Walla "to endeavor to prevent further evil."[6] Mr. Ogden left that same day, but his assignment was more complicated than Douglas indicated. He was to secure release of the survivors of the massacre and, if possible, the mission family from Lapwai. And if there was to be war (which, given the eternally prickly temper of the colonists, seemed probable), Ogden was to impress upon all tribes other than the offending Cayuse the wisdom of neutrality. A general conflagration would not only be bad for business, it could very well result in tribal confederation and calamitous attacks on the Willamette settlements.

Driving his *voyageurs* relentlessly, Ogden managed to make Walla Walla in under two weeks. By December 23 he convened his assembly. Bishop Blanchet's diplomacy had been marked by apostolic and somewhat nervous delicacy. P. S. Ogden was subtle as a fist. The Honourable Company was displeased. The chiefs blamed the murders and sundry previous thefts and insults visited upon Americans on the young men of the tribes. If the chiefs were governed by their young men they were not men themselves, for they lacked certain physiological appurtenances which real men possessed. The young braves plumed themselves on their bravery, but if they warred with the Americans that war would not end until every hostile Indian was cut off from the face of the earth. As for the sick, it was God, not Dr. Whitman, who had commanded they die. But the company had no part in this quarrel. He could not promise whether there would be war or no war. He had come to return the prisoners to their friends, and he would pay ransom. And that, he said, was all.

It was enough. The Cayuse were effectively split off from their most potent allies. For a quantity of blankets, shirts, tobacco and handkerchiefs, a few muskets with a little powder and one hundred musket balls, the fifty-seven survivors from Waiilatpu were surrendered, and for a rather smaller consideration, the Nez Percé delivered the Spaldings and retinue from Lapwai. Even before these last arrived on January 1 of the new year, rumors were circulating at Walla Walla that a rifle company had reached The Dalles from the Willamette. Ogden had barely time to load his refugees and whisk them downstream before the Cayuse War was a reality.

❧ III ❧

On Wednesday, December 8, James Douglas's letter enclosing Mc-Bean's account of the massacre reached Oregon City, exciting great anguish and outrage. The heart of the whole community, said the Reverend Mr. Roberts, throbbed with emotion. The legislature being already convened in regular session, Governor Abernethy referred the matter to that body as one requiring prompt action, suggesting the lawmakers apply to the Hudson's Bay Company and local merchants for loans to finance whatever plan they fixed upon. The governor was touching on a major embarrassment. The Provisional Government was bankrupt. The frugal Oregonians had set tax rates so low that proceeds were never sufficient to meet ordinary expenses. There was $43.72 in the treasury. Indebtedness, chiefly in issued scrip, exceeded $4000.

No campaign could have been mounted against the errant Cayuse had not J. W. Nesmith been a gifted improviser. Chairman of the assembly's militia committee, Nes wrote most of the war measures, contributed largely to the remainder and as self-constituted whipper-in drove his associates through a deal of business in an uncommonly short time. A company was voted, enlisted, organized under H. A. G. Lee, equipped with such military furnishings as were available and on December 9 went bobbing down the hurrying Willamette in a little flotilla of canoes and *bateaux,* with orders to seize and secure Wascopum Station. Commissioners were appointed to raise $100,000 against bonds secured only by the good faith of the territory and the general expectation that the federal government would eventually assume the obligations. The governor was authorized to raise a regiment of not more than five hundred volunteers, each recruit to furnish his own horse, gun and bedding and receive $1.50 per diem in promises. A fresh memorial was got up, asking the United States to extend its laws and protection over Oregon, and Joe Meek, member from Tuality, was selected to carry it east, together with word of the parlous situation in which the colony found itself. For which Joe was allowed $1000, provided he raise it himself, and as much additional as Congress might see fit to appropriate in reward for his services. Finally, the governor was authorized to appoint three peace commissioners whose duty it would be to persuade to neutrality the uncommitted tribes, particularly the Nez Percé.

Abernethy and the loan commissioners accompanied Lee's command as far as Fort Vancouver, nursing a frail hope that The Bay might underwrite the war. James Douglas was sympathetic, but instructions from London prevented him from extending any substantial line of credit. He did, however, furnish $1000 in powder and supplies necessary to complete the outfitting of Lee's company, taking a joint note given by Jesse Applegate, Abernethy and Asa Lovejoy.

Back at Oregon City a public appeal brought in only $3600, including $1000 in Methodist funds winkled from the reluctant Roberts, and some of the larger subscribers would redeem their pledges only if they were allowed bonds at a 25 percent discount. It being clear that bond sales would never raise funds sufficient to equip the troops and maintain them in the field, Commissary (and Quartermaster) General Joel Palmer and his agents were empowered to contract for goods and services, giving interest-bearing notes for the appraised valuation, and, when necessary, to levy forcibly upon the unwilling.

Though he had urged on the legislature the imperative need for prompt action, the anxious Abernethy himself procrastinated. To Pastor Roberts he confided that he would prefer simply to secure rescue of the prisoners and leave punishment of the murderers until the arrival of federal troops. But there were restless persons in the territory who were determined to go and chastise the Cayuse against all hazard and he thought it necessary to place them under proper control. So Abernethy explained himself to Roberts. The truth was more complicated. Contemplation of the hazards involved in a large-scale military venture unsettled the governor's mind and viscera. Only political pressures moved him to act. He met in closed session with the legislature December 25. That same day he issued his call for five hundred volunteers, appointed mustering officers in the various Willamette Valley counties and ordered each company, as soon as recruited, to march to a rendezvous point near Portland to place itself at the disposal of Colonel Cornelius Gilliam, 1st Oregon Rifles.

Neal Gilliam was a Floridian come west by way of Tennessee and Missouri, a Freewill Baptist preacher and forty-nine years old when he embarked on the last adventure of a picaresque career. He had bounty-hunted runaway slaves, served in the Blackhawk and second Seminole campaigns and, as a Missouri militia officer during the pitiless war which the Pukes waged upon the Latter-day Saints in 1838, been cited for commendable ruthlessness. He was a flawed man. His ambition was unbridled; his rashness approached idiocy; and he was swollen with bluster, some of it purposeful. Even before assuming active command Gilliam announced he would march to Vancouver, levy on The Bay for all necessary supplies and munitions and, if his demands were not directly met, pull down the fort around James Douglas's ears. When the moment came, he did nothing of the kind. But his well-broadcast bravado won him the admiration of dedicated Anglophobes whose support, once his soldierly triumphs were behind him, would be useful in the political arena.

Despite the exertions of the loan commissioners and commissary agents, supplying the volunteers was a laborious process. The soldiers furnished their own mounts but there was a dearth of pack animals. Everything must be carried up the Columbia by boat, battling the racing current and the icy winds gusting through the river's gorge, portaged from Lower Cascade and transferred to the south bank at Upper Cascade, where there was a rickety ferry. Not until the second week in February did Gilliam get everyone assembled at Wascopum Station, which, partially stockaded, had become Fort Lee. The colonel now had under his command six or seven companies (sources differ) totaling fewer than four hundred men, five hundred pounds of powder, fifteen thousand percussion caps and an elderly nine-pounder cannon; and Governor Abernethy's peace commissioners were also on hand: Commissary General Palmer (also superintendent of Indian affairs), Major Henry A. G. Lee and Doc Newell, speaker of the legislative assembly.

During eleven years in the mountain trade Newell had seen his share of nastiness and run against a good many hard cases, and his nature was not delicate. But the desperate character of the army alarmed him. Elements of it were rapacious and unhesitatingly brutal. A friendly Indian was shot dead simply for wandering into rifle range while tracking some strayed ponies. Some of the last of the overlanders to arrive the preceding fall had parked outfits and herds in the vicinity, intending to drive them to the Willamette once spring opened Sam Barlow's road. Gilliam's officers commandeered wagons and teams for transport and the cattle to feed the troops. Common soldiers rummaged through personal effects, breaking into trunks and boxes and wantonly scattering what they did not appropriate. "Little respect," Newell wrote in his journal, "appears to be paid to private property." [7]

Leaving the sick and a small garrison of able-bodied effectives at Fort Lee, Colonel Gilliam led his people east on February 14, backtracking the immigrant trail. It was a turbulent, ill-managed march. The colonel lacked aptitude for discipline. Volunteers looted commissary stores, slaughtered beef in defiance of orders, even stole tea and sugar from an ailing comrade. At one point nearly a quarter of them voted to desert unless all of the remaining flour was issued. Gilliam mounted a wagon and recharged their flagging zeal with a rousing speech on patriotic duty, after which he declared a day of rest. No mutineer was punished or even reprimanded. But the colonel's good nature was capricious. When thirteen Deschutes, led by a senior chief, filed into camp to announce their solidarity with the settlers, Gilliam was narrowly dissuaded from executing the lot.

Early the morning of the twenty-fourth couriers brought word that the Yakimas, on the advice of the priests who were their teachers, had voted not to war on the Americans. The army bivouacked the previous night at Well Spring, some twenty-five miles short of the Umatilla River, and when the march was resumed the peace commissioners rode well in advance of the column, carrying a parley flag, for there was abundant Indian sign. At Sand Hollows, where the eccentricity of nature fashioned hundreds of shallow bowls, they found the Indians themselves — Cayuse, and the Palouse who were the Cayuse's only reliable allies. Four hundred warriors, counting a scattering of the disaffected from other tribes, and gathered on a nearby hill were one hundred women come to cheer their menfolk.

Gilliam formed his command in an arc, flanks slightly withdrawn. An under-strength company of *Canadiens* and Britishers from French Prairie, recruited and captained by Tom McKay, anchored the southern end of the line. It was there the battle opened. Two prominent Cayuse rode out between the armies to shout the challenges ritual required. Gray Eagle was a shaman, a professional magician who boasted that his medicine made him impervious to Yankee lead. Five Crows was Spalding's and Whitman's only Cayuse convert. He had taken no part in the massacre but when it was over accepted the gift of a young immigrant girl, Lorinda Bewley, and used her as his wife until she was ransomed by Ogden. Tom McKay put a ball through Gray Eagle's brain. At the same moment Lieutenant Charles McKay, a Scot from Red River, shattered Five Crows's arm with a shotgun blast, causing the chief great pain and mortification and forcing him to retire in search of repairs.

This inauspicious beginning had its effect. Those Cayuse who had

no part in the massacre or doubted the wisdom of provoking a war —
Newell estimated they numbered a quarter of the whole party — sat
out the battle. The Indians who did fight fought with dogged courage
but increasing bewilderment. The young chiefs had told them the colonists were dogs and women to be beaten to death with clubs. Gilliam's
troopers shot fast and straight and didn't panic worth a damn. When
evening drew on, it was the war chiefs who ordered a withdrawal,
leaving the volunteers in possession of the field. They had suffered
five wounded, including Lieutenant Colonel James Waters, Gilliam's
second-in-command. The number of Indian casualties is unknown. All
of their injured and most of their dead had been carefully carted away.

The 1st Oregon slept on its arms that night, having no fresh water
nor wood for cook fires, for the camp was a place of unrelieved desolation. On the morrow the regiment resumed its march, meeting no
opposition. Instead groups of anxious Indians hung on the edges of
the dusty column, pleading for a parley. At sundown the Umatilla was
reached, and forded next morning. On February 28 the troopers set
up their tents outside Fort Walla Walla.

William McBean had good news. Chief Peu-peu-mox-mox had sent
assurances that his Walla Wallas wanted no part of the war. McBean
thought the peace commissioners could accomplish much good with
careful management. None of which satisfied Gilliam. Fathers Brouillet
and Rousseau were at the fort, having fled from their Cayuse mission
after being warned that they were no longer welcome. The colonel
questioned Brouillet stiffly about the priest's part in Archbishop Blanchet's recent efforts at effecting a settlement. Next day he ordered
pressed two kegs of Hudson's Bay gunpowder and sent a sizable detachment under Major Lee to insure delivery.

The army occupied Waiilatpu on March 3. The following evening
Joe Meek, who had ridden up from Oregon City with the troops,
slipped away east, taking ex-mountain man George Ebbert for partner,
a handful of passengers returning to the States, and a hundred-man
escort to protect the party until it reached the tumbled safety of the
Blues. On the fifth Gilliam ordered the mission buildings torn down
and the material used to construct the low parapets of what was to be
Fort Waters. Since his victory at Sand Hollows the colonel had grown
increasingly willful. Bill Craig had been sent to lead in the Nez Percé
for council but had not yet returned with them. Gilliam damned the
delay. He was vigorously displeased with the peace commissioners,

saying he would henceforth have his own way; that he had come to fight, and fight he would. But as regimental commander he was guilty of shameful laxity, doing nothing to curb waste and pilferage or to protect the property of the massacre's survivors. Items recovered were simply appropriated by the finders rather than turned over to the commissary general, as regulations required, because Gilliam refused to sustain Palmer's authority. "This army," Newell wrote, "is composed of different kinds of men. Some have come to act legally, others to plunder and others for popularity."[8]

Craig and 250 Nez Percé came in March 6 and counciled on the seventh, when the chiefs not only announced for benevolent neutrality but also undertook to advise the Cayuse to surrender the murderers in exchange for an end to hostilities. Nothing was accomplished, however, the Cayuse being so divided against themselves that no agreement was possible. On March 11 the peace commissioners, including Major Lee, left for the settlements. That same morning Neal Gilliam led about 260 effectives north to carry the war to the enemy. Five days later he was back, having taken a bad mauling. Deliberate imprudence had led him to interpose his troops between three hostile forces whose relentless attacks drove him for more than thirty hours in a bitterly contested retreat. He escaped serious losses only because a handful of sharp-shooters tenaciously held the approaches to the last ford over which he could splash to safety.

It was an embarrassing reversal. Nothing could water Gilliam's truculence, but his shaken officers advised discretion. They contended successfully that the army could conduct no major operation until it was reinforced and resupplied, and Captain Harvey Maxon's C Company, the regiment's largest, was ordered to The Dalles to bring up all available troops and the additional matériel presumed stockpiled at Fort Lee. Gilliam decided to go along, intending to visit Oregon City to argue his plans for future conduct of the war before Governor Abernethy. But at Well Spring a rope he was drawing from a wagon triggered a loaded rifle, killing him instantly. He was more mourned than missed. His judgments were erratic and his military accounts so muddled that the legislature voted them approved without audit to save his heirs from making good the deficit.

On reaching Fort Lee, Maxon discovered only a thinly equipped garrison company. Gilliam's accidental death and his own highly charged emotional state caused the captain to write so extravagant a description of the troops at Fort Waters — ragged, shoeless, lacking both powder and provender and surrounded by unnumbered savages — that its publication in the *Spectator* caused a fresh eruption of patriotic fever. Abernathy issued a call for more recruits. Fifteen young ladies of Oregon City announced they would accept the attentions of no man who failed to enlist in defense of God, home and virtuous womanhood. Matrons stitched together clothing to cover the nakedness of the soldier-boys. Loan commissioners and commissary agents labored unremittingly and against stiff odds; money was tight, wheat almost impossible to obtain and lead so scarce it was sometimes bought up a pound at a time. Two hundred and fifty men enlisted — Nesmith captained a company from Polk — and marched resolutely into the interior under Henry Lee, who had provisionally accepted a colonel's commission. At Waiilatpu they found the army very comfortably situated. Discovered caches yielded up stored grain, blankets and other necessaries. Whitman's old mill was restored and operating, James Waters had been elected to succeed Gilliam. Learning of this, the courteous Lee handed in his commission and volunteered to serve as second-in-command. A concession which made little difference, for the war was over. The weight of Nez Percé disapproval had crushed Cayuse spirits. The murderers were fled to the depths of the Snake country; other chiefs came in almost daily to plead for peace. The fighting was at an end.

A flying column was sent north to bring down the Walkers and Eells, who had taken refuge at Fort Colvile. Nesmith's company visited Lapwai to gather up such of the Spaldings' possessions as could be found. About sixty men volunteered to summer at Fort Waters, and another fifteen at Fort Lee, so as to provide protection for the settlers who would be rolling in from the other side of the continent. Everyone else was back in the Willamette Valley by mid-July when Governor Abernathy announced, on the advice of his new superintendent of Indian affairs, Henry A. G. Lee, that the Cayuse title was extinguished, and the tribal lands forfeit and henceforth open to white settlers.

The loan commissioners and commissary agents had raised, between them, approximately $30,000, less than 10 percent of it in cash. Soldiers were issued scrip. By 1854 the U.S. Congress had appropriated $150,000 to retire all major claims, though some individual claimants had to wait half a century for reimbursement. There is evidence of minor peculation and profiteering. (Flour shipped to the army from the governor's own mills was found to contain a high percentage of shorts, even though the grain had been raised by public subscription.) The Cayuse affair was the Oregonians' first Indian war, and by and large it was an unprofitable undertaking.

⚹ IV ⚹

On April 3, 1848, the Reverend Elkanah Walker sat down to write a cautionary letter to the Reverend David Greene, corresponding secretary of the American Board of Commissioners for Foreign Missions. He would not, Walker said, touch largely upon the horrid murders at the Whitmans' station, nor the treatment of women captives. Others better informed on these distressing matters would doubtless send the board more accurate information than was available to Walker himself. He wanted only to warn that great discretion should be used before giving publicity to some of the statements which might reach New York. "For," he said, "there is no reason to believe the Indians were prompted to commit the deed by anyone."[9]

He was writing from Fort Colvile. He, his family and the Eells had accepted the protection of Chief Factor John Lee Lewes. But the missionaries — Eells in particular — regularly visited Tshimakain to attend their crops and livestock. The senior Spokane chiefs had given them assurances that any Cayuse raiding party bent on massacre would be turned back, but the Indians were troubled and confused, and their tempers uncertain. Walker was himself depressed by the dangers closing in on him, yet he was anxious to keep the record straight. He had heard it reported from the Willamette Valley that Henry Harmon Spalding was not considered wholly sane. And while he hoped accounts of Mr. Spalding's conduct were much exaggerated, still he was aware that Spalding was easily excited, and apt to see things in a very strange light. Elkanah Walker had no affection for the priests. But he would not have them blamed for the bloody work at Waiilatpu.

Spalding, courtesy of Peter Ogden, had reached the safety of Oregon City January 10, and immediately set up a thunderous denunciation. The Roman Catholic hierarchy and The Bay were joined in monstrous conspiracy. Jesuits had incited the Cayuse to murder — for

Spalding, as for Lyman Beecher, his mentor at Lane Seminary, all
Catholic religious were Jesuits — and the massacre was the first dreadful fruit of a plot to destroy or drive out every Protestant American in
the territory. A great number of those who heard this flummery had
been preconditioned to anti-Catholicism by the nativist agitation which
had convulsed the States for two generations, and their perceptions
were further inflamed by fever generated by the war. Volunteers gathering to march up the Columbia swore they would shoot priests first
and Indians after. Archbishop Blanchet feared his schools and
churches in the Willamette Valley would be torched. The Reverend
Henry Spalding had found his calling.

He was momentarily embarrassed when, on January 20, the *Spectator*
printed all correspondence related to the incident at Waiilatpu and the
rescue of the survivors, including his own abject plea to the bishop of
Walla Walla. Governor Abernethy had tried hard to suppress Spalding's letter, but Ogden, who was making the papers available, would
not hear of it. Spalding himself considered publication one more example of priestly duplicity and dashed off an explanation which he
submitted to the paper. Young Curry had just been removed from the
editor's chair for insubordination, and attorney Aaron Wait had replaced him. Wait was confronted with his first major editorial decision,
and, mindful of his predecessor's fate, doubtless discussed the matter
with the governor before refusing Spalding's offering as being unduly
sectarian.

Abernethy was, in fact, willing enough that Henry Spalding have a
forum and even to contribute to its construction, so long as he could
avoid any appearance of connection with the concern. The arrangements took a little time. The American Board mission had acquired a
press for use in printing primers, hymnals and translations from the
Gospel in Salish and Sahaptin. At the time of the massacre the press
had been removed to Wascopum. Spalding acquired it, set it up at East
Tualatin Plains (now Hillsboro) in the home of John Smith Griffin and
used it to bring out the *Oregon American and Evangelical Union*. Griffin
was editor and publisher. Spalding, though he was careful to conceal
the fact, was owner. George Abernethy, even more careful than Spalding, put up the money.

The Reverend Mr. Griffin was the "self-supporting" Congregational
minister of whom Lieutenant Wilkes had formed so low an opinion
when he found him sponging off John McLoughlin's hospitality at Fort

Vancouver in 1841. Griffin's talents were slender. But he was gratifyingly free of principle, a dedicated xenophobe and better educated in rules of grammar than most of his Oregon contemporaries. The *Oregon American*'s salutatory is dated June 7, 1848, and carries Henry Spalding's apologia for his appeal to Bishop Blanchet:

> It has been said by some of my friends, in this country that they felt greatly mortified to see me in the dust, at the Bishop's feet, begging my life. A moment's review of history will show that not a strange thing has happened. This is not the first time that protestants (i.e. Heretics) have laid prostrate at the feet of the Pope of Rome. I saw my life, under God, in the hands of the Bishop and the priests. I had the right to ask it again. I seem to see the hands of these priests wet with the blood of my murdered associates, communicated by the hands of the murderers, as they stepped forward with bloody tomahawk in one hand, and delivered their children for the sacred ordinance of baptism . . . I saw the Bishop and his followers moving at pleasure through the country, and residing among the murderers unmolested . . . The Indians had declared that the protestants be murdered, but the Catholics spared. Was it unChristian to ask my life at their hands?[10]

As Elkanah Walker wrote David Greene, there were those who did not think Henry Spalding sane. It is a charitable view, and one which history has largely accepted. Consider Spalding's vicious description (to be repeated down the years) of Father Brouillet, who had saved Henry's life at the risk of his own. Consider the wild attack on Bishop Blanchet who had struggled, in dangerous circumstances, to achieve the settlement for which Henry Spalding begged in his letter. Each seems the product of a disordered mind. But Spalding unwittingly revealed himself. Shortly after the first appearance of the *Oregon American* he wrote Alvan Waller, lately the adversary of Francis Norbert Blanchet, a letter urging Waller to support the new paper: "While the public mind is awake to know the history of the Massacre & the *probable causes* [italics supplied] that led to it may we not with great advantage throw before them the thrilling fact of the subject of Romanism . . . Our beginning is small but we may be able to do better in a few years."[11] This is too cool for madness. Spalding's motivations were as calculating as Beecher's, the Morses' or a variety of like-minded zealots. When Eliza died in 1851, Henry caused to be carved on her gravestone "She always felt that the Jesuit Missionaries were the leading cause of the massacre."[12]

For the remainder of his long life (he died in 1874), Spalding warred upon the Catholics. But his greatest opportunity to score a permanent advantage was spoiled by inconstant fortune. Shortly before its adjournment the legislature of 1847–48 passed an act interdicting sale of powder to all Indians within the territory. James Douglas thought the measure iniquitous. Indians unable to conduct their regular hunts would turn to preying on settlers' cattle. Father Joseph Joset, superior of the Jesuit missions to the Flatheads, Coeur d'Alenes and related tribes north of the Oregon boundary, made a long journey to the Willamette to plead that the peaceful mountain tribes be exempted from the interdiction. Anticipating the next legislature would so amend the statute (it did, but not until 1849), and aware the prohibition was against sale or distribution, not transport, Joset ordered a ton of gunpowder to be sent from Fort Vancouver, enough to supply his Indians and missionaries for the next two years. Lieutenant Alexander Rodgers, commanding at Fort Lee, intercepted the shipment because he was told it was intended for delivery to the Cayuse, who would use it to reopen the war. Joset acquiesced in the confiscation, having little choice, though he wrote mildly that he had broken no law. The powder was quietly returned to The Bay, and the Jesuits' account duly credited. But Spalding was just then publishing his "history" of the Whitman massacre in the *Oregon American,* using language so violent that numbers of his ministerial colleagues, Elkanah Walker among them, raised worried objections, and a petition was being circulated to drive the priests out of the territory. There could well have been violence had not word come from California that James Marshall and Charles Bennet, both former Oregonians, while building a sawmill for Captain Sutter on the American River, had found gold nuggets in the millrace.

On August 7 the small schooner *Honolulu,* Newell commanding, reached the Willamette and skipper Newell began quietly to buy up spades, picks and every kind of digging tool. He was still in the river when Dr. Tolmie wrote James Douglas that a British frigate had arrived at Fort Nisqually with news of the gold strike near Sutter's Fort.

The Reverend Mr. George H. Atkinson was a young Congregationalist minister and had been in Oregon only two months. Already he had found a great deal he thought astonishing but the excitement which now boiled up simply bewildered him. Mechanics, loafers, farmers and merchants were preparing to leave for California or had already left. "Men from the sanctifying influence of the camp meeting, from the communion table, from the bosom of their families are leaving every comfort . . . with no provisions but flour to obtain gold. They go in thousands and leave good business, sacrifice property, pay high for goods, venture health, all for gold. Boys go . . . the elder of our ch[urc]h goes, also all our physicians . . ."[13] The good reverend was not exaggerating. Peter Burnett estimated that at least two-thirds of the male population of Oregon started for the goldfields in the summer and fall of 1848. The *Spectator,* the *Oregon American* and George Curry's little independent sheet, the *Free Press,* all were forced to suspend for want of printers. When the legislature was called in December, there were not members enough present to make a quorum.

❧ 9 ❧

A Festival of
Sons of Bitches

1849-1853

O N M A Y 4, 1849, Joe Meek, George Ebbert and what remained of
their party rode into St. Joe, Missouri, two months to the day out
of Waiilatpu. It was an astonishing effort. Snow had drifted to eight
feet in the Blues. Indians suffering from measles infected one of the
party. The rest slung him on a mule and went on, being unable to
spend time nursing. General Palmer had given them such supplies as
were available, mostly flour and jerked beef, but food was already
running low. McLoughlin furnished Meek an order against his own
account to be presented at Fort Hall, but when they reached that place
Captain Grant was absent and no one had the authority to issue provisions, so they went on empty-handed. Old Joe was reduced to stewing
a pair of polecats. A few days later a horse gave out. Meek and Ebbert
butchered it but the rest were at first too finicky to subsist on horsemeat. Hunger shortly cured them.

By the time the party reached the valley of the Bear even the last of
the horsemeat was gone. At the edge of desperation they ran upon the
camp of an old compadre, "Peg-leg" Smith, who, with a few French-
men for *vaqueros,* had given up the mountain trade to go to herding
cattle. Smith boiled a kettle of coffee, filled his friends with food and
killed beef so that they would have plenty of jerky to take on their way.
They stayed two days to smoke meat and allow their animals to forage.
At Jim Bridger's post they spent two days more and exchanged jaded
horses for fresh mounts. The rest of the way it was mostly routine:
night travel because the Sioux were up, a bloodless argument with

rapacious Pawnees, near starvation a good part of the time after they got east of the buffalo. Once they were reduced to boiling up their *parfleches*, the stretched, hairless buffalo-hide pouches in which Indians and mountain men stored their carriables. These, said Ebbert, being greasy from much use, made a very good meal.

Only Meek, Ebbert and Jacob Leabo — a patriot whom history has overlooked — went on to the national capital. If his story is to be believed, and there is presumably some truth in it, old Joe, by grandly announcing himself envoy extraordinary and minister plenipotentiary from the Republic of Oregon to the court of the United States, traveled the whole way from St. Joe as a guest of steamboatmen, coach lines and railroads. How Ebbert and Leabo fared is uncertain, but Meek arrived in Washington May 25, just two weeks after Judge Thornton, who had left Oregon five months before Joe and his party rode away from Waiilatpu.

Antebellum Americans preferred nonchalance to sophistication, which most of them suspected was something foreign and probably effete. Coincidences did not impress them. It was not thought remarkable that Senator Clay of Kentucky, the peerless leader of the Whigs, was connected by marriage to Senator Benton of Missouri, Grand Cham of the Western Democrats. Or that Mr. Meek of Oregon was cousin on his mother's side to Mrs. Sarah Childress Polk, wife of the President; or that Meek and C. Knox Walker, Mr. Polk's private secretary, were shirttail relations. Old Joe was one of the family. And if the reception was not quite so effusive as he afterward remembered — in his diary, the President always refers to Meek in formal terms — the entrée was unquestionably valuable. J. Quinn Thornton might consult pompously and at deadly length with Tom Benton or Senator Stephen A. Douglas of Illinois. Joe Meek had the ear and eye of James K. Polk, who had dared a war with Britain to get a settlement of the Oregon boundary and now was prepared to dare a war with John C. Calhoun to get Oregon organized as a territory. When Meek arrived, the President went carefully through the documents, official and unofficial, sent to him from the Willamette. Among them was one designed to explode the anxious expectations of Thornton, Abernathy and the Methodistic brethren.

More than one member of the provisional legislature had been chagrined to learn that Judge Thornton had slipped off to the States. Nesmith was incensed. Once the standard appeal to Congress had been voted, and Meek chosen to deliver it, Nes offered a second resolution intended to accompany the first, charging that Thornton's sole purpose in visiting Washington was to secure patronage for himself and his designing friends. This effort failed of passage, chiefly because Doc Newell, no close associate of Abernethy nor profound admirer of J. Quinn Thornton, argued that political bickering was unseemly when crisis threatened. But Young Curry was prevailed upon to defy his employers and publish the assembly proceedings in the *Spectator,* copies of which were given Meek to furnish to the President and circulate among the influential. Nes's maneuver succeeded, though at the cost of Curry's editorship and only with timely help from Thornton himself.

The previous January Stephen Douglas had introduced an Oregon territorial bill. It was not brought before the Senate until May and was argued over for three months, Calhoun and his Southern Democrats objecting to any reservation against the introduction of slaves into the territory. Meek whiled away the long summer entertaining Washington society with improbable yarns and raffish antics. Judge Thornton, quite innocently, became involved in intrigue, and with characteristic ineptitude managed matters to his own detriment.

The Hudson's Bay Company was desirous of selling its posts south of the Oregon boundary. The United States government was anxious to buy them. Early in 1848 Sir George Simpson visited Washington to help push along the deal. At the capital he was approached by George M. Sanders, part-time journalist, full-time manipulator. Simpson had written his superiors he considered $500,000 a generous price for the various properties. George Sanders suggested The Bay ask for $1 million, the remaining $500,000 to go to Sanders for greasing the deal. In March Sanders went to London where he made final arrangements; the Honourable Company would accept $480,000 in U.S. bonds, Sanders to receive 2.5 percent of that amount plus everything above it he could get from the American government.

While Congress was debating its way through the summer, Knox Walker brought Sanders to Thornton's lodgings in Washington, introduced the two and departed. Sanders, according to the judge's account, then offered Thornton a bribe to write letters to two members of the President's cabinet, declaring the $1 million valuation reasonable. The bribe, wrote Thornton after, was $25,000, and he threatened to kick Sanders downstairs; both statements doubtless exaggerations to magnify his own rectitude. Mr. Sanders departed on his own motion and J. Quinn Thornton promptly sent a hot account of the incident to President Polk.

The President found the communication offensive. Young Walker, whom Thornton sought to implicate, was not only Polk's private secretary, but also Mrs. Polk's first cousin, and the worst which could be demonstrated against him was that he had acted indiscreetly. The judge was asked to withdraw the letter. He refused. Instead he wrote the New York *Herald,* under the name "Achille de Harvey," charging corruption in high places. And made an enemy of James K. Polk, the man upon whom he was depending for appointment.

By mid-August the Oregon territorial bill had worked through both houses of Congress. Polk signed it August 14, and promptly appointed Meek U.S. marshal for the new territory. The President's choice for territorial governor was General James Shields, who once challenged Lincoln to a duel. When Shields declined, Polk appointed General Joseph Lane of Indiana.

Congress appropriated $10,000 to pay Meek for his services as messenger and his expenses while at the capital, buy gifts to reward those tribes which kept the peace, and be otherwise disbursed at the President's discretion. Meek, whose documents were in order, was paid without quibble. But when J. Quinn Thornton asked reimbursement for travel and lodging, Mr. Polk raised difficulties. The judge, so far as the record showed, was in Washington as a private citizen and had no proper claim against the government. The unhappy Thornton appealed to Douglas. Was the senator prepared, asked the President slyly, to affirm of his own knowledge that Thornton was a duly authorized representative of the Oregon Provisional Government? Douglas, who had no such knowledge, did so affirm. Judge Thornton was allowed $2750 and James K. Polk, harkening back to Nesmith's resolution, took satisfaction in knowing Stephen A. Douglas was capable of a serviceable lie.

⚶ II ⚶

Joseph Lane was born in Buncombe County, North Carolina, but grew up in Kentucky. As a boy he clerked in John J. Audubon's general

store at Henderson. Married at nineteen, young Lane moved to southern Indiana where he farmed, ran keel boats on the Ohio, and served
twenty-four years as a Democratic member of the Indiana legislature.
He had little schooling but managed to pick up as much education as a
clever man could in a busy life. When war with Mexico broke out he
was forty-five, the moderately prosperous father of a sizable and still
growing family. Though he ranked as captain in the state militia, he
enlisted as a private, depending upon oratory and connections for
advancement. He was not disappointed. At the mobilization point his
neighbors elected him regimental colonel. Shortly afterward Mr. Polk,
upon the advice of Robert Dale Owen, then an Indiana congressman,
appointed Colonel Lane brigadier general of the Hoosier volunteers.

Lieutenant Colonel Ethan Allen Hitchcock was a West Pointer with
thirty years' service in Florida and along the frontier, and he had a
professional soldier's distrust of volunteers. But his appraisal of the
Indiana brigadier (written after the war) was respectful. Lane was,
Hitchcock said, a fair example of a Western man: Commonsensical,
good-hearted, pushing and ambitious. This was a generous assessment,
for Lane's war record was marred by two acts of outrageous conduct,
one unmilitary, the other unthinkable.

The Hoosier brigadier fought acceptably at Buena Vista, displaying
exemplary courage under fire and taking a ball through one shoulder.
But two days before that battle he got into a fistfight with one of his
own colonels, the irascible and erratic James H. Lane, in full view of Jo
Lane's 3rd Indiana Regiment. After the two were separated the general stalked off to his tent, picked up a rifle and grimly announced his
intention of killing the colonel. He was dissuaded, though with difficulty, from doing just that. Zachary Taylor disciplined neither officer,
but he removed the 3rd Indiana from Jo Lane's direct command.

During the late summer of 1847 General Lane was transferred to
central Mexico and attached to the forces of General Winfield Scott.
At Huamantla Lane surprised and routed a slightly larger army personally led by General Antonio López de Santa Anna, and shortly after
relieved an American garrison besieged at Puebla. But following the
splendid victory at Huamantla Jo Lane turned his troops loose on the
town because his cavalry commander, Major Sam Walker, had allegedly been killed by a civilian sniper during a Mexican counterattack.
The sack of Huamantla — an awesome orgy of rape, murder, desecra-

tion, destruction and drunkenness — was the ultimate atrocity of a war made hideous by atrocities.

Santa Anna's defeat and subsequent removal as general-in-chief of the Mexican Army did not end the war. From Vera Cruz to the central plateau partisan bands and small troops of regulars continued to harass the American occupation forces. General Lane was given command of a few hundred well-mounted men and ordered to pacify the country. It was service for which he was admirably suited. In a series of lightning strikes — miniature campaigns even the normally critical Hitchcock thought remarkable — his hard-riding, hard-fighting troopers cleaned out almost every major pocket of resistance. His exploits won him the rank of brevet major general. The American press, harking back to the celebrated Swamp Fox of the Revolution, christened him "Marion of the Mexican War." His tour of duty ended, the general returned to Indiana very early in August, 1848, with a national reputation, presidential aspirations, and no wish to return to the prosaics of farm life. He was delighted to accept the governorship of Oregon Territory. Oregon was on the far side of the continent, but as governor Lane would control federal patronage and patronage was a necessary lever to a politician bent on advancement. On August 27, when Marshal Meek arrived at the Lane home in Newburgh with the official gubernatorial commission, the general was already making preparations for his leave-taking. Three days later, after embracing his infinitely patient wife, Polly, and saying good-by to nine of his ten children (twenty-four-year old Nat, the eldest son, was going along), Jo Lane and entourage boarded the steamboat for St. Louis.

⚜ III ⚜

They departed Fort Leavenworth September 10: the Lanes, the marshal, twenty-five mounted riflemen under Lieutenant George Hawkins, a military surgeon, teamsters, cooks and roustabouts, fifty-five men and gear enough to fill ten wagons. It was too late in the season to attempt the Platte River–South Pass route, so they rode south. At Santa Fé the grass ran out, making it necessary to abandon the wagons and pack everything on mules, which could find forage where horses and oxen could not. Matters went routinely until the party crossed over into New Mexico. Near Tucson two troopers deserted, and shot down two others sent to bring them back. Thereafter the country tested the company with bitter severity. The armies lately marching to and from California had swept the trail clean of game and ground cover. Cook's Wells, a major watering hole, was polluted by the rotted carcass of a mule. The general dipped a kettle in the tainted pool and boiled up coffee enough to go around, remarking that maggots were more palatable cooked than raw. Not everyone shared his wry stoicism. Both soldiers and civilians, unable to endure the hardships, slipped away along the march. Food supplies ran low. For a week they subsisted on beans. So many animals died of starvation, thirst and exhaustion that even the governor was reduced to walking, there being only mules enough to carry the luggage and equipment. Of the fifty-five men who left Fort Leavenworth nearly six months earlier, fewer then fifteen reached San Pedro.

A government vessel carried them to San Francisco, where they debarked early in February, 1849, ahead of the rush of gold hunters from the East and South. Meek was astonished to find the village crowded by over two hundred Oregonians, many with smiles and long pockets, waiting to get passage home. Thousands more were still working streams and ledges all over northern California. When Nat Lane developed gold fever, the marshal outfitted the young man and two or three others, in return for half the profits. Meek's share, when Nat delivered it that summer, came to three pickle jars of dust, about enough to cover the original investment.

A federal sloop of war was in the harbor and the marshal, who enjoyed his perquisites, suggested it be commandeered to carry the territorial officials north. Lane would not hear of it. He and Meek would go as common passengers aboard the brig *Janet,* at a cost of $100 each for miserably cramped accommodations on an overcrowded vessel which would, in eighteen days, take them no farther than Astoria. But there was, for the general at least, a compensation. Nesmith was also aboard, having "seen the elephant" and added a little to his means. Full, as always, of irreverent ribaldry and unsolicited advice, and anxious to instruct Jo Lane in the intricacies of Oregon politics.

The governor and his official party reached Oregon City toward evening, March 2, having traveled from Astoria by canoe, the governor taking his turn at paddling. That same night he wrote a proclamation announcing organization of the Oregon Territory, and Young Curry ran it off on the wooden press on which he had printed his ephemeral newspaper. There was an inaugural ball at William Holmes's spacious residence on the city's outskirts, at which Lane charmed the ladies with his homespun gentility and lightness of foot, and the gentlemen with his robust and forthright manner. On March 3, 1849 — James Polk's last full day in the presidential chair — Oregonians were at last granted that which they had so long sought: the United States government had extended over them its laws, and, in the persons of Lieutenant Hawkins and his eight remaining riflemen, its protection.

Having duly installed himself, the general buckled down to business. The area he was called to govern was rather larger than Texas. Apart from Indians and Kanakas, who did not count and were not counted, it was peopled by 298 foreigners and 8785 Americans, 2509 of the latter being males of legal age and qualified to vote. (One of Marshal Meek's first duties was to conduct a hurried census.) Though there was a steady trickle back from California, roughly four thousand still remained at the mines. Most of those returning brought at least a little dust to show for their pains; a few brought a great deal. Credit was immeasurably eased. California was becoming a demanding market for Oregon grain, produce, lumber and salmon. Until 1848 it was a rare year when eight vessels entered the Columbia. In 1849 there were fifty arrivals. At one time twenty vessels lay at anchor awaiting cargo, chiefly at Portland, now recognized to be the head of navigation. The territory should have been prospering, but was not. Most of the ships which beat their way to Oregon had come 'round the Horn to take advantage of the lucrative Pacific trade, off-loaded their merchandise at San Francisco and sailed north under ballast or with a few items so shoddy they could not be moved even in California. Necessary staples such as salt and saleratus were unavailable or outrageously expensive. But it was disparities in the price of gold which caused the greatest economic turmoil. In California it sold at an agreed $16 per ounce, in Oregon for as little as $7, so that much of the dust brought home by Oregonians was bought up for resale in San Francisco.

The last provisional legislature, meeting in February, attacked this problem by fixing gold at $16.50 the ounce and mandating establishment of a mint. Lane ruled against his government's participation on constitutional grounds, but raised no objections to formation of a private concern, the Oregon Exchange Company, which struck off $58,500 in $5 and $10 pieces, each bearing a crude representation of a beaver. Because the coins were made of unalloyed metal to insure currency, each was worth about 10 percent more than its face value, so that "beaver money" gradually disappeared from circulation. Specimens are today so rare as to be almost unobtainable.

Mr. Polk's other appointees were drifting in. Territorial Secretary Kintzing Pritchette appeared in April. So did William P. Bryant, chief justice of the territorial supreme court. Pritchette was a Pennsylvania lawyer dredged momentarily from obscurity. Bryant was an Indianian, a Whig turned Democrat, and purchasable. Peter Burnett, designated associate justice, had removed permanently to California and would shortly be first governor of that state. The other associate justice, Oliver C. Pratt, had somehow managed to reach Oregon City almost two months in advance of Meek and the governor, bringing the people first word that the Oregon bill was law and he had been selected to sit in judgment among them. Suave, sleek, swollen with self-esteem, incurably covetous, Pratt was slippery as a greased eel. Corners of his career are shadowed by little mysteries intended to conceal indecorous truths. One unexpected appointee was J. Quinn Thornton, who arrived carrying commissions for himself and Doc Newell as Indian subagents. Newell was perfectly acceptable; Thornton was not. He was neither experienced nor forceful enough to deal with native diplomats, each one of whom could smell the sweat of irresolution. Too fastidious to scuffle, too sensible to duel, he was not a man to Lane's liking. Moreover he was Nesmith's particular enemy — Nes and the governor being already on confidential terms — and had been chosen as a courtesy to Stephen A. Douglas, who strongly urged him for the judgeship which went to Pratt. Douglas and the general were already acknowledged rivals for the Democratic presidential nomination in 1852. In Jo Lane's view, J. Quinn Thornton was an embarrassment arrived inopportunely.

Using Meek's census as a basis for apportionment, Lane fixed June 6 for the election of members of the territorial assembly and council, and a congressional delegate. Until that time the newly installed bureaucracy served the public need. The general put aside his gubernatorial role and set out on a tour of inspection as superintendent of Indian affairs.

He had been appointed to both offices, and they were distinct. As

governor he was responsible to the secretary of state; as superintendent, to the secretary of war. He collected two salaries, each $1500 per
annum, which helped lighten his double burden. He was glad enough
to get away, greatly preferring Indian parleys to sitting behind a desk.
Setting out up the Columbia in April, he patched together a peace
between the Yakimas and Walla Wallas, distributed minor bribes in
return for promises that the immigrants that year would be allowed to
pass unmolested, and warned the Cayuse that the Whitman murderers
must be given up. It was as much as he could do without troops to
force compliance.

May brought unexpected trouble. A band of Snoqualmies stormed
The Bay's Fort Nisqually in an attempt to seize ammunition with which
to drive all whites from the lower reaches of Puget Sound. The attack
failed but one American, Leander Wallace, was caught and killed outside the gates, and another wounded. The settlers, about a dozen families of them, built two blockhouses, forted up and sent urgent word to
the general, asking his assistance. Lane was already marching north
with Lieutenant Hawkins and his five remaining riflemen (three had
absconded for the mines) when a dispatch announced the arrival of
the U.S.S. *Massachusetts* in the Columbia, bringing Brevet Major James
Hathaway and two companies of artillery.

Hathaway had stationed a company under Captain B. H. Hill at
Astoria, and brought the other to Vancouver, where he was bivouacked
behind the fort. The governor ordered Hill to Puget Sound to establish
a post (Fort Steilacoom) which would command Nisqually Plains. And
he wrote asking that the Snoqualmies be advised that troops were on
the way and those responsible for Wallace's death must be brought to
justice. The *Massachusetts* having proceeded to Portland, however, to
ship lumber for barracks in California, nothing could be done until
other transport for Hill's command was found.

Meanwhile June had arrived, and with it elections. The race for
delegates excited the greatest interest. A territorial delegate had no
vote but he could address the country from the floor of the House of
Representatives and attend committee meetings considering territorial
affairs. The Reverend John Smith Griffin thought himself eminently
qualified and, running on a nativist no-popery ticket, picked up eight
votes, including his own. Nesmith also ran, presumably with Lane's
blessing, though the governor publicly expressed no preference. The
two principal candidates were relatively late arrivals in Oregon; Judge

Columbia Lancaster and Samuel Royal Thurston both crossed the continent in 1847.

Lancaster was a native of Connecticut, one of the founders of Centerville, Michigan, and president and organizer of that community's first bank — which failed before opening its doors, to the chagrin of the shareholders. Sam Thurston was out of Maine, attended Dartmouth, graduated from Bowdoin. He practiced a little law and a little religion in Iowa, taking care the one did not interfere with the other. Having engaged to defend two rogues charged with counterfeiting, he and his law partner sat down to divide their clients' assets which they arranged in two piles, one consisting of $160 in hard cash, the other of a shotgun and $280 in queer money. Given his choice, Thurston took the bogus bills, and passed every one of them.

Lancaster was a Whig and Thurston a Democrat, which made little difference, neither party having an organization in the territory. What did make a difference was that Thurston had attended a Wesleyan seminary, was a Methodist exhorter and as fervent a nativist as Griffin, though infinitely more effective. All of these qualifications would have secured him support of the mission party even had Thurston not already given Abernethy secret assurances to further Methodist interests should he be elected. It was a compact, John Randolph might have said, between Blifil and blackleg; for Thurston, despite his church connections, was violent, unprincipled and in the habit of abusing his opponents in terms so rank as to put them out of countenance, and astonish even those of his partisans learned in the scatological and profane.

Dr. McLoughlin voted in the election, he having filed notice of intent to become an American citizen with Chief Justice Bryant's court just a week earlier. Thurston sardonically solicited the doctor's support. He didn't receive it, which made little difference. Only about 30 percent of the eligible voters went to the polls. This advantaged the Methodists, who came closest to being an organized party, and Sam Thurston won a narrow majority.

It was July before Captain Hill chartered the British bark *Harpooner* to transfer his men, guns and military baggage from Astoria to Steilacoom. Judge Thornton visited Puget Sound that same month as Indian subagent for the country north of the Columbia, to inquire into the recent Snoqualmie uprising. Lane instructed the judge to take a firm position, using the presence of Hill's artillerymen to awe the recalcitrant into submission. Instead Thornton offered the Snoqualmies close to $500 in Hudson's Bay blankets, a bribe whch so delighted the tribal council it offered to surrender six braves allegedly involved in the fracas at Fort Nisqually. (Thornton also ordered the arrest of the *Harpooner*'s Captain Morris for distributing the customary tot of rum to the Indians and part-Indians who unloaded the vessel at Steilacoom.) The governor was much incensed both by the flagrant disregard of his orders and the preposterous generosity of the gift, and determined to rid himself of J. Quinn Thornton. As superintendent of Indian affairs he made it a condition of employment that each subagent reside within the district assigned him. Thornton, unwilling to leave the comparative comforts of the Willamette Valley for the dangerous and near-deserted expanses of upper Oregon, resigned, writing pseudonymously to Horace Greeley's New York *Tribune* that while General Lane might be brave enough to fight he was not wise enough to rule, having thrown himself into the hands of men of low character and intemperate habits. Meaning, presumably, Nesmith.

The legislators convened in mid-July in a nationalistic mood and busied themselves renaming counties. Vancouver was once again Clark. Tuality became Washington. Champooick was henceforth Marion (honoring both the Revolution's Swamp Fox and his Mexican War reincarnation). A minor problem was got round. In a May proclamation establishing the federal courts, Lane had divided the territory into three judicial districts. The first district, bounded on the west by the Willamette and the north by the Columbia, was assigned to Bryant. The second district, consisting of the counties west of the Willamette and south of the Columbia, was Pratt's. But the third district, which included Lewis and Clark counties, both of them north of the Columbia, was not only without judge and court but was also the scene of the territory's most important case, the criminal trial of those allegedly involved in the shoot-out at Fort Nisqually.

So legislation was passed extending Justice Bryant's jurisdiction to Lewis County, to which he proceeded in September, taking with him a whole retinue of court officials, attorneys and even jurors. Two of the accused were convicted and hanged. The remainder were acquitted. Judge Bryant informed the governor of the outcome of the trial October 10, and shortly departed. The territory would see no more of him. Abetted by Sam Thurston he would contrive to draw his salary until January 1, 1851, but his whole time was spent in Indiana and Washington helping Delegate Thurston push an egregious swindle through Congress.

To his everlasting dishonor, Jo Lane was party to this massive thimblerig. The plot was concocted by George Abernethy to accomplish the undoing of John McLoughlin, and even in outline its workings are unclear. On April 29, 1849, George and William Abernethy, father and son, deeded Abernethy Island to the governor. This was the island the Methodists had seized and upon which they had built sawmills and gristmills in defiance of McLoughlin's claim of prior occupancy and improvement. A month later the Abernethys sold the same island and the sawmill to Chief Justice Bryant for a reported $35,000, a sum so far beyond the judge's available means it must be assumed that only a small part was rendered in cash and the remainder in what lawyers call "other valuable consideration." Bryant knew the Abernethys' claim to the island was contested, and was equally aware that McLoughlin could regain title only by a lawsuit brought in his, Bryant's, court. Shortly before leaving for the States the judge sold three-quarters of his interest to the governor and Nat Lane for $20,000 down and a $30,000 mortgage on Lane's Indiana farm. How Lane acquired $20,000 is unknown but he might very well have borrowed it from George Abernethy, giving in return a lien on the property, for it was to Abernethy that title eventually reverted.

The general was sanguine about his investment, writing Nesmith that he had entire control of a fortune, but that same winter floods destroyed or damaged almost every mill on the Willamette. Such of the Lanes' machinery as was not swept away was damaged, and stacked lumber simply floated off to the sea. By the time repairs were effected, and at ruinous cost, lumber prices in California had begun a precipitous slide. Not until late 1851, when he sold the family farm at Newburgh, Indiana, was Lane able to pay off Bryant's mortgage. But in the fall of 1849 the general's expectations were undiminished, which was as well. He had more immediate problems. The Oregon Rifle Regiment, or what remained of it, arrived at Oregon City under command of Brevet Colonel William Wing Loring.

When the regiment tramped out of Fort Leavenworth the previous May 10 it consisted of six hundred enlisted men and thirty-one officers, most of the enlisted men being raw recruits. It was escorting 160 wagons, had nearly 2000 horses and mules and was accompanied by the necessary complement of civilian teamsters, train agents, artisans and guides, and even a few women and children. The march was badly handled. Loring had begun his military career in the Seminole campaign and would end it as a general of division under the khedive of Egypt. He was demonstrably brave — he lost an arm leading the assault on Chapultapec Castle — but lacked certain qualities of command. His green troops resisted discipline, neglected sanitary precautions, sickened of the cholera, dysentery and heat fatigue and generally fared worse than most of the civilians who had been following the same trail for half-a-dozen years. Two of them, one a sergeant, plotted to kill the paymaster and rob the payroll wagon. They enlisted the help of Matt Deady, a large, awkward redhead working his way to Oregon as a teamster and part-time smith. But Deady was an attorney by profession and a schoolmaster by trade, and having learned what he could of the conspiracy, warned Loring. It was almost the only time luck favored the colonel. Provisions ran low. A supply column commanded by Lieutenant Hathaway and guided by Joel Palmer was sent from the Willamette to Fort Hall but missed connections. It was mid-October when Loring reached the Willamette, having lost more than a fourth of his wagons, 15 percent of his animals, and at least seventy men to illness, accident or desertion. The survivors were wasted, sun-blackened, ragged and not a few of them shoeless.

The colonel quartered his regiment at Oregon City for the early part of the winter. They did not make themselves welcome, being addicted to brawling and drunkenness. In December Loring closed down all the town's liquor outlets, drawing applause from the teetotalers but sadly vexing the majority of the male citizenry. Oregonians, who for a decade had been demanding that troops be sent to protect them, were rapidly becoming disenchanted.

Early in January, 1850, the *Spectator* announced that President Taylor had appointed Major John Pollard Gaines, lately Whig congressman from Kentucky, as new governor of the Oregon Territory. General Lane had expected to be removed but was determined before leaving office to bring the Whitman murderers to trial. After conferring privately with Douglas and Ogden, who offered assistance, and with McLoughlin and Archbishop Blanchet, who expressed approval, Lane demanded of the Cayuse that five of the guilty be surrendered. When the Cayuse temporized, the general delivered a blunt ultimatum: the tribe must come to terms or it would be destroyed. This was conclusive. Bay officials undertook to arrange a meeting at The Dalles.

Before this could be done 120 members of Loring's regiment deserted to the mines. By keeping a semblance of military order and
moving in large detachments, they were able to convince settlers in the
Willamette Valley they were on some legitimate military errand, and
even bought supplies against government credit. Through the columns
of the *Spectator,* revived the previous October under the editorship of
Wilson Blain, a Presbyterian clergyman, Lane offered a reward of $30
for every rifleman captured and returned, then galloped south in pursuit of the fugitives. He caught up with the rear elements, about two-
thirds of the whole, in the Rogue River Valley. Seventy of them agreed
to return with him, less because of his threats or his oratory than
because they were without provisions and had not proper clothing to
protect them against the wet and cold. Colonel Loring subsequently
succeeding in bringing in seven more. The remainder presumably perished, it being too early in the year to safely attempt passage of the
Siskiyous.

By the time the governor returned to Oregon City it was the third
week in April. He set off almost immediately to meet with the Cayuse,
taking with him a small escort who would serve to guard the prisoners
once they were in custody. The gathering at The Dalles was a somber
one. The tribe had brought fifty horses to pay attorneys' fees. Of the
five warriors selected to stand trial only two, Tiloukaikt and Tamahas,
were beyond question involved in the massacre. The other three were
almost certainly innocent. It made little difference. The Cayuse people
were so reduced by disease, by war, by wandering, they could resist no
further. The Americans wanted five men to punish for the crime at
Whitman's. They received five. Tiloukaikt explained it as well as it
could be explained. Asked why he and the others agreed to give themselves up, he replied: "Did not your missionaries teach us that Christ
died to save his people? Thus die we, if we must, to save our people."[1]

Lane spent two nights with the tribe, explaining that the five would
have all of the advantages of American justice, be presumed innocent
unless proved otherwise and be tried just as any white man would be
tried. The third morning he took them into custody, telling them to
say their final farewells to their friends and families, whom he thought
they would not see again.

The trial opened at Oregon City on May 22, with Judge Pratt sitting,
by special legislation, as district judge of the first judicial district.

United States District Attorney Amory Holbrook, the first of President Taylor's appointees to reach the territory, conducted the prosecution. Territorial Secretary Kintzing Pritchette led for the defendants, with a pair of barracks lawyers, a paymaster and one of Loring's captains, for associates. The principal defense was that since the crime alleged had been committed before organization of the territory, the court lacked jurisdiction. Pratt disposed of this argument handily, and denied a motion for change of venue to Fort Vancouver. Because of difficulty in securing unbiased jurors the examination of witnesses did not begin until late the second day. All of the testimony was sordid, much of it repetitious, some of it contradictory. Evidence put in by the defense seldom addressed the charges. After being out for seventy-five minutes the jury brought in verdicts of guilty against all of the accused. Judge Pratt set the executions for June 3.

Jo Lane signed the death warrants and at the same time delivered to the provisional secretary his resignation as governor, to take effect June 18. He was leaving with his popularity gratifyingly high. Thornton's derogatory letter had crossed and recrossed the continent and had been printed in the *Spectator*. Meetings were organized throughout the Willamette Valley — including one at Lafayette presided over by Matthew P. Deady, the honest teamster — to express support for the general and denounce his traducer. In Polk County ninety men signed a supportive memorial. Oregonians stood behind their outgoing governor with astonishing unanimity. He was gaining a national reputation as well, having recently been named by Indiana Democrats their candidate for the next presidential nomination.

Lane had set ahead the effective date of his resignation because he hoped, on his way to California and the mines, to arrange a truce between the Klickatats and the Rogue Indians, who were feuding, and conclude a treaty between the United States and the Rogues which would put an end to the robbery and violence visited on whites traveling through southern Oregon. The Rogues' mistrust of whites was born of the senseless murders committed years earlier by the Young-Kelley party, and there was little chance they could be bound to long-term commitment. They came to the council place charged with murderous intent and raised the war cry in the midst of the parley. Lane awed them by making a hostage of their principal chief, damning their bluster and dismissing them for two days, like so many errant children. They came back promising to be good — for a while. And the principal chief, with the governor's permission, thereafter called himself Chief Jo.

At Oregon City a petition was got up asking that the convicted Cayuse be reprieved. Kintzing Pritchette, who was prepared to assume the robes of office before Lane's resignation was effective, consulted Marshal Meek. Meek took the matter to Pratt, who ruled Pritchette without authority to act, there being no evidence General Lane had left the territory. And so on June 3 the murderers, real and supposed, were hanged. On a multiple gibbet built almost next door to John McLoughlin's house. All of them had been accepted into the Catholic faith during their last days, and a young priest accompanied them to the gallows, much to the outrage of such professional bigots as Spalding and Gray. Most of the five died relatively quickly, but an onlooker reported that one danced fourteen minutes at his rope's end.

⚜ IV ⚜

Sam Thurston kept a diary. It opens November 21, 1849, when he left his father's house in Maine, where he briefly visited, to take up his congressional duties in Washington. It closes, abruptly and without explanation, August 29, 1850. It is a record of nine months' feverish endeavor. He was struggling against the current of events.

For nearly thirty years the Missouri Compromise held the nation together despite the internal stresses threatening to rupture it. After the Mexican War those stresses increased alarmingly. During 1849 and most of 1850 the North and South engaged in a great debate. Was the federal government constitutionally empowered to forbid the introduction of slavery into the newly acquired territories? And if so, would it be in the general interest to impose such a prohibition? The contest was bitter. Intransigent Southrons boldly advocated disunion; Northern radicals demanded immediate Abolition. Each represented a sectional minority but both were sounding trumpets which, just a decade hence, would call men to battle. At length the aging Henry Clay came downstage to work his magic one last time. It silenced the uproar, hurried the demolition of the Whig Party and so hastened the emergence of the Republicans, but it solved nothing. Like all magic, it was illusion.

Samuel Royal Thurston stalked warily through this windy drama. He opposed extension of slavery on purely economic grounds. He had no patience for Abolitionists nor ear for those who argued the immorality of human bondage. He expressed these views, but only infrequently and never stridently. He was positioned too perilously to indulge in acrimonious debate. A Democrat, he could expect little patronage from Zachary Taylor's Whig administration. As territorial delegate he was barely a cut above consultant. He could gain passage of the measures he supported only by consistent and deferential lobbying.

Thurston was arrogant, and the need to humble himself, however slightly, must have soured his soul, but his accomplishments were impressive, whether for good or ill. He wrote a bill vacating Indian title to all lands west of the Cascade Range and herded it carefully through both houses. He wheedled an appropriation of $73,500 to be applied against the Cayuse War claims. He wrestled, manfully but vainly, to improve Oregon's postal service, both within the territory and with the States. He answered numberless inquiries from potential emigrants. He publicized the territory in Northern and Western papers, though seldom in the South. He franked government documents, navigational charts, maps, newspapers and letters to his constituents, continually mending his political fences.

The Donation Land Law was Thurston's great achievement. It combined admirable generosity with outright theft. Each male settler then in the territory was allowed 320 acres. Each married couple could claim 640 acres, one-half of which was property of the wife. Two sections in each township were set aside for school support, two townships for the support of a university. Thurston tried hard to dispossess or disqualify the British and French Canadian settlers, but was defeated in the Senate. He had better luck voiding John McLoughlin's claim, though it cost him enormous effort.

On January 1, 1850, he offered a resolution directing the House Judiciary Committee to define the possessory rights of the Puget Sound Agricultural Company, the Hudson's Bay Company and British subjects generally under the terms of the boundary treaty of 1846. Here was a point of departure for sustained vilification of the "foreign" element in Oregon: the two companies and their employees, the colonists from Red River, the French Canadians, the Roman Catholics and

above all Dr. McLoughlin. It was not an elevating performance though
the scope and sweep of Sam Thurston's mendacity is quite astonishing.
He was able to make use of a letter sent him by Daniel Lownsdale, who
had bought out Pettygrove's half-interest in Portland — a letter Thurston had obviously solicited before leaving Oregon. Lownsdale quoted
freely from that precious pair, W. H. Gray and Henry Spalding, charging that the Whitman massacre was instigated by the priests and The
Bay, and that McLoughlin was still chief at Fort Vancouver.

Thurston wrote Wyeth for confirmation of his own allegations that
Wyeth's trapping and trading concern was driven to the wall by Dr.
McLoughlin's unscrupulous tactics, and when Wyeth replied that the
doctor was the soul of honor, suppressed the letter. Like all men engaged in large-scale duplicity, Sam Thurston suffered of inflamed
suspicions. He convinced himself McLoughlin had an agent in
Washington. When Indiana's Senator Jesse Bright asked if the doctor
had supported him, Thurston, for delegate, Thurston immediately
concluded that Jo Lane had written letters derogating him to Lane's
old friend Bright. Curiously enough, just three weeks earlier Lane had
sent a letter, still in transit, to Thurston himself, expressing assurance
the delegate would never take Abernethy Island from a good American and give it to a foreigner.

The land bill was introduced in April and passed out of the House
Committee on Territorial Affairs the same week, but in late August it
was still bogged down in the Senate's Committee on Public Lands. The
delay vexed Thurston, who blamed it on improper influence exerted
by The Bay, and he recalled Judge Bryant to Washington, where the
judge had earlier spent some days lobbying, to testify that John Mc-
Loughlin had never filed notice of intention to become a citizen of the
United States and had announced his determination never to do so.
Bryant was eager to perjure himself in furtherance of his own interest.
It was enough — despite the fact he had deserted his post, the judge
was still chief justice of the Oregon Territory — and the land law which
passed September 23 included the section (11) over which Sam Thurston had sweated heavily to pay his political debts to George Abernethy
and Abernethy's friends:

> What is known as the "Oregon City Claim" excepting Abernethy Is-
> land, which is hereby confirmed to the legal assigns of the Walamet
> milling and trading companies, shall be . . . at the disposal of the legisla-
> tive assembly . . . [for] establishment and endowment of a university . . .

Provided, however, that all lots and parts of lots in such claim, sold or granted by Dr. John McLoughlin previous to the fourth day of March, eighteen hundred and forty-nine, shall be confirmed to the purchaser or donee, or their assigns . . ."[2]

The spoliation of John McLoughlin was complete.

Close attention to official business did not prevent the delegate from making plans to further his own career. He was a young man (only thirty-four in 1850), his future was promising and there were no fetters on his ambition. Prophecy sometimes touched him. As he lay sleeping the night of July 4, 1850, he saw a vision. Workmen busily undermined the foundation of the Capitol until it split lengthwise, beginning with the dome, and one side fell away. He awoke much troubled, believing the dream foreshadowed dissolution of the Union.

He mentions no other dream nor any of his aspirations, though the latter certainly occupied his mind. The first two weeks of March, 1850, however, he was at Springfield, Massachusetts, negotiating with Henry Russell and A. W. Stockwell for publication of a new paper at Oregon City. The *Spectator* had generally supported Thurston — except during the election, when it maintained a spurious neutrality — but the *Spectator* was George Abernethy's organ. Sam Thurston wanted a sheet wholly subservient to his own interests.

Russell and Stockwell were printers and compositors only. Thurston wrote Wilson Blain suggesting that Blain might consider moving over from the *Spectator* to handle the editorial side of the new enterprise, but even before he could receive Blain's reply, he had settled on a far more suitable candidate — Asahel Bush, a neophyte Massachusetts attorney with an excellent grounding in practical journalism and just then editing a weekly at Westfield, not far from Chicopee.

Sam Thurston's diary is tastefully discreet. He makes no mention of the lies he told or the political flimflams he perpetrated. Little that is personal appears. But on June 30, 1850 there occurred an event so momentous he included it:

"Washed all over."[3]

❧ V ❧

In 1845 the American Baptist Home Mission Board sent the Reverends Ezra Fisher and Hezekiah Johnson to the Willamette Valley. The pastors and their families suffered much hardship during the months after their arrival. Their clothing was ragged and inadequate, some of the children went barefoot through the winter and Fisher and Johnson were forced to hire themselves out as common laborers to stave off want.

In June, 1850, Mr. Fisher was able to write the board that great changes had taken place in Oregon. Gold from the California mines — he had visited them himself with modest success — had increased the demand for every kind of commodity and enormously inflated prices. Even by the exercise of stringent economies he could not live on his yearly allowance of $200. He would continue to preach and engage in missionary work. But exigency required he accept an appointment, at $600 per annum, as schoolmaster of a school established at Oregon City by fellow Baptists.

He included a list of items to be shipped him from New York: shoes of good quality, ladies' wear (not omitting parasol and gaiters), yard goods, dessert spoons, and for himself a hat, dress coat, summer vest, two pairs of pantaloons and silver spectacles suitable to his age and station. "People are becoming more extravagant in dress," said he, "and we must be able to appear in all circles."[4] Later the same year he urged the need for additional ministers and teachers to serve new towns springing up. Society was becoming politer; urbanization had begun.

There were young communities scattered from the middle fork of the Willamette to Puget Sound, each loosely gathered around the mill or store, or both, of some backwoods entrepreneur. Places of miscellaneous appearance. No streets. Cabins tucked at random in the underbrush. An inn with groggery attached. Perhaps a log school or church. The merchant-miller, having run a metes and bounds survey and platted a few town blocks, was patron, proprietor and, if his politics were right, postmaster.

There were exceptions. Many improvements were already in place when the best part of the Methodist Salem claim slipped into Dr. Willson's artful clutches. And there were a few professional developers. In

1850 Vermonter Lot Whitcomb was feverishly building up the town of Milwaukie, erecting sawmills and flouring mills, warehouses, a store; operating a ferry across the Willamette; pouring out money he had made speculating in Chicago real estate and selling Oregon lumber into California when the price was ripest. Lot was a boomer.

Seven miles downriver, on the opposite bank of the Willamette, Portland was struggling to keep pace. Little Stump Town, the derisive called it, a village not yet emerged from the timber. Its single street ran from forest to forest, unpaved, ungraded, with potholes deep enough to drown a good-sized child during the long rainy season. The place was under new management. Pettygrove and Lovejoy were never able to make it grow. Pettygrove sold to Daniel Lownsdale who sold equal shares to Stephen Coffin and William Williams Chapman. (What changed hands, as in all Oregon real-estate transactions prior to implementation of the land act, was presumptive title, subject to survey and patent by the federal land office.) Lownsdale and his associates believed they had acquired possessory rights to the entire town site, and were dismayed to learn Lovejoy had sold his half-interest to Ben Stark. After negotiations prolonged by the shiftiness of the parties, Stark settled for a triangular segment, cut from the extreme northeast corner of the claim, amounting to fewer than forty whole and fractional blocks. A curate's portion, but Ben had cogent reasons for accepting so much less than was due him. He was then in San Francisco. Lownsdale, Chapman and Coffin had the advantage of occupancy. An advantage which, as Amos Short demonstrated, could be decisive. Short became proprietor of Vancouver — as distinguished from Fort Vancouver — by jumping another's claim. And proved up by killing two representatives of the original claimant who presumed to protest.

Chapman, Coffin and Lownsdale were an ill-assorted set. Chapman was a Virginian, an attorney, formerly congressional delegate from Iowa Territory, and a Democrat of independent views. Stephen Coffin was a Maine man, a contractor and builder, a visionary, a Whig. Kentucky-born Daniel Lownsdale was a tanner by trade, a promoter by disposition, a man of overly flexible ethics. Between them they could raise considerable money, though never quite enough for their needs. The real money would come later, but a little too late for Lownsdale, Chapman and Coffin. None of them would get rich out of Portland.

They were not overly prosperous in the early months of 1850. The territory's California trade was being aggressively contested by Atlantic seaboard merchants shipping directly into San Francisco, and throttled by extortionate freight rates and a shortage of ocean steamers willing to visit the Pacific Northwest. Even Aspinwall's Pacific Mail Line, despite solemn undertakings, made no sustained effort to maintain regular services between California and the Columbia, and was particularly reluctant to send its steamers as far upriver as Portland. Sailing vessels, chiefly small coasters, visited the little town on the Willamette frequently. There were always masts rocking gently above the foot of Washington Street or above the wharf Captain John Couch had built near the southwest corner of his claim, which abutted the town site on the north. But steam vessels were only occasional visitors.

In 1849 Coffin had commissioned Henry Hunt, an energetic Columbia River lumberman, to go East to buy or have built a steamer suitable for the Portland trade. Hunt contracted at New York for a sizable vessel, saw her laid down and called her the *Columbia*. She was almost ready for outfitting when the money ran out, and he was forced to sell her to Aspinwall to avoid ruinous loss. But in June, 1850, the *Gold Hunter* tied up at Portland. She was a side-wheeler, 172 feet long, a year old and for sale. The asking price was $60,000. Portlanders raised $21,000, gave a mortgage on the ship to secure the remainder and jubilantly announced she would run to and from San Francisco carrying passengers and freight.

Down at Astoria James Frost was just completing his own side-wheeler, another *Columbia*. Her appointments were spartan — no galley or sleeping accommodations. But she was an honest-to-God steamboat with boiler, stack, whistle and even white pine planking brought from New England to grace the most heavily forested corner of the continent. Frost took his pride on her maiden voyage July 3, passed Portland next afternoon to the cheers of Independence Day celebrants and before nightfall reached Oregon City. Where he let it be known he would run twice-a-month service to and from Astoria, charging $25 per passenger or ton of freight, one way.

At Milwaukie the unquenchable Whitcomb was planning a superior riverboat. And he intended to have a newspaper too, as did the Portland proprietors. For the frontier real-estate speculator, a newspaper was a necessary tool. However short the subscription list, the overrun could be shipped to the States to impress potential immigrants with suitably inflated estimates of local prospects. The first issue of Whitcomb's *Western Star* came off the presses November 24. It was printed by William Austin Carter, edited by John Orvis Waterman and pronouncedly Democrat in tone. Two weeks later Thomas Jefferson Dryer brought out the *Oregonian* at Portland. Dryer was forty-three — rather elderly by Oregon journalistic standards — a New Yorker of varied experience, a Temperance lecturer when seized by sobriety and, despite his name, a dedicated Whig.

Milwaukie got a special gift for Christmas. Oregon's newest steamboat was tipped from her cradles into the waiting river. She was a first-class vessel: double-boilered, twin-stacked, with galley, dining salon and plenty of cabin space. Her machinery had been installed by Jacob Kamm, a young Swiss who had mastered his trade on the Mississippi. Her captain was John Ainsworth, another Mississippi graduate. She was christened the *Lot Whitcomb of Oregon* by Governor Gaines himself in the course of a day of massive self-congratulation, oratorical bombast and revelry. During the cannon salutes an unfortunate was blown to oblivion, but despite some distress provoked by this mishap, the launching was John P. Gaines's most successful public appearance in Oregon.

In the standard texts Gaines is characterized as vain, pompous, arbitrary and unavailable. He may have been reserved. He had reason enough. On the voyage out, two of his daughters died of yellow fever. The remainder of the accepted description is suspect. It issued from men who, because they opposed Gaines, did not hesitate to malign him. The governor's true deficiency was political. He was a Whig appointee in an overwhelmingly Democratic territory.

Gaines had arrived the previous August accompanied by what was left of his family, by Territorial Secretary Edward Hamilton, and by Associate Justice William Strong of the territorial supreme court. Because O. C. Pratt slipped away to California and the East immediately upon hearing that a new colleague was approaching Oregon, Strong served for eight months as the territory's sole judge. One of the new justice's first official acts was to order the public sale of the vessel *Albion*.

Her crew had been discovered at New Dungeness (not far from where Alex McLeod stumbled through his Klallam campaign a generation earlier), cutting spars and trading with Indians. Both unlawfully, for the ship was British, and being British, fair game. She was libeled, taken to Fort Steilacoom, and placed under bond. The bondsman promptly stole her cargo or connived at its theft by others. The *Albion* herself sold for $40,000, not a penny of which reached the public treasury. "Thar was barly enough," explained Marshal Meek, "for the officers of the court."[5] It being generally agreed that Meek had neither art nor rapacity to author so grand an embezzlement, suspicion fell on U.S. Attorney Amory Holbrook. No proof appeared beyond the fact that Holbrook had taken over the uneducated Meek's official accounts.

Asahel Bush reached Oregon at summer's end (still 1850) and immediately began undercutting his designated associates in the management of what Sam Thurston, doubtless with himself in mind, had decided would be the *Oregon Statesman*. Blain, Bush wrote Thurston, leaked secrets. Henry Russell was careless with money and made a bad impression. (Stockwell resigned from the enterprise early, saving himself from excoriation.) Bush's letters were *pro forma*. He rid himself of Blain and Russell within weeks, long before his complaints could reach Washington. Whatever Delegate Thurston's expectations, the *Statesman* was going to be the personal organ of A. Bush, proprietor, publisher and editor.

It would not come about quite yet. Press and materials were hung up somewhere between New York and Panama. Asahel flexed his frustrations, writing hot letters East. When the legislature met in December he got himself elected chief clerk of the lower house — the assembly — upon Sam Thurston's recommendation.

He made important friends that winter, and forged lasting connections. Matt Deady, erstwhile teamster and teacher, was now M. P. Deady, attorney-at-law and assemblyman from Yamhill County. He and Bush hit it off so well they shared rooms at Oregon City. Ben Harding, assemblyman from Marion, was a shy, good-looking lawyer, a gentle manipulator. He would be close to Bush until, after almost half a century, death separated them. Nesmith held no office that year but he could never resist the political fleshpots, and spent most of the session at the capitol. These three — Deady, Harding and Nes — were charter members of the Salem Clique — pronounced KLEE-que by the irreverent and spelled Cli-que by everyone — a disciplined little band of freebooters which, with A. Bush as brigand-in-chief, would tyrannize Oregon democracy and effectively govern territory and state for a decade.

The legislative session was tempestuous. The great issue was location of the territorial capital. Oregon City and Salem were the principal contenders. But several other communities, Portland and J. C. Avery's

Marysville (now Corvallis) among them, could muster votes enough to prevent either front runner from commanding a majority. More was at stake than civic pride. Congress had appropriated $40,000 toward construction of public buildings, none of which would become available until the location question was settled.

Colonel William M. King of Portland, Washington County, was speaker of the assembly. The colonel was distinguished by an illuminated nose and a conniving nature. A political associate who knew him well described the colonel as a man who "could marshal the selfish desires, interests and prejudices of men with consummate skill."[6] A former Pennsylvania canal contractor, he appreciated the profits to be made from suitably handled public works. Toward the end of January, with the legislature deadlocked and the session near its end, King summoned a select group of lawmakers to Portland. The result was an omnibus bill, introduced January 28 and passed two days later, which designated Salem the capital, gave Portland the penitentiary and placed the territorial university at Marysville. The upper house, the council, quickly acquiesced. The thing was done.

Not, however, to the satisfaction of Governor Gaines. The governor had no veto power. But he was final custodian of federal funds appropriated for the benefit of the territory. He sent down a special message to the legislature, pointing out that under the act organizing the territory each law should embrace but one subject, and that subject be embodied in its title. The location act was therefore an unlawful law, and he would not observe it.

The legislature's reply was shrill obfuscation. The governor was violating the sacred doctrine of separation of powers, interfering improperly with the legislative process and undermining the foundations of self-government, charges which Asahel Bush approved and which he would enlarge. His press arrived in March, 1851. The first number of the *Statesman* was issued March 28. Its language was so violent that Waterman suggested in the *Star* that Bush had been dining on pickles and case knives. Dryer and Gaines were Asahel's immediate targets, and he reviled both unmercifully. The governor gathered the shreds of his dignity about him and maintained a chilly silence. Dryer swore he would have a public retraction — at gunpoint, if need be. Greatly alarming Reuben P. Boise, a young lawyer who had known Bush in Massachusetts and a future member of the Cli-que, who bought a pistol and forwarded it from Portland to Oregon City so that his friend Asahel might be armed against those who resented the *Statesman's* editorial tone.

Dryer's fulminations caused Bush no unease, but a touchy political problem made him anxious. General Lane, returned from California, announced for territorial delegate. Sam Thurston, Bush's financial sponsor, was on his way to Oregon to stand for reelection. Bush was beholden to Thurston, but his new friends were drawing him into Lane's orbit. Deady was a solid Lane admirer. Nesmith and the general were as near cronies as the difference in their ages would allow. And Samuel Thurston's popularity was become increasingly fragile. The Oregon City section of the new land law had not won universal approbation. There was only scattered sympathy for the dispossessed John McLoughlin, but those who had purchased lots from the doctor subsequent to March 4, 1849, found their title expunged, their improvements lost and their property given over to support a nonexistent university. J. Quinn Thornton was one of those who protested. Thornton did not give a damn about Dr. McLoughlin but he had purchased from the old man after the cutoff date, and built on the property, and he was irate. He took more honorable exception to an attempt to bar former Bay personnel from the franchise and the right to hold under the land act even when they had given notice of intent to become citizens. Feeling ran so high that Wilson Blain felt called upon to send Thurston assurances that were the delegate molested at Oregon City, his upcountry admirers had promised to come down and burn the town.

Thurston was forced to defend himself before the winter session of Congress and did so in a fighting speech, denouncing his critics as rogues and scoundrels. Thornton, he wrote Bush, was a snake in the grass whom he, Thurston, would attend to personally. His vehemence delighted his more fervent supporters but disturbed those less totally committed. Lane, meantime, was quietly winning friends. A race between the two would be difficult to handicap. Bush wrote unhappily to Deady that in the event of such a contest the *Statesman* would remain neutral. Asahel was spared the test. Thurston contracted a tropical fever and died off Acapulco, April 9, 1851. A week later Lane's name was nailed to the paper's masthead as its candidate for the delegateship.

❧ VI ❧

Joseph Lane was Democrat to his marrow but during the campaign of
1851 his protestations of nonpartisanship gulled even Dryer, who supported the general in his columns. Down at Salem Dr. Willson raised a
feeble opposition. Willson was, like Lane, a Democrat, and also represented what remained of the mission party. He received less than 20
percent of the vote. The Democrats carried both houses of the legislature by overwhelming majorities.

The army was just then leaving, by request. Discipline had not improved. Even Major Hathaway attempted suicide during a bout of
alcoholic mania. More disconcerting to Oregonians was Colonel Loring's habit of creating huge military reserves by government fiat and at
places of commercial importance — Vancouver, The Dalles, Astoria.
When the colonel set off four square miles near Milwaukie, including
a tract planted in young fruit trees by nurserymen William Meek and
Henderson Leulling, protests multiplied. At Washington Thurston
had argued that supporting the rifle regiment was an impossible burden upon the territory. It would be cheaper to arm the settlers and let
them do their own fighting. The war department, with misgivings,
ordered Loring to march his people south to Benicia, and thence to
Missouri.

Bad judgment; worse timing. By now — the spring of 1851 — gold
had been discovered in extreme northern California and in the Rogue
and Illinois valleys of southern Oregon. Prospectors were pouring into
the area: a rough lot of necessity, many made desperate by circumstance and a few vicious by inclination. Brushes between miners and
Indians were commonplace. Travelers passing between California and
the Oregon settlements were subject to bushwhacking. In June Major
Phil Kearney, leading the last elements of Loring's regiment, fought a
nasty little battle with the Rogues at Table Rocks, two great mesas
rising a thousand feet above the valley floor. He might have been
roughly handled had not he been reinforced by volunteers led by the
ubiquitous Lane, on his way to inspect mining holdings near Mt. Shasta
before proceeding to Washington. Governor Gaines appeared in time
to accept thirty prisoners and arrange an impermanent peace.

The Rogues temporarily retired from hostilities to nurse their wounded and their damaged image, but other southern tribes continued fractious. The infant colony at Port Orford narrowly escaped massacre. An exploring party commanded by W. G. T'Vault lost half its number to ambush. New Superintendent of Indian Affairs Anson Dart was venal and promiscuous; many of his agents were inept and a few, like Henry Spalding, mere time-servers. There was, as yet, no war; but the threat of war shadowed the future. The people of Oregon, who had cheered the backs of the departing troops, suddenly felt uncomfortably alone.

Eighteen fifty-one was also a bad year for Lot Whitcomb. His steamboat grounded on the rapids opposite the mouth of the Clackamas. It required construction of wing dams to refloat her and costly repairs to fit her for service. He was discovering that publishing a losing newspaper is a quick way to insolvency. Debts piled up. Carter and Waterman took over the outfit in lieu of unpaid salaries. One dark night in May the editor and printer loaded press, type and materials on a small boat and floated down to Portland where, on June 5, they brought out the salutatory edition of the *Weekly Times*. Two weeks later Oregon City businessmen acquired control of the *Lot Whitcomb*. Lot had run out of luck and money. He would continue to struggle, but Milwaukie would never be Oregon's metropolis.

The 1850 census takers counted 821 noses in Portland but that same winter Tom Dryer claimed the town had a population of 1500. Presumably he included the Indians collected in sorry camps around the city's perimeter, most of them living on beggary though a few enterprising maidens sold professional services until the more obvious symptoms of social disease made them unappetizing even to resolute lechers. Dryer's exaggeration, however, was only one of degree. Portland was growing. Already it was bigger than Oregon City. It boasted a steam sawmill, nearly a dozen mercantile stores, a tin shop, a drug and paint store, a smithy and machine works, a Methodist church and a bowling alley. The Columbia Hotel (Orlando McKnight, Prop.) served a six-course dinner on Sunday, including a local delicacy, roast of bear. Portland was a go-ahead place.

In March, after only nine months' service, the *Gold Hunter* was taken off the San Francisco run. Local accounts unanimously blame the perfidy of California agents or shareholders, but there is a strong possibility the Portlanders were unable to come up with the balance due and the previous owners foreclosed. Coffin, Chapman and Lownsdale were just then busy promoting a new scheme, one which occupied much of their time and placed fresh demands on their credit.

Frank Pettygrove had seen that a road through the hills west of the town would attract trade from the rich Tualatin Valley, and had made a not overly strenuous effort to build one. The new proprietors proposed to grade and plank a road to the top of the convenient canyon cut by Tanner's Creek, push through a gap above the creek's source and build on to Hillsboro, Forest Grove and even Lafayette. The legislature of 1850–51 authorized incorporation of the Portland and Valley Plank Road Company. Stock subscriptions were sold as far south as Marysville. Expectations were high. The road would crush the hopes of St. Helens, just then preferred by the Pacific Mail Line as its Oregon terminus. But the company built little roadway, and that badly. Management fell into the hands of the unprincipled, accounting procedures were lax and stockholders criminally abused. After a little time the enterprise folded, causing a noisome scandal. There would be a road up that canyon (there is one to this day), but other companies would build it in other years.

Portland was chartered a city in 1851, and that year it acquired a handful of citizens who would be active in shaping its future: Henry Winslow Corbett, William Sargent Ladd, Cicero Hunt Lewis, Josiah Failing and his young sons, Henry and Edward. Accumulators, every one.

❧ VII ❧

The late legislative session had not only been inharmonious, it had been a closely run affair. Despite Colonel King's logrolling (and, it was rumored, bribes in the form of Salem town lots distributed by Dr. Willson), the location act passed the assembly by only a two-vote majority. Bush thought this evidence of disorderly management and was determined the next session would have the benefit of rigorous discipline.

He was irked with Deady. Deady had voted against the location bill in the assembly and the following spring, stumping for a seat on the council, argued stoutly that the law was void. Bush, who cared not a fig about legalisms, was so confounded by what he thought an irrational stand that he expressed a fear Deady would lose to his Whig opponent, David Logan, lately of Illinois. Logan was a masterful trial lawyer, a caustic speaker and an accomplished boozer. Deady got him drunk — a state in which Logan sustained himself without appreciable aid through much of the campaign — and won handily.

Bush had his own embarrassments. The legislators had selected him territorial printer. As such, he was required to print the territorial laws, but he had neither proper press nor a bindery. He proposed contracting the work to New York, touching off a loud row with Territorial Secretary Hamilton just when Asahel was hopefully pursuing Hamilton's daughter, Genevieve. The laws were sent to New York, and would be for several years, while Bush, through the beneficence of successive Democratic legislatures, turned a handsome profit.

During the recent campaign Asahel had joined Lane in damping appeals to national party sentiment. But the day following the election the *Statesman* carried a call for a convention at Salem to form a Marion County Democratic organization, a call which Bush probably inspired and editorially supported as a first step toward party organization throughout the territory. The disconcerted Whigs, echoing Jo Lane's late arguments, insisted Oregon was too remote from the States in national politics. Bush's retort was a marvel of insolence. The Whigs themselves were the incendiaries, he insisted, for by sending to the territory a swarm of federal appointees sworn to further Whiggish designs they had ignited party spirit.

Week after week the *Statesman* played the changes on this theme, demanding that Oregonians be allowed to elect their own officials. The unfortunate Gaines was castigated with relentless severity, accused of malfeasance, misfeasance, misprision, corruption and cowardice, all in the grossest terms. When Mrs. Gaines died in a tragic accident Bush printed routine regrets, but suspended hostilities only briefly before returning to the charge. The governor was in the position of being right when to be right was to be unpopular. He had consulted with Attorney General John J. Crittenden by letter. Crittenden returned an opinion that the location act was void because it was multifarious and that Gaines was justified in withholding the building funds. Dryer pronounced the matter settled. Bush inquired sarcastically whether the attorney general had been invested with judicial powers, since final verdict rested with the courts. Of course Asahel had no intention of laying the matter before any court not prepared to guarantee a favorable decision. None being available, he adopted an artful contrivance devised by O. C. Pratt.

On going East, Pratt had visited Galena long enough to impregnate his wife (relieving himself of the necessity of moving her to Oregon). At Washington he solicited his own appointment as territorial chief justice, and quarreled bitterly with Thurston, about whom he wrote incautious letters to J. Quinn Thornton. By April, 1851, Pratt was back in Oregon, having traveled most of the way in company with Chief Justice Thomas Nelson of New York, appointed to replace William Bryant.

For the first time the territory had a full complement of judges, who immediately fell into rancorous discord. Pratt not only became a busy partner in Bush's intrigues but also embroiled the courts in an absurd squabble over whether the Iowa statutes (which Congress had, by reference, made the laws of Oregon) were those in the compilation of 1839, as Congress provided, or those printed in 1843, which the territorial legislature had subsequently adopted. Nelson and Strong opted for the former. Pratt, anxious to ingratiate himself with Oregon Democrats, plumped resolutely for the latter.

The Blue Book controversy — the volumes, being bound in blue boards, were known as the Little Blue Book (1839) and the Big Blue Book (1843) — achieved a considerable notoriety in the legal history of the West. There being only two copies of the Big Blue Book in the territory, one wag quipped that in Judge Pratt's court there was little learning and less law. But there could be summary justice. Hearing a mechanic's claim against certain land, in which Pratt himself seems to have had an undeclared interest, the judge found both the complainant and his attorney, Colonel W. W. Chapman, guilty of contempt, ordered both imprisoned and Chapman stricken from the rolls of those qualified to practice before the courts of the territory. The unhappy Chapman offered to slit Pratt's throat and was taken into custody by the sheriff. Friends forcibly delivered Chapman from the Hillsboro jail that same evening, and next day, when the sheriff rode over to Portland from the county seat to collect his absconded prisoner, he was persuaded to depart unencumbered by a crowd of determined citizens. Chapman appeared before Nelson, who discharged him from contempt and ordered him restored to the rolls. Both Chapman and Pratt were Democrats, and Nelson a Whig, but Chapman could not swallow the omnibus act.

These antics were sufficient to amuse the cynical and keep the temperature of fervid partisans at a high level, but Pratt's real contribution to the overriding controversy was a letter which appeared in the *Statesman* September 16, coyly signed "Yam Hill." In it the judge laid down the dictum that the law was presumptively valid until the territorial supreme court ruled otherwise, and urged the court to hold session at Salem to decide the question. He was attempting a flimflam. Congress had designated the "seat of government" as the sole place where the supreme court could convene. By holding court at Salem the Whig justices would be recognizing the town as the territorial capital, no matter what contrary opinion they might later hand down. Even Deady was impressed, admitting that all would be well if Nelson and Strong would hold the next session at Salem. On the matter of the location act, however, he was immovable. And in October, barely three weeks after publication of the "Yam Hill" letter, he wrote Bush from Lafayette that he had gotten Pratt "to come out squarely against the statute when he was here in whole and in part."[7] It was a purely private admission. O. C. Pratt had no intention of allowing his judicial oath to interfere with his political commitments.

On December 1 the legislature convened and the territorial supreme court opened in winter session. Nelson and Strong met at Oregon City. So did the four Whig legislators and Democrat Aaron Wait, who was a local resident. The remaining Democrats, Deady included, assembled at Salem, with Judge Pratt in unctuous attendance.

Judges Nelson and Strong immediately heard arguments in the case of *Short* v. *Ermatinger,* counsel for appellant arguing that since the court was not sitting at the place designated "seat of the government" by statute, it was without jurisdiction. In separate opinions the two judges found the location act invalid, Strong remarking pompously that "it is dead without mourners and can lie unburied without offense."[8] At Salem the Democratic legislators promptly appealed to Pratt who, in answer to a resolution drawn up by Councilman Deady, gave it as his opinion that the location act required the lawmakers to meet at Salem, that even in the absence of such a law they could meet at Salem on their own motion and that the verdict handed down by Nelson and

Strong was a nullity since the supreme court was required by law to meet at the seat of government. The Salem legislators found this "decision" so satisfactory they instructed Territorial Printer Bush to run off three thousand copies for general distribution. The lawmakers passed a resolution, again prepared by Deady, asking that Congress ratify their acts and in the future allow Oregonians to elect their own governor, secretary and judges, those now imposed on them being unsatisfactory, O. C. Pratt excepted. And finally, to revenge themselves upon Chief Justice Nelson, they removed from his judicial district every county except Clackamas, putting the remainder of the territory south of the Columbia under Judge Pratt's jurisdiction — providing also that the dates for holding court in the various counties be advanced one week, so that if the chief justice continued to ride the circuit under the terms of the old law, he would find no business left to transact.

❦ VIII ❦

It was a literary season. An "Association of Gentlemen" issued the *Vox Populi* four times during the legislative session. Dated at Salem but printed on Bush's press at Oregon City, the paper carried some legislative news and advertisements of local merchants. The remainder was political bluster, a steady hectoring of Whig officialdom and heated demands that Oregonians be allowed to govern themselves. The wit was pungent and sometimes scatalogical: "It will be remembered that Nelson and Skookum [Chinook for *strong*] killed a 'defunct law' by sitting on it; in consequence of which *sitting*, said law lies *interred* without offense."[9] A solid hit, *Vox Populi* was the source of much congratulation among its sponsors and Democrats generally. But it was almost immediately eclipsed. On February 7, 1852, the *Oregonian* began serialization of *Treason, Stratagems and Spoils*, by "Breakspear," otherwise William Lysander Adams.

They called him Little Preach. He was born at Gainesville, Ohio, in 1821 and grew up a man of astonishing diversity: book pedlar, schoolteacher, lay minister of the Disciples of Christ persuasion (he had studied at Bethany College under Alexander Campbell himself), Prohibitionist, editor, politician, polemicist, eclectic physician, agnostic and apologist for demon rum. Despite his religious upbringing his invective was refreshingly free of restraint, his language never parson- ical, his humor broader than might have been acceptable in sternly Campbellite circles. His "Melodrame" (so he styled it), done in imita- tion of Shakespeare, was a five-act parody on the late maneuverings at Salem. The characters are leading Democrats disguised, with deliber- ate inadequacy, by other names. The scenes closely follow the chro- nology of actual events, but Adams shrewdly rearranged the roles. Instead of Bush's tool, as was the case, Pratt is portrayed as a master manipulator busily using Deady, Waterman, King, Bush and the rest to achieve his grand design, which is to detach the territory from the United States and join it to Utah and California to form a Mormon nation under Brigham Young.

In the 1850s Mormonism was to most Americans what Communism would become to their descendants a century later. To accuse a man of embracing it was to accuse him of practicing licentiousness and pro- moting treason. Little Preach's Mormon conspiracy, however, was no more than a sardonic comment on the true motives of the Democratic hierarchy, and not intended to be taken literally. Allusions to Judge Pratt's real-life delinquencies are another matter, obvious enough to have been recognized by any regular reader of the *Oregonian:* Pratt's forced resignation from West Point; Pratt charging the army $50 to carry a letter from Astoria to Vancouver; Pratt buying rough Spanish cattle from one Durham and selling them as blooded Durham stock, at an unconscionable price, to Sydney Moss; Pratt's coat, cane and valu- able papers seen scattered outside an Indian girl's wigwam on the outskirts of Portland early one winter morning. Adams did not omit mention of the transgressions of other victims of his satire, but it was the judge who offered the broadest target.

Treasons, Stratagems and Spoils was an instant sensation. Two pam- phlet editions, illustrated by woodcuts, were brought out before the end of April. Some of the labels Little Preach attached to his characters stuck for years. Bush was Chick (abbreviation of Chicopee, the little Massachusetts town where he first met Thurston), even among his cronies. Lovejoy was Hotspur. Most of the thirteen Democrats who appeared in the Melodrame accepted the lampooning gracefully. The judge was doubtless irked, but his inflated ego held him safely above embarrassment. Only John Orvis Waterman was openly provoked. Adams depicted Waterman as a chronically unsuccessful swain, which he was, and called him Peter. Greatly afflicting John Orvis, perhaps because, as George Belknap suggests, the connotation was sexual.

The *Statesman* took no official notice of Adams's triumph. Bush cannily refused to advertise that which he could not effectively answer. Instead he busied himself building party organization. A Democratic Central Committee was formed and Nesmith elected chairman. To the confusion of those Whigs and independent Demos who continued to repeat Jo Lane's no-party arguments of the preceding year, Asahel published a letter from the general urging party members to unite and organize. Lane had his own reasons for disavowing nonpartisanship. He was a presidential hopeful, Indiana's favorite-son candidate.

Bush's ruthless tactics created an atmosphere of extraordinary bitterness. He and Governor Gaines twice conducted minor skirmishes. When they bumped one another on an Oregon City street the governor raised his cane. Bush pulled his pistol. He pulled it again when Gaines threatened to cowhide him in Secretary Hamilton's office. The *Oregonian* railed unceasingly against the Durham Democracy — a backhanded reference to Pratt's cattle swindle — and its Mormon organ, but the June election was no contest. Against an opposition split between Maine Lawers (Prohibitionists), Independents and Whigs, the united Democrats swept the board almost clean. Two weeks later word arrived that Lane had talked a joint resolution through the Congress, affirming the proceedings of the legislature at Salem, effectively recognizing the town as territorial capital. The Cli-que was firmly in the saddle.

Despite being puffed in a well-written campaign biography by "Western" (probably Robert Dale Owen) and having Senator Jesse Bright's brother for his floor manager, Jo Lane was never a serious contender when the Democratic convention met at Baltimore. As the Indianians had expected, the major candidates canceled one another out, but when the compromise came the prize was awarded to Franklin Pierce, an amiable man of inconsiderable attainments. Lane campaigned hard for the ticket, damning the Whigs for having done nothing to honor or extend the country, praising Pierce extravagantly. Once his rhetoric got away from him and he announced that the day Franklin Pierce was inaugurated President he, Joseph Lane, would retire from public life.

After Pierce was elected over Whig Winfield Scott, who was a military genius but a political catastrophe, Lane wrote confidently to Deady that things would be put right in Oregon come March.

Since Nelson and Strong had been appointed to replace Bryant and Burnett, respectively, the terms of all three of Oregon's justices ended in the fall of 1852. During the summer Judge Pratt set out once more for the States to lobby for his own availability as next chief justice of the territory, to conduct a little business for Bush and to arrange to bring his wife and two children out from Galena. The judge's mental processes were always sensitive to his ambitions and he had come to a comforting conclusion: one essential point of W. L. Adams's burlesque was not burlesque at all. Orville C. Pratt *was* the First Chief of Oregon's democracy.

There is no other explanation for the unexampled hypocrisy in which he indulged himself at Acapulco, first visiting Sam Thurston's grave and then writing Bush a "soliliquy" full of praise of the late delegate and flowery laments over his untimely demise, all obviously aimed at capturing the affections of the late delegate's admirers. Bush, doubtless at Pratt's insistence, published this rubbish in the *Statesman,* being perfectly aware that the judge's violent attack on Thurston, sent from Washington almost two years before, had been given the widest possible circulation by that inveterate busybody J. Quinn Thornton. However grand his expectations, O. C. Pratt was going to have a short political shelf life.

⚔ IX ⚔

Charles Maley moved from Illinois to Oregon and in the winter of 1852–53 he wrote back a letter of complaints. It was raining so hard, Mr. Maley said, there was nothing for it but wade or swim. Prices were high and wages low: $15 to $20 per hundredweight for flour, $10 to $12 for beef, and common labor paid $1.50 a day. Pork was so lean you had to buy tallow to fry it in. "You think you have hard times in Illinois, but just come to Oregon if you want to get the elephant by the tail."[10]

His complaints were beforehand. Business generally was fairly good at the beginning of the new year but it deteriorated later, shortening both credit and tempers. When the Pacific Mail Line announced it was removing its terminus to St. Helens, irate Portlanders hanged the company's local agent in effigy. The wharves at St. Helens proved unaccountably susceptible to fire and before long the mail-line steamers were once more running into the Willamette.

Matt Deady had married the previous June to Lucy Henderson, just turned seventeen, a prim, pure, impossibly proper maiden with a permanently disapproving expression. There are no pictures of Lucy Deady smiling. Her somberness had its effect. Deady acquired the beginnings of dignity and a vague sense that he was helping make history. "Leave out your vulgarity when you address decent folk," he wrote Bush humorously. "Think how your memory will suffer, when the future Biographer will give your memoirs to the world, with your blackguard letters to me interspersed through the dog-eared volume."[11]

It was wasted advice. Bush's writing, private and public, remained vigorous as ever. Witness his editorial description of G. N. McConaha of Seattle: "A man whose very countenance is redolent with filth, from whose polluted lips it drips in an incessant stream, who has festered in brothels and wallowed in gutters half his life."[12] Colonel McConaha had sinned by commenting that the *Statesman* contained vulgar and offensive language.

As Lane had predicted, President Pierce was prepared to make things right. Oregon officeholders were turned out to make room for good Durhamites. Nesmith was made marshal in place of Meek. Ben Harding became U.S. attorney and Curry territorial secretary. Pratt was nominated to be chief justice, and Deady and Cyrus Olney, a former Ohioan, to be associate justices. Lane himself was to be governor. Pratt's name was shortly withdrawn, both Illinois senators, Douglas and General James Shields, informing the President they would oppose confirmation on grounds of personal privilege. Lane was told the reason for their opposition but refused to reveal it, though he did write Nesmith: "Think of him trying to speculate off the poor soldier who bared his breast to a savage foe and endured the privations and hardships of a campaign while he was sitting comfortably by his fire-side enjoying the fat of the land."[13] The chief justiceship went instead to George H. William of Keokuk, Iowa.

Pratt excepted, Oregon's Democratic chieftains were jubilant. Matt Deady had some momentary doubts about ascending the bench but manfully choked them back. In March Washington Territory was created, its southern boundary being the 46th Parallel from the Continental Divide to the Columbia, and midchannel of that stream to the Pacific. The change pleased citizens on both sides of the river. In April Oregon's first territorial Democratic convention was held at Salem, and Jo Lane chosen candidate for congressional delegate, receiving thirty-eight votes to eleven for Deady and five for Cyrus Olney. The selection might have been unanimous if the general had not written letters from Washington coyly insisting he would not stand for reelection. A month later Lane arrived, bringing his wife, Polly, and a train of relatives, near and remote, numbering twenty-seven. On May 16 he had the pleasure of replacing Gaines as governor, resigning three days later to run for delegate.

The opposition had refused to learn the lesson of the previous years. Alonzo A. Skinner consented to become a candidate after being urged to do so by those friends of all parties whom politicians have about them for just such a purpose. Lawyer, sometimes Indian agent and Whig, he was an infinitely abler man than Dr. Willson of two years before, but he had no apparatus and the Democrats had a fully operating machine. Bush ridiculed Skinner wickedly, dubbing him the lazy man's candidate; he jousted in print with Dryer (they had taken to calling one another "Ass-o-Hell" and "the Sewer man") and even rounded on poor Waterman, whom he accused of attaching himself to Jo Lane's coattails in the hope of getting a political handout. Waterman's unforgivable sin was that he wanted a piece of the territorial printing and Asahel was determined to have all of it.

Despite the disadvantages under which he was laboring, Skinner put up a vigorous contest and at times tempers got out of hand. Toward the end of the campaign he and Lane were at Althouse, a mining community near the California border, where they jointly addressed a meeting of citizens in Ball's saloon and bowling parlor. The candidates fell to arguing, and so did members of the audience. There having been considerable drinking — liquor being considered necessary to lubricate the democratic processes — a pair of partisans of the rival candidates exchanged blows. Setting off a general scrum during which one of the original combatants was beaten senseless and lost most of one ear, which was chewed off or removed by some equally efficient means. General Lane, who had immediately jumped into the melee in order to prevent a riot, gave up the effort and wandered wearily over to Franz Reinhart's bakery — in his shirt sleeves and carrying his battered stovepipe hat — to complain that Althouse was the hottest damned place he'd ever seen and that that was the roughest fight, too.

In the canvass, Lane polled more than 60 percent of the vote. The People's Party, as the opposition called itself, lost every council contest and elected only four assemblymen. The rout was so complete even Dryer was convinced, and in his first issue following the election called for Whig organization and outlined a Whig platform. Bush, after repeating Horace Greeley's pronouncement that Whiggery was dead in the States, commented acidly: "But like all animals of the reptile order, it dies in the extremities last; and him of the Sewer is the last agonizing knot of the tail." [14]

X

Deady once said of Colonel Nathaniel Ford that he was pregnant with his own future greatness. Doubtless self-conceived. The colonel was a Virginian, blown to Missouri by winds of restlessness. Like the late Cornelius Gilliam, he fought in Governor Lillburn Boggs's crusade against the Latter-day Saints, acquiring his military title and enough of a following to elect him sheriff of Howard County. His popularity seems not to have survived his departure, which was hurried. In 1844 he emigrated to escape acute pecuniary embarrassment and harassment by his creditors. Judgments were outstanding against him and executions were ordered against his property, but he was not disposed to allow sale of his chattels — including Robin and Polly Holmes and their baby daughter, Mary Jane — to satisfy his debts and obligations. He persuaded the Holmeses, to whom he no longer held legal title, to accompany him, promising that if they would serve him until he had opened up a farm in Oregon he would liberate the family.

They remained with him nearly six years. The Fords settled in Polk County, filed for 640 lush acres and with the help of the slaves built improvements. Polly gave birth to Roxanne and James and a babe unnamed in the records. In 1849 Robin spent a season at the California mines and faithfully turned over to Ford the $900 in gold dust he had accumulated.

In the spring of 1850 the colonel freed Robin, Polly and the infant child but retained Mary Jane, Roxanne and James, warning the parents that if he was troubled by complaints in the matter he would gather up the entire family, bundle it to Missouri and see it sold back into slavery. The Holmeses were desperately poor, unlettered and appalled by Ford's threat. It was two years — during most of which time the Fords refused to allow Polly Holmes even to see her children — before they sought legal aid. In April, 1852, upon motion of their father, Judge Pratt issued a writ of habeas corpus for the persons of Mary Jane, Roxanne and James Holmes.

Ford, a Democratic legislator of some prominence, was not hurried. A year passed before he was brought into court. Not that he had neglected the matter. In June, 1852, he wrote to James A. Shirley, a former friend in Howard County, suggesting that the execution levied against the Holmes family eight years earlier be renewed and sent to Oregon and the family taken back to Missouri under the fugitive slave law. By this means Shirley could make $1500 or $2000. Ford was prepared to pay all costs in Oregon and furnish all necessary evidence, and would do so happily, because the Holmeses, encouraged by a set of Abolitionists, were attempting to slander the colonel and his family.

Nothing came of this repellent proposal and in April, 1853, when Ford at last filed an answer to the original writ, he deposed virtuously that though he had been advised that he could return the Holmeses to Missouri and sell them as slaves, he had not done so, which was evidence of his charitable intent. He also deposed that he was holding the children as wards only until each reached the age of majority, and having supported them at great cost when they were small, he was entitled to their services now that they had reached a useful age. And anyway, Robin and Polly Holmes, being poor and ignorant, were unfit to bring up their own children.

We are almost at an end of the law's delays. On July 13 the case came before newly arrived Chief Justice George H. Williams, sitting as district court judge at Dallas, Polk County.

Judge Williams's most remarkable characteristic was his appearance; he was so homely as to cause comment. As a lawyer he was intuitive rather than scholarly. His personality was engaging. The Cli-que, which looked without trust on imported officials of whatever political denomination, accepted Williams with remarkable aplomb. He never became a member of the inner circle of Democratic manipulators, but neither was he cast into the outer darkness. In the Matter of *Holmes* v. *Ford,* he found for Robin and Polly Holmes.

Writing a half-century later, the judge said he had ruled slavery unlawful unless specifically authorized by state or territorial law — which may be. He had heard the arguments in chambers and seems to have issued no written opinion, so the only evidence was his memory. He also wrote that his decision had effectively ended slaveholding in Oregon, which is demonstrably false. There had been blacks in Oregon since the days of the mountain trade. How many were there in the 1850s is uncertain, the census records being unreliable, but the number was small. Probably more were slaves than free, and most of those who were slaves would remain so until the Civil War and the Thirteenth Amendment. All the same, Judge Williams's ruling was a landmark. Robin and Polly Holmes, brought to Oregon as slaves, had prevailed over an influential and (despite the poor-mouthing in his letter to James Shirley) well-to-do white in the courts of a territory whose organic law provided for the expulsion of all Negroes, whether free or bound.

Escapism was always an element in our westering. The movers who laboriously pushed the frontier across the continent were not only beckoned on by fair visions but also whipped by dissatisfaction and an urge to flee problems which seemed beyond solution. When the architects of the Provisional Government forbade residence of blacks in the Oregon country they hoped to set themselves permanently apart from the increasingly passionate controversy over slavery they left behind them in the States. By congressional action the provision became automatically, together with the remainder of the organic law, part of the territorial code. It was invoked only twice. In 1851 Winslow Anderson, apparently less for his color than for notorious conduct, was ordered expelled from the territory by Judge Nelson, as was one Jacob Vanderpool, mulatto. A year later the legislature, by special measure, exempted a much-respected black pioneer, George Washington Bush, from operation of the act.

Beyond question there were slaves in Oregon, and slavedrivers in Oregon, and bigots, some of whom were unpleasantly vocal. There was a minority who abhorred slavery, though few members of that minority — despite the strictures of Nathaniel Ford — were as yet Abolitionists. The ordinance against black residency remained on the books because a majority of Oregonians hoped to escape that hard decision whose making would shortly split the nation.

⚜ XI ⚜

Creation of Washington as a separate territory required a restructuring of Oregon's judicial districts. In the summer of 1853 Matt Deady learned he was assigned the southern counties, took up land at Camas Swale in Douglas County, not overfar from Winchester, and built a log house which it pleased him to call Fair Oaks. Lucy, great with child, remained at her parents' in Yamhill. She could not have safely been installed at Fair Oaks in any case, for there was a war building along the California-Oregon border.

An estimated twelve thousand immigrants reached the territory in 1852. Of those who traveled overland, most followed the route south from Fort Hall which had been laid out by the Scott-Applegate party in 1846. By the time they turned west from the Humboldt even the best-regulated trains were broken down to scattered groups of wagons, some much too small for safety in Indian country. The Pits and Modocs across whose lands they passed preyed upon them. Loss of life was small but the depredations were considered so serious that escort companies were formed at Jacksonville, the most effective being those captained by Ben Wright, who had turned up so providentially at Wascopum Station a dozen years earlier to help Daniel Lee and Henry Perkins conduct camp meetings. In northern California there was open war between the Shastas and the miners but the Rogues, who were Shasta allies, kept the treaty agreed upon in 1851. Indian Superintendent Dart and a commission which included Governor Gaines had negotiated a number of treaties vacating Indian title west of the Cascades, as the law provided, and arranging to move the pitiful remnants of the Willamette Valley tribes onto reservations. Later in 1852 it was learned that the U.S. Senate capriciously delayed ratifying any treaty made in Oregon and ordered negotiations halted until Indian policy in the territory could be reviewed.

The results could have been anticipated anywhere but in the national capital. Faith in the government's good intentions withered, particularly among the natives of southern Oregon. The fragile peace woven together by Dr. Dart and his agents was unequal to fresh strains. Incidents increased — little acts of casual violence involving a few Indians, a few whites. Each side brutalized women and children. Both practiced a chilling savagery. Warty, young son of an Umpqua chief, made an indecent proposal to a settler's daughter. Miners regularly forced their attentions upon native girls; the maiden in the case was uninjured, and Warty fuddled by drink. He was hanged anyway, and his body thrown on a bonfire to fry.

With the situation approaching flash point, the authorities found themselves awkwardly situated. Joel Palmer, new superintendent of Indian affairs, had not yet replaced Agent Alonzo Skinner, in charge of the southern district until he resigned to run for delegate. Despite the separate urgings of Gaines and Lane, the army had not yet returned to the area in sufficient force to maintain order. There was a tiny garrison at Fort Orford and another, hardly larger, at Fort Jones, California, southwest of Yreka. The previous September Lieutenant Colonel B. L. E. Bonneville, whose quartermaster was a homesick lieutenant named Grant, arrived at Fort Vancouver with what remained of the U.S. 4th Infantry, 268 officers and men — the rest lost to cholera and tropical fevers contracted while making the Panama crossing. But Bonneville was a military pedant no longer inclined to adventure, and his command was three hundred hard miles from the Rogue. From early June trouble hung in the air like the threat of summer storm. An Umpqua subchief called Taylor and three others were hanged by Jacksonville volunteers for allegedly murdering seven whites. After the executions the volunteers marched to a camp near Upper Table Rock where, it was rumored, the Rogues were holding two immigrant women captive. The rumor proved false but the Jacksonvillers shot up the camp, killing six of the occupants.

The hanging of Taylor and his supposed accomplices might have been justified but the murders at Table Rock were an affront the tribes could not allow to remain unavenged. Beginning August 4 the Rogues conducted a series of strikes at small settlements and remote ranches, killing about seven men and wounding others. The settlers reacted swiftly. Two hundred men were mustered in the Rogue River valley. A company of eighty was got up at Yreka. A request for guns and ammunition sent to Captain Brad Alden, commanding at Fort Jones, brought the captain himself and a dozen troopers. Colonel Bonneville unenthusiastically forwarded rifles, ammunition, a howitzer and six artillerymen led by Lieutenant August Kautz, under escort of forty volunteers captained by the intrepid Nesmith.

Kautz and his howitzer were delayed. Command fell to Alden, the only regular Army officer present. It was a burdensome honor. Though lacking both funds and authority to indebt the federal government, the captain was expected to raise all necessary supplies, and he was faced with the prospect of conducting a campaign without either maps or personal knowledge of the terrain. Alden must have been relieved when Jo Lane, who had been rusticating on his farm near Deer Creek, arrived on the scene, for he immediately tendered command to the general, who accepted without hesitation.

The Rogues had fortified themselves near the head of Evans Creek, about twenty miles north of Jacksonville, choosing their ground well. The steep sides of a ravine protected their flanks. Their front was masked by dense thickets behind which were log breastworks. Lane attacked the morning of August 24, touching off a brief, bloody action. Alden was fatally wounded, though he lingered for two years. The general took a ball through his right shoulder and scapula. Three of the volunteers were killed outright, and of the two wounded, one shortly died.

After a three-hour exchange in very heavy fire the Indians asked for a parley and, hearing Lane was on the field, requested that he confer with them. The general found the enemy troops in sadder state than his own. Eight were dead and the women were preparing to burn the bodies to protect them against defilement. Of twenty wounded, at least seven were mortally so. His old adversary, Chief Jo, who three years earlier had taken that name out of admiration for Lane, declared himself sick of war. A truce was arranged, it being agreed the parties would march to the vicinity of Upper Table Rock to negotiate a treaty. When the army marched south two days later, Chief Jo sent people to help carry the litters of the disabled.

The peace council was scheduled to open September 4, but Superintendent Palmer was delayed and some of the Rogue subchiefs had not arrived, so only preliminary negotiations were held on that date. In the interim Nesmith's company arrived, bringing Kautz and his howitzer and a commission from Acting Governor Curry appointing Lane brigadier general of the Oregon Volunteer Militia. Captain A. J.

Smith marched a detachment of dragoons over from Fort Orford. The general now had the military hammer, and those who believed the final solution of the Indian problem was mass extermination whispered he could do nothing better than wipe out the Rogue camp not a mile distant from his own. Lane gave no ear to such counsels and the troops under his immediate command were careful in observing the terms of the truce.

The bands of irregulars combing the countryside for cheap triumphs were unfettered by such scruples. Small groups of Indians were persuaded by fair words to put aside their arms, then murdered out of hand. It would be pleasant to be able to ignore these accounts, but they are officially documented. Each is unsavory. Most unsavory of all is that which reached the Rogue camp shortly after Nesmith and his command caught up with the army; a band of marauders captained by one Owens had tied a native to a tree and used him for target practice. For this story the only source is Nesmith, who had a weakness for yarning, but that the same Owens directed the slaughter of numbers of inoffensive natives is beyond dispute. Blood lust among even decent folk ran extraordinarily high. Martin Angell, an otherwise excellent citizen, shot down a passing Indian simply for being an Indian.

Somehow a peace was arranged. The Rogues sold the Rogue River valley for $60,000 — less $15,000 in indemnity for "depredations" — and one hundred square miles of reservation. Apart from the peacemakers no one was satisfied, and least of all those whites who advocated genocide a century before that appalling word was coined. A Jacksonville drunk wanted to gift Jo Lane with a petticoat, and there were others, less noisy but more dangerous, who quietly meditated violence. It would take another war to make a peace.

On September 4 Matt Deady paid a visit to the council grounds before riding on to Jacksonville, where he was to open court next day. The judge was burdened with a vexing problem but it is doubtful he found opportunity to discuss it with Lane, to whom it was also causing great embarrassment. Both had been victimized by Whig chicanery.

In December, 1852, the *Oregonian* predicted that President-elect Pierce would elevate Mordecai Paul Deady to the territorial bench. When Deady received his commission the following May, he was dumfounded to discover it was made out to Mordecai rather than Matthew. Though he was careful to make no public protest, the judge quickly learned that local Whigs were privy to the situation. The

Oregonian howled derisively. Deady was bitter against Lane for what he felt was at best unforgivable carelessness, and at worst treachery. The obvious explanation is the most probable. Lane had erred, though innocently. The two had associated politically since 1850, but seldom met, maintaining connections by correspondence. Deady habitually signed himself "M. P. Deady" (or simply "Deady" if the letter was informal), and though it would not have been tactful to admit it, the general may have accepted the *Oregonian*'s "Mordecai" because he knew no better. Meeting with the judge at Portland in October, just before departing for the East, Lane was full of assurances that immediately he reached Washington the matter would be put to rights. It could not have joyed the general that by the very steamer which was to take him to San Francisco there arrived at Portland Obediah B. Mc-Fadden, appointed associate justice of Oregon *vice* Mordecai P. Deady, removed as improperly commissioned.

McFadden was a Pennsylvanian, and Attorney General Caleb Cushing had seen in Deady's difficulty an opportunity to pass a patronage plum to the Buchanan wing of the party. The new judge disclaimed knowledge that he was sent to replace a brother Democrat against whom a great wrong had been done, but when it was suggested he withdraw, he refused. And he continued to refuse despite the abuse poured upon him by the *Statesman*. Matt Deady was in a boiling rage. He was particularly cankered by Dryer's barbs. A sympathetic Nesmith wrote his friend: "I am going to git up a festival of the Sons of Bitches, and give Toddy [Dryer] a promint [*sic*] place in the doings."[15] But despite Deady's growing conviction that Lane, if not the agent of these misfortunes, was an accomplice thereto, the general was true to his word. McFadden held a single term in southern Oregon before being transferred to Washington Territory to fill a vacancy. Deady was reinstated as associate justice, this time as Matthew.

The Honorable John W. Davis was for some time congressman from Indiana, speaker of the House of Representatives during the Mexican War and chairman of the national convention which nominated Franklin Pierce. In December, 1853, he turned up at Portland bearing a freshly minted appointment as territorial governor. His fellow Democrats gave him a mixed reception. Bush's arrogance was dividing the party into contending wings. The Hards were those who unmurmuringly carried out the dictates of the Cli-que. The Softs were those who did not. The Softs lacked organization. Their principal voice just now was the *Times,* "Peter" Waterman's not overly potent organ. They accepted the new governor cheerfully as an alternate source of patronage, from which Bush effectively cut them off. The Hards resented Davis's coming since he was displacing Acting Governor Curry, who was one of their own. But it was a matter of general congratulation that the doctor (he was a physician as well as a politician) brought with him some of the money Congress had appropriated for construction of public buildings, including $20,000 for that penitentiary to be erected at Portland. The business decline begun in mid-1853 had become a minidepression, and access to federal funds offered opportunities for the astute. Four years and two supplemental appropriations later local businessmen turned over the completed prison structure, built at a cost of $60,000, excluding unpaid bills and disallowed claims. Of the cells, six were considered strong enough to house convicts. The building material seems to have been astonishingly porous. Though the prison population was never large, twenty-two prisoners escaped in one fifteen-month period.

⚜ 10 ⚜

An Impossible Institution

1853-1859

I N OCTOBER, shortly before setting out for the States, Jo Lane undertook to mend a political fence. He wrote Asahel Bush an extravagant letter expressing his total confidence in Bush as a gentleman, friend and editor. The Deady debacle, just then reaching crisis proportions, was putting severe strain on relations between the general and the chief of the Cli-que.

Joseph Lane was not naive. He was a dab hand at dispensing soft soap, an article, Nes wrote him genially, with which Nature had abundantly supplied him. His trust in the Cli-que was so limited he arranged that Samuel Garrett, a young Indianian sojourning in Oregon, send confidential political reports to Washington. Garrett's devotion to Lane's interest was absolute, and in December the young man got himself elected clerk of the territorial council. The clerkship provided an excellent listening post, and Garrett had an acute ear and discerning judgment. When Waterman wrote Lane that McFadden was a prince of a fellow, he was using Deady's predicament to cut away at Bush, whom he accused of being determined to rule or run. Garrett, who gauged the measure of A. Bush's ambitions quite as accurately, advised the general to work for Deady's reinstatement and reap the credit for having uplifted a popular man.

Advice aside, there is little doubt but that Lane was sincere in his assurances to Deady. Quite apart from a genuine admiration for the judge, the general must have deeply resented Cushing's interference in Oregon patronage. Surveyor General Charles K. Gardiner (an old friend, if a letter to Nesmith can be believed) proved quite as unacceptable as his Whig predecessor, John B. Preston. Gardiner flatly refused to assist land claimants in preparing their applications unless they rewarded him with a fee, the alternatives being to hire an attorney or buy the services of Brother Preston, who had thoughtfully set up shop across the street from the land office. Gardiner had hardly entered upon his duties when demands for his removal began to rain down on the delegate's office, but despite Lane's best effort, the President was slow to act.

Governor Davis proved inoffensive, though not selective enough to satisfy the Bushites. He spoke courteously to Democrats of all complexions, and even to Whigs. Nes wrote Lane that he rather liked the old gentleman (Davis was fifty-five), but thought him of the Soft variety. That winter the legislature put a call for a state constitutional convention on the June ballot. The Hards were determined to have no more imported officials.

Attempts to organize an effective opposition failed dismally. Maine Law supporters had only Prohibition for a platform, but on that they stood adamantly, in most counties refusing to make common cause with the Whigs. Bush was so unconcerned he departed for the States early in the year, leaving the *Statesman* under the management of LaFayette Grover, just then a junior member of the Cli-que. In June the total opposition vote materially increased, but no Maine Law candidate was elected, and only eight Whigs. The call for a constitutional convention was roundly defeated, though that hardly disposed of the issue.

At New York Bush purchased a fine new press, arranged for printing and publication of the 1853–54 session laws, and went on to Washington to observe the performance of Oregon's territorial delegate at first hand. For the moment, Lane captivated him. The general's easy familiarity with national figures was impressive. Bush wrote enthusiastically to the *Statesman* that Lane worked harder and with greater success than any other territorial delegate in the Congress and exerted great and beneficial influence. Asahel's carefully cultivated cynicism was not proof against the general's genial charm.

⚜ II ⚜

David Logan had a genius for advocacy and a compelling thirst. When liquored he suffered moral lapses. His denigraters called him the Mingo Chief, because of a bent toward high oratory and low boozing shared with that other Logan, the Indian leader celebrated in Jefferson's *Notes on the State of Virginia*. Despite his dissipations, by 1854 Logan had become, after Dryer, the most prominent Oregon Whig. At the recent election he had won a seat in the legislature. On September 6 Alonzo Leland's *Democratic Standard* carried a sensational communication. Signed "Budget," it charged the Mingo Chief with having publicly raped an Indian woman at Jacksonville. "Budget" was Matthew P. Deady.

The *Standard* was a new sheet set up to further the ambitions of O. C. Pratt, and there is some evidence that Deady founded his allegation on information furnished by Pratt. Leland, his wits half-paralyzed by the storm which blew up around his head, was bullied into showing the original letter to Mark Chinn, Logan's law partner, and Chinn had no difficulty recognizing Judge Deady's distinctive hand. Pratt acted quickly to clear his own skirts, first publishing a card in the *Times* denying he had any interest in the *Standard,* and then writing Deady deploring Leland's lack of discretion. *"Bush,"* said O. C. greasily, "never could commit such a blunder!" [1]

Logan's answer appeared in the *Oregonian* of September 19, branding the story a total fabrication and criticizing Deady for disgracing his judicial position to damage a political foe. The letter has balance and dignity but the unfortunate Mingo Chief was unable to sustain the mood, staggering drunkenly through the next judicial term of the southern district, openly carrying a pistol and muttering threats against the judge's life. In November an unrepentant Deady sent Nesmith a detailed account of the incident:

> Some weeks since a friend of mine sent to Leland a certificate more than sustaining the Budget correspondence. I now know there is no mistake about it from eyewitnesses. The statement of the facts as I ascertain them are these [*sic*]. At noon on the Eighth of August, Logan was seen on the open ground at the end of one of the Main Streets of the town in full view of a large number of persons male and female. A squaw

came along Logan took after her and caught her by the blanket, the blanket pulled off and she escaped. He held on to the blanket she came back after it and he then caught her and threw her down unbuttoning his pantaloons and went through the motions. After he was through and up, she having been screaming all the time, he gave her some money and went off to the creek nearby and washed himself.[2]

Logan and Deady were both damaged by this unseemly affair. Logan was convicted in public judgment of gross indecency, Deady of demeaning himself. Only O. C. Pratt was advantaged, which may have been just what the ex-judge intended.

Orville C. Pratt was dishonest, deceitful, egocentric and cunning in roughly equal parts. He harped so on his impoverished condition that his friends called him Little Means, echoing his constant plaint. Yet as early as 1850 he was on personal and business terms with Sam Brannan — apostate Saint, San Francisco vigilante organizer and large-scale land promoter — and himself held substantial properties near Sacramento under management of Henry H. Haight, future California governor.

Since the publication of Little Preach's Melodrame, and most particularly since his own rejection as territorial chief justice, Pratt had become convinced that his own superior qualities and invaluable services to the Democratic party could best be recognized and rewarded by his election as congressional delegate to replace Joseph Lane. Having fixed upon this decision he wrote the astonished Lane that he, Pratt, would be candidate for delegate at the next Democratic convention and urged the general not to contest the nomination. When Lane ungraciously declined to withdraw, Pratt continued to press his private campaign, drawing little support and that chiefly from the Softs. As an aberration it had its comic aspects, but Pratt's maneuvers came at a troublesome season, for that fall the Cli-que found itself confronted by a vigorous and disciplined foe. The Know-Nothings had arrived in Oregon.

Since the 1830s no-popery agitation had been generally restricted to scurrilous literature, intemperate oratory and riots directed chiefly against the Irish. In 1849 it assumed a new and more ominous form with the organization of the Supreme Order of the Star-Spangled Banner, a secret, oath-bound society whose members were pledged to vote for none but native-born Protestants, work for a twenty-one-year probationary period preceding naturalization of immigrants, and combat the Catholic Church. Three years later the SSSB promoted the American party — commonly called Know-Nothing because members denied any knowledge of it — having the same oaths and ends. The new party spread with extraordinary rapidity, reaching California in May, 1854, and attracting powerful support in that state. Amory Holbrook, converted Whig, brought it north the August following, founding the Oregon Territory's first Wigwam at Oregon City.

There is little evidence that Holbrook was a dedicated anti-Catholic. His motives were political. Using the resolute nativists still clustered around Spalding, Griffin and Gray as a nucleus, he hoped to put together a combination of Whigs, Prohibitionists and dissident Democrats strong enough to unhorse Bush and end Cli-que domination. The moment seemed propitious. Pratt was in rebellion. The Whigs in Oregon, as elsewhere, were breaking apart over slavery. Maine Law advocates had been swamped in the 1853 elections. And there were a good many Democrats who feared Bush, but did not love him.

Other Wigwams were rapidly set up in almost every community in the territory and attracted adherents in large numbers. The *Oregonian,* though it remained nominally Whig, encouraged the new party. W. L. Adams was more forthright. In the first issue of his *Oregon Argus,* printed on the old *Spectator* plant, he bluntly announced that his paper would "take the American side in politics."[3] He opened his columns to anti-Catholic attacks, and inveighed against "foreign influences" — that is, the Hudson's Bay Company, which continued to maintain a post at Vancouver.

Bush, characteristically, met the threat head-on. He planted a spy in the Salem Wigwam. He published names of some of the leading Know-Nothings, Holbrook, Stephen Coffin and A. C. Bonnell among them. He secured and published the party's ritual, oaths, aims, grips and even its code, effectively robbing it of the secrecy which was its greatest strength. And with the *Statesman's* support and blessing, Assemblyman Delazon Smith of Linn introduced at the winter term of the legislature a *viva voce* bill, providing that each voter should announce his vote at the polling place in a loud, clear voice or hand his ballot to the precinct judge, who would announce it in the same manner. The measure was a direct attack on the Know-Nothing party's great strength.

The bill was Smith's introduction to territorial political maneuvering. Although only thirty-eight, he had behind him a singularly varied career. Born in New York State, he attended Oberlin, in Ohio, a pioneering coeducational school. Provoked by summary dismissal from the college, Delazon published *Oberlin Unmasked,* a sensational pamphlet in which he charged that the men and women students did more together than matriculate and even ministerial candidates were guilty of solitary vice. He practiced law and journalism in New York and Ohio until 1842, when President Tyler appointed him special commissioner to Quito. Recalled shortly after reaching his post, he managed to delay his actual removal for nearly two years by becoming "lost" in the tropical hinterlands. After returning from South America he emigrated to Iowa, where he became a leader of the bar, a maverick Democrat and editor of an agnostic newspaper until he experienced conversion and became a Methodist exhorter. To those who admired his bombast he was "the Lion of Linn." To those who did not he was "Delusion."

Despite the pressures Bush exerted and Delusion's impassioned rhetoric, the *viva voce* bill passed the assembly by only fourteen to twelve, and the council by five to three, a dangerously narrow margin considering the importance the Cli-que attached to the measure. A little later in the session the lawmakers openly revolted, voting to move the capital to Corvallis and the university to Jacksonville. It was, all round, a winter of excitements. Governor Davis was gone, having resigned in August. Offered a farewell banquet, he declined in a public letter, in which he chided his brother Democrats gently, advising them to substitute principles for personal considerations and even suggesting that "our opponents are entitled to their opinions equal with ourselves."[4] This time the President appointed Curry as governor and Ben Harding as territorial secretary, selections which should have improved Lane's standing with the Cli-que, but did not. The Washington interlude between Bush and the general had proved to be no more than a summer romance. Deady wrote Asahel that the editor's public praise of the general was arousing ridicule since it was well known that Bush had little use for Old Jo. For his own part, Deady said, he watched the Lane-Pratt contest like the unhappy wife watched the tussle between her spouse and the grizzly, cheering impartially: "Go it, husband! Go it, b'ar!" The judge was still sore over his temporary removal.

The truth was that the Hards would have preferred almost anyone to Lane, except Pratt. But there was no other candidate available who commanded the general's popularity, and the secret nature of the

Know-Nothing party made accurately estimating its strength utterly impossible. The Cli-que would stick to Lane because it was stuck with him.

❧ III ❧

Life on the Oregon frontier was not all religion, politics and business. There was romance as well, though it was apt to be of the rough-and-ready variety. A man married when he could. A girl married early, and during operation of the Donation Land Law brought with her a federal dowry in the form of acreage. Adam Wimple, thirty-four, wed Mary Allan, twelve. At thirteen she developed a roving eye. He murdered her and set fire to their cabin, after secreting her body under the floor. He was hanged. Charity Lamb and her seventeen-year-old daughter shared a passion for a drifter named Collins. When Lamb, as outraged father and cuckolded husband, strongly protested, Charity cut off his objections with an ax, qualifying herself as the first female resident of the Portland penitentiary. What happened to Collins and the daughter does not appear.

In this male-dominated society, courtship was usually the man's prerogative. But there were exceptions, as in the case of Dr. E. H. Cleaveland.

The doctor was a Jacksonville physician. In the fall of 1854 he journeyed to Washington Territory, leaving his "woman" (the word and quotation marks are Deady's) with the family of Agent George Ambrose at the Rogue River Indian Reservation. On his return home next spring he passed on to Jacksonville without stopping off to pay the lady his respects. What followed, Deady reported to Nesmith:

> By peep of day next morning the neglected fair one mounted a horse and started for town. On the way she borrowed a pistol. Arrived at town she marched to the Dr's office (where a crowd of young men were laughingly listening to the Dr's piquant description of the Walla Walla doves) and stepping cooly into the room commanded the Dr. to take a walk with her. The Dr. saw the storm in her eye and dreading bodily harm or at least a scene, immediately complied . . . In less than no time a justice was

sent for and before the Dr. was released from durance vile, he had meekly bowed his neck to the yoke matrimonial . . . Dr. Alexander and Ben Drew organized a company who, with long tin swords and other carricatured [*sic*] emblems of war went trooping about town to prevent artful widows and desperate damsels from spiriting away any more of the young men of the place.[5]

The cream of the jest was that Cleaveland was a prominent Whig and a member of the legislature, but the members of the Cli-que found little to joke about that spring. In 1853 Bush had moved the *Statesman* to Salem on the principle that the official territorial paper must be issued from the seat of the government. The same principle now forced him to move to Corvallis, which he found uncongenial, complaining to Deady that it was full of "tickyasse, pickeyune, grabbing people."[6] His mood was black for another reason. The steamer *Southerner,* outward bound from New York, had been lost at sea, carrying the *Statesman*'s new printing press and five hundred copies of the 1853–54 session laws to the bottom with her. The late legislature had released Bush from delivering the session laws, for which it paid him nothing and authorized him to print five hundred copies of the laws of the territory, including those of 1854–55, allowing him about $5000 for the work. But nothing could reimburse him for loss of the press.

On April 11 the Democratic convention, meeting at Salem, dealt brutally with O. C. Pratt's pretensions; Lane was nominated by a vote of fifty-three to six. On April 18 the Whigs met in the only convention they would hold in Oregon, and nominated John P. Gaines. The next day the American party, meeting at Albany, also nominated the former governor. Dryer was content with tacking Gaines's name once to the *Oregonian*'s masthead but the ebullient Adams — Bush derided him as "Air-goose Billy" — raised it twice in his *Oregon Argus,* once for each party.

The Democrats began badly. Lane had arranged the appointment of Robert Dunbar of Milwaukie, an old friend from Indiana days, as collector of customs at Port Orford, a position promised to Joseph Drew, a southern Oregon Hard with strong Cli-que ties. Both Nes and Deady were incensed, charging Lane with rewarding friendship above party regularity and attempting to build a personal following at the expense of the Democratic organization. The storm blew over, largely because Bush remained calm, but it demonstrated clearly that the Cli-que would never be satisfied with the major portion of the patronage;

it wanted all of it. And Jo Lane was being warned, by his son Nat and others he trusted, that the Cli-que's friends were not necessarily his own.

The campaign was conducted with a heat remarkable even for Oregon. Democrats sardonically saluted Gaines as "The Hero of Encarnación," that being the place where Gaines, out on reconnaissance, sensibly surrendered to an enemy cavalry force twenty times as large as his own. Whigs and Know-Nothings responded by styling Lane the "Mary-Ann of the Mexican War," but the epithet lacked inspiration. The candidates themselves agreed to debate around the territory, starting at Deer Creek for a swing through the southern counties, then north through the Willamette Valley to finish at Portland. They began meekly enough, striking no sparks, causing Deady and Drew great alarm that Lane would lose the south, which had always returned him heavy majorities. Gaines, Deady wrote Bush, was abusing Lane from the stump, and Lane was taking it meekly. When the general reached Corvallis, Bush spoke sharply to him, saying that there was an impression growing that Lane was fearful of the ex-governor. "He said," Bush told Deady, "that he [Gaines] was a g-d d---d old shit, but he had never said anything he [Lane] could construe into an insult — that if he gave him provocation he would cut his heart out."[7] What was more, Bush was able to report that Gaines and Lane had passed the lie at Dallas and engaged in some violence, unfortunately stopped by interveners before damage could be done. "They speak at Lafayette today, and I think they may have a fight. I am confident Lane can lick him, and he gets the advantage of him he'll pound him like hell, for he hates him most cordially."[8] There is something dreadfully unredeeming in the spectacle of young hotheads urging two elderly gentlemen — Lane was fifty-four, Gaines sixty — to beat one another to paste for the gratification of the body politic.

Bush might have been less bloodthirsty had he not been so unsettled by the Know-Nothing threat. He need not have worried. Lane won with an overwhelming 61 percent of the vote. Democrats gained twenty-eight of thirty assembly seats and controlled the council by a margin of seven to two. The triumphant *Statesman* boomed Lane for the Democratic presidential nomination in 1856.

The causes of the Know-Nothing debacle were not especially complex. Holbrook was never able to put together the combination he envisioned. The *viva voce* law — Delazon Smith had argued boldly it would cost the Whigs six hundred to eight hundred votes — cowed disaffected Democrats fearful of reprisals. A good many Whigs, repelled by the repressive character of the American party platform, either voted for Lane or did not vote at all. Gaines's unpopularity and Bush's bluster played their part. But so did Jo Lane's personal prestige, and he was as conscious of it as any man. The victory of 1855 would prove as costly as it was impressive. Because of it, Bush became more imperious and Lane more independent. The congressional delegate was on collision course with the high chief of the party machine.

≰ IV ≱

"There has never been any [Indian] difficulty in Rogue River," Deady wrote Bush in early September. "All these stories are got up by the Charlie Drew set to cover up and justify themselves. They would like to have a difficulty if they could."[9] Charles S. Drew was the loudest of a considerable group of whites on both sides of the California line demanding war, both to provide an excuse for dispatching the natives cluttering up the countryside and, business being slow, to afford opportunities for profitable speculation. Deady, however, was oversimplifying. All through the summer there had been difficulties. Every man walked warily along the most familiar trail. At Fort Jones 140 Indians — the majority widows and children of victims of white savagery — placed themselves under the protection of Captain Henry Judah. Chiefly through the devoted efforts of understrength garrisons at Fort Jones and Fort Lane, which overlooked the Rogue River Reservation, a peace of sorts was maintained until October 8. Early that day a company of Jacksonville irregulars made a predawn raid on a sleeping camp at Butte Creek, a short way off the reservation, killing twenty-three noncombatants — women, children and aged men — and seriously wounding numbers of others before wearying of carnage. Next day howling tribesmen swept down the Rogue Valley like the Assyrian upon the fold. Charlie Drew had his war, and an uncommonly vicious one it would be.

It was a long, cold winter, one of the bitterest on record, and a busy one. Oregonians spent it fighting on two fronts. The Yakima War

never reached into Oregon and for the purposes of this history it is
only necessary to say the war broke out as a result of an ill-advised
attempt by Washington Territorial Governor Isaac I. Stevens and Superintendent Palmer to vacate Indian title to the Inland Empire and
remove the interior tribes to reservations. A treaty to accomplish this
end had been concluded at Walla Walla in June, but the terms were
ungenerous and not even the Nez Percé pretended to be satisfied.
Kamiakin, senior Yakima chief, was leader of the dissidents, and rumors reached Olympia that he was gathering together allies and weaponry. Major Granville Hallers, with 150 regulars, was ordered to
reconnoiter the Yakima Valley. About fifty miles north of the Columbia he collided with a greatly superior force of hostiles and was barely
able to fall back on The Dalles, having lost his artillery (one howitzer),
his supplies and provisions, most of his animals and suffered twenty-
two casualties.

Governor Stevens was far off in Blackfoot country making treaties,
and Washington Territorial Secretary Charles Mason temporarily in-
herited executive powers. Mason offered Major Gabriel Rains, commanding at Fort Vancouver, a brigadier general's commission in the
Washington militia and general field command. Rains, in accepting,
levied on Washington for two companies and Oregon for four. Governor Curry, having contracted a bad case of war fever, ordered up
eight, though there were only rifles enough in the Fort Vancouver
armory to equip two. The rest of the troops were forced to supply their
own weapons as during the Cayuse War. Colonel J. W. Nesmith headed
a full complement of officers.

Bush was beside himself. Relying on Deady's judgment, he used the
columns of the *Statesman* to deride excited reports of fighting in the
southern counties, saying the accounts were deliberately exaggerated
by unscrupulous citizens intent upon raiding the federal treasury on
the pretense of putting down an Indian uprising. He was also mightily
irritated with Young Curry, writing Deady on October 21, "I am afraid
they are overdoing the northern war . . . Nat Lane, who has just returned from Portland . . . says that Dryer and Curry are so thick that
he couldn't get to speak to Curry to tell him they are making a d--n
fool of him . . . I am afraid Indian wars are rocks on which Curry will
split." [10]

A week later Deady wrote from Douglas County that Quartermaster
General M. M. McCarver was in the area, "giving or agreeing to give

three prices for everything. The bill will not be much short of half a million, while twenty thousand judiciously raised and expended would be amply sufficient."[11] And apropos Governor Curry he inquired sardonically, "Has Dryer swallowed his excellency? To judge from the *Oregonian,* when one farts the other complains of wind on his stomach."[12] Busy exchanging quips, both the judge and Asahel had lost touch with events. Big trouble was brewing in the southern counties. Haller's defeat had caused a perfect panic in Portland. The Yakima and Rogue River wars occurred simultaneously only by coincidence, but together they constituted the gravest threat the Pacific Northwest settlements would face.

Nesmith got his people to The Dalles about October 20. It was a creditable performance. Barely two weeks had passed since Haller's defeat. Almost immediately the colonel clashed with General Rains over Rains's refusal to help outfit Nes's command unless it agreed to enlist in the U.S. Army. Thereafter the Oregonians acted as an independent auxiliary. Rains crossed the Columbia on October 30, and marched north at the head of his regulars and Washington militia. Nesmith and his four companies followed two days later, Nes having written his wife he expected to spend the winter campaigning. But the Yakimas were uncooperative. Kamiakin craftily refused to be drawn into battle. By November 14 everyone was back at The Dalles after having, Nes grumbled, "a Hell of a time."[13] The war was humbug. "Curry as well as myself," he told Bush, "has been carryed away by the damned phrenzy of public clamour."[14] On December 4 he resigned his commission and rode home to Rickreall.

Brigadier General John E. Wool, commanding, Department of the Pacific, fought gallantly in the War of 1812 and with distinction at Buena Vista. He was soldierly, competent, crusty and outspoken. Shortly after reaching Fort Vancouver he found himself icebound. Frustration sharpened his tongue. His comments on the conduct of Haller and Rains were uncomplimentary. He opposed further winter campaigning. Bad weather would protect the settlements against attack. He advised Governor Stevens, still trapped in Blackfoot country, to cross over to the States and return to Olympia via Panama. He blamed the wars on outrages committed by whites and vowed to lobby against federal relief for losses sustained or payment of claims for property or services rendered in pursuing the hostilities. He agreed to transfer a regiment from Benecia to Washington Territory, though he was critical of the calling up of Oregon volunteers to fight the northern tribes, insisting Rains had troops enough if they were used effectively. A Chinook wind mercifully thawed the ice in the Columbia long enough for the general to sail back to California, loudly deploring that he could do nothing to halt a hare-brained venture ordered by Governor Curry, an expedition to retake Fort Walla Walla.

Chief Peu-peu-mox-mox of the Walla Wallas maintained a benign neutrality during the Cayuse War and even hanged one of the Whitman murderers himself, but during the summer of 1855 his patience with the whites ran out. The tribe's attitude became so threatening that Indian subagent Nathan Olney persuaded The Bay's James Sinclair to abandon Fort Walla Walla, after first dumping all munitions into the river, and urged the few ranchers in the vicinity to leave quietly for the settlements.

It was December 3 when about 350 troopers of the Oregon Mounted Volunteers, Lieutenant Colonel James K. Kelly commanding, trotted into the fort. They found the place pillaged, defaced and deserted. Next day's march was intercepted by Peu-peu-mox-mox himself with a considerable escort, one of whom carried a parley flag. When Kelly taxed him with the looting of the fort and the burning of the settlers' cabins, the chief said it was the young men, whom he could no longer restrain. He wanted no war. He accepted the stiff terms dictated by the colonel and agreed that he and six others be hostages to insure compliance by his people. That evening one of the hostages was sent to the Walla Walla camp to inform the tribespeople what was required of them. He never returned, and in the morning the village was found deserted. The increasingly distrustful Kelly continued his march toward Waiilatpu, where he intended to establish headquarters. He was still some way short of the mission site when, on the morning of the seventh, the warriors struck.

It was a four-day battle. The troopers drove the Walla Wallas several miles beyond Waiilatpu but the Indians, having fixed a line between the Touchet River on one side and high ground on the other, took a stand. Finding himself short of availables for guard duty, Kelly ordered the hostages tied. Peu-peu-mox-mox had surrendered his leadership and suffered multiple indignities, but he resisted being trussed like a turkey. He was clubbed to death and scalped, and the other hostages dispatched. The regimental surgeon pickled the old man's ears as mementos of a notable event.

Despite the loss of their senior chief, the Walla Wallas and their allies fought tenaciously for three more days, when a determined charge dislodged them and they fled the field. The triumphant Kelly prepared to winter his men not far from Waiilatpu.

Governor Stevens rode into camp December 20. His escape from the upcountry had been much facilitated by the Oregonians' victory and he was suitably appreciative. The volunteers he found in unenviable condition. Many were shod in roughly sewn moccasins, and the winds moaning down from the Blues carried paralyzing cold. For months they would subsist largely on camas, cous, peas and potatoes dug from scattered Indian caches. Not until early March did a relief column come up from the Willamette Valley.

❦ V ❦

Bush got up the petition in November, so that the regular 1855–56 session of the legislature, which would convene the first Monday of December, would be informed and could act. Asahel was in a poisonous humor. The Rogue River war had turned out to be a larger affair than he and Deady expected and those editorials blaming the original difficulties on mischievous whites had gone down badly in the southern counties. But it was Curry who must be brought to heel. The governor was guilty of insupportable heresy, having appointed a number of Know-Nothings to minor military commands (by now a Know-Nothing was anyone whose politics were unacceptable to the Cli-que), and the petition prayed His Excellency displace these unreliables with competent Democrats.

It was the kind of mindless proscription that Bush had inveighed against in the late political campaign, but he was never shackled to consistency. When the *Oregonian* mourned that anywhere but in Oregon war united men in common cause, Asahel was unmoved. Through the columns of the *Statesman* he dictated Democratic doctrine: no public offices of any kind for Know-Nothings. When Curry hesitated, the legislature acted, voting itself the power of military appointments. John K. Lamerick, an undistinguished Jackson County militia captain, was made brigadier general of the territorial army, a choice which inspired young Sam Clarke, just beginning a long career as journalist and historian, to produce a burlesque biography of the newly minted brigadier:

> His profession is the practice of faro, monte, chuckaluck and roulette . . . kan drink his liker and swere a blu streek.
> Having produced satisfactory pruff for the *Statesman* office . . . that he was the man to bully whig curnels inter resineing . . . and having showed his profishuncy in the Shangi drill he was elected, and promised to teach the arme to ____.[15]

Two other matters occupied the legislators' attention during the session: the Joaquin Young claim and the location of the capital. The Young claim was an elaborate scam which must be reduced to mere outline. It will be recalled that Ewing Young died in 1841. His estate, after having gone through a lengthy probate, escheated to the Provisional Government, no acceptable heirs having appeared. Most of the proceeds were used to build, at Oregon City, a jail which was promptly torched.

In 1855 appeared a claimant. His name was José Joaquin Young. He alleged himself the natural son of Ewing Young and Maria Josepha Tafoya of Taos, New Mexico. He seems never to have come to Oregon, leaving management of the case to his counsel, Alex Campbell. Toward the end of the 1854–55 session the legislature passed an act enabling Young to bring an action against the territory for the value of the Young estate.

Campbell offered certain affidavits as evidence. Two are worth consideration and both are dated at Taos, June 27, 1852. The first, signed by three residents of Taos (Kit Carson was one), attests that Ewing Young and Maria Tafoya had cohabited, and they, the affiants, believed Joaquin Young to be the issue of that relationship. The second is signed by Father Antonio José Martinez, a cleric of dubious repute. Father Martinez simply attests that there appears in the baptismal registry at Taos, at such a book and page, an account of his baptism of José Joaquin, child of Maria Josepha Tafoya, single lady, and said to be the natural son of Joaquin John (Ewing Young), a foreigner. The document is written with lawyerly care to preserve the good father from the sin of bearing false witness, and makes no mention that the entry was inserted long after the alleged event and probably in June, 1852.

No investigation was made at the time. None was possible. José Joaquin was born, by evidence presented, in April, 1833. Ewing Young departed Taos, never to return, in October, 1831. This fact was unknown in Oregon. In December the territorial supreme court found for the claimant, and Lawyer Campbell promptly applied to the territorial auditor for settlement. But in the meantime it was learned that the beneficiary of this windfall, roughly $5000, would not be José Joaquin but O. C. Pratt, who had acquired the young man's interest and who probably wired the entire swindle together while on his way east in 1852. An irate legislature voted to repeal the enabling act and in the course of the debate Uncle Fred Waymire, noted for his pungency, offered a pertinent comment. "Why go all the way to Santa Fé after an heir for Ewing Young?" asked he. "I think it could be proved that he has children here if they only could be found out; for like a great many of the original settlers, he was fond of the aborigines."[16]

The legislature, as required by the law passed at the previous session, convened at Corvallis to find itself confronted by a vexing contretemps. There was a fine capitol building, constructed at a cost of $33,000 in federal funds, at Salem. Congress let it be known that no monies would be authorized for the raising of another at Corvallis, or for paying legislators travel allowances to and from that place. Salem was hastily voted once more the seat of the government and on December 18 the territorial officials returned there (followed by a triumphant Bush and his newspaper plant), and installed themselves in the newly completed capitol. During Christmas recess the building was burned to its foundations by a fire of incendiary origin. No one was charged but there was widespread suspicion that the culprits escaped in the general direction of Corvallis.

≋ VI ≋

On the evening of February 22, 1856, a Tututni woman warned the men of Prattsville, a miners' settlement very near Gold Beach, that her people were planning to destroy the whites while they slept. Since the Tututnis had remained peaceable while the remainder of the southern tribes were in ferment, her listeners jeered her, threatened her with a whipping for telling bad lies, dismissed her with a warning and went laughing to their beds. To awaken to the screams of all hell breaking loose.

Several militia companies were in the area, some from California, and that night there was a dance. Of fifteen men who left that dance together, thirteen did not reach camp. Ben Wright, liquor salesman, evangelist, Indian fighter, agent and local hero, was beheaded and his heart cut out, says the legend, for culinary purposes. Thirty-one men and boys lost their lives in the initial attacks which, over a period of seven hours, laid waste to the thirty miles between Prattsville and Port Orford. Ranchers and miners who survived fled their holdings and dug in at Prattsville, which sustained a month's siege. Fighting ran like flames through the forests of the Illinois Valley and the defiles of the Coast range. It was June before order was restored and Superintendent Palmer could begin moving the tribespeople north to the newly established Grand Ronde Reservation in Polk and Yamhill counties. A proceeding which so infuriated residents of the Willamette Valley that the superintendent asked an escort of regulars from General Wool to protect his charges from massacre.

Asahel Bush was conducting his own private war against Palmer, who had incautiously confessed to Nesmith that he had joined a Know-Nothing Wigwam out of curiosity, but immediately resigned; against the unspeakable Gardiner, still in office; and most violently against Joseph C. Avery, who had led the revolt which removed the capital to Corvallis and must be punished for it.

General Lane was willing to cooperate with Bush's vendetta — to a point. Gardiner was replaced as surveyor general by Al Zieber, Bush's father-in-law. George Lawson, whom the general found personally offensive (either because he practiced spiritualism or because he asked permission to court young Winifred Lane), was removed from the southern land office. But Old Jo was becoming independent in patronage matters. Lawson's place was given, not to attorney Riley Stratton as the Cli-que recommended, but to Bill Martin, a Lane crony who was just a step above illiteracy. And Robert R. Thompson, hardly better educated, was made postal agent. Palmer was replaced by Absalom Hedges, whose qualifications were unremarkable, rather than the Reverend Edward Geary. A minor post was found for Waterman.

These appointments created consternation among the Hards. Deady reported that Martin's selection had caused a good deal of hard swearing along the Umpqua. Joseph Drew, who had been passed over for postal agent, could barely contain his fury. And he was not appeased when Lane wrote him that however faithful he was to the democracy, he could expect no patronage because the general had discovered Drew had been a Whig in New Hampshire. Only Bush maintained a morose silence. The Treasury Department refused to pay the $5000 voted by the legislature for printing the territorial laws because the expenditure had not been authorized by Congress. The only hope was a special appropriation. Just at that time Bush could not afford a break with Lane.

The general wrote that there was little chance the current session of Congress would appropriate funds to retire the war scrip issued by the territorial government. Bush's own assessment was even gloomier. "If Wool manages his case well enough," he told Deady, "and industriously and perseveringly he has facts enough, seeming and real, to forever prevent . . . payment."[17] Certainly General Wool intended to try. A noisy quarrel with Governor Stevens had convinced the old gentleman that the civil authorities of Oregon and Washington were unscrupulous, self-seeking time-servers, men who would encourage abuse of the Indians in order to line their own pockets and those of their accomplices.

Wool's rancor was twisting his judgment. Curry was excitable and Stevens large with self-esteem, but both were decent, honorable men. Isaac Stevens graduated from the Military Academy at the head of the class of 1839, served with distinction in Mexico and would die leading a Union charge at Chantilly. There were citizens, particularly in southern Oregon, who regarded an Indian war as an early-day WPA project, providing general employment and an infusion of public funds. And there was profiteering. In March, 1855, Franz Reinhart, the baker from Althouse, sold a good horse at nearby Waldo for $50. That same year the territorial quartermaster general was paying from $200 to $500 each. Flour, selling at Portland for from $10 to $14 a barrel, was priced at $20 at Jacksonville. At Portland J. Failing & Company accepted Oregon scrip for "readily merchantable" items only if allowed 3 percent interest per month. Henry Corbett settled for 2 percent in interest but routinely charged the territory twice wholesale price. This, as Arthur Throckmorton points out, was simply prudent business practice. Some merchants refused to accept Oregon scrip on any terms, being doubtful the federal government would underwrite the territory's war debts, doubts strengthened by John Wool's public pronouncements.

For Jo Lane the congressional session brought a series of defeats and frustrations. He managed to get the war claims referred to a commission to be appointed by Treasury Secretary Guthrie. The special appropriation for printing the territorial laws got nowhere (defeated by black Republicans, wrote the general, but Bush was disinclined to accept the explanation), and a bill enabling Oregon to organize a state government failed to come to a vote in the Senate. It was a presidential year and Lane worked hard for the election of James Buchanan over John C. Fremont, candidate of the newly founded Republican party, speaking up to three times a day though his health was uncertain and those old war wounds pained him.

The Republicans were already organized in Oregon, and Billy Adams kept up a steady trumpeting of "Free Speech, Free Labor, a Free Press, a Free State and Fremont" in the pages of his *Argus*. Dryer, determined to be the last of the Whigs, nailed the name of discredited Millard Fillmore to the masthead of the *Oregonian*. When the Republicans won Maine's state election handily, a disconsolate Bush wrote Deady that he thought Fremont would defeat Old Buck. He was determined, he said, to sell the *Statesman* at the close of the current volume, and urged Deady to buy it in partnership with Nesmith, who was willing. The judge was not interested; two men were too many to run such a paper. "As for money making," he commented dryly, "I expect the cream of things is gone."[18]

❧ VII ❧

On May 22, 1856, Congressman Preston S. Brooks of South Carolina entered the floor of the United States Senate and beat upon Senator Charles Sumner of Massachusetts with a gutta-percha cane, injuring the senator from Massachusetts so severely he was unable to attend his office for three years and never completely recovered. This in retaliation for a speech in which Sumner reflected unfavorably upon Senator

Andrew Butler of South Carolina, Brooks's uncle, who, being absent from Washington, could not attend to the beating himself.

Charles Sumner was not greatly loved even by those who approved his views, for he was coarse-grained, given to high invective and insufferably self-righteous, but the assault made him an Abolitionist martyr and Brooks the idol of Southern Ultras. Lane became involved when he acted as Brooks's second in negotiating a duel, which was never held, with Massachusetts Congressman Anson Burlingame. The affray caused a stir in Oregon. The *Statesman* virtually ignored it — Lane wrote Bush with bland inaccuracy that Sumner's injuries were superficial — but the *Oregonian* and the *Argus* erupted with indignation. The proslavery element was jubilant. "Thare is afiew of us out heare," Bill Martin wrote the general from Winchester, "having a cane made to Send to the Hon. Brooks . . . to replace the one he broke over Sumner."[19] Oregonians, like the remainder of the nation, were choosing up sides.

Since Judge Williams's ruling in the Ford case the slavery question had lurked near the wings. Now it was moving downstage, about to be wedded to the issue of statehood. The people of Oregon were alerted by the mindless turmoil in Kansas, first battlefield in a war not yet declared, where Free State and Slave State partisans were locked in bloody struggle. This was the bitter fruit of Stephen A. Douglas's doctrine of "popular sovereignty," and the repeal of the Missouri Compromise, both embodied in the Kansas-Nebraska Act of 1854. Oregonians were quick to read the lesson. Buchanan defeated Fremont, but Tom Dryer did not wait upon the election returns. Three times a proposal to call a constitutional convention had been submitted to the electorate; three times the *Oregonian* opposed it; three times it was voted down, though each time by a smaller margin. On November 1, 1856, Dryer reversed his stand and came out in favor of immediate statehood. "If we are to have the institution of slavery fastened upon us here," he wrote, "we desire the people resident in Oregon to do it and not the will and power of a few politicians in Washington City."[20]

The legislature convened in December to the bugles of rebellion. Softs combined with Opposition members to elect Colonel Kelly president of the council, and a Republican was chosen enrolling clerk. The session did much politicking but little ordinary business. A call for a constitutional convention was passed for submission at the June election, and this time was expected to pass, for the territorial newspapers almost unanimously supported it. The exception was Alonzo Leland's *Standard,* which remained defiantly heretical and because of its opposition would face a day of retribution.

The Cli-que had decided it must support Lane for delegate once more, though it could not swallow him without gagging. Joseph Drew prayed for deliverance from ever again being associated with such a damn demagogue. Delazon Smith thought the idea of a fourth term would repel voters. Delusion had ambitions of his own to nurture and wrote Lane — rather as Pratt had written in 1854 — on the merits of rotation in office, but stopped short of asking the general to step aside. Bush's discontent over failure of the printing appropriation bill soured him on Ancient Joseph's magic. When the convention met at Salem April 13 it duly nominated the general. It also resolved that each Democrat might speak freely and act according to his convictions on the slavery issue without impairing his party standard, so long as he did not espouse Abolitionism, black Republicanism or such-like abominations. It demanded strict adherence to the caucus rule. It complimented the *Times* as a worthy party journal and excommunicated the *Standard.* And it requested the nominee's open endorsement of these resolves. The platform, Nes told Deady, exhausted a great deal of enthusiasm, the candidate not a damned bit. Bush, however, was content. "I think we got Old Jo . . . where he can't play good Lord and the devil in the same breath."[21]

A newcomer was spectator to these proceedings. Ethelbert C. Hibben was an Indiana lawyer of small affairs, had acted now and again as Lane's clerk and press secretary and was come out, remarked a sardonic John McCracken, as a sort of John the Baptist to the nominee. He was impudent, perverse and, though in his thirties, ludicrously immature. He had been sent to advance the general's ambition to become a U.S. senator once Oregon had achieved statehood and carried letters of commendation from his patron. He also brought an unwelcome rumor that he was to take over management of the *Statesman.* "The plan," Nes wrote gleefully to Deady, "dont seem to meet with the views of the distinguished gentleman who at present 'drives that shit cart.' "[22]

Bad health had forced Absalom Hedges's resignation as superintendent of Indian affairs, and when Lane reached Portland on April 22 he brought word of Nesmith's appointment to the post for both Oregon and Washington, the territories having been combined for reasons of economy. The general acted swiftly to mend his political fences. A strong letter endorsed the entire Salem platform. Leland, when that unfortunate protested, was advised to avoid disharmony in the future. But the party was incurably infected with disharmony. Softs in five counties organized as "national Democrats" and refused to support Old Jo unless he disavowed the platform he had so recently endorsed. George W. Lawson ran as an independent Democrat on a Free State platform. The Republicans, being as yet imperfectly organized, fielded no candidate. Dryer, unwilling to admit Whiggery was dead, sat out the election. The *Statesman* routinely supported the general, but shortly before election day Bush accompanied Superintendent Nesmith to Washington Territory where Nes was to look into Indian affairs. Asahel's absence caused much comment and did not go unnoticed by the candidate, but had no effect at the polls. Lane whipped Lawson, as was expected, and the call for a constitutional convention passed by an overwhelming majority.

During the campaign the general had enlarged on Democratic principles, ignored Lawson and resolutely avoided discussing the leading issue, although at Winchester he expressed a doubt that a man could be a good Democrat and vote against slavery in Oregon. He was in friendly country. Jacksonville's outspoken proslavery sheet, Colonel T'Vault's *Table Rock Sentinel,* had an impressive circulation in the southern counties. In June the *Occidental Messenger* (commonly known as Avery's *Ox*), commenced publication at Corvallis. It was, if anything, more rabid than the *Sentinel.* Hibben was for slavery all the way. Though Dryer refused to associate with Republicans, he was pronouncedly Free State. Billy Adams's *Argus,* as the official Republican organ, was raucously so.

Bush kept close to the center of the path, soliciting letters on both sides of the question. He specifically asked Deady to present the proslavery argument. The judge flatly refused to involve himself in public controversy, but writing privately to a friend he succinctly stated his position. "If a citizen of Virginia can lawfully own a Negro . . . then I a citizen of Oregon can obtain the same right of property in this Negro . . . and am entitled to the protection of the Government in Oregon as in Virginia."[23]

The single most important contribution to the wordy debate which occupied the Oregon press that summer was a Free State letter from

Chief Justice Williams published in the *Statesman* toward the end of July. Shrewdly concentrating on the economic aspects of slavery, Williams argued that its introduction would be not beneficial but harmful. Slave labor degraded free labor, and the reverse. Slaves would be an impossible burden to their masters during the long, wet winter months when farm work was impossible. Blacks would find the climate insupportable and succumb to its chilly rains, or they would escape to make common cause with Indians against the whites. "The true policy of Oregon," said Williams, is "to keep as clear as possible of negroes, and all the exciting questions of negro serviture."[24]

For Deady, the question was a legal one. For Williams, it was one of economics. For Bush it was essentially a political problem, and one which crowded him into a tight place. None of the three considered the moral issue, and Asahel had only contempt for those who did, excoriating them in his columns as fanatics and maniacs prepared to dismember the Union to achieve their ends. Not until two weeks before the opening of the constitutional convention did the *Statesman* declare itself on the Free State–Slave State question, and in taking his stand Bush tried hard to come down almost equally on both sides:

> We believe [he editorialized] that the African is destined to be the servant and subordinate of the superior white race . . . that the wisdom of man has not yet devised a system under which the negro is as well off as he is under that of American slavery. Still . . . our climate, soil, situation, population, &c., render it . . . an impossible institution for Oregon.[25]

The constitutional convention opened at Salem August 17. About two-thirds of the members, chosen at the June election, were reasonably regular Democrats. The remainder was a markedly miscellaneous opposition: a Republican; two Whigs (Dryer and Dave Logan); a handful of independents of whom Jesse Applegate was the most noteworthy; an equal number of Free-Soilers. The Democrats, Soft and Hard, momentarily putting aside their differences, elected Matt Deady convention president. Though the judge had refused to take part in the *Statesman*'s forum, he had run for delegate on a proslavery ticket and openly announced his position. But he was astonishingly evenhanded. For a month and a day he presided over the deliberations at Salem. It is generally agreed he wrote more of the resultant constitution than any other man, though it cannot be said he was responsible for it all. And like several of the delegates, the judge pushed some doubtful causes. He successfully opposed a constitutional provision for the public funding of a university, though he would serve for nearly twenty years as president of the board of regents of the University of Oregon. He expressed in debate a distinct antipathy for corporations, regarding them as devices intended to swindle creditors by limiting individual liability. But he opposed imprisonment for debt, except for fraud, which was distinctly liberal in that day; he was adamant that, in the judicial system, the judges be interpreters of the law and the juries arbiters of the facts. He also insisted on *viva voce* voting; years later, after the state adopted the secret ballot, he would call that process cowardly. When the convention adjourned it left to the electorate's decision not only approval of the constitution but two other questions: whether Oregon should be admitted as a Free or Slave State, and whether free Negroes were to be allowed residence. Nesmith, whose political judgment was usually sound, wrote Deady he thought the new constitution would get a favorable vote but doubted the "peculiar institution" would make it. Not for lack of effort on the part of the proslavery press, which became increasingly vehement until Avery's *Ox,* just before the November plebescite, announced it would not accept an unfavorable vote as final. A stand which put at defiance the doctrine of popular sovereignty, the only thing holding the disparate elements of the Democratic party together.

Nes's judgment was accurate. The constitution was approved by a majority of more than two to one. Slavery was rejected by a margin of three to one, and admission of free blacks by more than seven to one. Oregonians, as Justice Williams had so smoothly put it, were determined "to keep as clear as possible of negroes." But the contest was not yet resolved.

❧ VIII ❧

John Orvis Waterman having been appeased with a federal surveyorship, immediately following the June election Ethelbert Hibben took over editorial management of the *Times.* And in August James O'Meara appeared at Salem with an offer to buy the *Statesman.*

Asahel Bush was weary, discouraged and momentarily vulnerable.

O'Meara's Democratic credentials were impressive. In New York he had been a minor cog in Fernando Wood's Tammany Hall machine. Upon moving to San Francisco in 1849 he had attached himself to the fortunes of Senator William McK. Gwin. Small, quick-tempered, intensely combative, he had a genius for personal journalism. After three weeks of dickering Asahel was persuaded to sign a letter of intent. O'Meara hurried back to San Francisco to put his affairs in order and conclude arrangements with Joseph Lane, who was offering $2000 in front money. The general no longer trusted the fidelity of his old friend Bush.

During the succeeding months frustrations would gall Lane more sorely than during all the remainder of his service as delegate. He had confidently predicted Oregon would be admitted to statehood early in the new congressional session, but the matter dragged. Objections were raised against the state constitution. Southern legislators balked at accepting the no-slavery clause; some Northerners were repelled by the proscription of free blacks. Nor was there any disposition to push federal assumption of the territory's war debts. The investigating committee appointed by the treasury secretary approved claims totaling $4.5 million and the secretary of war recommended payment. But the appropriation bill languished in committee. A measure to reimburse Bush for his supplemental printing got nowhere. The proposed allocation of funds for Nesmith's Indian superintendency was cut by $100,000.

The fault was not Lane's. He labored and lobbied as tirelessly as ever, but his efforts pressed futilely against the force of events. The Supreme Court's Dred Scott decision, holding that Congress had no power to interfere with slavery in any territory, wherever situated, had shocked the North. And now President Buchanan himself proposed to validate the discredited Lecompton Constitution and bring Kansas into the Union as a Slave State.

Lecompton was in that day capital of Kansas Territory. In the late fall of 1857 a constitutional convention assembled there. It was a proslavery convention because antislavery Kansans refused to take part in the election of delegates. It drew up a constitution which barred free blacks from residence, and submitted to referendum the question of slavery. In December, Free State men abstaining, slavery was approved. But in January, 1858, a second plebiscite rejected the entire constitution. Despite this negative vote President James Buchanan recommended that Congress ratify the Lecompton document and admit Kansas under its terms. Lane supported the President, both for reasons of principle and as a matter of party solidarity, but was dismayed when the legislators' preoccupation with the Kansas question delayed consideration of the Oregon bill. He had planned to leave for home early in order to take part in the campaign, but decided to stay on in the hope he could push admission through before the end of the session. His decision to stay in Washington was a reluctant one; reports reaching him from the territory were perplexing, some were contradictory and all were unsettling.

Because the mails were slow — three to five weeks from Portland to the District of Columbia — affairs in Oregon were going even more badly than the general realized. Hibben proved an embarrassment, honeyfogling Bush, complaining petulantly because Tom Dryer was well received in Portland society and he himself was not, and taking up Bush's vendetta against the *Standard* with such immoderate enthusiasm that he publicly spat in Alonzo Leland's face and missed terminal punctuation of his career only because Alonzo clumsily snagged his pistol in his own coat-skirts. An act of unvarnished insolence over which Ethelbert crowed lustily, but Messrs. Carter and Austin, proprietors of the *Times,* were not amused.

James O'Meara returned to the territory in late October, 1857, prepared to purchase the *Statesman,* but Bush, despite the signed agreement, refused to sell. Though Jimmy blamed Nesmith, whom he thought a malign influence, it is probable Asahel changed his own mind. O'Meara was vastly irked, but determined to play out the game. The unhappy Carter offered his half-interest in the *Times,* but the deal fell through. On January 1, 1858, however, O'Meara wrote the general that he had bought the *Standard.* With the help of a $750 advance from Captain John Cain, imported by Lane to be agent to the lower Columbia tribes and unofficial purse-holder, and $5250 in loans from Oregonians who, as O'Meara put it, became undoubted friends of Joseph Lane "since Capt. Cain proved to them you had no faith in Bush."[26]

Ethelbert Hibben had not been taken into Jo Lane's confidence. He was resentful when Cain and O'Meara told him Lane had helped finance acquisition of the *Standard* and been prepared to advance $2000 toward purchase of the *Statesman.* When it was suggested to him that the *Times* and the *Standard,* now that both were operated in the general's interest, should avoid future conflict, he sullenly refused. Until he received other instructions from Washington he would continue his present course.

Hibben meant what he said. The Democratic Central Committee, chaired by Nesmith, adopted a rule basing apportionment of delegates to the next territorial convention upon each county's vote for Lane in 1857 rather than, as theretofore, the county's total population. When O'Meara protested in his columns that large numbers of Softs would be debarred from the nominating process, the *Times* joined the *Statesman* in attacking him for being, like Leland, a promoter of disorganization and division. Changing the organ grinder, Hibben commented sarcastically, does not change the tune, so long as the cylinder is unchanged.

It was mid-February before the general learned that his two protégés were locked in violent dispute. On February 16 Lane sent Hibben a long letter intended for publication in the *Times*. Presumably it was intended to compose the differences between the two editors he was subsidizing, but he was, unfortunately, again in a mood to play good Lord and the Devil. He wrote loftily of rights and duties. He praised pertinent observations in the *Times* and lauded the general views of the *Standard*. And he pleaded for an end to discord.

The time factor defeated his efforts. In the journalistic epithetry of the day, James O'Meara was "Jeremy Diddler," after the inventive sponger in Kenney's farce, *Raising the Wind*. It was a backhand compliment to O'Meara's resourcefulness. He sensed that Bush and associates had overreached themselves and set about organizing the dissidents. There would be two Democratic nominating conventions that year.

The Hards met at Salem March 16, approved Buchanan's administration, popular sovereignty and the Dred Scott decision, and nominated Lafayette Grover for congressman and Bush for state printer. Lane delegates prevented nomination of Joseph Drew for governor, but could not nominate Curry. "Fiddler John" Whiteaker, a relatively obscure Lane County farmer and active slavery man, was the compromise candidate.

The *Times* of March 28 carried Lane's letter of the previous February 26. The members of the Cli-que were dumfounded. Nes wrote the general that his production was a senseless mess of trash; Bush, that he would not have published it for a thousand dollars. Nat Lane insisted the letter was a forgery and would not believe otherwise until he saw it with his own eyes. Son-in-law Lafayette Mosher, who had won the capricious heart of the beautiful Winifred, was equally incredulous. The Softs, now called National Democrats, read into it justification for their revolt against the Bushites. They held their own convention at Eugene on April 8, nominating E. M. Barnum for governor, Colonel Kelly for Congress, and O'Meara for state printer. The Republicans also nominated candidates but the entire slate withdrew, complaining of lack of party organization.

Bush, who did not underestimate his own unpopularity, was uneasy about his chances. A poor public speaker, he campaigned in company with Delazon Smith, who took charge of the oratory. Later, when the two had become enemies, Delusion said bitterly that he "packed the dumb dog over the state and barked for him because he couldn't bark for himself."[27] The worried Asahel asked Deady to make speeches in the southern counties urging his, Bush's, election, but the judge refused. Deady was himself candidate for a place on the state supreme court and had no wish to borrow enemies. In the election Grover and Whiteaker won easily, but Asahel ran embarrassingly far behind the ticket, defeating O'Meara by only 400 votes out of roughly 9500 cast.

In July the new state legislature met long enough to elect Lane and Delusion to the U.S. Senate and, there being no other business it could lawfully conduct, adjourned.

Bush had Grover's confidence and thought he had Smith's. But Delusion was true only to his own ambitions. The admission bill had passed the Senate but in the House of Representatives remained caught in committee at the end of the session. Asahel convinced himself that Lane was responsible for the delay. On August 3 the *Statesman* carried a letter signed "Metropolis," dated at Washington the previous June 17, but actually written by Bush. It charged that Lane worked to prevent passage so that at the next session he could draw mileage both as senator and delegate, thus pocketing an additional $8000. This was a libel to which even Deady could not subscribe. Late the same month Asahel sent the general a long letter. By now he knew Lane was behind O'Meara's effort to buy the *Statesman*, that Cain was operating in Lane's interest and that Lane owned one-sixth of the *Standard*. In language as cutting as it was polite, Bush catalogued Old Jo's errors and intrigues. The general's reply was a simple request that there be no further correspondence between them.

When Grover and Smith set out for Washington in late September, Bush instructed them to send him evidence that Lane was responsible for delaying the admission bill. He was infuriated when they reported back that there was no evidence, reacting with harsh words for what he thought to be their fulsome and unwarranted praise of Lane and their toadying to the general's wishes. When they retorted that Lane was not only a hardworking and influential delegate, but also a potential presidential candidate, Bush would have none of it, not even after Delusion reminded him of what he himself had written, both publicly and privately, during that visit to Washington in 1854.

By year's end Bush was moving away from support of the Buchanan administration and toward Stephen A. Douglas and popular sovereignty. He had been willing to accept the Lecompton constitution in order to get elected printer. Once elected he would support it no longer. What had begun as a local power struggle was becoming enmeshed in national issues.

There was one local issue, however, which still excited lively interests: the war claims. Territorial scrip circulated freely though at increasingly heavy discount, bringing 50 percent of face value when first issued, as little as 10 percent as the years passed. Large amounts of paper filtered into the hands of speculators, both on the Pacific Coast and in the East. Bush himself was dealing heavily not only in scrip but also in land warrants which, thanks to a Lane measure, were issued to veterans of Indian as well as other wars. That winter the *Statesman* gloomily predicted it would be two years before the claims were paid. In early February, 1859, the House Committee on Military Affairs referred the entire Oregon claim to the third auditor of the federal treasury for further trimming.

For Jo Lane the delay was a political catastrophe, but on February 10 the Oregon bill at last came on the floor of the House of Representatives and after three days of impassioned debate was passed by a vote of 114 to 103, the majority being furnished by a small number of Republicans who followed the lead of Massachusett's Eli Thayer. That night Lane was serenaded at Brown's Hotel by a crowd of celebrants and the U.S. Marine Band. Next day he and Smith drew for long and short terms. The general got the long term and would serve until 1860. Delusion and Grover would serve until the end of the current session, eighteen days away.

On February 14, the President signed the bill into law. Oregon was a state at last.

⚹ 11 ⚹

Most Uncivil War

1859-1862

B ECAUSE STATEHOOD had not yet been achieved in December, 1857, the territorial legislature met in regular session. Colonel Chapman and Colonel T'Vault presented petitions asking for a law to protect and assess slave property in the territory. Such a measure passed the council but failed to reach the floor of the assembly. Partisan feeling ran high. Assemblyman Dryer of Multnomah shied his inkpot at Assemblyman Lasater of Marion. Shortly afterward Lasater assaulted Dryer on a Salem street. Though he was both younger and larger than the editor, the member from Marion thoughtfully brought along two friends and the three pummeled Toddy Jep so brutally that he was forced to keep to his bed for days. The *Statesman* expressed deep satisfaction.

A new restlessness was upon Bush and he considered moving his paper to Portland, but was dissuaded by Judge Williams. The metropolis was not prospering. Despite business generated by the Yakima War, which was dragging slowly toward conclusion, trade was poor. Land titles in the city continued to be clouded by legal disputes between Daniel Lownsdale and the other proprietors. While loudly denouncing his erstwhile associates as practiced swindlers, Lownsdale quietly partitioned an undivided four-fifths interest in his property among his heirs. The remaining one-fifth he quitclaimed to his attorney, in trust (making no mention of the partition), with instructions it be sold to satisfy his creditors. After his death purchasers discovered they held title to 20 percent of what they had paid for. Stark was busily putting up buildings on his addition and so deeply in debt attorney W. W. Page warned Bush against loaning money to Benjamin, whom Page considered a slippery customer, unless it was secured by a real property mortgage. Hibben and Cain had returned to the States. The *Standard* suspended in January; O'Meara somehow resumed publication the next month, but the concern was decidedly rickety and would collapse in July.

It took more than a month for word of admission to reach Oregon. The *Statesman* carried a brief notice on March 22. Senators Lane and Smith, meanwhile, were putting together their own political machine. Nesmith and Zeiber were dismissed, their places filled by the Reverend Edward Geary and Colonel Chapman, men upon whom the general could depend. Matthew P. Deady was appointed to the U.S. district court. The Democratic state convention, held at Eugene in April, was controlled by a coalition of Lane and Smith delegates. Chapman defeated Nesmith for convention president, and Lansing Stout, a newcomer from California, won nomination for Congress over Grover. David Logan, who now described himself as a "popular Sovreignity [*sic*] — non intervention Republican,"[1] was the nominee of that party.

A special session of the legislature met in May to complete organization of the state government and elect a senator. Smith was, of course, a candidate to succeed himself, but an angry Bush was determined to defeat him. Democrats wrangled in caucus for days. At last Lane's intervention, together with a brandy sociable hosted by the general himself, earned Delusion the party nod by a vote of twenty-two to twenty-one. To no purpose, for the day before the end of the session the Cli-que adherents in the senate walked out, leaving less than a quorum and making any senatorial election impossible.

Old Jo and the disappointed Smith stumped the state together for Stout. On the Canyonville-Roseburg road they stopped at the Burnett House, then operated by Franz Reinhart, the Althouse baker, where they shared a bed with the more permanent occupants thereof. Bedbugs were awful bad at that time, Reinhart explains, and there was not a house or hotel in all Oregon not overrun by them.

Stout defeated Logan by a margin of sixteen votes out of more than eleven thousand cast. Marion County, where Bush and the *Statesman* exercised their greatest influence, went for Logan by a margin of three to one.

When Joseph Lane set out for Washington the last time, Matt Deady accompanied him. The judge wanted his court moved from Salem to Portland, now clearly the metropolis-to-be. And he hoped for reconciliation with his father who, Deady wrote long after, "often held the poorhouse and prison up to me as a warning and a prophecy."[2] The old man would repeat himself. To the end of his days Daniel Deady disapproved of his first-born.

Back in Oregon the split between the Bush and Lane wings of the Democratic party widened inexorably. The *Statesman* now fervently espoused Stephen A. Douglas and popular sovereignty, and spoke disdainfully of Buchanan. The Douglas minority bolted from the state central committee meeting in September and the state convention in November. The majority then elected Delusion to the chair and, skillfully managed by Mosher, selected Lane, Stout and Deady to represent Oregon at the 1860 Charleston convention and endorsed Jo Lane for President of the United States. That same month Delazon Smith began publication at Albany of the *Oregon Democrat,* a paper whose primary purpose was to eliminate the *Statesman* and destroy Asahel Bush, whom Delusion once described as the kind of man who would dig up his grandmother's bones to make jackknife handles.

ꙮ II ꙮ

Bitterness made for meanness of spirit. When Deady, writing from the national capital, told Nesmith that General Lane was afflicted by a painful felon (deep boil) on his hand, Nes retorted he had heard Lane's hand was very nearly as rotten as his heart. Bush had never forgiven Deady for refusing to campaign for him in 1858, and indeed relations between them would never again be as intimate as before. The *Statesman* poured a steady stream of abuse upon the heads of Lane and all those who upheld him. But behind the exchanges between personalities was a real issue, slavery, and that fact made possible a compromise which would have been unthinkable a year earlier.

Dr. Anson G. Henry had lived in Springfield, Illinois, and been friend and personal physician to A. Lincoln. After coming to Oregon in the very early 1850s he practiced both medicine and Whig politics and served in the territorial legislature. From 1852 he maintained correspondence with another, and closer, of Lincoln's friends, Colonel Edward D. Baker, who settled that year in San Francisco.

The English-born Baker practiced law in Springfield, sat in the Illinois legislature and was twice congressman. He saw action under Zachary Taylor during the Mexican War and was politically fortunate enough to be slightly wounded. Baker gave his name to the Lincolns' first child, who died young; after moving to California he established a lucrative practice in San Francisco. He was an orator of the ornate school, colorful as a circus poster, and a man of extraordinary improvidence. Offered $30,000 to defend the accused in a controversial murder case, Baker demanded half his fee in advance and lost it that same night at the faro tables.

As early as 1857, just before the Oregon constitutional convention, Henry urged his Illinois friend to move north. The colonel was tempted — according to one account he bought his ticket and boarded ship — but wisely changed his mind. The time was not yet.

In late 1859 came a second summons, and this one had more substance. Henry had enlisted the support of Billy Adams. Dave Logan, though somewhat reluctantly, added his approval to the urging. Even Tom Dryer had belatedly discovered that Whiggery was dead, and the *Oregonian* joined the Republican party. By now Baker's reputation was much enhanced. His speeches made him famous. His eulogy to Senator David Broderick, killed in a duel by California Supreme Court Justice David Terry, was much praised. Terry was notorious for his association with the criminal element which terrorized San Francisco. Broderick was a Tammany-trained machine politician who brought New York methods to California. Formerly they had been friends. But Senator Broderick opposed his colleague and Terry's friend, Senator Gwin, on the issue of slavery. This was the chord upon which Baker strummed in his address. Broderick became a Free State martyr, and Edward D. Baker a Republican hero.

Baker arrived at Portland December 15, 1859, and remained in the state nine days, long enough to visit Salem and Bush. Simeon Francis, sometime editor on the Springfield *State Journal* and newly come to Oregon, wrote Lincoln that Baker hoped to be elected to the United States Senate and that he, Francis, thought the colonel would be successful. Baker arranged to rent a house in Salem. In early February his family moved up from California. Baker followed shortly in company with Tom Dryer who, lately come to the realization that Republicanism could be profitable, had gone south to escort the new champion.

There was an election in June. Though Stout had barely warmed his seat, the Democrats nominated a strong proslavery candidate, George Sheil, for Congress. The Republicans nominated Logan though Billy Adams, still constricted by those moral scruples fastened on him by Alexander Campbell, did not approve. Edward Baker campaigned assiduously, astonishing the backcountry folk with his high-toned words (he was not given to public invective) and flawless delivery. Sheil defeated Logan by a narrow vote, but no matter. In the legislature the Douglas Democrats could count eighteen votes, the Lane Democrats one more. But the hammer was in the hands of the Republicans, who numbered thirteen. Edward Baker was elected U.S. senator to succeed Delazon Smith, and J. W. Nesmith to succeed Joseph Lane.

Because of his failure to secure reelection, Lane's viability as a presidential candidate greatly declined. During the last months of 1859, President Buchanan and Secretary of War Floyd thought Breckinridge of Kentucky and Lane the leading contenders, with Lane having the edge. Despite his Oregon defeat, however, the general might have made it as a presidential candidate had he not decided to stand upon principle at an inopportune moment. When Stout, who was representing him at the Charleston convention, wired Lane that the Southern delegates were prepared to leave rather than accept the nomination of Stephen Douglas, Old Jo telegraphed back that Stout should go out and stand with Lane's proslavery friends. He qualified the instruction further on in his message, but Lansing was literal-minded and Lane lost any chance for nomination or election. There is evidence that Lane, a Northern man with Southern principles, was the only potential candidate who could unite the Democratic party, in which case Abraham Lincoln would be no more than a historical footnote. Instead Jo Lane became the vice-presidential candidate on a Breckinridge-Lane ticket which lost even in Oregon, though by so slight a margin even Lincoln called it the narrowest in political bookkeeping. For the remainder of his term Old Jo continued to speak out for the things in which he believed — slavery, and compromise.

On his fifty-ninth birthday he wrote his son Lafayette that he had had, in his times, ups and downs. Born poor, without wealth or influential friends, without proper education, without a family to support him, he had achieved prominence and some distinction. Now he was ready to retire, "unless the War Cry shall be raised by the Northern sectional party to coerce seceding States . . . If war shall ensue," he wrote Lafayette, "I will not retire till peace shall perch on the independence of the Southern states . . . I believe secession is certain and necessary."[3]

Lane did not think war would come, but it did. Joseph Drew wrote Deady not to encourage his proslavery friends to further California Senator Gwin's conspiracy aimed at creating a Pacific Republic — echo of Shively's suggestion those many years before — but he need not have worried. So long as slavery was legal, Deady supported it, but he could not support secession, which was insurrection. Insurrection was treason. Matthew P. Deady would have no part of treason.

Ancient Joseph served out his term to the last day, which irritated Nesmith, who was waiting to succeed him. He had promised to enlist in the Southern cause but yielded to the weight of years. In Oregon James O'Meara had taken over the Jacksonville *Sentinel* and conducted it in favor of slavery until his money ran out and he sold it to Henry Denlinger. Denlinger and O'Meara disagreed as to which had the right to unpaid subscriptions. O'Meara lay in wait for his rival — who was a damned Republican — but Henry managed to wrestle away Jimmy's pistol, which he used to perforate Jimmy's coattails and that part of Jimmy immediately underneath. Delusion, intolerably pained by fractured ambition, came to blame Lane and Lane's friends for his own senatorial defeat. In November, 1860, he went on a protracted spree at Portland and died of acute alcoholism, aged forty-four. Tom Dryer deeded the *Oregonian* to printer Henry Pittock in payment of wages due, carried Oregon's electoral votes to the national capital where he put them to Lincoln and Hamlin's account and was rewarded with the post of commissioner to the Kingdom of Hawaii.

Jo Lane reached Portland, by malicious fortune, on the steamer which brought word of the Confederate assault on Fort Sumter. Apart from the Deadys, who had him to supper, old friends avoided him. Driving a team and wagon, the general slowly made his way south to his home in Douglas County, preceded by rumors he had come to promote rebellion. At Dallas he was hanged in effigy. At Corvallis, where Southern sentiment was strong, he was welcomed with a reception. Lane stayed on a few days to enjoy his honors, but he already knew he was a vanished man. Near Winchester his pistol accidentally discharged as he was climbing out of his wagon, wounding him severely. Jesse Applegate, Republican, took him in and nursed him back to health.

The military departed. Captain Thomas Jordan, Quartermaster's Corps, who had just recently hoped to be Democratic senator from Oregon, would shortly be General P. T. Beauregard's chief of staff. Captain Rufus Ingalls, incurably avaricious, would be Sam Grant's most dependable quartermaster. Colonel Joseph Hooker left his superintendency of military road construction in southern Oregon to offer his services to the Union. Lee would victimize him at Chancellorsville. Little Phil Sheridan left Fort Yamhill and the Grand Ronde Agency to become Lincoln's most brilliant cavalry commander.

John Lane left West Point to accept a Confederate commission, and General Lamerick of Rogue River fame became a Confederate paymaster, but by and large Oregonians sat out the war. Not that they were unaffected by it. Partisan passions split apart men who had been bosom companions. Nesmith, Old Jo's first friend in Oregon, wanted the general locked up at Alcatraz. The apple was eaten, the innocence gone.

There was sorrow in Eden.

Notes

Bibliography

Index

Notes

NOTE: *Oregon Historical Quarterly* appears as *OHQ* after the first mention; Oregon Historical Society Collections appears as *OrHi*.

INTRODUCTION

1 William Faux, *Memorable Days in America,* in Reuben Gold Thwaites, ed., *Early Western Travels, 1748–1846,* 32 vols. Chicago, 1904–07; vol. xi, p. 21.
2 Ibid., p. 178.
3 Alexis de Tocqueville, *Democracy in America.* Henry Reeves, trans., Francis Bowen, ed., 2 vols. Cambridge, 1862; vol. i, p. 379.
4 Reprinted in *Christian Advocate and Journal and Zion's Herald,* March 14, 1834.

1. ACROSS THE DISTANT MOUNTAINS

1 "Selections from Editorial Articles from the *St. Louis Enquirer* on Oregon and Texas . . . 1818–1819," Missouri Historical Society.
2 John Quincy Adams, *Memoirs,* Charles Francis Adams, ed., 12 vols., Chicago, 1875; vol. iv, p. 275.

2. HIS MAJESTY'S MARCHES

1 Peter Skene Ogden, *Ogden's Snake Country Journals, 1824–25 and 1825–26,* in E. E. Rich and A. M. Johnson, eds., *Publications of the Hudson's Bay Record Society,* 31 vols., London and Winnipeg, 1938–; vol. xii, p. 49.

3. OVERLANDERS — PIOUS AND IMPIOUS

1 Nathaniel J. Wyeth, *The Correspondence and Journals of Captain Nathaniel Jarvis Wyeth, 1831–36,* in Frederick G. Young, ed., *Sources of the History of Oregon,* vol. 1, parts 3 through 6, Eugene, 1899; N. J. Wyeth to Leonard Jarvis, February 6, 1832, p. 33.
2 *Christian Advocate and Journal and Zion's Herald,* March 1, 1833.
3 Jason Lee, "Diary of the Reverend Jason Lee," *Oregon Historical Quarterly,* vol. xvii (1916), pp. 116–46, 240–66, 397–430; entry of July 3, 1838, p. 408.

4 Wyeth, *Correspondence and Journals,* to Rev. Clark Perry, November 12, 1833, p. 80.
5 Ibid., to Elizabeth Stone Wyeth, February 26, 1834, p. 118.
6 Ibid., to Elizabeth Wyeth, March 3, 1834, p. 128.
7 Lee, "Diary," entry of May 5, 1834; *OHQ,* vol. xvii, p. 119.
8 Cornelius J. Brosnan, *Jason Lee, Prophet of the New Oregon,* New York, 1932; p. 60.
9 Ibid., p. 62.
10 Wyeth, *Correspondence and Journals,* journal entry of September 23, 1834, p. 233.

4. OREGON AS EDEN

1 Brosnan, *Jason Lee, Prophet,* Lee to Fisk, March 5, 1836, p. 80.
2 25th Congress, 3rd Session, *House Report Nos. 101, 3 and 4,* and *Supplemental Report, 4–7.*
3 J. Lee to D. Lee, April 25, 1838; Oregon Historical Society Collections, Mss. 1211.
4 Lee, "Diary," July 30, 1838; *OHG,* vol. xvii, p. 415.

5. GERM OF A GREAT STATE

1 William H. Gray, *A History of Oregon, 1792–1849,* Portland, San Francisco and New York, 1870; p. 194.
2 25th Congress, 3rd Session, *House Report No. 101, Appendix 1,* J. Lee to C. Cushing.
3 Ibid.

6. THE CHILDREN OF ADAM

1 Arthur L. Throckmorton, *Oregon Argonauts,* Portland, 1961; p. 26.
2 Frances Fuller Victor, *The River of the West,* 1950 (fascimile reprint of 1870 edition); p. 321.
3 Gray, *History of Oregon,* p. 354.
4 Ibid., p. 358.
5 Ibid.
6 J. Lee to G. Hines, July 1, 1844; *OrHi,* Mss. 1215.
7 George Gary, "Diary of the Reverend George Gary," Charles H. Carey, ed., *OHQ* xxiv (1923), 68–105, 168–87, 269–333, 386–433; p. 274.
8 John McLoughlin, *McLoughlin's Fort Vancouver Letters, 1825–46,* in E. E. Rich, ed., intro. by W. Kaye Lamb, *Publications of the Hudson's Bay Record Society,* vols. iv, vi and vii, London, 1941–44; vol. vii, p. 99.

7. OREGON, CALIFORNIA, TEXAS AND POLK

1 John Quincy Adams, *Writings of John Quincy Adams,* Worthington Chauncey Ford, ed., 7 vols., New York, 1913–17; to Abigail Adams, June 3, 1811, vol. iv, p. 128.

2 Gary, "Diary," p. 388.
3 *Oregon Spectator*, April 2, 1846.
4 J. Quinn Thornton, *Oregon and California in 1848*, 2 vols., New York, 1849; vol. i, p. 161.
5 Gary, "Diary," p. 390.

8. MOST HORRID BUTCHERY

1 "Archives of the American Board of Commissioners for Foreign Missions, Vol. 248 — Letter 28," *OHQ* xxii (1921), p. 35.
2 *Spectator*, Dec. 10, 1847.
3 Henry H. Spalding, "Lectures: Early Oregon Missions, Their Importance in Securing the Country to America," no. 6, p. 2; *OrHi*, Mss. 1201, typescript copy.
4 *Spectator*, January 20, 1848.
5 Ibid.
6 Ibid., December 10, 1847.
7 Robert Newell, *Robert Newell's Memoranda*, Dorothy O. Johansen, ed., Portland, 1959; p. 106.
8 Ibid., p. 111.
9 E. Walker to the Reverend David Greene; *OrHi*, Mss. 1204, photostat.
10 *Oregon American and Evangelical Union*, June 7, 1848.
11 Spalding to A. Waller, August, 1848; *OrHi*, Mss. 1210.
12 Henry H. Spalding and Asa Bowen Smith, *The Diaries and Letters of Henry H. Spalding and Asa Bowen Smith*, Clifford M. Drury, ed., Glendale, 1958; p. 345.
13 George H. Atkinson, "Diary of Rev. George H. Atkinson, D. D., 1847–1858," E. Ruth Rockwood, ed., *OHQ* xl (1939) 52–63, 168–87, 265–82, 345–61; xli (1940) 6–33, 212–26, 88–303, 386–404; xl, p. 361.

9. A FESTIVAL OF SONS OF BITCHES

1 Hubert Howe Bancroft, *History of Oregon*, 2 vols., San Francisco, 1886–88; vol. ii, p. 95.
2 *Oregonian*, July 5, 1951.
3 Samuel Royal Thurston, "Diary of Samuel Royal Thurston," intro. by George H. Himes, *OHQ* xv (1914), pp. 153–205, p. 200.
4 Ezra Fisher, "Correspondence of the Reverend Ezra Fisher," S. F. Henderson, N. E., and K. S. Latourette, eds., *OHQ* xvi (1915), 65–104, 277–311, 379–412; xvii (1916), 55–76, 149–76, 267–339, 431–80; xix (1918), 134–63, 235–61, 351–72; xx (1919), 95–137; xvii, p. 321.
5 Victor, *River of the West*, p. 505.
6 Reuben P. Boise, *Transactions of the Oregon Pioneer Association, 1876;* "Annual Address," p. 29.
7 M. P. Deady to A. Bush, October 8, 1851; Bush House Papers, Oregon State Library.
8 *Spectator*, December 9, 1851.
9 *Vox Populi*, January 16, 1852.
10 *Oskaloosa* (Iowa) *Herald*, March 25, 1853.

11 Deady to Bush, January 19, 1854; *OrHi*, Mss. 581, typescript.
12 *Statesman*, September 2, 1853.
13 J. Lane to J. Nesmith, December 26, 1854; *OrHi*, Mss. 577.
14 *Statesman*, July 4, 1953.
15 Nesmith to Deady, January 8, 1854; *OrHi*, Mss. 48.

10. AN IMPOSSIBLE INSTITUTION

1 O. C. Pratt to Deady, September 11, 1854; *OrHi*, Mss. 48.
2 Deady to Nesmith, November 2, 1854; *OrHi*, Mss. 577.
3 *Oregon Argus*, April 21, 1855.
4 *Oregonian*, August 5, 1854.
5 Deady to Nesmith, April 12, 1855; *OrHi*, Mss. 577.
6 Bush to Deady, May 21, 1855; *OrHi*, Mss. 48.
7 Bush to Deady, May 22, 1855; *OrHi*, Mss. 48.
8 Ibid.
9 Deady to Bush, September 5, 1855; Bush House Collection, Oregon State Library.
10 Bush to Deady, October 21, 1855; *OrHi*, Mss. 48.
11 Deady to Bush, October 30, 1855; Bush House Collection, Oregon State Library.
12 Ibid.
13 Nesmith to Bush, November 14, 1855; *OrHi*, Mss. 581.
14 Nesmith to Bush, November 26, 1855; *OrHi*, Mss. 581.
15 *Oregonian*, February 16, 1856.
16 *Statesman*, December 18, 1855.
17 Bush to Deady, May 17, 1856; *OrHi*, Mss. 48.
18 Deady to Bush, November 17, 1856; *OrHi*, Mss. 581, typescript.
19 Wm. J. Martin to Lane, October 28, 1856; Lane Collection, Indiana University.
20. *Oregonian*, November 1, 1856.
21 Bush to Deady, May 19, 1857; *OrHi*, Mss. 48.
22 Nesmith to Deady, May 3, 1857; *OrHi*, Mss. 48.
23 Deady to Ben Simpson, July 28, 1857; *OrHi*, Mss. 48.
24 *Statesman*, July 28, 1857.
25 *Statesman*, August 4, 1857.
26 J. O'Meara to Lane, January 1, 1858; Lane Collection, Indiana University.
27 Walter C. Woodward, *The Rise and Early History of Political Parties in Oregon, 1843–68*, Portland, 1913; quoted at p. 136.

11. MOST UNCIVIL WAR

1 David Logan, "22 Letters of David Logan," Harry E. Pratt, ed., *OHQ* xliv (1943), pp. 252–85, p. 277.
2 Matthew P. Deady, *Pharisee Among Philistines: The Diary of Matthew P. Deady, 1871–1893*, Malcolm Clark, jr., ed., 2 vols., Portland, 1975; vol. i, p. 259.
3 J. Lane to L. Lane, December 14, 1860; Lane Collection, Indiana University.

Bibliography

Published Primary Sources

NOTE: *Oregon Historical Quarterly* appears as *OHQ*

Adams, John Quincy, *Memoirs of John Quincy Adams,* Charles Francis Adams, ed., 12 vols., Philadelphia, 1875.

————, *Writings of John Quincy Adams,* Worthington Chauncey Ford, ed., 7 vols., New York, 1913–17.

Adams, William L., *Treason, Stratagems and Spoils,* George N. Belknap, ed., Yale University Library, New Haven, 1968.

Allen, A. J., *Ten Years in Oregon. Travels and Adventures of Dr. E. White and Lady,* Ithaca, 1848.

Atkinson, George H., "Diary of Rev. George Henry Atkinson, D. D.," E. Ruth Rockwood, ed., *OHQ* xl (1939), pp. 52–63, 168–87, 265–82, 345–61; xli (1940), pp. 6–33, 212–26, 288–303, 386–404.

Ashley, William Henry, *The West of William H. Ashley, 1822–1833,* Dale L. Morgan, ed., Denver, 1964.

Bailey, Margaret Jewett, *Grains, or, Passages in the Life of Ruth Rover, with Occasional Pictures of Oregon, Natural and Moral,* Portland, 1854.

Beaver, Herbert, *Reports and Letters of Herbert Beaver, 1836–1838,* Thomas E. Jessett, S. T. D., ed., Portland, 1959.

Brouillet, Jean Baptiste Abraham, *Authentic Account of the Murder of Dr. Whitman,* 2nd ed., Portland, 1869.

Burnett, Peter H., *Recollections and Opinions of an Old Pioneer,* New York, 1880.

Clark, Robert C., "Aberdeen and Peel on Oregon," *OHQ* xxiv (Sept., 1933), pp. 236–40.

Clyman, James, *James Clyman, Frontiersman,* Charles L. Camp, ed., definitive ed., Portland, 1960.

Dale, Harrison S., ed., *The Ashley-Smith Explorations and the Discovery of the Central Route to the Pacific,* Cleveland, 1916.

Douglas, David, *North American Journal, 1823–27,* London, 1914.

Drury, Clifford M., ed., *The Diaries and Letters of Henry H. Spalding and Asa Bowen Smith Relating to the Nez Percé Mission, 1838–42,* Glendale, 1958.

Drury, Clifford M., ed., *First White Women Over the Rockies; Diaries, Letters and Bibliographical Sketches of the Six White Women who made the Overland Journey in 1836 and 1838,* 3 vols., Glendale, 1963–66.

Ebbert, George W., "George Wood Ebbert," *OHQ* xix (Sept., 1918), pp. 263–67.

Farnham, Thomas J., *Travels in the Great Western Prairies, the Anahuac and Rocky Mountains and in the Oregon Territory*, in *Early Western Travels, 1738–1846*, Reuben Gold Thwaites, ed., vol. xxviii, Cleveland, 1906.

Faux, William, *Memorable Days in America*, in *Early Western Travels, 1748–1846*, Reuben Gold Thwaites, ed., vols. xi-xii, Cleveland, 1905.

Fisher, Ezra, "Correspondence of Reverend Ezra Fisher," S. F. Henderson, N. E. and K. S. Latourette, eds., *OHQ* xvi (March, Sept., Dec., 1915), pp. 65–104, 277–311, 379–412; xvii (1916), pp. 55–76, 149–76, 267–339, 431–80; xix (June., Sept., Dec., 1918), pp. 134–63, 235–61, 351–72; xx (March, 1919), pp. 95–137.

Frost, John H., "Journal of John H. Frost, 1840–43," Nellie B. Pipes, ed., *OHQ* xxxv (1934), pp. 50–73, 139–67, 235–62, 349–75.

Gary, George, "Diary of Reverend George Gary," Charles H. Carey, ed., *OHQ* xxiv (1923), pp. 68–105, 168–87, 269–33, 386–433.

Gay, Theressa, *Life and Letters of Mrs. Jason Lee*, Portland, 1936.

Gray, William H., *A History of Oregon, 1792–1849*, Portland, San Francisco and New York, 1870.

Hafen, LeRoy R. and Ann W. Hafen, eds., *To the Rockies and Oregon, 1839–1842*, Far West and Rockies Series, vol. iii, Glendale, 1955.

Hancock, Samuel, *The Narrative of Samuel Hancock, 1845–1860*, New York, 1927.

James, Edwin, *Account of an Expedition from Pittsburgh to the Rocky Mountains performed in the Years 1819, 1820 . . . under Command of Maj. S. H. Long*, in *Early Western Travels, 1748–1846*, Reuben Gold Thwaites, ed., vols. xiv–xvii, Cleveland, 1905.

Kelley, Hall Jackson, *Hall J. Kelley on Oregon*, Fred Wilbur Powell, ed., Princeton, 1932.

Landerholm, Carl, trans., *Notices & Voyages of the Famed Quebec Mission to the Pacific Northwest*, Portland, 1956.

Lee, Daniel and John H. Frost, *Ten Years in Oregon*, New York, 1844.

Lee, Jason, "Diary of Reverend Jason Lee," *OHQ* xvii (June, Sept., Dec., 1916), pp. 116–46, 240–66, 397–430.

Lockley, Fred, "Case of Robin Holmes vs. Nathaniel Ford," *OHQ* xxiii (June, 1922), pp. 111–37.

Lockley, Fred, "Some Documentary Records of Slavery in Oregon," *OHQ* xvii (June, 1916), pp. 107–15.

Logan, David, "22 Letters of David Logan, Pioneer Oregon Lawyer," Harry E. Pratt, ed., *OHQ* xliv (Sept., 1943), pp. 253–85.

McLoughlin, John, *Letters Written at Fort Vancouver, 1829–1833*, Burt Brown Barker, ed., Portland, 1948.

———, *McLoughlin's Fort Vancouver Letters, First Series, 1825–38*, in *Publications of the Hudson's Bay Record Society*, vol. iv, E. E. Rich, ed., London, 1941. *Second Series, 1839–44*, vol. vi., London, 1943. *Third Series, 1844–46*, vol. vii, London, 1944.

Methodist Episcopal Mission, "A Document of Mission History," Robert M. Gatke, ed., *OHQ* xxxvi (Mar. and June, 1935), pp. 71–94, 163–81.

———, "Methodist Annual Reports Relating to the Willamette Mission (1834–1848)," Charles H. Carey, ed., *OHQ* xxiii (Dec., 1922), pp. 303–64.

———, "The Mission Record Book of the Methodist Episcopal Church, Willamette Station, Oregon Territory, North America, commenced 1834," *OHQ* xxxiii (Sept., 1922), pp. 230–66.

Munger, Asahel and Eliza Munger, "Diary of Asahel Munger and Wife," *OHQ* viii (Dec., 1907), pp. 387–405.

Newell, Robert, *Robert Newell's Memoranda,* Dorothy O. Johanson, ed., Portland, 1959.

Ogden, Peter Skene, *Ogden's Snake Country Journal, 1824–25 and 1825–26,* in *Publications of the Hudson's Bay Record Society,* vol. xiii, E. E. Rich and A. M. Johnson, eds., London, 1950.

——, *Ogden's Snake Country Journal, 1826–27,* vol. xxiii, K. G. Davies and A. M. Johnson, eds., London, 1961.

——, *Ogden's Snake Country Journal, 1827–28, 1828–29,* vol. xxviii, Glyndwr Williams, ed., London, 1971.

Palmer, Joel, *Journal of Travels over the Rocky Mountains to the Mouth of the Columbia River,* in *Early Western Travels, 1748–1846,* Reuben Gold Thwaites, ed., vol. xxx, Cleveland, 1906.

Parker, Samuel, *Journal of an Exploring Tour Beyond the Rocky Mountains,* 4th ed., Ithaca, 1844.

Polk, James K., *The Diary of James K. Polk during his Presidency, 1845 to 1849,* Milo M. Quaife, ed., 4 vols., Chicago, 1910.

Reinhart, Herman Francis, *The Golden Frontier: The Recollections of Herman Francis Reinhart, 1851–1869,* Doyce de Nunis, Jr., ed., Austin, 1962.

Robertson, Colin, *Robertson's Letters, 1817–22,* in *Publications of the Hudson's Bay Record Society,* vol. ii, E. E. Rich and R. Harvey Fleming, eds., London, 1939.

Russell, Osborne, *Journal of a Trapper,* Aubrey L. Haines, ed., Portland, 1955.

Schafer, Joseph, ed., "Documents Relative to Warre and Vavasour's Military Reconnaissance in Oregon, 1845–46," *OHQ* x (March, 1909), pp. 1–99.

Simpson, [Sir] George, *Fur Trade and Empire; George Simpson's 1824–1825 Journal,* Frederick Merk, ed., Harvard Historical Studies, Cambridge and London, 1931.

——, *London Correspondence Inward from Sir George Simpson, 1841–42,* in *Publications of the Hudson's Bay Record Society,* vol. xxiv, Glyndwr Williams, ed., London, 1973.

——, *Narrative of a Journey Round the World,* London, 1847.

——, *Simpson's Athabaska Journal and Report, 1821–22,* in *Publications of the Hudson's Bay Record Society,* vol. i, E. E. Rich, ed., London, 1938.

——, *Simpson's 1828 Journey to the Columbia,* in *Publications of the Hudson's Bay Record Society,* vol. x, E. E. Rich, ed., London, 1947.

Smet, Pierre-Jean de, S. J., *Life, Letters and Travels of Pierre-Jean de Smet, S. J.,* Hiram M. Chittenden and Alfred T. Richardson, eds., 4 vols., New York, 1905.

Thompson, David, *Narrative of David Thompson, 1784–1812,* Richard Glover, ed., The Champlain Society, Toronto, 1962.

Thornton, J. Quinn, *Oregon and California in 1848,* New York, 1849.

Thurston, Samuel Royal, "Diary of Samuel Royal Thurston," *OHQ* xv (Sept., 1914), pp. 153–205.

Tolmie, William Fraser, *The Journals of William Fraser Tolmie, Physician and Fur Trader,* Vancouver, 1963.

Victor, Frances Fuller, *River of the West,* Hartford and Toledo, 1870.

Wilkes, Charles, "Diary of Wilkes in the Northwest," Edmond S. Meany, ed., *Washington Historical Quarterly,* xvi (1925), pp. 49–61, 137–45, 206–23, 290–301; xvii (Jan., June, and Sept., 1926), pp. 43–65, 129–44, 223–29.

Williams, Glyndwr, *Hudson's Bay Miscellany, 1670–1870,* in *Publications of the Hudson's Bay Record Society,* vol. xxx, Winnipeg, 1975.

Work, John, *The Journal of John Work,* William S. Lewis and Paul C. Phillips, eds., Cleveland, 1923.

Wyeth, John B., *Oregon, or a Short History of a Long Journey,* Cambridge (Mass.), 1933.

Wyeth, Nathaniel J., *Correspondence and Journals of Nathaniel Jarvis Wyeth, 1831– 36,* Frederick G. Young, ed., in *Sources of the History of Oregon,* vol. i, parts 3– 6, Eugene, 1899.

Young, Frederick G., "Ewing Young and his Estate with Documentary Records," *OHQ* xxi (Sept., 1920), pp. 270–315.

———, "Financial History of Oregon; Provisional and Territorial Periods," *OHQ* vii (Dec., 1906), pp. 360–432; viii (June, 1907), pp. 129–90.

NEWSPAPERS AND PERIODICALS

Christian Advocate and Journal and Zion's Herald, New York.
Democratic Crisis, Corvallis.
Democratic Standard, Portland.
Free Press, Oregon City.
Missionary Herald, Boston.
Nile's Register, Baltimore.
Occidental Messenger, Corvallis.
Oregon American and Evangelical Union, Tualatin Plains.
Oregon Argus, Oregon City.
Oregon Democrat, Albany.
Oregon Spectator, Salem.
Oregon Statesman, Oregon City, Salem, and Corvallis.
Oregon Weekly Times, Portland.
Oregonian, Portland.
Table Rock (post-1858, *Oregon*) *Sentinel,* Jacksonville.
Vox Populi, Salem.
Western Star, Milwaukie.

SHORT LIST OF SECONDARY SOURCES

Bancroft, Hubert Howe, *History of Oregon,* 2 vols., San Francisco, 1886.

Barker, Burt Brown, *The McLoughlin Empire and Its Rulers,* Glendale, 1959.

Bauer, K. Jack, *The Mexican War, 1846–1848,* New York, 1974.

Blair, Harry C. and Rebecca Tarshis, *Lincoln's Constant Ally, The Life of Colonel Edward D. Baker,* Portland, 1960.

Brosnan, Cornelius J., *Jason Lee, Prophet of the New Oregon,* New York, 1932.

Brown, J. Henry, *Political History of Oregon,* Portland, 1892.

Bryce, George, *The Remarkable History of the Hudson's Bay Company,* London, 1904.

Carey, Charles H., *A General History of Oregon,* 2 vols., Portland, 1935.

Chittenden, Hiram M., *The American Fur Trade of the Far West,* 2 vols., Academic Reprints, Stanford, 1954.

Clark, Keith and Lowell Tiller, *Terrible Trail: The Meek Cut-off, 1845,* Caldwell (Idaho), 1946.

Clark, Malcolm, jr., "The Bigot Disclosed: 90 Years of Nativism," *Oregon Historical Quarterly*, lxxv (June, 1974), pp. 109–90.

De Voto, Bernard, *Across the Wide Missouri*, Boston, 1947.

———, *The Year of Decision*, 1846, Boston, 1943.

Drury, Clifford M., *Henry Harmon Spalding*, 2 vols., Caldwell, 1936.

Duncan, Janice K., " 'Ruth Rover,' Vindicative Falsehood or Historical Truth?" *Journal of the West*, xii, no. 2 (Apr., 1973), pp. 240–53.

Galbraith, John S., *The Hudson's Bay Company as an Imperial Factor, 1821–1869*, Berkeley and Los Angeles, 1957.

———, "John N. Sanders, 'Influence Man' for the Hudson's Bay Company," *Oregon Historical Quarterly*, liii (Sept., 1952), pp. 159–76.

Hafen, LeRoy R., ed., *The Mountain Men and the Fur Trade of the Far West*, 10 vols., Glendale, 1965–72.

Hendrickson, James E., *Joe Lane of Oregon, Machine Politics and the Sectional Crisis, 1849–1861*, Yale Western Americana Series, 17, New Haven and London, 1967.

Holmes, Kenneth L., *Ewing Young, Master Trapper*, Portland, 1967.

Irving, Washington, *The Adventures of Captain Bonneville in the Rocky Mountains and the Far West*, New York, 1837.

———, *Astoria, or Anecdotes of an Enterprise across the Rocky Mountains*, Philadelphia, 1836.

Johannsen, Robert W., *Frontier Politics and the Sectional Conflict; The Pacific Northwest on the Eve of the Civil War*, Seattle, 1955.

Kelly, Sister M. Margaret Jean, *The Career of Joseph Lane, Frontier Politician*, Catholic University Press, Washington, 1942.

Loewenberg, Robert J., "Elijah White vs. Jason Lee: A Tale of Hard Times," *Journal of the West*, vol. xi (Oct., 1972), pp. 636–72.

———, *Equality on the Oregon Frontier: Jason Lee and the Methodist Mission, 1834–43*, Seattle and London, 1976.

———, " 'Not . . . by feeble means:' Daniel Lee's Plan to Save Oregon," *Oregon Historical Quarterly*, lxxiv (Mar., 1973), pp. 71–78.

Lyons, Sister Letitia Mary, *Francis Norbert Blanchet and the Founding of the Oregon Missions (1838–1848)*, Catholic University Press, Washington, 1940.

Mills, Randall V., *Stern-Wheelers up Columbia*, Palo Alto, 1947.

Morton, Arthur S., *A History of the Canadian West to 1870–71*, ed. and rev. by Lewis G. Thomas, Toronto, 1973.

Rich, E. E., *Hudson's Bay Company, 1670–1870*, trade ed., 3 vols., New York, 1961.

Sullivan, Maurice S., *The Travels of Jedediah Smith*, Santa Ana, 1934.

Throckmorton, Arthur L., *Oregon Argonauts: Merchant Adventurers on the Western Frontier*, Portland, 1961.

Tocqueville, Alexis de, *Democracy in America*, Henry Reeve, trans., Francis Bowen, ed., 2 vols., Cambridge (Mass.), 1862.

Turnbull, George S., *History of Oregon Newspapers*, Portland, 1939.

Victor, Frances Fuller, *The Early Indian Wars of Oregon*, Salem, 1894.

Western (pseud.), *Biography of Joseph Lane; Not Inappropriately Styled by His Brother Officers and Soldiers, "the Marion of the War,"* Washington, 1852.

MANUSCRIPT COLLECTIONS

Abernathy, George, Oregon Historical Society, Mss. 929
Abernathy, George & Co., Oregon Historical Society, Mss. 920
Adams, William L., Oregon Historical Society, Mss. 64
Applegate Family, Oregon Historical Society, Mss. 1089
Bryant, William P., Oregon Historical Society, Mss. 823
Bush, Asahel, Bush House Papers, Oregon State Library
Bush, Asahel, Oregon Historical Society, Mss. 581
Curry, George Law, Oregon Historical Society, Mss. 700
Deady, Matthew P., Oregon Historical Society, Mss. 48
Ermatinger, Francis (Frank), Oregon Historical Society, Mss. 29
Foster, Philip, Oregon Historical Society, Mss. 996
Griffin, John Smith, Pacific University Library, Forest Grove
Grover, Lafayette, Oregon Historical Society, Mss. 581
Haight, Henry H., Henry E. Huntington Library, San Marino
Henry, Anson G., Oregon Historical Society, Mss. 638
King, William M., Oregon Historical Society, Mss. 1142
Lane, Joseph, Indiana University, Bloomington
Lane, Joseph, Oregon Historical Society, Mss. 1146
Meek, Joseph L., Oregon Historical Society, Mss. 926
Nesmith, James W., Oregon Historical Society, Mss. 577
Protestant Missionaries in the Pacific Northwest, Oregon Historical Society,
    Mss. 1200–1223
Shively, John W., Oregon Historical Society, Mss. 1127
Stark, Benjamin, Oregon Historical Society, Mss. 1155
Thornton, J. Quinn, Oregon Historical Society, Mss. 371
Thurston, Samuel R., Oregon Historical Society, Mss. 379

Index